Transforming Economies and European Integration

Transforming Economies and European Integration

Edited by

Rumen Dobrinsky

Deputy Director General, XXI Century Foundation, Centre for Strategic Business and Political Studies, Sofia, Bulgaria

and

Michael Landesmann

Professor of Economics, Johannes Kepler University, Austria and Research Associate, Department of Applied Economics, University of Cambridge, UK and The Vienna Institute for Comparative Economic Studies (WIIW)

Edward Elgar

Aldershot, UK • Brookfield, US

Published by
Edward Elgar Publishing Limited
Gower House
Croft Road
Aldershot
Hants GU11 3HR
UK

Edward Elgar Publishing Company
Old Post Road
Brookfield
Vermont 05036
US

British Library Cataloguing in Publication Data
Transforming Economies and European
Integration
I. Dobrinsky, Rumen II. Landesmann,
Michael
337.14

Library of Congress Cataloguing in Publication Data
Transforming economies and European integration / edited by Rumen Dobrinsky and Michael Landesmann.
p. cm.
"The book is the outcome of an international conference ... held in Sofia, Bulgaria, 27–28 May 1994, and organized by the XXI Century Foundation"—Pref.
Includes bibliographical references and index.
1. Europe, Eastern—Foreign economic relations—European Union countries—Congresses. 2. European Union countries—Foreign economic relations—Europe, Eastern—Congresses. 3. Europe—Economic integration—Congresses. 4. Europe, Eastern—Economic conditions—1989- —Congresses. I. Dobrinsky, Rumen, 1950- II. Landesmann, Michael A. III. XXI Century Foundation.
HF1532.7.Z4E857 1995
337.1'4—dc20 95–6825
CIP

ISBN 1 85898 204 9

Printed and bound in Great Britain by
Hartnolls Limited, Bodmin, Cornwall

Contents

Figures

Tables

Contributors

István Ábel, Budapest University of Economics/CEPR.
Richard Baldwin, Graduate Institute of International Studies, Geneva/CEPR.
Marek Belka, Institute of Economics, Polish Academy of Sciences/University of Łódź.
Tito Boeri, OECD, Paris.
Jaromir Cekota, OECD, Paris.
Daniel Daianu, National Bank of Romania, Bucharest.
Rumen Dobrinsky, XXI Century Foundation, Sofia.
Gancho Ganchev, XXI Century Foundation, Sofia.
Rumen Gechev, University of National and World Economics, Sofia.
Giovanni Graziani, University of Brescia.
László Halpern, Institute of Economics of the Hungarian Academy of Sciences, Budapest.
Peter Havlik, The Vienna Institute for Comparative Economic Studies.
Radu Herghelegiu, Department of European Integration, Government of Romania.
Michael Landesmann, University of Linz/ University of Cambridge.
Françoise Lemoine, Centre d'Etudes Prospective et d'Informations Internationales, Paris.
Garabed Minassian, Institute of Economics of the Bulgarian Academy of Sciences, Sofia.
Lubomir Mitov, World Bank Resident Mission, Sofia.
Fiorella Padoa Schioppa Kostoris, Institute of Studies for Economic Planning, Rome.
Stefano Scarpetta, OECD, Paris.
Klaus-Dieter Schmidt, The Kiel Institute of World Economics.
John Sheehy, European Commission, Brussels.
Richard Stern, RAND Corporation, Santa Monica.
Jan Švejnar, Institute of Economics of the Czech Academy of Science, Prague/ CERGE, Prague/University of Pittsburgh.
István P. Székely, United Nations, New York/ Budapest University of Economics/ CEPR.
Alexander Tomov, XXI Century Foundation, Sofia.

Preface

One of the ultimate goals of the process of economic transformation in the countries of Central and Eastern Europe (CEE) is their integration into the European economy. Europe is currently passing through a dramatic historical period in which issues of international integration and disintegration are of crucial importance. In spite of the difficulties encountered on the way to broader European integration, this process is going on, taking new shapes and new dimensions. The opening up of CEE economies, after decades of political and economic isolation, was one of the unprecedented challenges to the European integration process. In this regard, the success or failure of the process of economic and social transformation in Eastern Europe and East–West European integration, including the prospects of membership in the European Union, can have a major impact on the future of the continent.

This book focuses on the interdependence between the pattern and prospects of economic transformation in CEE and the wider issue of European integration. It is an attempt to address some of the important aspects of this process from different perspectives: from the point of view of academic economic and political science research as well as from the point of view of current economic policy discussion. In designing the book, the principal objectives of the editors were to review the current state-of-the-art of the process of East–West European integration; to reveal bottlenecks and obstacles to the process; to identify key economic policy issues and outline the prospects of European integration regarding the transforming CEE economies.

The book seeks to provide analytical insight into some of the most widely debated developments in the European economy such as the political economy of European integration in view of the envisaged expansion of the European Union; East–West trade after the opening up of Eastern Europe; industrial restructuring and labour market adjustments resulting from the intensification of the process of economic integration; and the role of financial reforms and financial flows in this process. Special emphasis is placed on the role of European integration for speeding up the transition process in the countries of CEE.

In the main, the book is the outcome of an international conference on the same topic held in Sofia, Bulgaria, 27–28 May 1994, and organized by the

XXI Century Foundation in Sofia. The editors are grateful to the ACE Programme of the European Commission and to the Open Society Fund, Bulgaria, for financial support for this conference, to the XXI Century Foundation for the excellent organization and to the Vienna Institute for Comparative Economic Studies (WIIW) for important editorial help in the final stages of completing the manuscript of this book.

Rumen Dobrinsky
Michael Landesmann

Abbreviations

CAP	Common Agricultural Policy (of the EU)
CEE	Central and Eastern Europe
CEE-6	Bulgaria, Czech Republic, Hungary, Poland, Romania, Slovak Republic (before the split of Czechoslovakia: CEE-5)
CEE-4, Visegrad-4	Czech Republic, Hungary, Poland, Slovak Republic (before the split of Czechoslovakia: CEE-3)
CEEC(s)	Central and Eastern European country(ies)
CEFTA	Central European Free Trade Agreement
CIS	Commonwealth of Independent States
CMEA (COMECON)	Council for Mutual Economic Assistance
CSFR	Czech and Slovak Federative Republic
EA(s)	Europe Agreement(s) (Association Agreements with the EU)
EBRD	European Bank for Reconstruction and Development
EEA	European Economic Area
EFTA	European Free Trade Association
EMU	Economic and European Monetary Union
ERM	Exchange Rate Mechanism
ESI	export specialization index
EU	European Union
FDI	foreign direct investment
FTA	free trade agreement
FSU	Former Soviet Union
GSP	General System of Preferences
IA(s)	Interim Agreement(s) (between CEECs and the EU)
IIT	intra-industry trade
ILO	International Labour Organization
IPR	Import penetration ratio
LDCs	less developed countries
LFS	labour force survey
MFA	Multi Fibre Agreement
MFN	most favoured nation (status)

NACE	industry classification used by the European Statistical Office
NAFTA	North American Free Trade Area
NTB	non-tariff barriers
OLI	ownership, locational and internalization
OPT	outward processing traffic
PCE	previously centrally planned economies
PIT	'Partners in Transition' (OECD initiative)
PW(s)	public work(s)
QR	quantitative restrictions
RCA	revealed comparative advantage
SOCB(s)	state-owned commercial bank(s)
SOE(s)	state-owned enterprise(s)
TB	tariff barriers
UA	unemployment assistance
UB(s)	unemployment benefit(s)
UI	unemployment insurance
UN ECE	United Nations Economic Commission for Europe
WEU	West European Union

1. Introduction

Rumen Dobrinsky and Michael Landesmann

The end of the 1980s brought the most significant change in postwar Europe and, probably, in the world too: the demise of totalitarian rule in the Central and Eastern European countries (CEECs) and the former Soviet Union. After decades of political isolation and economic degradation, the peoples of this region were eager to start catching up with the developed world which had in the meantime moved many years ahead in terms of economic progress and living standards. The process of transition from totalitarianism and central planning to pluralistic democracy and market economy which is under way in these countries poses one of the most unprecedented challenges both to the peoples of these countries and their policy makers.

The process of economic transformation affects practically all aspects of economic reality in the former communist states. One of the ultimate goals of this process is the integration (or rather the reintegration) of their economies with the European and with the world economy. The decades of economic isolation from their natural economic partners and the artificially imposed economic and trade arrangements within the CMEA had immensely distorted the structure of their foreign economic relations.[1] Rebuilding economic ties with the western part of Europe is thus an integral part of the transition process. This book is an attempt to address some of the issues and problems faced by the transforming CEECs on their way to European integration.

Both economic theory and economic reality have provided proofs of the mutual benefit of liberalized trade relations for the participating countries. However, nowadays, free trade is seen only as one of the elements of the process of economic integration among nations. The current understanding of the economic integration of nations is, as István P. Székely puts it in Chapter 10, a state of relations among countries in which the impact of country borders on the decision-making processes of economic agents is insignificant.

The development of sophisticated international structures such as the post-Maastricht European Union (EU) based on the concept of a Single European Market, or NAFTA in North America, is the best illustration of the evolution in both political thinking and practical results of modern concepts of economic integration. Although not without controversy and setbacks (remember the failures in implementing narrow bands in the European Exchange Rate Mechanism), efforts towards deeper and wider European integration are continuing and progress is remarkable.

Reality confirms that what is now the EU is turning out to be the most viable among the international economic structures that have existed during different periods in postwar Europe. It is often cited as the most successful regional integration scheme of the world (Winters, 1993). Besides, unlike any other existing scheme, integration within the EU extends far beyond free trade within a customs union. Some of the most important – and unique – EU provisions of this kind are factor mobility within the EU, the common agricultural policy (CAP), the common external trade policy, the common competition policy, the common structural policy promoting underdeveloped regions, the monetary union and the harmonization of standards, to mention just a few.

In reality, the depth of the Maastricht integration arrangements has created a qualitatively different economic situation in Europe, in which those who were left outside the boat could clearly sense the disadvantage of their position (Baldwin, 1994). This in turn sparked off a process of further widening of the EU leading to the accession of most of the EFTA members which in itself is further evidence of the EU's success.

Under these circumstances it is understandable that the CEECs, after the rupture of their previous multilateral arrangements within the CMEA, have sought closer ties specifically with the EU. Indeed, as stated by Alexander Tomov in his discussion notes on Part One of the book, for many East Europeans, including high-ranking politicians, at least at the start of transition, European integration was synonymous with full membership in the EU. Thus EU–CEE relations are naturally a central issue in this book.

At first sight, at least in the eyes of the East, the prospects for pan-European integration seemed achievable before the turn of this century. The Association Agreements of the CEECs with the EU (the Europe Agreements) seemed to support this optimism. However, when the short period of euphoria after the initial political changes in the East was over, there came a time of more sober judgement. In essence, this spirit is reflected in all essays in the book.

In Chapter 2, Daniel Daianu reflects on the broad evolutionary aspects of the process of European integration in the context of global economic dynamics. He sees, however, serious difficulties in the process of pan-European integration both in the East and in the West. To make his argument, he introduces the notions of economic *vitality* (denoting 'the sustainability of relatively high rates of competitive economic growth') and economic *viability* (meaning 'satisfactory per capita income and income distribution which does not disrupt the social fabric'). Problems in the two parts of Europe are of a different nature, but both obstruct the pan-European process. In spite of the progress made during the postwar era, Daianu argues, Western Europe is suffering from diminishing *vitality*, resulting in 'chronically losing ground in world competition'. Conversely, the problems in the eastern part of the continent stem from weakened *viability*, an outcome of the transition crisis. This represents at the same time an opportunity and a threat for Europe. Joint efforts to link the West European quest for new vitality and the East European quest for viability, provided proper policies are devised, might induce synergies which could be beneficial for the whole of Europe. On the other hand, any lack of action in the heterogeneous European space may result in a 'clash of civilizations'. Daianu appeals for *collective strategies* in Europe based on vision and genuine cooperation, calling this type of pan-European action a *Grand Alliance*.

Despite the popular appeal and the apparent, or at least declared, high-level political will for widening the process of pan-European economic integration towards the CEECs, there are, at present, still serious obstacles to this process. In Chapter 3, Jaromir Cekota explores some of the most important 'barriers to East–West European integration'. One of the most substantial barriers is related to the costs of East–West integration and, ultimately, to the question of who pays these costs. The only example of genuine and rapid Eastern reintegration – the reunification of Germany – provides a sound basis for estimating the astronomical costs which would be implied, if this type of policy were pursued in the rest of Eastern Europe. It is more than obvious that Western taxpayers would never be inclined to bear such a burden. Hence, Cekota argues, 'integration of the CEECs should not be an expensive process involving massive handouts' to East Europeans.

Another obstacle in the West, as specified by Cekota, is the fear of rising unemployment caused by the influx of Eastern products as a result of liberalizing trade with the CEECs. In fact, Chapter 9 provides partial answers to this problem. In this chapter, Giovanni Graziani analyses some aspects of the impact of liberalized trade with CEE on the EU manufacturing industry on the basis of a detailed sectoral analysis. One of his main findings is 'the recognition that the actual threat to EU industry seems to be much smaller than is usually thought and limited to very specific sectors'. Besides, as emphasized by Graziani, 'for most of the sectors concerned, competitive pressure by the CEECs is only a supplementary factor to a challenge already taking place on the world market'.[2] He also argues that any negative impact should be compared with the benefits of the possible expansion of EU exports to CEE. The liberalization of trade with CEE provides Western producers with many new niches and hence aggregate benefits may very well outweigh the 'losses'. Nonetheless, the partial 'losses' and the need for structural adjustment in the West have already led to the mobilization of strong protectionist pressures in some West European countries.

One of the real innovations of the Maastricht treaty was the goal of a monetary unification within the EU. It was embedded in practical requirements for the EU member states (the so-called Maastricht convergence criteria). These criteria will now also be applied to new candidates wishing to join the EU. Cekota examines in Chapter 3 whether and to what extent the CEECs meet the Maastricht convergence criteria and concludes that only the Czech Republic (in an optimistic scenario of economic development) might be ready to meet these criteria before the turn of the century. For the other CEECs it might take ten to fifteen or more years to do so.

Following this line, Richard Baldwin presents in Chapter 4 an assessment of the prospects of an Eastern enlargement of the EU in the context of the pan-European integration process. He argues convincingly that the economic implications of an eventual speedy accession of the CEECs to the EU would be of such magnitude that they would be intolerable both for the peoples and for the policy makers in the current EU member states. Among the arguments put forward by Richard Baldwin, to mention only some, are: the implied budget burden on the 'old' members (resulting from the membership of populous and poor countries); the inevitable redistribution of the EU structural funds and CAP spending, to the disadvantage of the current recipients; the resulting changes in the distribution of voting power within the EU, which might completely change not only the decision-making process but also the setting of the EU agenda.

On the basis of strong empirical evidence Baldwin argues that it may take fifteen to twenty years before the first CEECs may be prepared for full membership in the EU. In his discussion notes, Alexander Tomov is in broad agreement with these points, stressing that, in spite of the political will, the economic barriers will effectively preclude the CEECs from EU membership in the foreseeable future.

Is there another, mutually beneficial way out of this situation? In Chapter 4 Richard Baldwin puts forward a very intriguing proposal on how to 'break the tie' of the CEE–EU integration process. He calls for an 'Association of the Association Agreements' (AAA), embedding the existing Europe Agreements and an intermediate step to the CEECs' full membership in the EU. The AAA, consisting of the EU and the CEECs, would require the CEECs to liberalize trade amongst themselves and would amount to a free trade zone covering the EU and CEE. This amounts to a gradual accession process to the EU similar to that of EFTA countries in the past.

The integration of CEE with the European economy and, in particular, with the EU, involves a process of 'economic interpenetration' between these two parts of Europe. In Chapter 5 John Sheehy analyses the main aspects of this process and its prospects, focusing on the recent evolution of CEE–EU trade. After 1989 and especially after the dismantling of the CMEA, there was a spectacular growth of CEEC trade with the EU, more specifically of CEEC exports to the EU. As a result, the EU already is the main trading partner of these countries. However, the importance of the trade links is highly asymmetric for the two sides: altogether, CEE accounts for a meagre 4–5 per cent of the EU's total trade with non-EU member states.

Sheehy further argues, on the basis of empirical evidence, that whereas the changes in CEE exports to the EU were more of a quantitative nature (export expansion with little change in the composition of flows), those in CEE imports from the EU implied substantial restructuring of the trade flows. He notes especially the inflated importance of CEE consumer goods imports from the EU.

Another issue addressed by Sheehy is whether, if at all, the CEECs' Association Agreements with the EU had any significant impact on CEE–EU trade patterns and if the remaining EU protection in some 'sensitive' sectors constitutes a serious barrier to CEE exports in these sectors. Interestingly enough, the results of his analysis seem to indicate a negative answer to both these questions. At least in the initial stage there is no statistically significant evidence that the sectorally differentiated changes in protection have affected the CEECs' export performance; on the other hand, the remaining EU quantitative restrictions do not appear to act as binding constraints on CEE exports in the sensitive sectors. Thus, at least in the short run, the problems appear to stem from rigidities on the CEECs' supply side, namely from the failure of CEE producers to respond promptly to changes in market conditions. This may also very well be one of the explanations for the modest changes in the commodity composition of CEE exports to the EU.

Undoubtedly the developments in East–West trade and, in particular, CEE–EU trade are of paramount importance for the process of East–West integration. These developments are analysed from different perspectives in several chapters of this book. In Chapter 6, Rumen Dobrinsky analyses some of the changes in the patterns of CEE–EU trade in the transition period. He also attempts a rough comparison of the commodity composition of exports of CEECs and of EU member states.

Dobrinsky finds that since the start of economic transformation there has been a notable diversification of CEE–EU trade and ascribes it to the emergence of new trade in this period. The commodity composition of the CEECs' exports, however, using different quantitative measures, shows rather high similarity amongst the individual countries. They are thus competing for broadly the same or similar niches in the EU market. Furthermore, it turns out that in a number of sectors in which all CEECs enjoy comparative advantages *vis-à-vis* the EU, they face strong competition on the part of the other CEECs and protectionist measures on the part of the EU.

The factor content of CEE exports to the EU is another indication of the current state of CEE–EU relations. All CEECs still appear to specialize in products of high energy content (due to inertia resulting from previous access to cheap Soviet energy), low skill content and very low R&D content. If compared to the factor content of EU total exports, the pictures for the two sets of countries are almost mirror images. Again, so far transition has not brought about significant changes in the factor content of CEE exports to the EU.

It is not realistic to expect that the composition and structure of CEE trade will change fundamentally while the income gap with respect to Western Europe remains in its current range. As long as this gap remains, Dobrinsky concludes, the principal driving forces of trade are likely to remain distinctly different in the two parts of Europe.

In Chapter 7 Michael Landesmann discusses the issue of whether we might be witnessing the beginning of a process of strong differentiation across different regions of CEE regarding their capability of catching up with the West. Based on the results of recent growth theory which suggest a bifurcation in which some countries or regions might be able to catch up and others will fall further behind, he analyses recent empirical evidence of changes in the pattern of trade between CEE and the EU. He finds strong evidence for an accentuation of specialization patterns in CEE towards more labour-intensive branches and away from capital-intensive branches (see also the evidence on this point in Chapter 6), as one would expect following a process of trade liberalization between countries characterized by developmental gaps between each other. However, Landesmann finds that these shifts are of significantly different size and that the general shift away from R&D and skill-intensive branches does not apply, for example, to the ex-CSFR and Hungary. Also, the general shift towards more intra-industry trade (which one would expect to characterize a catching-up process) is more pronounced in the case of the ex-CSFR and Hungary, while in the other economies the trends are towards more inter-industry specialization. Hence the limited data, given the short statistical time series available since 1989, suggest that there is both evidence for increasing specialization patterns in East–West trade relationships (there are also signs of a high degree of *intra*-industry specialization) but also some evidence pointing in the direction of a catching-up process in certain countries/regions, but not in others.

In Chapter 8 Peter Havlik explores in more detail the export/import asymmetry in the adjustment process regarding CEE trade with the EU already mentioned. The quantitative evaluation of recent changes in the structure of the CEECs' exports to and imports from the EU confirm the striking difference in the dynamics of the two flows. This means that the demand side in the transforming economies has apparently been much more responsive to the changes in the macroeconomic environment than the supply side.

This point has two aspects. The first is related to the question of whether any significant reorientation of trade from ex-CMEA markets to the EU did take place in that period. The answer to such a question is somewhat disputed, but it is possible to say that much of the previous trade within the CMEA was simply lost by the CEECs.

The second aspect concerns the producers' behaviour during transition. As pointed out by Lubomir Mitov in his discussion notes (p. 164), during the initial years of transition CEE exports were predominantly generated by large state-owned enterprises (SOEs). In general, the performance of large SOEs in this period was characterized by slow speed of adjustment to the changing market environment. Restructuring and adjustment of SOEs was impeded by some systemic factors such as the loss of traditional markets, disturbances in the supply of some inputs, lack of managerial and marketing skills for operating in a market environment, malfunctioning and imperfections in some markets. It is not surprising then that not much change was observed in the commodity composition of CEEC exports to the EU.

One of the intriguing problems arising from the liberalization of trade by the CEECs is which industries have been more successful than others in expanding their EU market shares. Havlik addresses this issue on the basis of a 'shift-and-share' analysis, whereby he quantifies the impact of different factors on the CEECs' export growth. One of the conclusions of his assessments is that more than 80 per cent of the increment in exports of manufactured goods by Czechoslovakia, Poland and Hungary in 1989–92 could be ascribed to 'competitive gains' on EU markets, that is to faster growth of exports in these sectors than the growth of other suppliers. However, as observed in the discussion notes of Lubomir Mitov and Marek Belka, this could have been a one-time effect of transitory nature ('the outcome of a unique concurrence of circumstances').

In a similar line of reasoning, in Chapter 9, Giovanni Graziani analyses CEEC industries showing the largest shares in exports to the EU. He identifies three such industries: footwear and clothing, metal production and chemicals (mainly petrochemicals and industrial chemicals). The first group is especially interesting due to the emergence of intensive outward-processing traffic (OPT) between EU-based firms and CEE-based subcontractors in recent years. OPT has thus been one of the main determinants of the recorded 'boom' of trade flows in certain sectors, in both directions.

In summarizing the EU's 'benefits' and 'harms' from trade liberalization with the CEECs, Graziani concludes that 'any new non-tariff barriers in EU trade with CEE would inevitably restrict the CEECs' export access and consequently diminish the chances of economic transition in these countries, which are extremely dependent on export revenue'. This conclusion may be regarded as counterbalancing the one by John Sheehy about the marginal impact of EU protection measures on CEE exports quoted above.

In a broader perspective, East–West European integration would require the full opening up of all markets on both sides towards each other. As observed by István P. Székely in Chapter 10, this would mean that 'the flow of goods and capital and the movement of labour across national borders is not hindered by institutional imperfections and regulations ... and significant differences in risk components...'. Székely goes on to make the illuminating point that international economic integration presupposes 'economic integration within national borders'. The fact is that financial markets in the former centrally planned economies (if they existed at all) were highly segmented and this now becomes a serious obstacle to their reintegration into European financial markets. This may also have grave consequences for the overall process of East–West economic integration.

Thus financial reform in the CEECs will play a critical role both for the process of economic transformation in these countries and for their reintegration into the European economy. Székely highlights in Chapter 10 the importance of financial sector reforms in economic transformation and integration: 'financial markets and institutions play a central role in the integration of different markets within and across national borders'. Besides, through intermediation, the financial sector has to guarantee the efficient allocation of the relatively scarce financial resources available for the process of economic restructuring in the transforming CEECs.

However, financial reforms in CEE encounter serious difficulties. Progress in this area seems to be hampered by the emergence of a vicious circle in the financial sector: the banking system as a whole is not operating efficiently due to lack of competition and slow privatization; investors (especially strategic foreign investors) do not show any notable interest in state-owned CEE banks because the latter are burdened with large amounts of bad loans; the current accumulation of bad loans reduces the banking system's efficiency even more. The expected recovery in some CEECs may improve the situation of their banking systems. Székely argues that this may be the chance for speeding up financial reforms and thus the whole process of economic transformation in these countries.

The process of economic transformation and liberalization also brought about important changes in the CEECs' labour markets. The most significant of them, sadly, was the emergence of high and, as it seems, probably persistent unemployment in most of these countries (with the exception of the Czech Republic). Tito Boeri and Stefano Scarpetta highlight in Chapter 11 some features of the labour market in the CEECs and some characteristics of unemployment in these countries.

One of the dazzling features of labour market adjustment in the CEECs (definitely different from the situation in Western Europe) is the stagnant nature of the unemployment pool, characterized by low in- and outflows. One of the results is a large spread of long-term unemployment (especially among young people, as revealed by Boeri and Scarpetta) with its serious economic and social consequences. This situation in turn requires specific labour market policy measures to help the return of the unemployed to gainful employment. This is by no means an easy policy task under the conditions of transformation depression in CEE. Besides, there is a need to find an efficient combination of passive (benefit-based) and active (directed towards job search) labour market policy measures.

The unemployment benefit systems in the CEECs have occasionally been criticized for being too 'generous' and thus creating disincentives for work. This argument is seriously challenged by Boeri and Scarpetta who evaluate the level of unemployment benefits in most CEECs as often falling below the minimum subsistence levels in these countries. Consequently, unemployment benefits 'may well fail to provide the minimum income support required to devote enough time to job search'. Boeri and Scarpetta argue that carefully designed active labour market policies may help at least to speed up the turnover of the currently stagnant unemployment pool. Even if this does not lead to increases in job offers, it would have a favourable social impact as it will reduce the duration of unemployment spells for the long-term unemployed.

In their discussion notes, Fiorella Padoa Schioppa Kostoris and Jan Švejnar provide additional arguments and evidence on the incidence of unemployment in the CEECs and the implied policy measures. Without challenging the main arguments of Boeri and Scarpetta, Kostoris asserts that the main policy instrument to combat unemployment in CEECs is the stimulation of exports as a way of raising aggregate demand. Švejnar warns that due to measurement problems the recorded levels of short-term unemployment in the CEECs may be underestimated; this may in turn lead to erroneous policy measures.

Given the current state of the CEE economies, foreign direct investment (FDI) can play a very substantial role in their revival, in speeding up the transformation process and in their reintegration into the European and the world economy. This aspect of East–West economic integration is addressed by Klaus-Dieter Schmidt and by Richard Stern in the two closing chapters of the book. Indeed, as rightly noted by Schmidt, one hopes that FDI may 'perform a catalytic role in restructuring and privatizing the state industry' and serve as 'an engine in transforming the CEECs into Western-style market economies'.

According to some of the theoretical approaches, FDI is undertaken when a firm perceives ownership and location advantages and the latter can be utilized best within the firm's internal structure. FDI is only one among numerous possibilities of operating abroad; a firm undertakes FDI when it considers this to be a more efficient way of conducting foreign operations. The transforming economies' abilities to attract FDI depend on a number of conditions, in particular their natural endowments and the inherent business risk factors.

As demonstrated by Schmidt, during the short period since the start of economic transition, dramatic differences in FDI flows to different parts of Eastern Europe and the former Soviet Union (FSU) have emerged. However, the analysis of this differentiation shows that it is substantiated by the emerging differences in economic transformation paths observed in the countries of the region. Schmidt argues convincingly that factors such as institutional and political stability, the level of development and the market size and future growth prospects of a country are much more important in the firms' investment decision process than concessions and subsidies by the recipient country.

Stern notes that FDI has traditionally been viewed, especially in less developed economies, as 'an external source of capital which can be used to augment domestic savings' and 'fill the investment gap'. He argues, however, that this is not likely to happen in Eastern Europe, at least in the short run. This argument is substantiated by comparing the estimated (by different authors) investment needs of the countries in the region and actual flows. In spite of the speculative character of some of the quoted estimates, the gap between needs and actual flows is spectacular[3] and this is not likely to change in the foreseeable future.

Following this line of reasoning, Stern suggests that what the CEECs need under these circumstances is to try to increase the overall effect of the scarce FDI they are able to attract. He views FDI mainly as a means of technology transfer: if deployed in certain 'critical' sectors of the economy, these can contribute best to economic growth in the medium and long term.

Taken as a whole, the book addresses only some selected, though important, aspects of the dichotomy 'economic transformation – economic integration'. Obviously, it reflects the state-of-the-art in these selected topics at a certain point in time. The dynamics of change in Europe, particularly in its eastern part, are such that the publication lag may render some facts and arguments obsolete. In any case, it is an attempt to provide an objective assessment of progress in the topics addressed, leaving scope and space for future research.

NOTES

1. It is instructive to compare the CEECs' current volumes and directions of trade with prewar figures (see, for example, Baldwin, 1994, and Collins and Rodrik, 1991).
2. It is illustrative to note that other recent studies point in the same direction. Thus, Faini and Melo (1994) found that the effect of EU trade liberalization on employment in the EU, evaluated on the basis of potential labour displacements in EU countries, will practically be negligible.
3. The actual flows of financial resources from the western to the eastern part of Germany after reunification (the annual level of these flows exceeds the cumulative stock of FDI to all CEECs and the FSU, taken together, since the start of transition) is a good illustration of this gap.

REFERENCES

Baldwin, R.E. (1994), *Towards an Integrated Europe*, London: Centre for Economic Policy Research.

Collins, S. and Rodrik, D. (1991), *Eastern Europe and the Soviet Union in the World Economy*, Washington, DC: Institute for International Economy.

Faini, R. and Melo, J. de (1994), 'Trade with Eastern Europe: adjustment and opportunities', paper presented at the 9th Annual Congress of the European Economic Association, Maastricht, 3–5 September 1994.

Winters, L.A. (1993), 'The European Community: a case of successful integration?', CEPR Discussion Paper Series No. 755, London: Centre for Economic Policy Research.

PART ONE

The New Dimensions of European Integration

2. Europe under a double challenge

Daniel Daianu

THE THREE CIRCLES OF TRANSITION

The year 1989 was a watershed moment in the flow of history as it signalled the start of post-communist transformation in Europe and the end of the cold war. Post-communist transformation marks the close of this century; its assumed and stated goal is to stop the decay of the former communist countries, to transform their non-viable economic systems into well-functioning market economies and, eventually, change their political systems into pluralistic democracies. This undertaking is a historical challenge facing Europe. However, this challenge is accompanied by a growing malaise engulfing the continent. There are signs indicating that the large European economies have been chronically losing ground in world competition during the past decades and their dynamics seem to have been replaced by diminishing vitality. Additionally, German reunification and the regional and international implications of the collapse of communism have put exceptional pressure on the direction, speed and the accepted patterns of implementing the process of further European integration as defined by the Maastricht treaty. Whereas Eastern Europe (this term is used in the broad, traditional sense here) and the newly established states strive to achieve economic viability in a relatively hostile international environment, the West European countries appear to be mainly concerned with regaining their vitality. The combination of problems of a differing nature faced by the two regions substantially complicates the task of policy makers in all countries concerned.

In a narrow sense post-communist transition deals with the changing anatomy and physiology of the former command systems. In a broader sense, it refers to the whole array of consequences of the dismantling of communism on the European continent. One telling example is the upheaval of the political establishment in Italy, which was enhanced by the relatively sudden disappearance of the ideological and military confrontation between the two blocs in Europe. The implosion, or metamorphosis (as in Italy), of major Western communist parties, is another significant consequence.

Moreover, for Europe as a whole, post-communist transition must be judged in conjunction with trends which had been discernible for more than twenty years – in terms of processes which allow (or do not allow) timely institutional and technological change brought about by internal and external competitive pressures. Thus a recent OECD study emphasizes that 'the truth is that the culprit is not change, but the rich countries' inability or unwillingness to cope with it'.[1] The same study remarks that '...the industrial countries, especially in Europe, have allowed their economic arteries to harden' for at least the last twenty years.[2]

The double connotation of transition in Europe is not sufficient for grasping the evolution of this continent within the context of the world economy. We have been witnessing a process of redistribution of economic power in the world space with its economic gravity centre shifting steadily and, apparently, inexorably, towards the Pacific Rim. *The Japan That Can Say No* (Ishihara, 1991) became an open reality in February 1994 when, for the first time in postwar bilateral relationships, the Japanese prime minister mentioned possible retaliatory measures against eventual unilateral steps taken by the USA.

International economic policy opinion has not failed to take into account the rise of Asian economies. Thus a report by the Bretton Woods Commission (chaired by Paul Volcker), which had been set up to celebrate the 50th anniversary of the IMF and the World Bank, recommends that the voting structures in the international financial organizations be changed to reflect the rising power of Asia.[3]

Neither should one forget China, which is seen by many observers as an emerging economic superpower in the next century. The awakening of China will doubtless reinforce the process of overall redistribution of economic and political power in the world, with its multitude of geopolitical and economic consequences. Chancellor Helmut Kohl's visit to Beijing in 1993 exemplified not only the new and growing German assertiveness in pursuing its regional economic and political interests, but also signalled the way Germany is looking at the new China.[4]

Likewise, the fact that the Clinton administration had to give up attempts to use the Chinese most-favoured-nation status as a means of political pressure reflects the irresistible power of economic logic in today's world politics. More than ever foreign policy means foreign economic policy. In this respect, let us remember how Japan was looked at by some Western countries in the aftermath of the oil price shocks during the 1970s – when it was accused of practising a single-minded oil diplomacy. Today even the USA seems to be forced to adopt a similar posture in international relations.[5]

With the benefit of hindsight we can see how unrealistic and misleading a vision can be that proclaimed *The End of History* (Fukuyama, 1990) by focusing on the demise of communism only. Besides, the clash of ideologies is not over and cannot be left behind in the past – the distinction left vs right has defined and will continue to define the political process in all democracies and it would be very naïve to consider that socialist leanings are fading away in the former command societies.[6]

From a certain perspective, ironically, the post-cold war world looks less stable: the proliferation of military and ethnic conflicts, widespread economic recession and trade protectionism, the rise of Islamic fundamentalism, the escalation of nationalism, tribalism and right-wing extremism (neo-fascism) are very worrying signs. We can talk of three concentric *circles of transition* (crisis) in the world: one that comprises the former communist states; a larger one that covers the whole of Europe; and a third one that looks at processes in the space of the world at large.

TRYING TO DEFINE *VITALITY* AND *VIABILITY*

In an ideal world of perfect competition, of insignificant borders, a preoccupation with 'macro'-behaviour would not be justified. The real world is different. Even arguments put forward in terms of a 'new industrial revolution' and of tendencies of a globalization of economic activities reducing the scope for national economic policy making cannot conceal a fundamental truth: the real world is made up of national entities which develop and pursue national goals and have their particular traits and dynamics. Moreover, the real world reveals imperfect competition and shifts in comparative advantages resulting from astonishing catching-up processes and successful institutional design.

There is no shortage of concepts and highly elaborate explanations attempting to capture analytically the differentiated economic evolution of national entities in global space.

In the late 1970s Charles Kindleberger (1978) talked about the 'aging economy', trying to clarify the institutional roots of decelerating dynamics. Some years later, in his book *The Rise and Decline of Nations* (1982), Mancur Olson suggested that 'institutional sclerosis' was the basic cause of societal decline. He highlighted the development of 'coalitions of vested interests' which capture the public domain and ossify the decision-making process, thereby negatively affecting societal productivity. It is noteworthy that this concept was later used to analyse the economic euthanasia of command systems.[7] 'Overstretch' is seen by Paul Kennedy (1992) as the main explanatory factor behind the collapse of 'great powers' (empires). Put differently, nobody is big enough to enjoy sustainable (permanent) and expanding supremacy, unless endowed with celestial vitality. For example, the downfall of the former Soviet Union can be linked with the process of institutional dissolution, triggered by the virus called *glasnost*. But it is indisputable that the political opening itself was conceived by the Soviet leaders as a means to induce an invigoration of the economic system overstretched by military competition with the USA.

Michael Porter (1990), using concepts of industrial organization theory, puts the emphasis on clusters of capabilities and on endogenous growth to elucidate the competitiveness of nations. From a different perspective, George Lodge (1990) emphasizes the existence of and the need for *national strategies* to achieve, or restore, competitiveness. Alice Amsden (1989) and Robert Wade (1990) reason in the same vein.

By comparing the Asian 'economic miracles' with the Anglo-Saxon (Western) world, Lester Thurow (1993) distinguishes between 'producer' and 'consumer' economies. He argues that the former are most likely to become domineering economic forces in the world because of their institutional and cultural structure which favours savings/investment and the build-up of highly educated human capital. The 'consumer' economies, on the other hand, show a relatively low propensity to save and behavioural short-termism – the latter also being cited as an outcome of inadequate structures of corporate governance. The school of evolutionary economics (Nelson and Winter, 1982; Lesourne, 1991) seeks to throw light on the institutional determinants of differentiated dynamics across national economies. From such a theoretical perspective John Cornwall wrote his *Theory of Economic Breakdown* (1990).

The explanations listed above refer to the developed part of the world economy and are largely the intellectual byproduct of the Western anxiety about the dynamism exhibited by the Asian economies.[8] One could easily add to this the classical arguments on the congenital malfunctioning and inefficiency of command systems mainly provided by Ludwig von Mises and Friedrich von Hayek (as protagonists of the Calculation Debate in the 1920s and 1930s) and, more recently, by Janos Kornai (1980). All these theoretical explanations imply two concepts: *vitality* and *viability*.

To put it succinctly, one could say that *vitality* means the sustainability of relatively high rates of competitive economic growth. This also implies the existence of long-term equilibrium in the balance of payments. Competitive economic growth involves intensive innovation (or creative imitation) and a steady accumulation of highly educated human capital. The neo-growth theory (Romer, 1986), with its emphasis on the accumulation of knowledge, externalities and imperfect competition, provides a very illuminating theoretical underpinning of this phenomenon. One could trace this explanation to Gunnar Myrdal's process of 'cumulative causation' and try to identify what allows a poor performer (a poor country) to break the vicious circle, and a good performer (a rich country) to be diverted from the 'corridor' of sustainable prosperity.

As for *viability*, I would propose the following possible definition: maintaining satisfactory per capita income and income distribution which does not disrupt the social fabric. In a broad sense this definition would refer to the entropic degradation of the environment as well.

Both definitions assume a certain stability in the evolution of society: change can be managed, for it is either internally generated (if there are active agents of change), or society has the capacity of absorbing it in a non-disruptive way. Matters become much more complicated in the case of societies which are in the throes of social upheaval, or which are undergoing dramatic institutional and structural change. It is logical to presume that societal transformation, i.e. large-scale organizational and institutional change, is accompanied by fuzziness, volatility and institutional fragility. Under such circumstances economic, social and political stability is more than hard to achieve – it may easily turn into wishful thinking and a policy nightmare.

A viable economy is not necessarily a vital one. The British secular decline is a relevant example in this respect, though one can hardly question the solidity of British society. In fact, there are pundits who fear the spreading of an accentuated 'British disease' – something I would call *civilization fatigue*,[9] a sort of Spenglerian symptom – throughout the old continent.

EASTERN EUROPE, THE FIRST, OR INNER CIRCLE OF TRANSITION: WHY IS TRANSITION SO HARD?

The general mood has changed dramatically throughout Europe since the end of the 1980s. In Eastern Europe the euphoria which followed the collapse of the communist regimes is being replaced by uncertainty and increasing frustration regarding the pace and results of transition. People are beginning to realize that post-communist transformation is a much more complex and complicated process than initially thought and that time cannot be speeded up at will.

Defining and enforcing a new structure of property rights, formulating and passing legislation, making institutions work (institutions seen as 'rules enjoying wide social acceptability', in the phraseology of Douglas North, 1981), achieving durable macro-stabilization via structural adjustment and industrial restructuring, are intertwined prerequisites for attaining economic viability. But these are time-consuming and painful endeavours.

What is unique about post-communist transformation in Europe is that it implies several simultaneously evolving processes: large-scale institutional changes, economic restructuring, structural adjustment and macro-stabilization, and, last but not least, modernization. In addition post-communist transformation lacks the institutional ingredients of a market environment and experiences enormous distortions in the allocation of resources. Additionally, one should not forget that the Asian economies enjoyed the benefits of the golden years of a growing world economy (the 1950s and the 1960s) and that the success of several Latin American countries in the 1980s was favoured by a consumption-driven expanding US economy. The current international environment is significantly different and magnifies the shocks produced by the sudden disappearance of Eastern markets. I shall now focus on what I consider to be rather neglected issues in the current debate: understanding the relative backwardness and, in consequence, the institutional fragility of the evolving societal framework and the magnitude of the required reallocation of resources.

While the system-related (institutional) dimension of transition is of paramount importance, one can detect a further impulse which has driven the evolution of East European societies throughout this century. This is the attempt to catch up with the West, an idea which obsessed national politicians during the interwar period and, later, also the communist leaders of these countries. Nowadays this aspiration is reflected in the CEECs' ardent desire to join the EU.

Why is the desire to catch up so strong? One can often hear presumably knowledgeable professionals passing judgements on the transformation process who seemingly neglect the heavy legacy of backwardness of these societies – a state of affairs which goes far back in history.[10] As observed by a keen student of the region: '... Eastern Europe was in some sense economically backward long before it was absorbed into the broader Western world market. This backwardness has roots in the very distant past...' (Chirot, 1989, p. 3). Similarly, Ivan Berend (1994, p. 110) remarks: 'What is missing in most of these analyses is a deeper understanding of long-term historical trends in East–Central Europe'.[11]

However, a note of caution is required. The post-communist societies of Europe are societal entities which show similar structural traits but also major discrepancies. The latter can be attributed to the dissimilar pre-communist legacy (the most conspicuous example is Czechoslovakia which was a leading industrial country during the interwar period) and the different brands of national central planning, in terms of relaxation of direct controls and economic policy choices. The historical differences explain why market institutions vary qualitatively across CEECs and also why macro- and micro-disequilibria differed among them on the eve of 1989. Undoubtedly Hungary, Czechoslovakia and Poland had a substantial competitive edge in starting and managing the process of transition. Unsurprisingly, these countries fared better than the rest in their stabilization programmes.

Backwardness should be seen as bearing considerably on the potential for overcoming the performance deficit of institutionally poorly arranged societies.

On the one hand it points to the lack of knowledge of individuals and of society as a whole and to the constraints obstructing genuine institutional change, and on the other hand it suggests that there is much scope for a system to deviate from what may be conceived as an ideal course of evolution. The stress put on the burden of the past is meant to warn against its dragging effects and the dependency on an unfavourable path from which is not easy to break away.[12] Backwardness makes it harder to overcome the fragility of market institutions in the making and it enhances the danger that the dynamics of change might get out of control.

It is fair to point out that the high degree of literacy of East European societies, their large segments of well-trained workers, the existence of a numerous technical intelligentsia and the links with the developed world offered by the information age provide positive counterbalancing factors. Nonetheless it would be short-sighted and counterproductive to disregard the industrial and cultural distance that separates the East from the West.

The institutional fragility aspect has already been mentioned. Apart from the insufficient analytical attention paid to institutional build-up in the transforming societies in Europe, one must consider the seeds of instability produced by this very fragility. There is a train of thought which argues that as long as property rights are not clearly defined and enforced, durable macrostabilization will be out of reach (Lipton and Sachs, 1990). This is a relevant line of reasoning although it is incomplete in that it does not take into account the magnitude of inherited misallocation of resources and the strain this causes within the system.

The poor capacity of immature institutions to perform properly can also be mentioned in this context. For example, the debate 'universal vs. specialized banks' is quite relevant to the concerns created by immature market institutions in terms of enhanced instability and uncertainty in the system.[13] From a broader perspective one could raise the issue of the *governance capabilities* of these countries' political and economic élites, namely, the question to what extent they are capable of inducing and managing change (transformation) when so much fuzziness, volatility and uncertainty prevail.

Another issue which, in my view, is not sufficiently highlighted in the public debate, is the dimension of the inherited misallocation of resources in Eastern Europe. Here I am referring to the sheer scale of the disequilibria at the new relative prices, and to the magnitude of the required restructuring compared with the system's ability to undergo wide-ranging and quick changes. What is amazing is the nonchalance of many professionals with respect to the consequences of the magnitude of required restructuring. When one sees Western governments – and their social constituencies – tinkering on the fringes and deeply reluctant to undertake relatively minor adjustments, the strain under which the former command economies operate becomes understandable.

The inherited structure of the economies and the misallocation of resources have put the decision-making systems in the CEECs under exceptional strain once the combination of internal and external shocks (engineered by reforms or simply triggered by uncontrolled processes of systemic dissolution) had occurred. 'Structure' here refers to the network of institutional arrangements (including rules of conduct that are socially ingrained) and of vested interests (based on material/productive interdependencies and the distribution of property rights) which creates the logic of motion in the system and makes individual enterprises its captives. Vested interests are also the result of the configuration of industry inherited from the command system.[14] This industrial structure, with its extremely high concentration and its reliance on chain links, explains the degree of market monopolization in the transforming economies. In this respect one may talk about *structural power*, which is well illustrated by the power of debtors over creditors. This power is not of a conspiratorial nature (the cartel is unconscious) because it relies on the system's rules of functioning.

Command planning, with its inherent incapability of rational calculation and its forced industrialization, left a legacy of resource misallocation which became visible by price liberalization and the functional opening of the economy. The new prices show what was previously kept hidden by administrative prices and strong redistribution of income: a very wide range of profitability rates of economic entities. As a consequence one may observe a wide dispersion of units which could be grouped into several distinctly different categories: negative value-added enterprises; inefficient, but positive value-added units (which, in turn, can be subdivided into non-viable and potentially viable firms); and inefficient enterprises.

The wide range of profitability rates and the wide dispersion of enterprises with highly diverging performance mean that, should financial discipline be strictly enforced, a large number of units would have to go bankrupt. This would be the start of a profound reallocation of resources but aggregate output would go down substantially since market destruction is significantly more intense than market construction, at least during the first stage. There are two important aspects involved in this process: first, the scope of reallocation and, second, the speed required to maintain a certain balance between exit and entry,[15] so that the growth of the healthy private sector should not be unduly impaired. A plausible assumption is that the wider the scope and the faster the desired speed of the process, the higher the imbalance and tension within the economy. Actually, when 'low supply responsiveness' of transition economies is mentioned in debates, one points to this imbalance.

The problem of the scope and speed of resource reallocation can be posed for an economy operating at any level of employment: a significant change in relative prices would bring about resource reallocation. But it makes sense to presume that the lower the level of employment, the higher the reluctance to change will be. In this regard it may be interesting to recall the experience of the industrialized countries which had to absorb the oil price shock in the 1970s. These countries enjoyed the luxury of undertaking the necessary adjustment at a relatively leisurely pace due, essentially, to the quality of functioning of their economies, their status as world price makers for manufactured goods and the recycling of petro-dollars. Incidentally, monetary policy was also used to delay change, which led to a surge of world inflation.

The post-command economies are fundamentally price takers; they had to absorb a major worsening of their terms of trade (except the Russian Federation and, probably, Kazakhstan) once world prices started to govern all their trade transactions. They also had to face a relatively sudden collapse of Eastern trade following the dismantling of the COMECON arrangements. Additionally, there was a sharp contraction of domestic trade and, consecutively, of aggregate supply/demand as a result of the skyrocketing information and transaction costs for many enterprises. Owing to the extreme fuzziness concerning property rights, it is not unjustified to assume that *X-inefficiency* (Leibenstein, 1966) has been on the rise in may enterprises – a phenomenon accompanied by pervasive asset stripping. For the transforming economies the strain caused by the magnitude of required resource reallocation, combined with primitive and fragile institutional arrangements and the lack of organizational capital (Murrell, 1992), was compounded by severe exogenous shocks.

What are the implications of the existence of this strain? One is that these economies can very easily become exceedingly unstable and that their capacity to absorb shocks is pretty low. Another implication is that policy makers face extremely painful trade-offs and that in most cases, unless sufficient external support is available, the room for manoeuvre is practically non-existent. Basically, policy makers have to sail between the Scylla of high inflation (or hyperinflation, in the structurally more rigid economies) and the Charybdis of huge unemployment, both being highly undesirable politically and socially. Russia provides one of the most dramatic examples of this miserable trade-off: 'Economic chaos could produce a political collapse in at least two ways – through the descent into hyperinflation, or through a catastrophic rise in unemployment not cushioned by a social safety net' (Sachs, 1994).[16]

On this track it becomes apparent how critical the international environment is for the dynamics of transition. Unfortunately, the international environment is pretty unfavourable and the trends are not encouraging at all. It is unquestionable that the rising nationalism in international policy making, the growing protectionism, the global economic recession and the level of real interest rates on world capital markets do not facilitate post-communist transformation and accentuate the strain in the transforming economies. A concrete example of the distance between myth and reality in the rhetoric of support is the extent of access East European producers have to EU markets for most of their main export items. In this case there is a relationship between the needed sectoral adjustment in Western Europe[17] and trade as a tool for systemic adjustment (transformation) in post-communist countries. Reducing strain in the latter involves increasing short-term difficulties in the former, and the decision on how to deal with such a trade-off cannot be but political. But with Western Europe still stunned economically by the German reunification blow and by increasingly weak governments, the prospects of gaining wider access to EU markets are not very encouraging at present, in spite of high-level pronouncements and gestures.

East European governments are under strenuous time pressure: for them 'it is raining while the house is roofless'. They cannot afford the luxury of procrastinating and those who waste time will be heavily penalized. Besides, increasing worries are created because of the depressed levels of output, very low investment ratios and hardly any real wage increases; these are trends which could undermine the prospects for long-term growth. One should also mention an increasingly intense struggle over the distribution of wealth and an erosion of the consensus on a certain kind of societal change under conditions when large segments of society are made up of losers – phenomena that are not good signs for safeguarding the consistency of and support for economic policy making. An ever more pervasive social fatigue, coupled with the instability caused by ethnic and military conflicts in several parts of the region, can play havoc with transformation and lead national systems astray.

Path-dependency is a very meaningful expression under these circumstances. A sequence of major policy blunders and unfavourable external shocks can put a system on a trajectory that is misdirected and hard to correct. There is also the 'Russian factor', a variable whose magnitude and dynamics defy prediction – though some would argue that, in spite of all adversities, the march towards capitalism in that country cannot be stopped in the long term (Yergin and Gustaffson, 1994).

One needs also to consider that the degree of instability in the East is amplified by the extent to which the countries of the region feel their security threatened. When military conflicts occur, when borders are questioned, when ethnic tensions heighten, such a feeling is more than justified. All these factors enhance the development of a social and political psychology which makes the task of working out and implementing sound economic policies much harder.

WESTERN EUROPE, THE SECOND, OR MIDDLE CIRCLE OF TRANSITION: WHAT IS BEHIND CURRENT PESSIMISM?

Euro-pessimism is not new. This syndrome seems to recur in European history: suffice it to remember the hostile reaction to the international offensive by American corporations in the 1960s. A good barometer of the mood of the political class and of the business community in France at that time was Jean Jacques Servan-Schreiber's bestseller *Le Défi Américain*[18] (1967). One could argue that the 1960s were the decade that gave Europe the decisive intellectual impetus for the formation of companies aiming at developing an international identity, which could enable them to compete with American and, later, with Japanese transnational corporations. One could also say that the 1960s represented a period when the member countries of the (then) EEC started to develop an awareness which went way beyond the initial strategic goals pursued by the communities (the integration of former West Germany into pan-European structures and the containment of communism).

The Maastricht treaty and the European Monetary System (EMS) were a response to the syndrome of Eurosclerosis felt so deeply in the late 1970s and early 1980s. Both were meant to help Europe cope with the globalization of the world economy and the dynamism of the Pacific Rim. The fight between organicists and constructivists (in Hayek's terminology) was won by the technocracy in Brussels which argued in favour of a big institutional push: the achievement of the European Union. This vision, however, proved to be limited in the sense of being incapable of accommodating – both conceptually and operationally – two shocks: the collapse of communism in Europe and the reunification of Germany.

The *de facto* emasculation of the EMS (the collapse of the Exchange Rate Mechanism) was a logical consequence of the stress produced within the EU member countries by the economic impact of German reunification and the lack of coordination of economic policies. But this event can be seen as the peak of an iceberg. Rising economic nationalism, lack of policy coordination, sizeable and hard-to-contain budget deficits, unusually large and increasing unemployment rates (from an average of 3 per cent in the 1970s to more than 11 per cent currently), non-competitive industrial segments, burdensome welfare nets and restive trade unions, are symptoms of what appears to be a lasting disease – and not a cyclical phenomenon.

Especially worrying is rising unemployment which creates considerable social and political tensions and can harm the functioning of the institutions of democracy. Thus, after the success of the 'National Alliance' in the Italian elections of May 1994, the speaker of the Italian parliament declared that 'unemployment, which led to the rise of fascism and Nazism in the 1930s, poses a greater danger to democracy in Europe than anything else'.[19] It is no wonder then that the main theme of the G-7 summit meeting in Detroit (in March 1994) dealt with unemployment. An unavoidable conjecture is that rapidly growing unemployment in the East European region poses even greater dangers to the process of building up democratic institutions in post-communist societies.

Increasingly, weak governments and disenchantment by electorates with their political establishments (a growing 'cognitive dissonance' in political life which can be discerned in the USA and Japan as well) suggest a serious malaise in Western societies. It is disconcerting to see both left and right-of-centre governments being unable to steer their economies in a way that would indicate resolution and ability to deal with structural problems. The student demonstrations in France in April 1994 – for many reminiscent of the wave that swept the country in 1968 – and the way the French government had to give in to student demands have more than a symbolic significance. The resurgence, both politically and at the polls, of right-wing extremist parties in many European countries is more than disturbing. Chauvinism in its most aggressive form appears to be spreading all over the continent. Even in the countries considered to be role models of democratic procedures and religious and ethnic tolerance, right-wing extremism is on the rise (the case of the Netherlands is relevant). These trends complement the rise of nationalism and of right-wing extremism in post-communist countries in a very disturbing way.

It is not yet clear what impact these negative trends will have on the process of European economic integration. It would be dishonest, however, not to acknowledge that they create a great deal of unease and concern for the future dynamics of the process. It has always been an open secret that there are disagreements among the member countries as to the final destination of the integration journey. The fear now voiced by many is that, in spite of the further institutional sophistication of the EU and its expansion by three EFTA members, deep countercurrents are at work. There is also a growing sense of unease as to the actual distribution of influence within the EU as a consequence of Germany's reunification.

The policy towards Eastern Europe has mostly been reactive. The fact is that the West perceives the Eastern countries as a highly unstable and contaminating zone. In my opinion this policy has been more shaped by the desire for containment, or by an attempt to set up a sort of a buffer zone (with a hard core represented by the Visegrad-4), rather than by the understanding that Western involvement needs to be active and visionary – relying on a philosophy of integration.

The Copenhagen statement (of June 1993) signalled a significant conceptual breakthrough in this respect. Nonetheless, actual support is still much below what is needed to keep alive the momentum of reforms in the East and secure the stability of the continent. For instance, there are plans in Brussels to undertake large-scale public work projects in order to deal with rising unemployment in the Western countries. At the same time, the similar but more perturbing phenomenon of unemployment could derail reforms in the East. If one also considers the very low investment ratios and the badly needed improvement of infrastructure in the post-communist countries, a logical question arises: why is there no common European strategy to deal with this issue? For, if there it is now recognized that sooner or later Eastern Europe (or parts of it) will join the EU, it makes sense to develop strategies together and undertake joint national and regional public work projects in the transforming economies. This would help reforms considerably, it would build up social and political support for the process of economic transformation and it would help to homogenize infrastructure at a European level.

The danger both for the West and for the East lies in the inability of policy makers to conceptualize and make operational the intricate connections between the quest of advanced democracies to regain vitality and the quest of the emerging democracies to achieve economic viability. Taken together, the challenge for Europe now is how to speed up its industrial adjustment so as to cope with the offensive of Asian economies – 'the developmental market economies' as Yujiro Hayami (1992) calls them.[20]

A *GRAND ALLIANCE* IS NEEDED (THE THIRD, OR OUTER CIRCLE OF TRANSITION)

Europe is at a critical juncture of its history. There is a question of identity: how does, or how should Europe look after the collapse of communism in the East? In this regard the step taken by the EU in May 1994 to offer closer links with its security arm to nine countries of Eastern Europe[21] can be viewed as another major initiative (after the Partnership for Peace) aimed at defining the post-cold war frontiers and at tying the East more firmly to the West.[22] Jonathan Eyal[23] remarked in this respect: 'The political message is much more important than the practical one at this stage... Basically, it is now accepted that this is where Europe ends'.[24] This is a fairly bold statement bearing in mind that after the fall of the Berlin Wall in 1989, which can be seen as an ideological, political and social 'Big Bang', Europe has taken the posture of an expanding universe. In my view it is still too early to say where the frontiers of the new Europe are likely to settle. On the other hand one could argue that Eyal's words reflect a particular vision whose rationale is revealed by a certain logic of development of the European Union. In any case, this political vision needs to be given economic substance and, hence, organic links need to be forged between the West and the East. The West needs to match its rhetoric with more support for the East. A step in the right direction is the 'partnership' agreement concluded between the EU and Russia, which aims at the establishment of a free-trade zone towards the end of the century.[25] Likewise, the signing by Russia of the Partnership for Peace accord is a welcome event.

There is much need for *collective strategizing*. Though many statesmen have realized the linkage between the quest by Western countries for new vitality and the quest for viability of the emerging democracies, the gap between rhetoric and real action is striking. This linkage can inject new dynamism and do away with European lethargy if it is seen as a historical window of opportunity and if proper strategies and policies are devised. But it can also drag Europe down further if the current trends of poor communication, protectionism, shunning and beggar-your-neighbour policies continue.

West Europeans and East Europeans need a *Grand Alliance* – to paraphrase Graham Allison's 'Grand Bargain'. In a broader sense, the Western world needs to structurally embrace Eastern Europe, Russia, Ukraine and other former Soviet republics in order to avoid what Samuel Huntington (1993) suggestively called a possible 'Clash of Civilizations'.[26]

Europe needs vision, wise and bold leadership, and genuine cooperation. In our so highly interdependent continent strategies of *sauve qui peut* are dangerous. In a broader perspective, the Western world needs to help preserve an open world economy and provide a conceptual thrust for creating a stable post-cold war world order.

NOTES

1. See Reginald Dale's commentary 'The way to get the good jobs back', *International Herald Tribune*, 3 May 1994.
2. Ibid.
3. See Alex Brummer, 'Bretton Woods call for rethink on exchange rates', *Guardian Weekly*, 19 June 1994.
4. It is worth noting that Chancellor Helmut Kohl returned from Beijing with full hands: apart from the nurturing of political relations, economic deals amounting to almost $3 bn were announced. I have no information about any other European statesman having been able to achieve something comparable in business terms.
5. In 1994 for instance President Clinton himself turned into the most effective salesman for Boeing in the $6 bn Jumbo deal with Saudi Arabia.
6. There are sufficient grounds to expect a resuscitation of socialist ideas, under the ideological guise of social democracy in the former communist countries. In my view, the results of the recent elections in several of the countries in the region are not incomprehensible and do not reflect a temporary swing only.
7. Mancur Olson and Peter Murrell (1991) use the notion 'all encompassing interest' for this purpose.
8. As remarked by James Fallows (1994, p. 5), one difficulty for the West in understanding

the changes in the world is that 'Western societies, especially America, have been using the wrong mental tools to classify, shape, and understand the information they receive about Asia. They try to fit the facts into familiar patterns and categories – and they are hurt and frustrated when predictions derived from these patterns do not come true'.

9. In a very gloomy tone Zbignew Brzezinski (1993, p. xiii) says: 'The global relevance of the West's political message could be vitiated by the growing tendency in the advanced world to infuse the inner content of liberal democracy with a life-style that I define as permissive cornucopia... In contrast, outside the richer West, much of human life is still dominated by fundamental concerns with survival and not with conspicuous consumption'.
10. According to A. Solimano, in 1937 the nominal per capita income in Great Britain, Sweden, Germany, Belgium, Netherlands, France and Austria was estimated at $440, $400, $340, $330, $306, $265 and $190, respectively. The corresponding estimates for Czechoslovakia, Hungary, Poland, Romania, Yugoslavia and Bulgaria were $170, $120, $100, $81, $80 and $75, respectively (Gelb and Gray, 1991, p. 65).
11. I espouse the same line of reasoning in my article 'Transformation and the legacy of backwardness' (Daianu, 1992).
12. I remember in this respect how baffled some of my Romanian colleagues were when Ken Jowitt stated that 'Latin American countries have been in transition for more than a century' (remark made during the Romanian–American economic round table, Bucharest, 16–17 April 1991). He referred not only to erroneous economic policies (Argentina comes easily to one's mind for it belonged to the group of advanced economies before the Second World War) but also to institutional bottlenecks typical of certain levels of economic development.
13. As Jacek Rostowski (1993) put it, 'The lack of banking skills in the post-communist economies (PCEs) thus introduces a fundamental instability into their monetary systems. Until this problem is resolved, macroeconomic instability will remain hard to attain'. Similarly sceptical is Ronald McKinnon (1991).
14. The command system as a complex dynamic system is characterized by chain links, in contrast to a market economy which relies, essentially, on parallel links.
15. When considering this balance Olivier Blanchard and Philippe Aghion (1994) speak of an 'optimal speed'.
16. '...high inflation tends to be dynamically unstable, planting the seeds of even greater inflation in the future. On the other hand, tough stabilization without large-scale foreign financial support is also likely to fail, if high unemployment and inadequate social support produces political instability' (Sachs, 1994).
17. The steel processing industry and agriculture make the big headlines.
18. 'The American Challenge'.
19. Cited by Reuters in the report 'Senate chief blames neofascist', *International Herald Tribune*, 13 May 1994.
20. Hayami (1992) remarks: 'As developmental market economies become successful in industrial development, they begin to compete in the world trade of manufactured commodities. If this speed is too fast and exceeds the capacity of industrial adjustment on the side of advanced economies, it tends to create strong political demand for protectionism. The real danger arises when the protectionist bloc tries to achieve its political goal by escalating economic conflicts to ideological confrontation'.
21. The countries are: Bulgaria, the Czech Republic, Estonia, Hungary, Latvia, Lithuania, Poland, Romania and Slovakia.
22. See Tom Buerkle, 'EU offers 9 Eastern nations a step to security line-up', *International Herald Tribune*, 7–8 May 1994.
23. Director of the Royal United Services Institute for Defence Studies in London.
24. Cited by Tom Buerkle, op. cit., note 22.
25. See Gardner (1994).
26. The demographic dynamics suggest that, over the longer term, the *Europeanness* of the USA may change not insignificantly. This phenomenon may help create an economic and cultural 'bridge' between Western countries and the emboldened East Asian societies; but

it may further stimulate a certain reorientation of the USA toward the Pacific Rim – a tendency which may complicate the multi-relationship with Europe. Thus, Fukuyama (1994) considers that 'There is something in American (as opposed to European) culture that has been stimulated by the dynamism of Asia... There is a kind of cultural creation going on in the business world that is foreign to Europe, and that in time will make America seem more foreign to Europe'. For the implications of demographic dynamics in the USA see also Kennedy (1993, chap. XIII).

REFERENCES

Amsden, A. (1989), *The Next Asia's Giant*, New York: Oxford University Press.

Berend, I. (1994), 'Annus Mirabilis – Anni Mirabiles?', *Contention*, **8**, Winter, 109–28.

Blanchard, O. and Aghion, P. (1994), 'On the speed of transition in Eastern Europe', mimeo.

Brzezinski, Z. (1993), *Out of Control*, New York: Charles Scribner's Sons.

Chirot, D. (ed.) (1989), *The Origins of Backwardness in Eastern Europe*, Berkeley: University of California Press.

Cornwall, J. (1990), *The Theory of Economic Breakdown*, Cambridge: Oxford University Press.

Daianu, D. (1992), 'Transformation and the Legacy of Backwardness', *Economies et Sociétés*, **44**, May, 181–206.

Fallows, J. (1994), *Looking at the Sun. The Rise of the New East Asian Economic and Political System*, New York: Pantheon Books.

Fukuyama, F. (1990), *The End of History*, New York: Free Press.

Fukuyama, F. (1994), 'For the Atlantic allies today, a fraying of the sense of moral community', *International Herald Tribune*, 6 June.

Gardner, D. (1994), 'EU and Russia close to partnership pact', *Financial Times*, 12 May.

Gelb A. and Gray, C. (1991), 'The Transformation of Economies in Central and Eastern Europe', Washington, DC: The World Bank.

Hayami, Y. (1992), 'Japan and the model of developmental market economies: a historical perspective on the new world confrontation', paper presented at the Congress of the International Economic Association, Moscow, August.

Huntington, S. (1993), 'The Clash of Civilizations', *Foreign Affairs*, **50**(3), Summer, 22–50.

Ishihara, S. (1991), *The Japan That Can Say No*, New York: Simon and Schuster.

Kennedy, P. (1992), *The Rise and Fall of Great Powers*, New Haven: Yale University Press.

Kennedy, P. (1993), *Preparing for the XXI Century*, New York: Random House.

Kindleberger, C. (1978), 'The Aging Economy', *Weltwirtschaftliches Archiv*, **114**(3).

Kornai, J. (1980), *Economics of Shortage*, Amsterdam: North-Holland.

Leibenstein, H. (1966), 'Allocative Efficiency vs. X-Efficiency', *American Economic Review*, **56**(3), 392–410.

Lesourne, J. (1991), *Economie de l'Ordre et du Désordre*, Paris: Economica.

Lipton, D. and Sachs, J. (1990), 'Privatization in Eastern Europe: the case of Poland', *Brookings Papers on Economic Activity*, **2**, 293–333.

Lodge, G. (1990), *Perestroika for America*, Cambridge, Mass.: Harvard University Press.

McKinnon, R. (1991), *The Order of Economic Liberalization*, Baltimore: Johns Hopkins University Press.
Murrell, P. (1992), 'Evolutionary and radical approaches to economic reform in Eastern Europe', *Economics of Planning*, **25**(1).
Nelson, R. and Winter, S. (1982), *An Evolutionary Theory of Economic Change*, Cambridge, Mass.: Harvard University Press.
North, D. (1981), *Structure and Change in Economic History*, New York: Norton.
Olson, M. (1982), *The Rise and Decline of Nations. Economic Growth, Stagflation and Social Rigidities*, New Haven: Yale University Press.
Olson, M. and Murrell, P. (1991), 'The devolution of centrally planned economies', mimeo.
Porter, M. (1990), *The Competitive Advantage of Nations*, New York: Free Press.
Romer, P. (1986), 'Increasing Returns and Long Run Growth', *Journal of Political Economy*, **94**, 1002–37.
Rostowski, J. (1993), 'Creating stable monetary systems in post-communist countries', mimeo.
Sachs, J. (1994), 'Russia's struggle with stabilization: conceptual issues and evidence', paper presented at the annual World Bank Conference on Development Economics, Washington, DC, 28–29 April.
Servan Schreiber, J.J. (1967), *Le Défi Américain*, Paris: Denoel.
Thurow, L. (1993), *Head to Head*, Cambridge, Mass.: MIT Press.
Wade, R. (1990), *Governing the Market*, Princeton: Princeton University Press.
Yergin D. and Gustaffson, T. (1994), *Russia – 2010*, New York.

3. Barriers to European (East–West) integration

Jaromir Cekota

INTRODUCTION

This chapter investigates the barriers to full integration of Central and Eastern Europe into the security, economic and political structures of Western Europe.[1] To assess the prospects for European (East–West) integration in the 1990s and beyond, it is necessary to understand the objectives and outcomes of the recent 40-year (the cold war) period. This protracted confrontation between East and West came to an end with the massive concessions by the Soviet Union in the late 1980s, including the Red Army's withdrawal from Afghanistan, the German unification on Western terms, and the termination of Soviet political control over Eastern Europe. The main objective of Western strategy – the defeat of Russian communism – was fully achieved when the USSR itself imploded in 1991. Interestingly enough, the anti-Soviet coalition failed to develop a coherent political and economic programme of postwar reconstruction.

The end of the cold war was symbolized by the fall of the Berlin Wall in November 1989. Within a year all countries of CEE controlled formerly by the Soviet Union were ruled by democratic governments which promised to integrate them into the EU. The radical shift of the CEECs towards Western Europe was not a great surprise to most observers. After all, in the CEE area the communist system was more or less imposed by the USSR in the years following the Second World War rather than reflecting electoral preferences, with the arguable exception of the Czech Lands. All CEECs considered here (Bulgaria, the Czech and Slovak Republics, Hungary, Poland and Romania) were more or less integrated into capitalist Europe before the Second World War.

The political commitment to democracy and markets displayed by voters in Central and Eastern Europe in the late 1980s and early 1990s reflected a genuine desire to return to capitalism. The collapse of the CMEA trade arrangements forced all CEECs to find alternative markets for their exports.

With the demise of the CMEA in 1991 many CEE enterprises found themselves in the sea of change, suddenly exposed to new trade winds generated by hard currency transactions at world prices. The post-communist countries of Central and Eastern Europe joined major international institutions such as the IMF, the World Bank and GATT. Four of them became associated with the OECD in the framework of the 'Partners in Transition' (PIT) programme.[1] Since 1991 trade treaties with the EU (the Europe Agreements) and EFTA (free-trade agreements) were negotiated and signed in 1992 and 1993, followed by the mutual free-trade agreement (CEFTA) of the four Central European countries (the Visegrad-4) in late 1992 (implemented in April 1993).

Following the dissolution of the Warsaw Pact, the CEECs strove to achieve full membership in NATO. However NATO membership was neither offered nor promised to them but all post-communist countries became eligible for admission to the 'Partnership for Peace' initiative involving themselves as well as the NATO members.

Within a few years, the post-communist CEECs accomplished a radical institutional turnaround moving definitely closer to the West. The question is whether the momentum towards full integration can be sustained given the rapidly changing configuration of political and economic forces on the European continent. Clearly, Russia has been seeking to assert itself as one of the great powers. It is certainly a great power in the sense that it could obliterate any state with its still mighty nuclear arsenal. Russia also benefited in narrow economic terms from the collapse of the Soviet Union: Moscow is no longer obliged to supply anyone with natural resources and energy inputs at below world market prices.

In the new multipolar world of the post-cold war era, the USA remains the only superpower in a class of its own.[2] Russia, Japan, China and the EU can be considered to be great, albeit second-class, powers. European integration in this context defines a great power in the state of becoming: unlike its rivals, Western Europe is still organizing itself as a great power *sensu stricto*. This chapter does not attempt to describe this broad process; it merely provides a series of observations pertaining to some barriers which inhibit its progress.

The next section outlines political and economic barriers to integration which manifest themselves in Western Europe. Such barriers in Eastern Europe are discussed in the subsequent section. The concluding part of the chapter provides a speculative assessment of further European integration in the second half of the 1990s.

BARRIERS IN THE WEST

Political Barriers

Costs of integration

The disappearance of the proverbial iron curtain has created a real chance to overcome the traditional division of Europe but the end of the cold war in itself has not removed the perennial East–West divide. What has changed is the ease of movement across national borders for people, ideas, goods and services. However it is apparent in the mid-1990s that a truly *irrevocable* process of economic and political unification with the Western world is taking place only in one ex-communist country. The citizens of the former GDR (East Germany) are the only people of the defeated Soviet bloc blessed with instant membership in the club of Western democracies. Full membership has real privileges, for it provides not only many perks, but also the means to defend them.[3]

Ideally all nations of Western Europe ought to be as generous as the Germans.[4] For better or worse, this is not the case. Even in West Germany many citizens have second thoughts on the unification as its price keeps rising. This points to political barrier number one: Western taxpayers fear that full and rapid integration of CEE into the EU would be too costly. Given the presence of genuine democratic institutions in the West, it is clear that this fear will be translated into actual political decisions. For the architects of European integration, the corresponding lesson is obvious: integration of the CEECs should not be an expensive process involving massive hand-outs to Czech steel-workers, Polish coal-miners, Hungarian farmers, Slovak arms-producers, and so on.

A new spectre

Although the threat of communism has apparently ceased to exist, a new spectre is haunting Europe, the spectre of high and persistent unemployment. Most West European citizens perceive mass unemployment as the most important economic problem which translates into another political barrier to further integration of the CEECs. From a purely academic point of view, one might argue that exports from Western Europe to the CEE area grow faster than the flow of goods and services in the opposite direction; therefore the East–West trade liberalization of the early 1990s probably resulted in net employment gains in the West. However most citizens of the West European countries do not necessarily form their political preferences on the basis of liberal economic theory.[5] Hence mass unemployment in the West is bound to undermine the political resolve to integrate the CEECs into the EU because the public would fear more job losses.

What should policy makers in Western Europe do to tackle the unemployment problem? There is obviously significant room for improvement in the area of labour market reforms[6] but I suspect that there is a limit to the political acceptability of reforms that would be necessary to radically alter the prospects for new job creation. Sustained economic growth would therefore seem all the more necessary to achieve low unemployment in advanced economies. The role of technical change is prominent in this context. More precisely, what matters is the *type of technical advance* taking place in these economies.

Empirical studies indicate that technical progress has traditionally been both cost-reducing and labour-saving. With the benefit of hindsight, one can argue that in the 1950s and 1960s the cost-reducing effects of technical change were stronger than its labour-saving effects.[7] This was conducive to high profitability of business investment which generated a strong, self-sustaining growth process in most advanced economies. Over the 1970s and 1980s the cost-reducing effects were relatively weak: the famous *productivity growth slowdown* reflected this tendency. What is really important to the matter at hand is the predominant nature of technical change in the 1990s.

It is possible that productivity growth will accelerate during this decade; for instance, the ongoing microelectronic revolution might cause this to happen if its cost-reducing potential results in significant economies of production costs. Should this scenario prevail in the near future, a spontaneous and vigorous growth may reappear in the private business sector in coming years, igniting a new era of prosperity with full employment. Such a productivity-growth reversal would substantially ease political resistance in the West to further integration. But this scenario is only a hope; its materialization by no means certain.

National security

The traditional security vacuum in CEE reappeared at the end of the cold war. It is unclear how to resolve this problem. On the one hand, no country of Western Europe seems to be willing to get involved in a war defending anything or anyone in CEE: the conduct of the EU concerning the war in Bosnia is certainly consistent with this hypothesis.

On the other hand, the post-Second World War experience has taught West Europeans that the voluntary economic and political integration of free nations leads to lasting peace. Integration of the CEECs into the EU would presumably make a future war between Hungary and Romania, for example, just as unthinkable as a military conflict between Germany and France today. Clearly, full integration could reduce defence outlays, providing welcome relief to the strapped Western taxpayers.

Economic Barriers

Sensitive imports

Non-tariff restrictions pertaining to West European imports from the CEE area appear to be based on political considerations so that one can speak of the *primacy of politics in the West.* Most frequently restrictions on sensitive imports (specific agricultural, chemical, steel and textile products) are discussed in this context. According to a recent OECD study, sensitive product exports to the West have grown in importance for the CEECs in the late 1980s and early 1990s.[8] Access to West European markets in the sensitive sectors is thus vital to short-term trade performance of all economies in transition, although the long-term comparative advantages in these industries remain unclear.

The removal of Western restrictions on sensitive imports would clearly help but policy makers have to consider the activities of well-organized pressure groups (farmers, fishermen, steel-workers and so on). Asymmetric trade agreements between Western Europe and the CEECs, which generally favour the latter, contain provisions for gradual easing of such restrictions. On the whole, other trade measures are probably at least as important as the sensitive-import constraints.[9]

Other barriers to trade

In addition to non-tariff measures pertaining to sensitive products, the CEE exporters still face some tariff barriers, although the EU as well as EFTA agreements with the CEECs have reduced these greatly. Of greater significance, as revealed by a recent OECD sponsored survey, non-restrictive trade regulations in the West, including health and safety measures, marking and packing requirements, and quality certification procedures, impose effective trade barriers on exporters from CEE.

Lack of information inhibits East–West trade strongly; corporate managers responsible for purchasing decisions in Western Europe are often unaware of the availability of competitive Eastern goods and services whereas many potential CEE exporters know scarcely anything about the OECD area trade rules and conventions. Nevertheless, trade among the CEECs and Western Europe has dramatically increased over the last four to five years, although it is next to impossible to obtain detailed trade data that are both recent and accurate. The expanding trade enhances the prospects for further integration.

BARRIERS IN THE EAST

Political Barriers

Incomplete harmonization

The free-trade agreements (FTAs) of the CEECs with the EFTA and EU are similar in the sense that both sets of agreements include provisions about public procurement, intellectual property rights, rules on competition, preferential treatment and provide for an asymmetric implementation of tariff and non-tariff barrier reductions. However there are notable distinctions: the FTAs between the CEECs and EFTA cover only industrial and processed agricultural products, while trade in other agricultural products is subject to bilateral negotiations. The scope of the Europe Agreements (EAs) is much broader: they embody several provisions of a political nature and important steps towards the harmonization of legal, economic and political systems of the CEECs with those prevailing in the EU countries.

The PIT countries (Czech Republic, Hungary, Poland and Slovakia) have reformed radically their economic and legal systems, establishing constitutional foundations of the market economy and parliamentary democracy.[10] The remaining two CEECs (Bulgaria and Romania) have moved in the same direction, although their new economic and political institutions appear to be less robust than those in the PIT countries. In any case *formal harmonization* of political structures and legal norms is well under way in all six countries of CEE which have become associate members of the EU through the EAs.[11]

Political barriers imposed by the still insufficient harmonization of legal and other institutional standards seem to result in most cases from constraints imposed by the limited administrative capacity to implement new provisions rather than from the lack of good will on the part of policy makers. Any massive overhaul of institutional arrangements takes time even in countries with a sufficient supply of experienced political and legal experts who can rely on a well-trained corps of civil servants. Therefore it should not be surprising to us that the CEECs cannot impose Western institutions instantly.[12]

However, a more important point is that legal and other institutions reflect the properties of the underlying form of economic organization. More precisely, the actual functioning of institutions reflects the essential properties of the existing economic order. For instance, most economies in transition have binding bankruptcy legislation on the books but experience an incredibly low number of bankruptcies in comparison to their Western counterparts. Similarly, rigorous banking acts fail to produce desired effects. Clearly, economic behaviour which produces such startling outcomes in the framework of a market economy must be driven by other objectives than profit maximization.[13]

Immature civil society

The presence of democratic institutions and the growing regulatory framework of a market economy can be viewed as necessary, but not sufficient, conditions for the existence of civil society. In the pragmatic sense civil society can be defined as a community in which a sufficient majority of citizens respect voluntarily a few basic rules of democracy including private property and other human rights. Although it is impossible to design a 'democracy barometer', some qualitative comparisons should be feasible. On the whole, all CEECs made significant progress towards civil society within a relatively short time. Some intolerance towards minorities (both ethnic and political), some questionable court decisions, some violations of human rights and some corrupt practices have been observed in each country of CEE but the overall report card certainly looks encouraging: no country – including those in OECD – can claim to have a perfect score in these matters.

If the majority of CEECs citizens continue to internalize values of civil society, then another barrier to their integration into Western Europe is bound to disappear. In this sense the speed of integration will be determined by the people rather than by the élites. It is true that the EAs signed by the EU with the six CEE states attempt to lock in the achievements of political and economic reforms of the post-communist era; it is also true that the development of authentic civil society cannot be based merely on a carrot-and-stick approach, no matter how sophisticated the structure of inducements and deterrents might be. In the final analysis, civil society in CEE cannot evolve without some degree of economic prosperity generated by genuine market forces; fascism or some other nasty form of nationalism presents the alternative social arrangement driven by both economic crisis and spiritual poverty.

Economic Barriers

Slow systemic transformation

The discussion presented above indicates that, in contrast to Western Europe, the principal barriers to integration which exist in CEE are mainly economic rather than political. This primacy of economics defines the relevant limits to full integration of the CEECs into the EU.

To illustrate this fact I have prepared Table 3.1 which demonstrates that no transition economy considered in this chapter meets the *basic* full-convertibility requirement for economic and monetary integration into the EU (the Maastricht convergence criteria).[14] All CEECs have established strong central banks, adopting statutes similar to those of the German *Bundesbank*. Thus one of the Maastricht convergence criteria has been met. In addition to that, Romania and Slovakia have met another requirement (low public debt) while the

Table 3.1 Do the CEECs meet the Maastricht convergence criteria?

Criterion	Bulgaria	Czech Republic	Hungary	Poland	Romania	Slovakia
Full convertibility	No	No	No	No	No	No
Strong central bank	Yes	Yes	Yes	Yes	Yes	Yes
Low inflation	No	No	No	No	No	No
Low public debt	No	Yes	No	No	Yes	Yes
Low government deficit	No	Yes	No	No	No	No
Low interest rates	No	No	No	No	No	No
Stable currency	No	Yes	No	No	No	No

Sources: National sources; OECD estimates and projections; Qvigstad (1992).

Czech Republic has also achieved low government deficits and stable currency.[15]

However, even in the Czech case it may take two to three years before the koruna becomes fully convertible and four to five years before inflation as well as interest rates approach those of the best EU performers, assuming an optimistic scenario of economic development. The other three PIT countries (Hungary, Poland and Slovakia) might become fit for full economic integration perhaps within ten years; Bulgaria and Romania perhaps within fifteen years, providing that similarly optimistic scenarios materialize.

Deficient capital stock

All CEECs inherited from the communist era capital stocks of diverse dates and structures that were simply not conducive to rapid integration with Western Europe. Instead, both human and physical capital stocks were characterized by properties suitable for integration with Russia. For instance, a casual observer can notice that even today, several years after the fall of the Berlin Wall, many government officials as well as private-sector executives appear to be fluent in Russian but struggle with any Western language. Similarly, many factories still seem to be well equipped to supply Soviet-type trade agencies rather than Western markets. Transformation of infrastructure (telecommunications, transportation and energy networks) proceeds at a very slow pace in comparison to East Germany.[16]

The comparatively slow transformation of capital stocks reflects weak domestic and foreign investment (except, perhaps, in the case of Hungary). Net capital formation financed by foreigners would certainly accelerate if the CEECs became full members of the EU; conversely, rapid accumulation of good-quality capital stocks would help these countries in their sometimes frantic efforts to unite with Western Europe. The upshot is that for the time being the economic transformation will have to rely mainly on domestic efforts. There is much room for improvement.

For example, the shortage of physical capital structures such as modern, well-equipped factories geared towards production of marketable goods can be alleviated to some extent by operating them around the clock. The maximum rate of utilization of such production units should not be impeded by labour codes and social policies which emulate those of Western economies where shortages of suitable productive capacity pose no serious problem.[17] In addition, the authorities in charge of fiscal and monetary policies in the CEECs can certainly do more to encourage domestic savings while improving incentives to invest. Further, businesses ought to be encouraged to acquire the skills necessary to cope with non-restrictive trade regulations prevailing in the world markets because ignorance of such regulations remains probably the most important barrier to further growth of exports.[18] Strong export growth seems to be the only feasible strategy for a real economic recovery and sustainable growth leading to subsequent improvement of living standards in CEE.

CONCLUSIONS

The arguments presented above imply some conclusions relevant to the medium-term prospects of integrating the six countries which have signed the EAs (Bulgaria, Czech Republic, Hungary, Poland, Romania and Slovakia) into Western Europe. Conclusions pertaining to the EU are presented at the outset of this section; they are followed by conclusions relevant to the six CEECs.

First, full integration of the CEECs into the EU structures is desirable on geopolitical grounds. Currently three of these countries are situated on the eastern and southern borders of the Union (Czech Republic, Poland and Bulgaria); with Austria joining the EU, Hungary and Slovakia will also have common borders with the Union. The geopolitical significance of Romania is defined by its substantial population, land mass and strategic location between Hungary and Bulgaria which makes possible the eventual transformation of the EU into a geographic whole.[19]

Second, the EAs between the EU and the six CEECs provide a suitable framework for further integration. The productivity gap between the CEECs and the Union is huge and real economic convergence cannot be expected in the near future. At the same time, it must be emphasized that the PIT countries (Hungary, Poland, the Czech and Slovak Republics) have made remarkable institutional progress towards integration with Western Europe, establishing a solid legal and political framework of modern society within a relatively short period of a few years. Bulgaria and Romania seem to be moving in the same direction, albeit with more difficulties, caused by their worse initial conditions for transition to capitalism.

Third, it is extremely important that the EU countries reward political and economic liberalization in CEE with more generous trade concessions. This approach would avoid any significant tax burden on the present members of the EU while helping the CEECs to maintain the pace of reforms leading to the gradual development of civil society and efficient markets. Just as it is wise for a person to make a living by hard work rather than by the charity of others, it is expedient for a nation to earn income by producing and exporting instead of having to beg international institutions for financial assistance. A forward-looking policy for European integration should not underestimate the economic importance of self-esteem.

Fourth, it is just as important to penalize countries for fiscal and/or political misconduct by withdrawing favourable trade concessions, freezing or even reversing the process of integration. True collective security can be achieved if, and only if, aggressive governments are punished swiftly for hostile actions which threaten to destabilize their peaceful neighbours; this principle is indivisible.

Fifth, the EU ought to intensify as soon as possible cooperation with the CEECs in the areas of military, energy-related and economic security. Unlike Russia, the EU can claim a great power status on the basis of its economic strength. The West European industrial powerhouse remains a rather ineffective military power. To improve security at its borders, the EU ought to contribute both funds and know-how necessary to develop closer ties to the CEECs. Perhaps these transition countries could be offered membership in the West European Union (WEU), perhaps a completely new joint defence organization could be set up.

As far as CEE is concerned, there are only a few clear-cut conclusions which apply evenly to all six countries which signed the EAs. Therefore it is necessary to differentiate sometimes between the Visegrad-4 (PIT) countries on one side, and the remaining two CEECs on the other.

First, the case for swift integration into the EU would be tremendously advanced if the PIT countries were to expand and deepen their own integration. The establishment of the mutual free-trade agreement (CEFTA) was a good idea; further extension of the CEFTA by means of FTAs concluded between the Czech Republic, Slovakia, Hungary and Slovenia ought to be continued, involving Bulgaria and Romania as well. It is hard to see why the last three countries should not become full members of CEFTA. Further, the CEFTA countries would be well advised to abolish mutual restrictions on sensitive goods right away. It is difficult to lobby effectively in Brussels for more trade concessions on sensitive goods if, for instance, Poland continues to obstruct imports of Czech cars by high tariffs, while the Czech Republic keeps in place quotas on imports of Polish coal.

Second, all CEECs ought to intensify immediately their cooperation in the sphere of military security. This cooperation could lead to the establishment of a formalized collective security organization, parallel to CEFTA. Clearly, the demonstrated readiness to defend themselves would be conducive to the success of diplomatic efforts pushing the WEU or NATO to provide CEE with credible security guarantees. Sooner or later, such guarantees might lead to full membership in Western security structures.

Third, mutual cooperation of the CEECs ought to include economic security, especially in the area of energy supplies. For instance, Bulgaria and Romania should be encouraged to join the PIT countries in their effort to upgrade their electricity systems to Western standards; once this conversion were completed, the CEE area electricity grid could link up with the West European system through Austria, Germany and Greece. Similarly, the CEECs should coordinate their stockpiling and emergency supply plans pertaining to strategic raw materials (especially oil and natural gas), utilizing to the full technical assistance available from the Paris-based International Energy Agency (IEA) and other sources. In this context, full OECD membership for the PIT countries in a few years could be of extreme importance, enabling them to join the energy supply-management system coordinated by the IEA. Of course, membership presupposes that the four applicants accept a number of OECD disciplines restricting their freedom of manoeuvre in the area of economic policy.

Fourth, all governments of the CEECs must contain the rise of rabid nationalism (neo-fascism) by all constitutional means available, applying the full force of the law against those who are guilty of criminal acts such as violent attacks against gypsies, Jews and other minorities. Similarly, the authorities should rigorously enforce basic human rights guaranteed by the new constitutions, even if the exercise of some of these rights might result in outcomes unpleasant to the government of the day.

Fifth, all citizens of the six CEECs considered in this chapter would benefit tremendously from learning, and internalizing, a simple principle of introductory economics: let bygones be bygones. One cannot repeat this advice often enough. Without the widespread willingness of both governments and residents of these countries to accept it, no integration with Western Europe can be possible in the foreseeable future.

NOTES

1. The author works in the Central and Eastern Europe Division of the OECD Economics Department. The Division has produced regular economic surveys of the post-communist countries which participate in the OECD programme 'Partners in Transition' (Czech Republic, Hungary, Poland and Slovakia) and occasional surveys of Bulgaria and Romania (see, for example, OECD, 1992; 1993; 1994). Therefore the discussion of barriers to and prospects for further integration of Central and Eastern Europe into the West is restricted to the countries mentioned above. The author's views are his own and do not represent official positions of the OECD secretariat or of OECD member governments.
2. For a description of the shift from the bipolar to multipolar world see Kennedy (1988).
3. Some observers have pointed out that there are costs too. Many East Germans perceive themselves as 'poor cousins' who have very limited scope to shape their own destiny. Nevertheless, the majority of East Germans do not favour a revival of the former German Democratic Republic which implies that the benefits exceed the costs of full integration with West Germany.
4. The West German generosity is defined *ex-post* by the fiscal effects of unification with the GDR. This clarification is necessary because the *ex-ante* motives for the broad support of unification in West Germany were not always altruistic. Be that as it may, there was hardly any other option. From the legal point of view unification was simply mandated by the constitution (*Grundgesetz*) of the Federal Republic.
5. If they did, full economic integration would have taken place already. Of course, some jobs in Western Europe have disappeared as domestic production was displaced by

Eastern imports. Persons who lost these jobs are not necessarily identical to those who gained jobs in the wake of export expansion. Therefore opposition to cheap imports from the CEE area is understandable from the viewpoint of the job losers.

6. According to the oft-cited OECD findings, between 1970 and 1992 the EU created 10 million new jobs: 3 million in the private sector and 7 million in the public sector. In contrast, the US economy created over the same period some 39 million new jobs including only 6 million in the public sector. It is widely believed that the higher degree of labour market flexibility in the US accounts for its superior rate of job creation. The OECD Jobs Study – Evidence and Explanations, Paris: OECD, 1994.
7. These effects were analysed in a competent critique of my earlier work on technological change, see Özol (1991).
8. See CCET (1994), chaps I and IV.
9. For instance, in 1993 the Czech Republic outperformed all other CEECs in export growth. Nevertheless most Western quotas available to Czech exporters were not fully utilized.
10. See Commission of the EC (1993b), Annex E – Overview of law reforms in East Germany, Poland, the former Czechoslovakia and Hungary.
11. The first two EAs (Hungary and Poland) were ratified on 1 February 1994. The other four EAs (Bulgaria, the Czech and Slovak Republics, Romania) which entered into force on 1 February 1995 are somewhat different, including explicit provisions dealing with human rights which were not present in the two EAs negotiated earlier. However title III of these EAs, which contains the relevant free-trade arrangements, has been implemented already.
12. It is understandable that the legal reform has advanced faster and more smoothly in Hungary than in the remaining CEECs because the Hungarian authorities have accumulated a great deal of administrative experience with gradual reforms of the Soviet-type system since the late 1960s.
13. The actual functioning of post-communist economic systems remains poorly described and even more poorly analysed. This 'reality without theory' presents a tremendous intellectual challenge to serious practitioners of economics. Of course, one has to beware of the obvious temptation to 'fit' the baffling experience of post-communist economies into the Procrustean bed of some well-developed theory designed to describe something else.
14. The criteria (also known as EMU 'membership rules') are as follows. All restrictions on the movement of capital shall be prohibited. Establishment of an independent central bank. Price inflation shall not exceed that of the three best performing EU economies by more than 1.5 percentage points. General government debt shall not exceed 60 per cent of GDP. General government deficit shall exceed neither 3 per cent of GDP nor the level of government investment ('the Golden rule of public finance'). Long-term interest rate shall not exceed that of the three best inflation performers by more than 2 percentage points. Normal currency fluctuation margins in the ERM and no devaluation the previous two years. For a recent report on economic and monetary convergence within the EU see Commission of the EC (1993a).
15. At present only one member country of the EU (Luxembourg) meets all Maastricht criteria. However all economies of Western Europe are well ahead of the CEECs in respect of the basic criterion (convertibility), and most of them are moving in the right direction as far as the other requirements are concerned.
16. In addition to that, all citizens of the former GDR speak fluently at least one Western language.
17. For a comprehensive analysis which demonstrates why this is the case see Georgescu-Roegen (1970).
18. In addition to the lack of trade skills, barriers to exports found in the CEECs include the underdeveloped infrastructure, the constantly changing financial and regulatory environment and the absence of effective export-promotion policies. For a concise discussion of such barriers see CCET (1994), pp. 72–5.
19. I expect that the further expansion of the Union is bound to include Slovenia and possibly Croatia in South–Central Europe, the three Baltic states between Finland and Poland, and

Turkey in the East. This would provide united Europe with solid North–South and East–West economic, political and security dimensions.

REFERENCES

CCET (1994), *Integrating Emerging Market Economies into the International Trading System*, Paris: OECD.

Commission of the EC (1993a), 'Broad economic policy guidelines and convergence report', *European Economy*, **55**, Brussels: Commission of the EC, Directorate-General for Economic and Financial Affairs.

Commission of the EC (1993b), 'Shaping a market-economy legal system', *European Economy Reports and Studies*, **2**, Brussels: Commission of the EC, Directorate-General for Economic and Financial Affairs.

Georgescu-Roegen, N. (1970), 'The economics of production', *American Economic Review*, **60**, 1–9.

Kennedy, P. (1988), *The Rise and Fall of the Great Powers*, New York: Random House.

OECD (1992), *OECD Economic Surveys: Poland*, Paris: OECD.

OECD (1993), *OECD Economic Surveys: Hungary*, Paris: OECD.

OECD (1994), *OECD Economic Surveys: The Czech and Slovak Republics*, Paris: OECD.

Özol, C. (1991), 'The surrogate wage function and capital: theory with measurement', *Canadian Journal of Economics*, **24**, 175–91.

Qvigstad, J.F. (1992), 'Economic and monetary union (EMU): a survey of the EMU and empirical evidence on convergence for the EC and the EFTA countries', Occasional Paper No. 36, Geneva: EFTA Economic Affairs Department.

4. Paths towards an integrated Europe: problems and prospects*

Richard Baldwin

INTRODUCTION

Communism's demise destroyed the political barriers dividing Europe and shattered East European economic structures, including trade arrangements. Integration and reconstruction are under way but the outcome is still uncertain. If all goes right, economic success in the East could foster prosperity and peace throughout the continent. If all goes wrong, prolonged economic distress in the East could produce catastrophic consequences for Europe. Western Europe can do little to ensure Eastern prosperity; the CEECs must shoulder most of the work and pain. Building a sensible path towards pan-European integration is one way Western Europe can help. This should be a priority.

RECONSTRUCTION WITHOUT A PLAN

Pan-European integration is proceeding but no one seems to be in charge. Despite this, much progress has been made. The promised liberalizations, especially the EU–CEEC Association Agreements signed with the CEE-6, are important steps. However the current system has three important shortcomings:

1. Some Eastern nations have not yet been included.
2. The bilateral Association Agreements are 'spokes' separately linking each CEEC to the West European 'hub'. This hub-and-spoke bilateralism tends to marginalize CEECs economically and politically.

* This chapter is based on the Executive Summary of Richard Baldwin's book: *Towards an Integrated Europe*, London: Centre for Economic Policy Research, April 1994. Published with the permission of ©Centre for Economic Policy Research, 25–28 Old Burlington Street, London W1X 1LB.

3. There is no immediate step between the Association Agreements (Europe Agreements) and full EU membership.

Not-yet-included Nations

Most industrial trade in Western Europe is duty-free, so duty-free access to CEECs merely levels the playing field. The EU intends to sign Europe Agreements (EAs), or free-trade accords also with Slovenia and the Baltic states, so a solution has been promised.

Hub-and-spoke Bilateralism

A railway system, with the capital city as its centre, favours investment in the capital. Similarly, hub-and-spoke bilateralism discourages foreign and domestic investment in CEECs. This may slow Eastern growth. West European firms are harmed by the other side of this investment-deterring effect. Trade barriers between CEECs – and the possibility of future barriers – inhibit normal commercial practices; for example, supplying the region from facilities concentrated in one Eastern country. Intra-CEEC agreements are an imperfect solution. Given the track record of such agreements among developing countries, investors cannot be sure that these piecemeal deals will become effective.

The investment-deterring effect may have enduring repercussions. Suppose a large Central European market emerges. Where will the new industrial concentrations be? Industry is its own best customer, so firms tend to locate near concentrations of other firms. This 'herding instinct' means that once a location gets a head start, other locations must struggle to catch up. This is a problem since five or ten years of hub-and-spoke bilateralism gives German and Austrian locations a head start on locations in Slovenia, Poland, Hungary, the Czech Republic and Slovakia. Hub-and-spoke bilateralism may also marginalize CEECs politically.

No Intermediate Stages

EU special-interest politics is likely to prevent an Eastern enlargement for a long time. Without an intermediate stage to allow continued progress, reintegration would stall at the EA stage for decades. Frustrating the aspirations of millions of Central and East Europeans for this long would create political problems for Western Europe. It would also mean missing important economic gains.

At Least Two Decades Before Membership

Simple arguments imply that an Eastern enlargement is improbable for decades. These arguments are set out below.

Budget burden

Because CEECs are so poor, so populous and so agricultural, an early Eastern enlargement would be costly. The 64 million people in Visegrad-4, for example, are 2.5 times more agricultural and only 30 per cent as rich as the EU-12 average. Admitting Visegraders would increase annual EU spending by an estimated 63.6 billion ECU. Financing this would require a drastic cut in EU spending, or an increase (about 60 per cent) in incumbent contributions. Raising taxes or deficits for this would be unpopular with voters. The spending cost would fall on two extremely powerful interest groups – EU farmers and poor regions, since they receive 80 per cent of EU spending. As a matter of self-defence, coalitions of farmers and poor regions are likely to veto an Eastern enlargement until CEECs become much richer and much less agricultural. This problem is worse for earlier and greater enlargements.

Structural funds

A region's income must be below 75 per cent of the EU average to be eligible for the most generous structural spending. If the EU average grows at 2 per cent and Visegrad-4 growth was three times that pace, it would take two decades before the Visegraders passed the 75 per cent cut-off. If they managed to grow 'only' twice as fast as the EU, it would take three decades. The periods are longer for poorer CEECs.

CAP spending

The Visegrad countries are blessed with fertile land, well suited to the products most heavily protected by the CAP (for example dairy). Consequently their accession is likely to bankrupt the post-McSharry CAP. One careful study puts the annual cost of extending the CAP to the Visegraders at US$47 bn in 2000. Rising incomes might never change this. Visegrad farmers could be as productive as French or Danish farmers in twenty years, so the most relevant fact is that a Visegrad enlargement would boost the EU land mass by more than a fifth. Further CAP reform is inevitable, but an early Eastern enlargement would significantly alter the nature of the necessary reforms.

Voting issues

Under current practices, the Visegrad group would receive more Council of Minister votes than the incumbent poor four (Spain, Portugal, Ireland and Greece). This would drastically alter EU politics. The problem increases with the size of the enlargement. EU voting reform is foreseen in 1996. One likely reform is to trim the over-representation of small nations. The extent of this could depend on how soon, and how far, the Union enlarges to the East. Small incumbents may have to choose in 1996 between preserving power and enlarging eastwards.

The human factor

Assuming that the obligations of EU membership require capable and experienced people, it is not enough to adopt EU law. Entrants must be trained and experienced personnel must interpret, apply and enforce the laws. Government officials in all CEECs are inexperienced in the design and enforcement of health, safety and environment standards in a market economy. Gaining the necessary experience takes years.

Migration

Estimates suggest that no more than 3–6 million Visegraders would migrate westwards. If they spread themselves thinly about the Union, few problems would arise. If they all settle in Germany and Austria, there would be many problems.

Defence and security issues

If Poland joins, the Union would have a border with Belarus, the Ukraine and Russia (Kaliningrad). This would greatly enrich the foreign policy issues that the EU must resolve. It would also transfer some of the CEECS' security problems to the Union.

Deepeners versus wideners

Maastricht made bold, but vague, commitments to deeper social, economic and political integration. Voting by EU members over the coming decades will decide how the commitments are met. An Eastern enlargement would have important, but unpredictable effects on the outcome.

Early membership on the cheap

One solution to the budget burden of an early Eastern enlargement would be to exclude entrants from structural spending until they were rich enough not to need it, and from agriculture for however long incumbent EU farmers insist. This 'solution' is a recipe for great political complications. Excluding entrants from almost all EU spending programmes is unprecedented. Once the joys of marriage wore off, this second-class status for CEECs could disrupt the EU. To put it colloquially: unpleasantness is unavoidable if second-class ticket holders can vote on what first-class passengers will have for dinner. Specifically, a long transition means that CEECs would vote on reform of structural spending and the CAP. One wonders what stance they would take towards programmes from which they were excluded.

All this suggests that an early Eastern enlargement is likely to be vetoed due to pressure from farmers, poor regions and/or small countries. Of course, the future is full of surprises. Extreme political events could convince West European voters to open their pocket books and admit some CEECs.

THE CHALLENGE

The basic long-run design of European integration was decided at the EU's 1993 Copenhagen Summit. All CEECs with EAs can join the EU, eventually. These agreements and the various CEEC–CEEC trade deals dictate where pan-European integration is now. Europe needs a well marked path that gets it from here to there.

The required path must correct the system's three shortcomings to avoid political difficulties and seize the economic opportunity presented by Communism's demise. It should be a multispeed path to account for the great diversity among CEECs. Above all, it must be politically viable. Eastern politics impose three large constraints. First, CEECs resist the recreation of a CMEA, so one natural route – an Eastern free-trade area – is blocked. Second, the path must make the journey to membership easier, not harder; membership is a top CEEC priority. Third, there is no leader among CEECs, so the EU must take the initiative. Western politics impose more constraints. The path to full EU membership for CEECs must avoid four 'political land mines': agricultural trade, competition for structural spending, migration, and voting in the Council of Ministers. As argued, an Eastern enlargement is unlikely for at least two decades (absent earthshaking political events). Consequently, a makeshift road will not do. Whatever the path to membership is, it will govern pan-European integration for a very long time.

A PROPOSAL

The proposal envisions two phases. The first would redress the hub-and-spoke bilateralism by embedding the existing EAs into a proposed 'Association of Association Agreements' (AAA). The second would create an intermediate step – resembling the European Economic Area (EEA) Agreement without migration – for CEECs that needed it. If the most optimistic timetable for EU enlargement holds, some CEECs – certainly not all – may go straight to membership. The intermediate step would turn the European trade arrangement into three concentric circles. Membership in all three circles should evolve.

Association of Association Agreements

Goals

The AAA should rationalize the EU's and CEECs' piecemeal trade liberalizations. It should also redress Europe's hub-and-spoke bilateralism and create a more coherent institutional framework. Finally, it should immediately increase the EU's engagement in the short- and medium-run economic integration of Europe. This stage would concern only CEECs with EU Association Agreements.

Content

The EU and all CEECs with EAs would be members. The AAA would require CEECs to liberalize equally with all AAA members. This would give CEEC-based firms access to other CEEC markets that was no worse than that accorded to EU-based firms. The Europe Agreement process and the internal political processes of individual CEECs would continue to govern the pace of liberalization. Poland's progress, for example, in lowering tariffs would not be tied to the progress of other CEECs. The AAA would merely require the liberalization to be extended to all AAA members. The proposed AAA would also regionalize the EAs' provisions on national treatment of establishments, trade in services, government procurement, and financial payments and transfers. The confluence of the Treaty of Rome and the proposed AAA would create a duty-free zone for industrial goods. An industrial firm located in any AAA member state would have (after transition periods) duty-free access to any other AAA market.

Does the AAA postpone enlargement?

High-level politics will decide the date and extent of the first Eastern enlargement. The AAA does not touch on such questions; it addresses more modest problems. CEECs fear that joint treatment is a pretext for postponing enlargement, so the issue must be addressed. There is little joint treatment in the AAA, since it only regionlizes the bilateral liberalization generated by the Europe Agreements. Progress by individual CEECs would continue to be dictated by their internal politics. The proposed AAA might marginally hasten enlargement by boosting CEECs' trade and incomes, and by providing them with a track record on multilateral cooperation in an EU-dominated organization dealing with complicated economic issues. Accession talks are slowed by discovery and discussion of special features of each entrant's economy. By increasing the EU's involvement immediately, the AAA might shorten the eventual accession talks.

An institutional framework

The proposed institution, 'the AAA Authority', should improve Europe's current patchwork of institutional arrangements. It would deal with EU–CEEC and CEEC–CEEC economic relations, namely in goods and services, rights of establishment, the liberalization of payments and financial transfers, competition rules, state aids, government procurement and the approximation of laws as covered in the EAs. In each of these areas the AAA Authority would:

1. play a surveillance and enforcement role to ensure that promised liberalization actually occurred and was not offset by subtle changes in domestic laws or regulations;
2. have a coordinating function for many transition periods and derogations in the EAs;
3. coordinate EU technical and financial assistance; and
4. assist with the human capital formation necessary to operationalize the approximation of laws foreseen in the EAs.

The EU must dominate the AAA Authority for legal and political reasons, and CEECs wishing to join should be happy with this. The EU would be visibly more engaged in helping CEECs to carry out Europe Agreement measures. The proposed Authority should not be a junior Commission; it should respect the basic Commission mandates.

Benefits of the AAA

Although it would entail no immediate increase in East–West liberalization, the new framework would promote trade and investment on a pan-European basis. The heightened credibility, consistency and predictability of trade policy throughout the AAA region would be good for European business. International commerce abhors uncertainty over future trade and investment policies and lack of transparency. Elimination of hub-and-spoke bilateralism should encourage investment in CEECs and help EU firms to do business there. This would spur CEEC growth. The AAA Authority would help CEECs to form the human capital necessary to run and regulate a market economy. The AAA may also take on additional tasks. It may be a good vehicle for adopting sensible cumulation in rules of origin. It could also provide a forum for rational discussion of safeguard measures. Even without altering the letter or spirit of EA safeguard provisions, such a forum might produce more satisfactory outcomes for all parties.

THE NEXT STAGE: AN INTERMEDIATE STEP

EU farmers and poor regions are likely to veto an Eastern enlargement for at least two decades. The second stage proposes an intermediate step to allow pan-European integration to proceed. The importance of this step is that it does not require the two-decades-before-membership premise to apply to all CEECs. Optimists hope that Hungary, Poland, the Czech Republic and perhaps Slovenia can join in the year 2000 with a long transition period. Even if this occurs, many CEECs will not make the first wave. For these, the wait may be much longer than two decades.

The EU grants much better access to EFTA members of the EEA than to CEECs. Some CEECs should be ready for this deeper integration by, say, the end of the decade. Similarly, if CEECs grow rapidly, EU firms will want Single-Market access to CEECs. The proposed intermediate step – an 'Organization for European Integration' (OEI) – would guarantee CEEC and EU firms such access. The OEI should not replace the AAA since not all CEECs would be ready simultaneously.

Duty-Free Trade to Single Market Integration

The proposed OEI would help to fulfil the Europe Agreement promise 'to make progress towards realizing between [the EU and each CEEC] the other economic freedoms on which the Community is based'. The EAs are specific about tariff and quota removal. They are asymmetrically vague about moving beyond this. It is clear what CEECs must do (approximation of laws and so on). It is not clear what the EU must do. Extending the Single Market to CEECs will not be an easy task, as the EEA negotiations revealed. For example, the EEA forbade contingent protection (for example, anti-dumping), allowed any product approved in one EEA country to be sold freely in all and permitted EEA companies registered in their home country to operate in any EEA country without prior approval of the local authorities. Clearly this sort of access requires that many rules be enforced credibly and uniformly. This demands a strong institution. The EEA was basically stillborn, so a new more appropriate framework is needed.

No immediate action

Unlike the AAA, the second stage would require no immediate action. Several years must pass before any CEECs are ready. Nevertheless, good road builders know that it is wise to decide the whole route before laying the first cement.

Shape of the new agreement

The proposed OEI would avoid all four 'political land mines' mentioned above. As with the EEA, OEI members would participate in the EU's Single Market without agriculture, without transfers and without voting. Unlike the EEA, migration would also be excluded.

New institution

A strong body (perhaps an extended AAA Authority) would be necessary to deal with competition policy, state aid and mutual recognition of technical standards and regulation. This administration authority should be modelled on the parts of the EU Commission dealing with enforcement and surveillance of the Single Market. Of course, the proposed Administration Authority could not impinge on the mandates of existing EU institutions, so some sort of multi-tier arrangement would be necessary. The awkward two-pillar legal structure of the EEA Agreement is not a good model, but it is indicative. The EFTA Surveillance Authority polices EFTA countries. The EU Commission polices EU nations. The EU has no direct involvement in the EFTA Surveillance Authority. This last item should be changed. As in the AAA Authority, the proposed 'OEI Administration' should be dominated by the EU. The CEECs that want to join the EU should welcome assistance in helping them to adopt Community standards on all Single Market issues. The EU should be interested in extending this assistance to promote trade, investment and growth.

A Pan-European Trade System with Three Concentric Circles

This intermediate step would create a pan-European trade system of three concentric circles. The EU would be the central circle with the smallest membership (at least until the Copenhagen vision is fully realized). The OEI would be the next largest comprising all the EU member states plus the leading CEECs that were not yet Union members. The outer circle, the AAA, would delimit the boundary of a European duty-free zone of industrial products.

Currently, opening this system to Belarus, the Ukraine, Moldova and Russia seems to be politically infeasible. If the political situation changes, there is no economic reason for excluding them from the AAA. On the contrary, there would be important economic benefits in doing so. Deeper-than-AAA integration for the 200 million citizens of these nations is a matter for futurologists.

Discussion of Part One

Alexander Tomov

THE BARRIERS ON THE WAY TO EUROPEAN INTEGRATION ARE GREAT BUT THEY CAN BE SURMOUNTED

I think that the basic conclusions drawn in the three chapters of Part One are important and of great significance for the CEECs. They are of a sensitive nature, too.

In the period 1990–91, we were cherishing many illusions and we believed in something which did not come true. We were convinced, and this conviction had been cultivated in our thinking, that integration with Western Europe would be achieved by the end of the century on the basis of a clear political will on both sides. By the term 'integration' we understood, *inter alia*, our admission to the EU as members of equal status, in spite of our lower level of economic development. I would not try to conceal the fact that we received a number of promises and pledges by a number of Western politicians that it would be possible for Poland, Hungary and Czechoslovakia to join the EU around 1995–96, while Bulgaria and some other countries could expect to do so by 1998–99. The examples of Greece and Portugal were inspiring us.

Consider the path of Bulgaria during the years of economic transformation. In this period Bulgaria successfully implemented many important reforms: internal convertibility of the national currency, liberalization of prices and of foreign trade, and the reform of the banking system. Many important legislative acts were adopted in this period, and three standby agreements with the IMF were implemented. The private sector in the economy grew steadily: from 9.1 per cent of GDP in 1990 to 19.4 per cent of GDP in 1993.

The conclusion is, however, that these achievements are not sufficient to overcome the existing barriers, well documented by Jaromir Cekota in Chapter 3. This suggests, in turn, that the idea of our joining the EU before the end of the century is absolutely utopian. Furthermore, it now seems unrealistic to expect that this would happen within the next ten to fifteen years, as rightly concluded by Richard Baldwin in Chapter 4.

Many of the other CEECs are experiencing similar difficulties. So the question of which barriers to East–West economic integration are the most substantial becomes of paramount importance. I would like to add some further considerations to the discussion on the obstacles to East–West integration.

First, there are barriers of a geopolitical type, related to the global restructuring of political power in the world. Immediately after the 'velvet' revolutions in CEE the question of the future geopolitical position and role of the small CEECs seemed to have an easy answer, assuming a speedy accession to the EU and NATO. Very soon, however, it became clear that this could not be achieved so easily and that Russia would not favour such a solution. It is obvious that Russia is not willing to have a new 'iron curtain' at its borders and that it would not accept new economic barriers either.

The global US initiative 'Partnership for Peace' put the problem in a different perspective, namely one of a large, united Europe, with Russia maintaining close ties with Europe. This is something which is of utmost significance not only for NATO, regarding the problems of peace in Europe, but also for the prospects of European economic integration. The number of politicians who (following the logic of the newly emerging geopolitical structures) see the role of CEE as a buffer zone between Western Europe and Russia, is increasing. If Russia became a member of the EU, this would change its image dramatically and would diminish its influence to a large degree. If, on the other hand, the small CEECs were integrated in the EU and, especially, if this were done on the basis of the Maastricht treaty, this would alienate Russia from the world community and could give rise to increased hostilities.

The conclusion we can draw on the basis of these geopolitical considerations is that the process of integration of the small CEECs into Europe will not be fast but gradual and will not take place on the basis of political will but mainly on the basis of economic adjustment. This will make the process of economic transformation in these countries even more costly, difficult and painful.

Second, the barriers on the way to East–West European integration stem from the big gap in the levels of economic development in these countries. In particular, the poor quality of the CEECs' products made the reorientation of their trade to Western markets after the collapse of the CMEA nearly impossible.

For many people the prospects of immediate trade integration of the CEECs seemed bright at the start of the economic transformation, but this turned out to be illusory and today this illusion has been totally discarded. It is unfortunate that a great number of political leaders in the CEECs did not realize this in their initial euphoria. Bulgaria is a typical example of such political short-sightedness. Due to political pressures, Bulgaria completely neglected its trade relations with the former CMEA partners. As a result, the share of former CMEA member countries in total exports fell from 84 per cent in 1989 to 28 per cent in 1993. Nearly 40 per cent of industrial enterprises became loss makers, largely due to the loss of markets. All this had a devastating effect on the economy.

The question whether the CEECs could have preserved closer economic ties deserves special attention. As Bulgarian deputy prime minister in 1991 I can confirm that after the disintegration of the CMEA I participated in efforts to create a new East European trade zone, to form an integral part of the European economic space. This idea was supported by the governments of Bulgaria, Czechoslovakia, Poland and Romania. There was a task force meeting in Varna in July 1991 which prepared the first drafts of the documents. The major problem then was the eventual membership of the USSR and the implications of this membership. The general opinion was that USSR representatives should be invited; they actually took part in the discussions. Unfortunately after the attempted coup in Moscow in August 1991 this initiative died. The subsequent Bulgarian government gave it up altogether. The three (later four) Visegrad countries started to seek their own ways of reviving their economic relations and pursue their common aim of integrating with Western Europe. According to my own estimations, the total losses to Bulgaria from the disintegration of CEE's economic structures amounts to over US$10 bn. I am convinced that the damage to other CEECs is substantial too.

The share of Bulgarian enterprises which, at this stage, are not capable of producing goods that can be sold on Western markets is above 90 per cent. Consequently, we can only penetrate into small and specific segments of these markets. This means that a policy of restoring our economic ties with the CEECs and the countries of the former USSR should precede our integration with Western Europe. This largely conforms to the conclusions drawn by Richard Baldwin in Chapter 4. Specific market strategies in the West and recapturing the markets in the East is the policy mix capable of overcoming the barrier stemming from the gap in economic levels.

Third, the barriers on the way to European integration are of a technological nature. It was clear that CEE was lagging behind in its technological development. For example, the share of high-tech products in Bulgarian manufacturing output was one-quarter to one-fifth of the corresponding share in Austria or Italy. Unfortunately, the way in which economic reforms in the East have been carried out does not foster the removal of this barrier. On the contrary, the gap is expanding further. The Bulgarian manufacturing sectors most affected by the adjustment process were electronics, mechanical engineering and electrical engineering. Unfortunately, they were only specialized for the Soviet market and could not cope with the competition on the world market.

The direct and indirect impact of this gap, following the process of economic liberalization in the CEECs, seems to have been neglected by both Eastern and by Western governments. Today the share of high-tech products in Bulgarian manufacturing output has dropped to one-third of its previous (very low by international standards) level. A large number of electronics and engineering enterprises are about to be closed, their well-educated and well-trained workforce having no chance to apply their knowledge and skill in the country.

Furthermore, although I accept J. Cekota's logic in Chapter 3, I think that while the Maastricht criteria are relevant to West European economies, if they are applied to CEECs, the latter will never become members of the EU. Transitional criteria are needed that fit the real geopolitical situation on the continent and the actual level of economic development in the CEECs. A new Marshall Plan is badly needed for mobilizing investment into CEE and for stimulating the privatization process in these countries. It is clear that the way ahead is one of concrete steps aiming at the harmonization of Eastern and Western economic structures. Otherwise a new gap between the East and the West could be created, first, by discriminating against the movement of Eastern people and, second, against the movement of Eastern goods.

PART TWO

Restructuring of East–West Trade in Europe

5. Economic interpenetration between the European Union and Central and Eastern Europe

John Sheehy

INTRODUCTION

In the main, this chapter presents briefly some of the results of a project with the same title which the European Commission has been financing and managing in 1992–93 (European Commission, 1995).[1] The motivation for the project has been to try to evaluate the nature and intensity of the economic repercussions stemming from the CEECs' process of marketization and opening up to international markets in the European Union.

The chapter begins by sketching the trade-flow changes in manufacturing goods that have occurred since the transition process began at the end of 1989 in the CEECs. It goes on to discuss trade between the EU and the CEECs in the context of the liberalization measures agreed between the EU and the CEECs in the Europe Agreements. After that come sections on the maximum possible welfare impact facing the EU from enhanced trade with the CEECs in the medium run and on FDI – another potentially important element in developing the economic interpenetration of the two halves of Europe. The final two sections look, on the one hand, at the degree of structural adjustment facing one member state where the impact of changes in the CEECs is likely to be disproportionately high – namely Italy – and, on the other hand, at developments in a 'sensitive' sector – textiles and clothing ('sensitive' in the sense that trade liberalization as set out in the Europe Agreements and subsequently are slower and more constrained than is generally the case).

The goal of this chapter is to provide an overview of the main aspects of the ongoing process of economic integration between CEE and the EU. This broad subject limits by necessity the possibilities for a deeper analysis of the nature of this process. However most of the issues addressed in this chapter will be analysed in more detail and/or from different perspectives in several of the following chapters.

RECENT DEVELOPMENTS IN MANUFACTURING TRADE BETWEEN THE EU AND THE CEECS

Until 1989, each CEEC's trade was dominated by the former Soviet Union in particular, and the ex-CMEA in general. A significant proportion of each CEEC's exports to the ex-CMEA consisted of highly processed, advanced manufactures (especially engineering products) in return for imports of raw materials and, especially, cheap energy. There was a more diverse structure towards the West. After 1989, and especially after the CMEA's collapse in 1991, trade between the CEECs and with the former Soviet Union nosedived. Contemporaneously, compensating to some extent for the regional trade crunch, CEE trade with Western markets has grown enormously, especially with the EU. As a result, the share of each CEEC's manufacturing exports going to the EU has doubled since 1989, from 20–25 per cent to over 50 per cent in 1992.

Indeed, the intensification of trade between the EU and the CEECs has been unprecedented. Take the case of EU imports from the CEECs first or, in other words, CEE exports to the EU. Before 1989, the growth of the CEECs' exports to the EU was the lowest of any group of countries exporting to the EU. Between 1980 and 1988, extra-EU exports[2] to the EU grew by 103 per cent in current prices, but CEE exports to the EU grew by a much more sedate 60 per cent. After 1989, however, the growth of CEE exports to the EU was only exceeded by South East Asia's export growth to the EU. Between 1989 and 1992, extra-EU exports to the EU grew just 12 per cent in current price value terms while CEE exports to the EU increased by 80 per cent.

However these overall results mask some startlingly divergent individual CEEC performances. The best export growth performance since 1989 has been recorded by former Czechoslovakia (up 129 per cent by 1992) and Poland (up 111 per cent) while Romania registered a 19 per cent decline. Moreover, having started from a low base, the CEECs still remain rather marginal trade partners of the EU. In terms of their share of the Community's extra-EU manufacturing imports, the CEECs have risen from 2.8 per cent in 1988 to 4.6 per cent in the first three quarters of 1993 (see Table 5.1) with Poland followed by Czechoslovakia together responsible for over 3 per cent alone.

The pattern for EU exports to the CEECs (CEE imports from the EU) is similar but even more pronounced. Between 1980 and 1988, the current price value of EU exports to the CEECs grew only 24 per cent while EU–extra-EU exports grew 69 per cent. Conversely, in the period between 1989 and 1992, EU exports to the CEECs recorded an 87 per cent increase, 80 percentage points more than the growth of total EU manufacturing exports to non-EU (up only 7 per cent).

Table 5.1 *EU manufacturing trade with CEE (values in mn ECU, current prices; market shares in % of total extra-EU trade)*

	CEE		Bulgaria		Czechoslovakia		Hungary		Poland		Romania	
	Value	Market Share	Value	Market Share	Value	Market Share	Value	Market Share	Value	Market Share	Value	Market Share
EU imports												
1980	5146	3.56	242	0.17	1139	0.79	1131	0.78	1709	1.18	924	0.64
1985	7532	3.23	362	0.16	1875	0.80	1616	0.69	2149	0.92	1530	0.66
1988	8222	2.80	350	0.12	1950	0.66	1816	0.62	2552	0.87	1555	0.53
1989	9303	2.76	398	0.12	2228	0.66	2182	0.65	2842	0.85	1654	0.49
1990	10525	3.06	441	0.13	2401	0.70	2547	0.74	3962	1.15	1174	0.34
1991	13598	3.63	600	0.16	3678	0.98	3138	0.84	4973	1.33	1209	0.32
1992	16736	4.43	762	0.20	5102	1.35	3554	0.94	5984	1.58	1334	0.35
1993[a]	12674	4.55	572	0.21	3840	1.38	2468	0.89	4662	1.67	1132	0.41
EU exports												
1980	6808	3.53	681	0.35	1126	0.58	1424	0.74	2206	1.14	1371	0.71
1985	8648	2.63	1378	0.42	1730	0.53	2254	0.69	2324	0.71	963	0.29
1988	8412	2.58	1300	0.40	1969	0.60	2123	0.65	2460	0.75	559	0.17
1989	10079	2.73	1323	0.36	2142	0.58	2673	0.72	3299	0.89	642	0.17
1990	10522	2.84	818	0.22	2343	0.63	2624	0.71	3717	1.00	1021	0.28
1991	15213	3.99	895	0.24	3428	0.90	3136	0.82	6663	1.75	1091	0.29
1992	18875	4.79	977	0.25	5628	1.43	3745	0.95	6967	1.77	1557	0.40
1993[a]	15914	5.27	777	0.26	4582	1.52	3173	1.05	6051	2.00	1332	0.44

Note: [a] January–September.

Source: Eurostat and European Commission Services.

Table 5.2 Sectoral breakdown of EU manufacturing trade with CEE (NACE 2-digit level), %

		CEE		Bulgaria		Czechoslovakia		Hungary		Poland		Romania		Total extra-EU	
Sector		1988	1992	1988	1992	1988	1992	1988	1992	1988	1992	1988	1992	1988	1992
EU imports															
21	Metalliferous ores	0.5	0.2	0.0	0.1	0.2	0.1	0.0	0.1	1.4	0.4	0.0	0.0	1.9	1.4
22	Metals	14.7	12.7	14.7	15.3	14.1	13.8	10.7	6.5	17.1	15.9	16.3	9.0	10.6	7.6
23	Mineral extraction	0.4	0.7	0.3	0.5	1.5	1.2	0.1	0.1	0.1	0.9	0.0	0.0	0.8	0.6
24	Mineral products	4.0	4.8	2.0	2.8	7.1	8.0	2.6	2.7	2.8	3.5	4.1	5.3	0.9	1.2
25	Chemical industry	11.6	9.2	22.5	11.2	14.4	9.6	12.2	10.8	9.9	8.5	7.6	5.9	8.9	9.4
26	Man-made fibres	0.7	0.7	0.7	0.7	1.0	1.0	0.5	0.4	0.2	0.4	1.4	0.9	0.5	0.4
31	Metal articles	2.9	5.9	0.8	2.0	2.4	7.0	3.3	5.1	3.3	6.6	3.1	2.9	2.1	2.5
32	Mechanical engineering	5.6	6.2	8.4	6.0	8.5	7.9	5.8	7.3	4.4	4.6	3.0	3.6	8.3	8.6
33	Office machinery	0.1	0.3	0.9	0.4	0.1	0.4	0.2	0.6	0.1	0.1	0.0	0.0	6.5	6.5
34	Electrical engineering	4.8	6.1	3.9	4.7	3.8	5.8	7.7	11.1	4.4	4.1	3.3	3.1	13.1	13.5
35	Motor vehicles	3.4	4.7	0.3	0.6	3.7	7.4	1.0	3.3	5.4	4.4	3.0	1.0	5.7	6.3
36	Other means of transport	1.3	1.1	0.2	0.3	0.5	1.2	0.0	0.2	3.7	1.5	0.2	1.4	4.1	5.3
37	Instrument engineering	0.4	0.5	0.5	0.4	0.4	0.5	0.5	0.7	0.3	0.3	0.2	0.2	2.9	3.1
41	Food, drink and tobacco	12.1	8.5	13.9	9.7	5.0	2.7	21.7	15.5	15.3	10.5	4.3	2.9	6.5	5.6
43	Textiles	5.5	5.3	6.4	8.6	6.5	5.8	5.8	5.7	3.4	3.5	7.1	8.4	4.7	5.1
44	Leather goods	0.8	1.1	1.0	1.9	0.9	1.1	1.3	1.3	0.5	1.0	0.5	0.5	1.1	1.0
45	Clothing and footwear	13.6	16.4	8.2	22.6	6.8	9.5	16.2	17.8	13.2	17.0	20.9	33.5	4.9	6.1
46	Timber, wooden furniture	10.6	8.8	3.9	3.8	10.0	6.7	4.6	4.7	9.4	11.6	22.0	18.9	3.6	3.4
47	Paper products	2.5	2.2	2.8	1.8	6.5	4.0	1.0	1.2	1.1	1.6	1.3	0.3	5.7	5.1
48	Rubber and plastics	2.0	2.3	1.7	2.8	3.1	3.1	2.6	2.8	1.4	1.6	1.3	1.4	2.1	2.4
49	Other	2.5	2.5	6.9	3.8	3.7	3.3	2.2	2.1	2.4	2.4	0.6	1.0	5.3	5.3
	Total manufacturing	100.0	100.0	100.0	100.0	100.0	100.0	100.0	100.0	100.0	100.0	100.0	100.0	100.0	100.0

EU exports

21	Metalliferous ores	0.3	0.1	0.3	0.6	0.3	0.1	0.2	0.1	0.1	0.0	2.0	0.7	0.1	0.1
22	Metals	5.6	3.0	8.7	2.3	3.1	3.4	5.0	2.9	6.0	3.1	7.3	2.2	7.0	4.9
23	Mineral extraction	0.2	0.2	0.1	0.1	0.2	0.3	0.1	0.1	0.4	0.2	0.4	0.1	0.3	0.2
24	Mineral products	1.7	1.8	2.1	1.3	1.4	1.7	1.6	1.9	1.5	2.2	3.1	1.3	2.3	2.2
25	Chemical industry	21.7	12.4	20.5	12.9	21.1	10.5	21.3	13.6	23.6	14.1	20.6	7.9	12.7	12.4
26	Man-made fibres	1.0	0.3	1.1	0.7	0.7	0.3	1.5	0.4	1.0	0.2	0.2	0.3	0.4	0.3
31	Metal articles	2.4	3.8	2.7	1.9	2.4	3.8	2.7	4.2	2.0	4.0	2.5	3.3	3.5	3.6
32	Mechanical engineering	24.9	19.3	28.2	14.5	32.6	25.7	21.4	16.6	24.7	16.9	4.5	17.0	16.9	17.2
33	Office machinery	1.5	2.7	0.9	1.4	3.0	3.7	1.4	2.4	1.0	2.4	0.4	1.2	2.5	2.5
34	Electrical engineering	8.8	11.4	8.8	8.2	11.0	14.1	10.2	11.2	6.9	10.6	4.3	7.6	10.3	11.4
35	Motor vehicles	2.8	7.7	4.1	9.4	1.8	8.7	3.2	9.4	2.8	6.4	1.6	4.9	9.5	8.1
36	Other means of transport	0.4	2.2	0.3	9.2	0.3	1.6	0.2	0.4	0.2	1.1	2.7	9.2	4.2	6.1
37	Instrument engineering	1.9	1.9	1.8	1.5	2.2	2.2	2.1	2.2	1.7	1.7	0.7	1.0	2.1	2.2
41	Food, drink and tobacco	6.9	7.2	7.4	10.6	7.2	4.9	3.8	4.3	9.6	9.3	5.3	11.5	6.6	7.1
43	Textiles	8.5	10.3	3.4	10.3	4.1	5.7	10.8	11.7	8.6	11.6	27.5	18.0	4.1	4.1
44	Leather goods	1.0	1.2	0.1	0.9	0.3	0.8	2.5	2.5	0.4	0.8	2.7	2.0	0.8	0.8
45	Clothing and footwear	1.5	2.8	0.8	4.1	1.0	2.1	2.1	4.3	1.3	2.1	3.0	4.4	2.9	3.1
46	Timber, wooden furniture	0.5	1.1	0.6	0.7	0.6	1.2	0.5	1.5	0.2	1.1	0.8	0.5	1.5	1.4
47	Paper products	2.0	3.0	2.5	2.6	1.4	2.4	2.6	3.0	1.8	3.8	1.4	1.7	2.5	2.6
48	Rubber and plastics	3.2	3.9	2.9	3.1	2.3	3.4	3.7	3.7	3.4	4.7	4.7	2.9	2.9	2.9
49	Other	3.1	3.5	3.0	3.8	2.9	3.6	3.2	3.5	3.1	3.6	4.5	2.4	7.0	6.9
	Total manufacturing	100.0	100.0	100.0	100.0	100.0	100.0	100.0	100.0	100.0	100.0	100.0	100.0	100.0	100.0

Source: Eurostat and European Commission Services.

Once again, however, there have been some striking divergences in the performance of the individual CEECs. Former Czechoslovakia has seen EU exports to it grow 163 per cent between 1989 and 1992, followed by Romania where the growth during the same timespan was 111 per cent. At the other end of the scale, Bulgaria actually saw a drop in the value of its imports from the EU (down 26 per cent in the same period). Nonetheless, one consequence of these developments is that the importance of the CEECs as a target for EU exports has grown from 2.6 per cent of all EU exports to non-EU countries in 1988 to 5.3 per cent by October 1993. Another consequence has been that whereas CEE–EU trade was virtually balanced in 1988, the EU has since enjoyed growing trade surpluses with the CEECs, especially after 1991.

Turning to the sectoral pattern of CEE manufacturing exports to the EU (see Table 5.2), one notable feature is the relative concentration in just a few sectors. The five largest NACE 2-digit sectors[3] account for 55.6 per cent of CEE exports to the EU in 1992 compared with only 45.4 per cent of total extra-EU exports to the EU. These five export sectors were clothing and footwear (16.4 per cent of the manufacturing exports' total), metal products (12.7 per cent), chemicals (9.2 per cent), timber products and wooden furniture (8.8 per cent) and food products (8.5 per cent) – all either rather heavy industrial sectors or traditional consumer goods industries. On the other hand, sectors such as mineral ores, office machinery and instrument engineering, incorporating a high natural resource content or a high R&D and/or qualified labour content, are unimportant in terms of CEE exports.

Amongst the CEECs, Romania's trade in 1992 was the most concentrated of all with clothing and footwear alone providing 34 per cent of its manufactured exports to the EU and its five largest export sectors accounting for 72 per cent. This may make Romania relatively more vulnerable to changes in EU demand than the other CEECs. Conversely, former Czechoslovakia's trade is the least concentrated of the CEECs in its export pattern to the EU, with its five largest sectors providing 49 per cent of its total. The concentration of CEECs trade with the EU will be analysed in more detail in some of the following chapters.

Overall, the CEECs seem quite similar in terms of their export structure to the EU, although there are some country differences. Textiles, especially clothing and footwear, are very much more important for Bulgaria and Romania than for other CEECs (23 per cent and 34 per cent of their 1992 manufacturing exports, respectively). Mechanical engineering is rather more important for Czechoslovakia and Hungary (8 per cent and 7 per cent, respectively).

The sectoral patterns of CEECs' exports to the EU have changed little despite the enormous growth noted above. This is surprising because in the initial period after 1989 there was considerable speculation that the CEECs would try to reorient the exports that they used to send to the ex-CMEA markets to the EU instead. The implication, of course, is that there has not been much reorientation of trade flows from East to West (except, perhaps, former Czechoslovakia where trade reorientation to the West is argued to have been accomplished quite successfully, although it is likely to be a short-term phenomenon due to extreme price competitiveness). Evidence about Hungary suggests that only about 19 per cent of the recent growth in trade to non-CMEA countries could be attributed to reorientation of trade flows that had previously gone to the ex-CMEA. On the other hand, it does appear from

Table 5.3 EU manufacturing trade with CEE: coefficients of structural change[a] at the NACE 3-digit level

	1988/87	1989/88	1990/89	1991/90	1992/91
EU imports from:					
Bulgaria	37.1	32.7	22.5	33.7	37.3
Czechoslovakia	11.0	10.7	12.3	30.5	21.0
Hungary	9.7	10.9	13.9	19.2	16.8
Poland	19.3	17.0	18.9	20.3	17.9
Romania	21.7	10.9	27.9	20.7	23.6
CEE	11.8	9.3	12.2	14.6	14.6
EFTA	5.9	4.7	6.6	6.4	5.5
USA	9.4	10.7	6.8	7.7	9.9
Japan	7.1	5.4	4.9	7.2	8.2
EU exports to:					
Bulgaria	26.3	23.9	30.1	49.9	42.8
Czechoslovakia	16.9	13.2	20.6	33.7	21.7
Hungary	13.4	14.6	18.9	20.8	15.9
Poland	15.6	22.5	35.1	35.9	25.6
Romania	27.2	36.2	42.1	55.4	35.4
CEE	12.1	14.8	20.0	26.8	14.4
EFTA	6.8	4.0	4.6	5.2	5.8
USA	15.8	8.9	8.1	14.8	6.7
Japan	10.6	12.7	14.8	11.8	15.8

Note: [a] Defined as: $\sum_i |s(i, t) - s(i, t{-}1)|$, where $s(i, t)$ is the trade share of sector i in year t, %.

Source: Eurostat and European Commission Services.

Table 5.3 that the rate of change of the CEECs' export structure in their trade with the EU has accelerated in the 1990s and that the rate has been significantly faster than the rate of change of export structure of other EU trade partners.

What is quite clear from Table 5.3 is that the CEECs' export patterns with the EU have not been changing as radically as have their imports from the EU. It can be observed that there has been both rapid growth and a dramatic shift in the CEECs' import structure due to a big increase in the importance of consumer goods. From Table 5.2 one can see that, for example, motor vehicles took a 7.7 per cent share of EU exports to the CEECs in 1992, up from only 2.8 per cent in 1988.

Given that the CEECs are small enough to face virtually infinitely price-elastic export supply curves and that consumers in the CEECs often either faced shortages or uncompetitive products, or both, during the socialist planning era, this is not a surprising development. It is to be expected that the CEECs' rapid reduction of most constraints on imports since 1990 should have led to a near one-off adjustment in the sectoral pattern. The slowdown in the rate of adjustment of the CEECs' import structure in 1992 may be evidence that most of the adjustment has now already taken place. In the future, however, as the CEECs recover, it is to be expected that there should be an increase in the importance of investment goods in imports.

Currently, the most important EU exports to the CEECs are processed products – mechanical engineering, electrical engineering and chemicals – but also food products and textiles. The latter probably reflects the growing importance of OPT trade – the process of exporting textiles especially (but also unfinished clothing) from the EU to the CEECs for subcontractors to transform into finished products and re-export to the EU (discussed below).

As, on the one hand, the marketization process in CEECs unfolds and, on the other, trade barriers between them and the EU come down (discussed below) it could be that their future comparative advantage is becoming clearer as market signals and forces begin to operate. If so, it is interesting to look at a traditional indicator of revealed comparative advantage, the export specialization index,[4] and its development since 1988 for the CEECs in relation to the EU (see Table 5.4).

In 1988, there were at least four sectors at the NACE 2-digit level which stand out as being export sectors to the EU in which the CEECs were very specialized by comparison with EU imports from non-EU countries. These were mineral products, timber products and wooden furniture, clothing and footwear and, finally, food products. In the ensuing period to 1992, some significant changes took place. Mineral products remain as an export sector in which the CEECs are highly specialized. Clothing and footwear have also remained a CEE specialization. However food products and wooden products

Table 5.4 Export specialization indices[a] *of CEE exports to EU at the NACE 2-digit level*

Sector	CEE		Bulgaria		Czechoslovakia		Hungary		Poland		Romania	
	1988	1992	1988	1992	1988	1992	1988	1992	1988	1992	1988	1992
21 Metalliferrous ores	0.2	0.1	0.0	0.1	0.1	0.1	0.0	0.1	0.7	0.3	0.0	0.0
22 Metals	1.4	1.7	1.4	2.0	1.3	1.8	1.0	0.9	1.6	2.1	1.5	1.2
23 Mineral extraction	0.6	1.3	0.4	0.9	2.0	2.1	0.2	0.1	0.2	1.5	0.0	0.1
24 Mineral products	4.2	4.2	2.1	2.5	7.6	6.9	2.7	2.3	3.0	3.0	4.4	4.6
25 Chemical industry	1.3	1.0	2.5	1.2	1.6	1.0	1.4	1.2	1.1	0.9	0.9	0.6
26 Man-made fibres	1.5	1.7	1.5	1.7	2.1	2.6	1.0	1.1	0.5	1.0	3.1	2.4
31 Metal articles	1.4	2.4	0.4	0.8	1.2	2.8	1.6	2.0	1.6	2.7	1.5	1.2
32 Mechanical engineering	0.7	0.7	1.0	0.7	1.0	0.9	0.7	0.9	0.5	0.5	0.4	0.4
33 Office machinery	0.0	0.0	0.1	0.1	0.0	0.1	0.0	0.1	0.0	0.0	0.0	0.0
34 Electrical engineering	0.4	0.5	0.3	0.4	0.3	0.4	0.6	0.8	0.3	0.3	0.3	0.2
35 Motor vehicles	0.6	0.7	0.1	0.1	0.6	1.2	0.2	0.5	1.0	0.7	0.5	0.2
36 Other means of transport	0.3	0.2	0.0	0.1	0.1	0.2	0.0	0.0	0.9	0.3	0.0	0.3
37 Instrument engineering	0.1	0.2	0.2	0.1	0.1	0.2	0.2	0.2	0.1	0.1	0.1	0.1
41 Food, drink and tobacco	1.9	1.5	2.1	1.7	0.8	0.5	3.3	2.8	2.4	1.9	0.7	0.5
43 Textiles	1.2	1.1	1.4	1.7	1.4	1.1	1.2	1.1	0.7	0.7	1.5	1.7
44 Leather goods	0.8	1.1	1.0	2.0	0.9	1.2	1.3	1.4	0.5	1.0	0.5	0.5
45 Clothing and footwear	2.8	2.7	1.7	3.7	1.4	1.6	3.3	2.9	2.7	2.8	4.2	5.5
46 Timber, wooden furniture	3.0	2.6	1.1	1.1	2.8	2.0	1.3	1.4	2.6	3.4	6.2	5.6
47 Paper products	0.4	0.4	0.5	0.4	1.1	0.8	0.2	0.2	0.2	0.3	0.2	0.1
48 Rubber and plastics	1.0	1.0	0.9	1.2	1.5	1.3	1.3	1.2	0.7	0.7	0.6	0.6
49 Other	0.5	0.5	1.3	0.7	0.7	0.6	0.4	0.4	0.5	0.5	0.1	0.2

Note: [a] For a definition see text.

Source: Eurostat and European Commission Services.

no longer appear so strong. Both have registered non-negligible declines in their share of total CEE exports – from 12.1 per cent in 1988 to 8.5 per cent in 1992 for food products and from 10.6 per cent to 8.8 per cent for wooden products in the same period.

Meanwhile there has been a significant increase in the export specialization index for metal products. This reflects an important increase in this sector's share of overall CEE exports from 2.9 per cent in 1988 to 5.9 per cent in 1992. A caveat is necessary here. Trade restructuring in the CEECs is going to be very dependent on domestic industrial restructuring. The latter often leads to social tension due to factor immobility, so it cannot be rushed, which means that the structure of CEE exports to the EU is likely to persist over the next five to ten years. This means that CEE comparative advantage is only likely to emerge gradually. Furthermore, the events of 1989 were a 'Big Bang' and are still relatively recent. Thus the results so far may turn out to be outliers over a twenty-year perspective.

THE IMPACT OF THE EUROPE AGREEMENTS ON CEECS' ACCESS TO THE EU MARKETS

One factor contributing to the growth of trade between the CEECs and the EU could be measures to lower the trade barrier which have rapidly been taken since 1989. This process has climaxed in the signing of six agreements which aim to create a free-trade area within ten years and ultimately lead to the accession of the CEECs to the EU. Even before their ratification by all EU and CEECs' legislatures, nonetheless their trade provisions already apply under so-called Interim Agreements (IAs). The IA signed with former Czechoslovakia has been replaced with two separate IAs. As a result of these IAs, the CEECs have moved since 1989 from being the least favoured non-EU countries in terms of trade access to EU markets to being the most favoured. It is interesting to consider these IAs to see whether they are having an identifiable effect on trade flows, in particular on the sectors where trade liberalization is proceeding fastest.

The path to be followed to achieve free trade in industrial products is rather asymmetric, with the EU dismantling its own trade barriers faster and earlier – generally within five years – than each of the CEE signatories. In fact, the EU was able to eliminate immediately all trade barriers, whether tariffs or quantitative restrictions, on most industrial goods except for some 'sensitive' sectors – including agriculture, textiles, clothing and steel – where temporary trade barriers remain in place. As a result, around 50 per cent of CEE exports to the EU (in 1992 value terms) enter without restriction, although the individual CEECs' experience varies between Bulgaria, where 56 per cent of exports can enter unrestrictedly, and Romania, where only 25 per cent of exports can do so. The latter result is almost entirely explained by the different role that textiles play in the export structure of individual countries.

The pattern of all types of significant trade protection measures applied by the EU against CEE imports basically follows the MFN tariff schedule. In other words, non-tariff barriers (NTBs) are insignificant when tariffs are zero or low, but become increasingly important in sectors where tariffs are medium to high. Unfortunately, the CEECs' most important exports to the EU generally come under this regime of high tariffs and NTBs.

On the other hand, in the sensitive sector of textiles, quantitative restrictions (QRs) do not seem to be binding constraints on CEE exports to the EU except in the case of the former Czechoslovakia. For the other CEECs, the QRs were only partially used up. The problem seems to lie more in the inadequacies of the CEECs' supply side although some producers within the CEECs are apparently claiming difficulty in accessing EU markets.

Furthermore, evidence shows that as QRs have been loosened, quota utilization ratios have remained static, suggesting some kind of QR effect. On the other hand, it was suggested that difficulties facing CEE producers seeking sales on the EU markets could be due to problems in the domestic export licensing administration of the CEECs.

However, what is clear is that with the collapse of the former CMEA there is an attempt being made in the CEECs to redirect trade away from their traditional partners and towards the EU in particular. Under these circumstances, the remaining QRs may yet become effective constraints for a broad range of CEE products, in which case their removal would certainly benefit the CEECs.

The reduction in EU tariff barriers in line with the IAs will lead to an enhanced real income effect for the CEECs. However the relative reduction in tariffs in the first year is lower, the higher the MFN tariff level, which means that the relative discrimination by the EU against the CEECs' most important exports to the EU actually increased in the initial period. The overall effect of this on the CEECs' sectoral pattern of developing export flows depends, however, on price elasticities of demand in the EU.

The IAs provide a framework for a progressive liberalization of industrial imports by the EU from the CEECs and the tariff reduction compared to MFN tariffs is better than under the General System of Preferences. However, the EU may be being least liberal in freeing trade in exactly those sectors where the CEECs are most competitive. Moreover, safeguard clauses exist in the IAs which could be invoked by the EU in an illiberal manner if it is felt that significant injury is being done to an industry in one or more EU member states. However such fears may be exaggerated, with only one such measure taken since the agreements came into force.

To what extent then, are CEE exports related to the varying degrees of EU protection facing them? This was tested using standard correlation tests between export performance and measures of protection. The export performance indicators used were the CEECs' export specialization indices at the NACE 2-digit level. The measures of protection used were tariff rates and import coverage ratios for QRs and other NTBs. It was found that the CEE exports are clearly concentrated in sectors which have been highly protected by the EU, and this has been the case both before and during the transition period.

On the other hand, no significant results were found which would show that sectorally differentiated changes in protection in the most recent period had led to changes in the export performance of those sectors by the CEECs. Nonetheless, Landesmann (1993) has found that there may be some evidence that exports are being diversified away from high EU protection sectors to lower ones in former Czechoslovakia.

THE WELFARE EFFECT OF CEE TRADE DEVELOPMENTS ON THE EU

One of the most often debated issues related to the process of further East–West economic integration is that of the welfare effect of this process on the EU. Within the Interpenetration project, Smith, Venables and Gasiorek (1993) analysed the economic effects on the EU of enhanced trade with the CEECs on the basis of a general equilibrium model. The model consists of a perfectly competitive composite sector and fourteen other imperfectly competitive sectors, thirteen of which are in manufacturing and one in financial services. The imperfectly competitive sectors consist of a number of firms, each producing several varieties of a differentiated product used in both final and intermediate demand. There are five primary factors of production: capital, two types of skilled labour and two types of manual labour. Capital is assumed to be internationally mobile whilst labour is not. Only the effects of expanded trade in manufacturing goods on the EU are considered.

Three different projections of CEE–EU trade are used to motivate the model. For all three projections the overall growth of CEE–EU trade is the same, and is based on estimates produced by Hamilton and Winters (1992). The difference in the projections lies in the distribution of the trade growth across EU member states and sectors. In the first projection, it is assumed that the overall growth of trade between the EU and the CEECs is uniformly distributed across countries and sectors. In the second projection, the distribution is based on the trade changes which have actually occurred between 1985 and 1992 (although it is likely that the first three years of the reform will turn out to be outliers over the fifteen- to twenty-year adjustment period facing the CEECs). Finally, the third projection postulates uniform trade growth across sectors but member state distribution which reflects the work done by Hamilton and Winters.

The effects of enhanced trade with the CEECs depend heavily on the projections used and, by extension, on their underlying assumptions. Nonetheless, some interesting conclusions can be derived from the exercise. First, even if trade is assumed to grow at a considerable rate, the base level of CEE-EU trade is currently so small relative to the size of the EU economy that the output and welfare effects on the EU are marginal. This is all the more so because trade between the CEECs and the EU is to quite a high degree intra-industry by nature. However the projected output changes in the EU may, nevertheless, not be insignificant. Still, most such output changes are likely to be positive and even the negative changes should be easily absorbable by the EU, especially given that the changes are likely to occur over a ten- to twenty-year period.

The modelling exercise provides no evidence that particular regions could suffer disproportionately in the EU.[5] What is clear is that consumers in the EU will invariably gain from enhanced trade with the CEECs, even if producers do not always, and that consumer gains will certainly exceed any producer losses. Further sensitivity checks have shown that even if trade between the EU and the CEECs grew eight-fold, rather than four-fold as assumed in the study, the effect on the EU would still be small.

The general conclusion of this exercise seems to be that the EU should not seek to slow the liberalization of trade between the CEECs and the EU; on the contrary, most parties are likely to gain from the speeding up of this process.

FOREIGN DIRECT INVESTMENT IN THE CEECS

There is some sensitivity in the EU that emerging markets in the CEECs may prove to be so attractive to potential foreign investors seeking new production locations that they will be persuaded to invest there, whereas in the absence of the CEECs they would have invested in the EU. This is especially sensitive for the southern EU member states which are generally agreed to have enjoyed enhanced economic growth thanks to significant FDI flows in the 1970s and 1980s.

FDI statistics covering the CEECs are extremely problematic due to the inconsistency of different sources and the doubtfulness of registration statistics.[6] Nonetheless, the picture emerging from the data available on the stocks and flows of foreign capital so far invested in the CEECs (for more details see Chapter 12) puts Hungary first;[7] Czechoslovakia and Poland follow. Interestingly, foreign investments into Poland accelerated in the most recent period (whilst they stabilized to Hungary and contracted to former Czechoslovakia) which could reflect the fact that it is the first CEEC to achieve economic growth since reforms began. Romania and, especially, Bulgaria have received very modest foreign investment inflows.

According to business surveys,[8] foreign investors have most commonly entered CEECs' markets via joint ventures or joint venture acquisitions. This involves linking up with an existing enterprise in the CEECs. The advantages of taking this route are that the investments involved can be quite small, liability for past environmental damage cannot be apportioned to the foreign investor, and existing distributional channels and regional business know-how can be tapped.

Nonetheless, the proportion of investment entering via greenfield developments is significant. The advantage of this route for investment is the avoidance of inheriting past management styles or production structures. Indeed, even where investment enters via merger or acquisition activity, the data clearly show that a controlling share is usually acquired because that makes it easier to impose Western working practices, techniques and strategies.

The EU is a major source of FDI everywhere in the CEECs. Within the EU, Germany usually leads, especially in Czechoslovakia where its importance has grown due to the VW–Skoda link-up. However, elsewhere in the CEECs, Germany is being caught up by other EU member states. In Poland, for example, Italy is an important investor owing to the large FIAT and Lucchini steel investments. Outside the EU, the USA is an important source of foreign investment for the CEECs. In general, US investments tend to be fewer but larger than investments from the EU.

Concerning the question of CEE–southern EU member states' competition for FDI, recent work suggests that for the moment there is no problem. Surveys indicate that large companies investing in the CEECs are not funding their activity by cutting back FDI to Southern Europe. There is investment creation, not diversion. Furthermore, some studies carried out on Spain (see, for example, Bajo-Rubio and Sosvilla-Rivero, 1994; Martin and Gual, 1994), suggest that the prime motive for FDI to that country is locational and made to exploit the large and growing domestic market and the availability of skilled labour, whereas FDI to the CEECs is attracted by low wages. It might be concluded, therefore, that a country like Spain is not competing for FDI with the CEECs.

THE CONSEQUENCES OF CEE OPENING UP FOR ITALIAN INDUSTRY

Within the Interpenetration project Italy was taken as a case study to analyse the impact of CEE opening up on the industry of an EU member state. Italy is a significant trade partner for all the CEECs, usually coming second or third within the EU. On the other hand, no CEEC is a significant trade partner for Italy. Nonetheless trade between the CEECs and Italy has grown rapidly in the 1990s and faster than the EU average. Moreover, Italian exports to the CEECs have been growing faster than imports from the CEECs.

Concerning potential competition on the EU market, the CEECs and Italy are both specialized in clothing, household textiles, wood products, glassware and foundries. On the Italian domestic market, meanwhile, the CEECs have been achieving a faster rate of import penetration than any other part of the world, especially in footwear, textiles, leather products and wood manufactures. However, in no sector do the CEECs achieve a high degree of import penetration.

Nonetheless it is possible to see that the CEECs will most likely add to the increasing competition already confronting Italian industry in sensitive sectors from developing countries. However some of the Italian sectors most penetrated by CEE exports are characterized by high and increasing intra-industry trade, which means that the adjustment costs for Italian industry may be lessened – accepting the proposition that intra-industry trade involves less adjustment than inter-industry trade.

There are also excellent opportunities for Italian exporters to the CEECs. Already the Italian mechanical engineering sector has enjoyed a large and growing export surplus with the CEECs, followed by textiles, chemicals, electrical engineering and motor vehicles. It is notable that two of these sectors – textiles and motor vehicles – are characterized by OPT-type trade, with Italy exporting semi-finished products to the CEECs for final assembly and reimport by Italy.

Meanwhile, Italian FDI to the CEECs has been on the increase in recent years, attracted by low labour costs and historical links. In a survey of Italian companies interviewed, over half expect a positive impact on their business thanks to the changes in the CEECs.

Overall, the threat to Italian industry from the CEECs is much lower than often thought, and limited to specific sectors. Moreover, even in one such sector, clothing, the apparent threat is actually related to a strategy adopted by Italian producers of enhancing textile exports. For all the threatened sectors, the CEECs are only adding a little to competitive pressures which had already been apparent on world markets and to which Italian industry has been adapting. On the other hand, if trade access to EU markets is not given to the CEECs they will not achieve export-led growth which could stoke CEE demand for Italian products.

A SENSITIVE SECTOR: TEXTILES AND CLOTHING IN THE EU AND THE CEECS

The issue of the textile and clothing sectors is very sensitive from the point of view of both the EU, especially its South European EU member states, and the CEECs. In the EU, the two sectors account for about 9 per cent of industrial employment, but provide up to one-third of manufacturing employment in Greece and Portugal. The EU's recent recession has hit these sectors particularly hard, with production down 4.7 per cent between 1988 and 1992 in textiles, and by 6.4 per cent in clothing, worse than for manufacturing as a whole. In the same period, employment in the sectors contracted 14 per cent, while investment has shrunk by 32 per cent in textiles and 25 per cent in clothing.

For the CEECs, meanwhile, the sectors are sensitive because they are quite important in employment terms – employing about 10–12 per cent of the working population. Despite the collapse of CMEA export markets and plunging domestic demand as national income fell, the sectors have shrunk only a little since 1989 thanks to substantial export increases towards Western markets, especially the EU. Now, over 20 per cent of CEE manufacturing exports are provided by these two sectors.

Other important reasons explaining sensitivity on both sides include the dynamic growth in trade of textiles and clothing between the EU and the CEECs since 1988. Between 1988 and 1992, the volume of EU exports of textiles to the CEECs grew by an annual average rate of 22 per cent while clothing grew by 41 per cent. Meanwhile, CEE exports to the EU of textiles grew by 12 per cent per year, while clothing grew 20 per cent annually.

Perhaps the most striking feature marking relations in these sectors between the EU and the CEECs, however, is the rapid growth of OPT operations involving EU firms and their counterparts in the CEECs. As a result, EU clothing imports from the CEECs covered by OPT arrangements rose from 46 per cent of all such imports in 1988 to 62 per cent in 1992. This may explain the growth in EU textile exports to the CEECs, a large proportion of which are intended for local making-up operations and subsequent reimportation into the EU. Hence, the picture that emerges is of two-way trade motivated to a significant extent by the growing internationalization of production location.

A key reason lying behind this development could be that labour costs in the EU textiles and clothing sectors are high by international standards. This is especially serious for clothing, as they are often considered to be a key component affecting competitiveness. The CEECs have a real competitive advantage over the EU in this area, even when one uses unit labour costs to account for productivity differences in the CEECs. There are, of course, so-called non-price competitiveness factors which are important, such as the sophistication and quality of output and delivery time and reliability, which may allow a high-cost producer to maintain competitiveness. However, the CEECs are thought to score relatively well on all such indicators. Indeed, that would give added reason to explain why EU producers are engaging in more and more OPT trade.

Concerning the trade regime governing textiles and clothing, together with concessions provided by the member states at the Copenhagen Summit of the EU in 1993, the EU is moving quickly to free trade between itself and the CEECs in the textiles and clothing sectors. Both QRs and tariffs are being cut in steps and will be abolished for all textiles and clothing products by 1997. However both sides have recourse to safeguard clauses.

At the same time, as noted above, the utilization of QRs by the CEECs appears to be rather low, suggesting that even now they do not represent a serious trade barrier to CEE exports of textiles and clothing and that their reduction may not lead to significantly increased flows. On the other hand, the evolving trade regime now offers immediate tariff-free access for EU imports of OPT products, which may act as an incentive to further relocation of production from the EU to the CEECs where labour costs are lower.

Despite the dynamism of OPT developments, FDI in these sectors has not been significant inside the CEECs. This reflects the subcontractual nature of OPT activity whereas the CEECs would probably prefer more capital involvement.

CONCLUSIONS

Marketization in the CEECs and trade liberalization between those countries and the EU have provoked both interest and anxiety inside the EU about the potential consequences on its industrial sectors in terms of greater competition, possible output losses and new opportunities. The Interpenetration project was set up to investigate what consequences might arise.

One of the main conclusions is that the bulk of the impact due to the dramatic developments in the CEECs' internal affairs and their trade relations with the EU since 1989 will come from growing East–West trade flows. Up to 1989, the CEECs' export structures to each other and to the former Soviet Union were quite different from their export structures to Western markets, in particular that of the EU. Exports to the former group consisted primarily of apparently highly processed and advanced manufactures, whilst exports to Western markets were more diverse and dominated by more basic manufactures. Furthermore, trade within the former CMEA dominated the CEECs' export flows – only around 20–25 per cent of total manufactured exports went to the EU.

Since 1989 the situation has radically changed. The CEECs' exports collapsed with the disintegration of the ex-CMEA and the structure of their exports to countries that made up that grouping has shifted to more basic products. Combined with sharp export growth to Western markets generally and the EU in particular, this has meant that over 50 per cent of CEE industrial exports went to the EU in 1992. The development of CEE imports has been similar but even more remarkable. Nonetheless, despite the considerably enhanced importance of the EU to the CEECs as an export destination, those countries remain rather marginal trade partners with the EU even if their importance roughly doubled between 1989 and 1992.

The substantial volume changes did not result in dramatic changes in the structure of CEE exports to the EU after 1989. It is CEE imports from the EU which have shown the most startling changes, with a huge swelling in the importance of consumer goods imports. On the other hand, it does appear that the CEECs' pattern of exports to the EU has changed faster since 1989 than the export patterns of other EU trade partners with the EU.

It is interesting to ask whether the rapid process of mutual trade liberalization between the CEECs and the EU since 1989, culminating in the EAs (and consequently the IAs), has had any role to play in explaining trade developments in this period. Correlation tests carried out show that CEE exports to the EU are concentrated in sectors which have been highly protected by the EU, both before and during the transition period. However, there is no statistically significant sign that sectorally differentiated changes in protection in the most recent period have had any affect on export performance by any CEEC (except, possibly, former Czechoslovakia). In this context it is also interesting that, given the criticism of the IAs that they continue to discriminate most against the CEECs' most important export sectors, in the particular example of textiles QRs do not seem to be binding constraints on CEE exports anyway – although they make the sector seem very protected within the EU. Rather, the problem seems to be on the CEECs' supply side.

Another issue over which there is some sensitivity is that of FDI to the CEECs. Whereas it is accepted that FDI to the CEECs is an important element in the process of making those countries' production techniques more internationally competitive and helping to integrate the CEECs into world trade, nonetheless there is some concern that such FDI may be diverted away from the poorer Southern member states of the EU, where it has been playing an important role in enhancing economic growth. To the extent that such diversion occurs, then economic growth in those EU member states could be curtailed.

So far, FDI flows to the CEECs have been very modest so any diversion effect must also have been modest. In any case, there is some evidence suggesting that the opening up of the CEECs is leading to FDI creation as enterprises see those countries as a new opportunity, not an alternative opportunity. This is backed up by research suggesting that the driving forces of FDI are quite different in the CEECs as compared to some of the Southern EU member states. Hence they cannot be regarded as direct competitors in attracting FDI.

Assuming that as time goes by, marketization in the CEECs consolidates and the supply side improves so that markets in the CEECs work at least as well as they do in Western markets, then estimates suggest that trade liberalization between the EU and the CEECs may lead to a four-fold increase in the level of CEE exports to the EU. Modelling the effects of this leads to the conclusion that the impact on the EU will overall be positive, especially for consumers. Most EU sectors will also benefit. Even those which suffer output losses as a result will be buffered by the opening up of export opportunities to the EU and the ten- to twenty-year adjustment period likely. However, because the CEECs are small relative to the EU, the welfare gains or losses experienced by the EU are also going to be quite small.

NOTES

1. The author is an official of the Directorate-General for Economic and Financial Affairs at the European Commission. The advice, suggestions and comments of Pierre Buigues, Lászlό Halpern, Radu Herghelegiu and other participants of the Sofia conference on 'Transforming Econòmies and European Integration' are gratefully acknowledged. Any views expressed are those of the author alone and are not attributable to the Commission.
2. The term 'extra-EU' is used to denote all non-EU member states.
3. See Annex for the NACE classification of industrial activities.
4. Following Balassa (1965), the export specialization index (export performance ratio) for commodity (sector) *j* of country *i*, denote it as ESI_{ij}, was specified as:

$$ESI_{ij} = \frac{x_{ij}}{X_i} : \frac{M_j}{M},$$

   where x_{ij} is country *i*'s exports of commodity (sector) *j*;
   $X_i = \sum_j x_{ij}$ is country i's total exports;
   $M_j = \sum_i x_{ij}$ is EU's total imports of commodity (sector) *j* from 'extra-EU', which is the same as the total exports of commodity (sector) *j* by the group of countries (extra-EU);
   $M = \sum_i \sum_j x_{ij}$ is EU's total imports from 'extra-EU', which is the same as the total exports of the group of countries (extra-EU).
5. However a weakness of this argument may be that the proximity of different parts of the EU to the CEECs is neglected in the model so that the projected regional effects could be too modest.

6. See OECD (1993), Stern, Bunt and Thomas (1992), UN–ECE (1993).
7. Of all the CEECs Hungary is the only country whose record seems internationally comparable with countries which have enjoyed significant inflow of foreign investment – notably Portugal.
8. See, for example, Business Central Europe (1994), Business International and Creditanstalt (1992), Deloitte Touche Tohmatsu International (1992), Genco, Taurelli and Viezzoli (1993).

REFERENCES

Bajo-Rubio, O. and Sosvilla-Rivero, S. (1994), 'An econometric analysis of foreign direct investment in Spain, 1964–89', *Southern Economic Journal*, **61**(1), July.

Balassa, B. (1965), 'Trade liberalization and "revealed" comparative advantage', *The Manchester School of Economic and Social Studies*, **33**(2), 99–123.

Business Central Europe (1994), 'Foreign investment survey', Business Central Europe, London: The Economist Group.

Business International and Creditanstalt (1992), '1992 East European investment survey', Vienna: Business International.

Deloitte Touche Tohmatsu International (1992), 'Why companies go international: the international strategy of middle market companies', Brussels: Deloitte & Touche Europe Services.

European Commission (1995), 'Economic interpenetration between the EU and Central and Eastern Europe', *European Economy*, Brussels: European Commission, Directorate General for Economic and Financial Affairs (forthcoming).

Genco, P., Taurelli, S. and Viezzoli, C. (1993), 'Private investment in central and eastern Europe: survey results', London: European Bank for Reconstruction and Development.

Hamilton, C. and Winters, L.A. (1992), 'Opening up international trade with Eastern Europe', *Economic Policy*, **14**, 77–116.

Landesmann, M. (1993), 'Czechoslovakia – an examination of trade structure and EC trade protection', paper presented at the IV Workshop on Economic Interpenetration Between the EC and Eastern Europe, Brussels, 13–14 December 1993.

Martin, C. and Gual, J. (1994), 'Trade and foreign direct investment with central and eastern Europe: its impact on Spain', Discussion Papers Series No. 1006, London: Centre for Economic Policy Research.

OECD (1993), 'Foreign direct investment in central and eastern Europe: policies and trends in fourteen economies in transition', Paris: OECD.

Smith, M.A.M., Venables, T. and Gasiorek, M. (1993), 'Modelling the effect of Central and East European trade on the European Community', paper presented at the IV Workshop on the Economic Interpenetration Between the EC and Eastern Europe, Brussels, 13–14 December 1993.

Stern, J., Bunt, K. and Thomas, N. (1992), 'Foreign direct investment in central and eastern Europe', London: NERA.

UN–ECE (1993), 'Statistical survey of recent trends in foreign investment in east European countries', Geneva: UN Economic Commission for Europe.

Discussion of Chapter 5

Radu Herghelegiu

INTRODUCTION

To approach the issue of 'Economic interpenetration between the EU and Central and Eastern Europe' – the basic pillar of European integration – requires not only analysis of the quantitative aspects of economic flows (such as trade and foreign investments) but also the dynamic measures which should be taken for achieving the final goal of European economic integration: a more powerful Europe, from West to East. In order to reach this target, the huge development potential of CEE should be revealed by implementing coherent, adequate short-, medium- and long-term strategies.

In doing so, one should always bear in mind the linkages between the evolutionary process of the EU and the internal changes implied by the transition and the economic reforms in the CEECs. As far as Romania is concerned, extensive work is under way to ensure the consistency of the reform process with the goal of the country's full integration into Europe.

Among the important aspects of the transformation process related to European integration, I would like to accentuate the following:

- The transition to democracy and a market economy has to keep pace with the commitments undertaken by the countries in the Association Agreements with the EU (the EAs).
- The legislative reforms should ensure the proper functioning of the EAs.
- The implementation of the EAs is conditioned by the speeding up of the process of macroeconomic stabilization and by support for the economic reforms.
- The facilities agreed within the EAs have to be consolidated and put into operation by concrete actions in the fields of commercial and financial activities.
- The effectiveness of the national mechanism for integration presupposes coordination of actions of the government structures with the public and the private sectors.

- The development of commercial, economic and political cooperation with other associated CEECs is one of the means to accelerate the transition processes in every country and to prepare the conditions for full membership.

THE INSTITUTIONAL FRAMEWORK OF ROMANIA'S COOPERATION WITH THE EU

The economic interpenetration is conditioned by major and comprehensive institutional agreements. After the political upheavals and the profound changes in CEE, Romania, as other countries in this region, negotiated with the EU several important agreements, such as:

- Trade and Cooperation Agreement, in force as of 1 May 1991. It was the first agreement promoting mutual trade, commercial and economic cooperation.
- A Europe Agreement (EA), finalized on 1 February 1993, which provides for the gradual establishment of a free-trade area over a period of ten years and for far-reaching cooperation in all areas of economic activity. The asymmetric character of the EA ensures that EU grants trade concessions earlier than Romania does.
- An Interim Agreement (IA), signed on 1 February 1993 and in force since 1 May 1993, related to the economic aspects of the EA, applicable until the ratification of the EA by all EU member states.
- Additional Protocol, signed on 30 April 1993, concerning trade with textile and clothing products, annexed to the EA and IA.
- Additional Protocol to the EA and IA, signed on 21 December 1993 and in force on 1 February 1994. It contains further concessions granted to Romania, following the European Council Summit in Copenhagen in 1993.
- Agreement concerning the mutual protection and control of wine denomination and Agreement for setting up tariff quotas for certain wines. These Agreements were signed on 26 November 1993 and have been applied since 1 February 1994.

These agreements had a significant positive impact on Romanian trade with the EU; besides, they stimulated the flow of FDI to Romania and created an improved environment for financial assistance from G-24 and the PHARE Programme of the EU.

It is worth mentioning that the economic interpenetration between CEE and the EU can be stimulated by connecting the CEECs to the European infrastructure networks (telecommunication, road and railway transport) and by granting assistance in implementing the complex process of approximation of the CEECs' laws to those applicable in the EU. In this respect, the decisions of the Edinburgh and Copenhagen Summits established the guidelines and concrete steps to follow with a view to achieving such goals.

DEVELOPMENTS IN ROMANIAN TRADE WITH THE EU

Traditionally Romania has had important and active commercial ties with the EU. The evolution of Romania's trade with the EU in the period 1980–93 is shown in Table D5.1.

Table D5.1 Evolution of Romania's trade with the EU, 1980–93 (US$m, current prices)

Year	Turnover	Exports	Imports	Trade balance
1980	4714	2624	2090	534
1981	4380	2475	1905	570
1982	3252	2120	1132	988
1983	3170	2429	741	1688
1984	3674	2808	866	1942
1985	3259	2414	845	1569
1986	2608	1885	723	1162
1987	3163	2591	572	2019
1988	3007	2533	474	2059
1989	3130	2699	431	2268
1990	2835	1670	1165	505
1991	2814	1435	1379	56
1992	3620	1398	2222	–824
1993	4664	1924	2740	–816

As can be seen, Romania recorded a large trade balance surplus during 1982–89, but after 1989, after the liberalization of imports, the surplus turned into deficit.

As a result of the fundamental move of Romania towards integration in the EU structures and due to the liberalization of reciprocal trade, the direction of Romanian foreign trade has shifted significantly towards the member states of the EU. Thus the share of the EU in the total Romanian trade turnover increased from 35 per cent in 1992 to 42 per cent in 1993.

Regarding the composition of Romanian exports to the EU, the largest share belongs to traditional products such as clothing, footwear and wooden products. An increasing role is played by the outward processing (OPT) arrangements, due to the labour costs in Romania. On the import side, consumer goods, foodstuffs, engineering products and textiles are the most important. As the trade barriers are gradually lowered and the need for investment in Romania increases, the pattern and volume of trade will certainly undergo further changes.

The time that has elapsed since the IA has been in force (May 1993) is rather short and, consequently, one cannot expect spectacular increases in the volumes and changes in the patterns of trade. However it is obvious that the new agreements contain many catalytic factors which will contribute to an enhanced economic cooperation between Romania and the EU.

László Halpern

It is a positive development that the European Commission initiated a project carrying the name of the chapter that I have the privilege to discuss. What is also very important is that the participants in this project have been outstanding scholars with broad knowledge of both the empirical and the theoretical aspects of international trade.

The chapter presents a well-documented and very rich analysis of the trade relations between CEECs and the EU and provides a forecast of these ties.

It is very difficult to disentangle the short-term and the long-term tendencies of foreign trade in transition countries. In this respect the author has tried to base his analysis as much as possible on neoclassical trade theory. However the question of whether this theory offers satisfactory answers to the problems of transition remains an open one.

I have some concerns about the treatment and the role of manufacturing sectors. One cannot assume that the relevant structural information in transition can be assessed properly on a sectoral level. It is only true if the variation within the sectors is significantly lower than across them. Quality, price, and factor requirements may reveal the opposite (take as examples Trabant vs. Mercedes, intra-firm trade, OPT and so on).

It is important to note that the notion of trade specialization in the chapter stands for export specialization. It would be interesting to show the import specialization measures as well. They could reveal a number of interesting features of CEECs' imports. There is another, more serious aspect of the traditional export specialization measures. Can they be interpreted as revealing comparative advantage? In the case of transition it is rather dubious. There are so many firms in CEECs struggling for mere survival, or continuing to export even when they are technically bankrupt. It is also difficult to assess whether the exports in a sector result from a declining, or from an emerging activity, or – what is more plausible – a combination of both. In order to produce realistic forecasts it would have been useful to know the time trends of the export shares.

The direct measure of comparative advantage is based on factor data for EU member states. This means that the results can only be interpreted in a very narrow sense: what would be the comparative advantage of CEECs if their resource requirements were those of the EU average? It is quite obvious, though, that there can be important differences between CEECs and Western countries.

6. Economic transformation and the changing patterns of European East–West trade

Rumen Dobrinsky

INTRODUCTION

The economic transition brought about substantial trade restructuring in the CEECs. In the pre-transition period the trade of these countries was of a dual nature: trade within the CMEA (mainly with the ex-USSR) orchestrated by the long-term multilateral agreements among the CMEA member countries and implemented under artificially imposed conditions, and trade with the rest of the world performed under more or less normal market conditions (with the exception of some cases of special agreements with developing countries).

Among other things the collapse of the ex-CMEA-driven trade with manufactured goods caused dramatic changes in the volume and in the commodity composition of trade in the countries from the region. For the first time in decades the economies of the CEECs were fully exposed to the realities of international trade and international competition.

A recent study undertaken under the auspices of the European Commission (European Commission, 1995) focuses on the emerging new patterns of trade between the CEECs and the EU member states in the light of the newly signed EAs. One of the important findings of this study was the general conclusion that the CEECs were not able to perform substantial trade reorientation of ex-CMEA trade to the EU market and as a result of the collapse of the CMEA they lost (to differing degrees) significant export flows (see Chapter 5). The recent changes in the trade patterns of these countries *vis-à-vis* the EU on the export side indicate more or less a continuation of previous trends whereas more dramatic changes occurred in CEE imports.

This chapter analyses some aspects of the process of trade restructuring in CEE with a special focus on the factor content of trade flows. Another specific accent of the present study is the attempt to draw some lines of possible comparison between the structure of CEE trade flows and those of the EU proper. The principal goal is to try to reveal whether the recent changes in the trade structure of CEECs (in a dynamic perspective) bring this structure closer to the 'typical' structure of a West European economy or vice versa.

METHODOLOGICAL BACKGROUND

The traditional theoretical approach to international trade (the neo-factor proportions hypothesis) broadly based on the Heckscher–Ohlin theory suggests that the composition of trade of a given country depends on the relative endowments of factors (and hence, on the relative factor prices) in the trading countries. Accordingly, a country will tend to export those goods which embody relatively large amounts of its abundant and therefore (relatively) cheap factors and will tend to import goods which embody relatively large amounts of its relatively scarce (and hence expensive) factors (Ellsworth and Clark Leith, 1984, p. 61). The neo-factor proportions hypothesis gives a satisfactory theoretical explanation of heterogeneous or inter-industry trade among countries (Johns, 1985).

The growing trade within one and the same sector (intra-industry trade) gave rise to other theoretical approaches such as the neo-technological hypothesis (Hufbauer, 1970) or the 'differentiated goods theory' (Gray, 1973), sometimes combined in the so-called 'theory of Linder goods' (Gray, 1980). According to these theories trade between industrialized countries with similar factor endowments and especially intra-industry trade in manufactures is driven by other factors than the relative endowments of factors in the countries. It is hypothesized that such trade is brought about by the impact of product-specific and/or firm-specific inputs creating cost or design advantage where no factor-price cost advantage exists (Gray, 1980).

A number of studies indicate, however, that the commodity composition of trade as well as its determinants depend to a high degree on the level of economic development of the countries (Balassa and Bauwens, 1988; Gray, 1980; Nolle, 1990; Preusse, 1985; Yeats, 1989). Moreover, a study by Michaely (1981) suggests that countries of different income levels are positioned differently in terms of the factor intensity of their trade flows, which he measures by the so-called 'index of the income level of trade flows' (introduced by Michaely); a change in the relative income position of a country brings about corresponding shifts in its export (import) commodity structure. The results of the latter study hint at the existence of 'typical' export and import structures for a given level of relative income in a country. This confirms earlier results of Balassa (1966) who found a high degree of similarity in the structure of manufacturing exports among West European countries.

A specific line of research in the applied analytical approaches towards the trade specialization of countries and country groups is based on the concept of 'revealed comparative advantage' (RCA) first introduced by Balassa (1965) and further elaborated in a number of studies (for a useful overview of the various approaches and developments in this area see Vollrath, 1991). The introduction of the 'revealed' comparative advantage concept (as opposed to the theoretical concept of comparative advantage) was mainly justified by the failure of the traditional theoretical approaches to generate quantifiable indicators of comparative advantage which could be used in applied studies.

The initial application of the RCA approach was limited in scope and was aimed at finding a way to measure and quantify the relative standing of individual sectors from the commodity structure of trade of a given country within a group of countries (or the world as a whole) based on the observed patterns of trade of that specific group of countries.[1] Further it was attempted to analyse and evaluate the determinants of RCA in terms of other aspects of economic performance and economic policy (Balassa, 1979, 1986; Hulsman-Vejsova and Koekkoek, 1980; Wolter, 1977; see also the review by Hartigan, 1981). The focus of most of these studies was on testing either the neo-factor proportions hypothesis or the neo-technology hypothesis (or both at the same time) vs. the indicators of RCA.

The recent developments in international trade theory are linked to a major shift from the classical assumptions of perfect competition and constant returns to scale of the traditional theory to the assumptions of imperfect competition and increasing returns to scale, which are considered as more relevant to economic reality. The 'new' theory of international trade, which is largely based on the analysis of the interactions of individual firms in different countries, tries to find plausible explanations of intra-industry trade between similar countries, particularly in the advanced technology sectors (Sapir, 1993).

In this context, three main lines of analysis are followed in the chapter:

1. Comparison of commodity composition of trade of CEECs with that of West European countries. As pointed out above, both theoretical and empirical works suggest that there is a strong relation between the level of economic development and structure of trade. Thus a quantitative evaluation of the degree of similarity of the commodity structure of trade of former centrally planned economies with that of developed market economies can provide an indirect (though very rough) measure of their current relative economic standing.
2. Analysis of the impact of revealed comparative advantage as a determinant of trade in CEECs and in West European countries. Both recent theoretical and empirical works suggest that comparative advantage plays

a diminishing role as a determinant of international trade among industrialized countries, in particular, in manufactured goods. Though the notion of RCA is different in nature and interpretation from the classical notion of comparative advantage, basically it reflects the same fundamentals of trade determination. In this respect a quantitative assessment of the role of RCA as a determinant of CEE trade and a comparison with industrialized Western countries, both in statics and in dynamics, can provide some further insights on the current situation and the possible future trends in CEECs.

3. Factor intensities and composition of trade. The two main underlying hypotheses of international trade theory – the neo-factor proportions and the neo-technological hypotheses imply a different role of factor endowments as determinants of trade. To the extent that it is possible to define measurable indicators of theoretical notions this could be traced in the factor intensity of trade flows (under the assumption that a higher factor intensity of exports from a country reflects the relative abundance of this factor in the country and vice versa for imports). By defining quantifiable factor intensity indicators it will be attempted to assess the factor content of trade flows and to compare the patterns in CEECs with those in West European countries.

Some precautionary words should be said about the limitations of the analysis presented here which stem from the scope and nature of the available empirical data. Trade data have always been a serious limitation to analysing trade performance of CEECs, especially when we go back to the period of central planning. National statistics in many of these countries did not produce trade data on the basis of international standards and classification. So for the purpose of this study I use a very limited segment of trade data for these countries: the trade flows to and from the EU member states, as reflected by the mirror statistics of the latter. The available data for this study only cover trade in the manufacturing sectors. The NACE 2- and 3-digit classification of economic activities is used to define sectoral trade (21 and 108 sectors, respectively). For simplicity, henceforward the explicit reference to this fact will be omitted; however it should be borne in mind that the trade flows which are analysed only comprise trade in manufactured goods.

As a benchmark of comparison I use the total trade flows (exports and imports) of the twelve EU member states by the same sectoral breakdown. This adds one more limitation to the possibility of comparison and actually the quantitative results for the CEECs and for the EU member states are not directly comparable. In spite of that, the decision to select these EU trade flows was based on the fact that the intra-EU trade *per se* is largely driven by the removal of trade barriers among the member states. Besides, the determinants of intra-EU trade in the latest years have changed largely, as suggested by the 'new' trade theory mentioned above. In this regard, the motivation of intra-EU trade is substantially different from that of trade between CEECs and EU member states.

As one of the goals of this study is to analyse the implications of the economic transition in CEECs on their trade performance I have selected two points in time. The first is the middle of the 1980s, about the time when Portugal and Spain joined the EU. The second point is the beginning of the 1990s, the first years of the economic transition in the CEECs.[2]

CONCENTRATION AND SIMILARITY OF CEE AND EU TRADE FLOWS

The extent to which the commodity structure of trade is dominated by a relatively limited number of traded commodities can be measured by the Gini–Hirschman coefficient of concentration of trade.[3] Concentration is relatively more pronounced on the export side if a country is specialized in the export of certain commodities. Small countries as well as lower-income countries tend to have higher concentration coefficients.

High concentration coefficients can also (though not necessarily) be an indication that factor endowments play a significant role as determinants of trade flows. If a country tends to export those goods which embody relatively large amounts of its abundant production factors and to import goods which embody relatively large amounts of its relatively scarce factors (as stems from the factor proportions hypothesis), there will be a higher concentration of both exports and imports in certain commodities. However a higher concentration of trade may result from specialization based on other principles as well.

In dynamics, a declining concentration coefficient means that the commodity trade structure becomes more even, the large shares becoming smaller and the small share becoming larger. This is usually an indication of a process of emerging new trade, or trade creation. On the contrary, an increasing concentration coefficient means that large shares become larger whereas small shares become smaller. When measured over a specific market this might be an indication (though not necessarily) of a process of trade diversion. When calculated over the total exports or imports it is simply an indication of increased specialization of trade.

The interpretation of the calculated concentration coefficients of CEECs' trade with the EU and of EU member states' total trade (Table 6.1) is not straightforward. In general on the export side the CEECs' concentration coefficients are slightly higher than those of the EU member states whereas

Table 6.1 Indicators of concentration and intra-industry trade, CEE and EU

	Gini–Hirschman coefficients of concentration of trade[a]				Grubel–Lloyd indices of intra-industry trade[a]	
	Exports		Imports			
	1984–85	1991–92	1984–85	1991–92	1984–85	1991–92
CEE trade with the EU						
Bulgaria	0.280	0.214	0.187	0.177	0.341	0.417
Czechoslovakia	0.210	0.172	0.198	0.169	0.436	0.527
Hungary	0.273	0.213	0.183	0.167	0.462	0.529
Poland	0.237	0.218	0.176	0.159	0.351	0.420
Romania	0.271	0.325	0.199	0.176	0.396	0.318
CEE	0.208	0.191	0.177	0.158	0.468	0.486
EU total trade						
Belgium/Luxembourg	0.202	0.209	0.195	0.177	0.805	0.807
Denmark	0.200	0.189	0.152	0.150	0.583	0.642
France	0.166	0.193	0.159	0.177	0.774	0.811
Germany	0.191	0.186	0.162	0.168	0.672	0.757
Greece	0.229	0.260	0.185	0.172	0.359	0.322
Ireland	0.254	0.242	0.182	0.170	0.645	0.622
Italy	0.153	0.157	0.187	0.185	0.574	0.606
Netherlands	0.190	0.170	0.155	0.163	0.752	0.755
Portugal	0.199	0.225	0.187	0.192	0.455	0.438
Spain	0.206	0.252	0.194	0.184	0.592	0.699
U.K.	0.175	0.175	0.165	0.166	0.757	0.790
EU	0.160	0.165	0.160	0.164	–	–

Note: [a] For definition see text.

Source: Own calculations based on Eurostat COMEXT.

regarding imports they are roughly on the same level. In dynamics the measures of concentration of trade in the CEECs declined from 1984–85 to 1991–92 (with the exception of Romanian exports) whereas there were different trends in the EU member states in this period.

The decline in the trade concentration in the CEECs is an indication of the diversification of their trade with the EU and the emergence of new trade which is taking place after the collapse of the CMEA when a process of reorientation of trade flows was begun. All CEE transition economies tried to redirect some of their ex-CMEA exports to other markets and, in particular, to the EU. Although they were not particularly successful in this regard (Dobrinsky, 1993; Rosati, 1993), some reorientation of exports did take place, leading to new trade and a more diversified export structure. Only Romania appears as an outlier of this tendency. However, the concentration of Romanian exports increased, which is probably an indication of trade diversion in sectors in which the country used to be specialized.

At the same time many ex-CMEA suppliers were substituted for more competitive ones, largely from Western Europe. As a result the import structures became more diversified and the import concentration ratios declined.

One interesting phenomenon is that in all the three newcomers to the EU (Greece, Portugal and Spain) the concentration of exports increased substantially after they joined the EU (besides, the level of export concentration is also relatively high). This might be interpreted in the sense that the enhanced access to the EU market gave an impetus mainly to their most competitive products, which increased their relative share in their total imports. However, only judging by this indicator one cannot draw a more definite conclusion as to which was the underlying internal determinant of this specialization; I shall return to this issue later.

An important structural indicator of trade specialization is the Grubel–Lloyd index of intra-industry trade (Grubel and Lloyd, 1971, 1975). Intra-industry trade, or the simultaneous export and import of similar products, cannot be explained by the traditional comparative advantage theory of international trade. Actually, the identification of this phenomenon was one of the motivations for putting forward the neo-technological hypothesis of trade as well as for the development of the 'new' theory of trade. In accordance with these theoretical principles intra-industry trade takes place mainly among industrialized countries and is motivated by product differentiation, increasing economies of scale, imperfect markets and consumers' taste for variety (Vona, 1991).

The calculated Grubel–Lloyd indices of intra-industry trade for the CEECs and for the EU member states (Table 6.1)[4] reveal another aspect of their trade performance. Within the EU-12 one could clearly identify two subgroups: the 'old' EU-9 members plus Spain, which are characterized by relatively high values of the Grubel–Lloyd index, in conformity with the theoretical postulates; and two of the 'new' members – Greece and Portugal – which appear as 'outliers' with much lower indices of intra-industry trade (in both cases the latter have decreased since joining the EU). This is already a second indicator that the determinants of trade in these two countries may differ from those of the other EU member states.

The CEECs (with the exception of Romania) recorded an increase in their Grubel–Lloyd indices from 1984–85 to 1991–92. Among them Czechoslovakia[5] and Hungary had the highest indices of intra-industry trade; the levels of the latter in 1991–92 were close to those in some EU member states (such as Denmark, Italy and Spain) in 1984–85 and higher than those in

Greece and Portugal. Bulgaria and Poland in 1991–92 displayed Grubel–Lloyd indices comparable to that in Portugal and the index of Romania was comparable to that of Greece (Table 6.1).

In principle the change to higher levels of intra-industry trade in most of the CEECs since the start of the transition might be an indication of a process of economic reintegration with Western Europe, in which trade determinants other than the traditional comparative advantage begin to play an increasing role. Such a process is most clearly observed in Czechoslovakia and Hungary. However, because the Grubel–Lloyd indices are not calculated on the level of individual products but on the sectoral level, this increase in the measured intra-industry trade, as will be shown in Chapter 9, may also account for other developments such as the intensification of 'outward processing traffic' (OPT).

A further step is to compare the actual commodity composition of the trade flows of individual countries. The results of such a comparison need careful interpretation because the determinants of trade may differ substantially from country to country, even among countries of a comparable level of economic development. Due to these limitations such comparisons are not likely to provide evidence for more general conclusions. However, without exaggerating the analytical potential of such an exercise, it can enlighten some specific features of the trade structure of CEECs and EU member states.

The quantitative evaluation of the degree of similarity has been performed on the basis of a version of the similarity index.[6] In this chapter, I present only the similarity indices for the export commodity structures of the CEECs and the EU member states, calculated on the basis of the 108-sector NACE 3-digit sectoral classification (Tables 6.2 and 6.3 for the two time points, respectively). Again, the numbers do not provide straightforward clues and need careful examination.

The results of this evaluation reveal that geographic proximity seems to be an important determinant of the similarity of the export structures. Among determinants of similarity, according to the results of the evaluation, are the income level as well as the size of the economies.

One specific feature of these results is that the group of CEECs appears quite homogeneous in terms of the similarity of their export structure, presumably as a result of the simultaneous impact of all factors mentioned above. The opposite is true for the twelve EU member states among which it is possible to distinguish different subgroups of countries with resembling export structures. This picture should be interpreted in terms of the heterogeneity of the determinants of similarity in the EU member states.

As regards the cross-comparison between CEECs and EU member states, the exports commodity structure of the lower-income EU countries such as Greece and Portugal is characterized by a higher degree of similarity to the

Table 6.2 Similarity indices of CEE and EU export structures, 1984–85

	Total exports												Exports to the EU					
	UK	Spa	Pt	Nl	Ita	Irl	Gre	Ger	Fra	Dk	B/L	EU	CEE	Rom	Pol	Hun	Cze	Bul
Bul	0.355	0.525	0.449	0.591	0.431	0.328	0.486	0.410	0.468	0.308	0.604	0.484	–	0.658	0.559	0.619	0.788	–
Cze	0.411	0.623	0.537	0.644	0.552	0.325	0.348	0.554	0.595	0.358	0.670	0.615	–	0.565	0.535	0.588	–	
Hun	0.309	0.324	0.423	0.611	0.391	0.433	0.406	0.330	0.388	0.679	0.426	0.427	–	0.606	0.672	–		
Pol	0.361	0.531	0.459	0.520	0.409	0.269	0.580	0.442	0.491	0.455	0.553	0.499	–	0.672	–			
Rom	0.261	0.386	0.608	0.360	0.490	0.198	0.465	0.340	0.358	0.320	0.403	0.389	–	–				
CEE	0.418	0.567	0.610	0.660	0.577	0.360	0.546	0.507	0.572	0.550	0.628	0.604	–					
EU	–	–	–	–	–	–	–	–	–	–	–	–						
B/L	0.668	0.834	0.400	0.696	0.619	0.382	0.338	0.823	0.828	0.379	–							
Dk	0.517	0.268	0.293	0.617	0.476	0.516	0.230	0.420	0.510	–								
Fra	0.849	0.832	0.479	0.723	0.744	0.475	0.313	0.939	–									
Ger	0.764	0.855	0.436	0.684	0.703	0.414	0.234	–										
Gre	0.250	0.401	0.523	0.298	0.424	0.134	–											
Irl	0.578	0.320	0.257	0.671	0.376	–												
Ita	0.727	0.636	0.659	0.555	–													
Nl	0.680	0.547	0.406	–														
Pt	0.391	0.473	–															
Spa	0.565	–																
UK	–																	

Source: Own calculations based on Eurostat COMEXT.

Table 6.3 Similarity indices of CEE and EU export structures, 1991–92

	Total exports												Exports to the EU					
	UK	Spa	Pt	Nl	Ita	Irl	Gre	Ger	Fra	Dk	B/L	EU	CEE	Rom	Pol	Hun	Cze	Bul
Bul	0.362	0.270	0.643	0.452	0.532	0.261	0.645	0.361	0.331	0.381	0.419	0.432	–	0.671	0.897	0.773	0.712	–
Cze	0.562	0.582	0.576	0.627	0.705	0.307	0.403	0.697	0.560	0.370	0.698	0.719	–	0.492	0.709	0.675	–	
Hun	0.388	0.290	0.612	0.625	0.564	0.435	0.501	0.421	0.370	0.602	0.416	0.493	–	0.633	0.776	–		
Pol	0.367	0.331	0.563	0.467	0.512	0.239	0.568	0.414	0.360	0.398	0.440	0.458	–	0.724	–			
Rom	0.164	0.162	0.591	0.211	0.382	0.135	0.460	0.190	0.178	0.266	0.215	0.232	–	–				
CEE	0.445	0.396	0.654	0.577	0.640	0.316	0.553	0.510	0.435	0.476	0.523	0.568	–					
EU	–	–	–	–	–	–	–	–	–	–	–	–						
B/L	0.710	0.806	0.362	0.652	0.605	0.368	0.269	0.839	0.695	0.446	–							
Dk	0.577	0.279	0.272	0.719	0.564	0.547	0.279	0.535	0.519	–								
Fra	0.899	0.702	0.364	0.658	0.675	0.434	0.226	0.836	–									
Ger	0.851	0.830	0.411	0.736	0.779	0.440	0.233	–										
Gre	0.248	0.192	0.629	0.308	0.389	0.176	–											
Irl	0.615	0.258	0.210	0.740	0.383	–												
Ita	0.748	0.568	0.618	0.628	–													
Nl	0.783	0.441	0.322	–														
Pt	0.343	0.428	–															
Spa	0.604	–																
UK	–																	

Source: Own calculations based on Eurostat COMEXT.

export structures of the CEECs. However, a similar result is also observed for some higher-income countries such as Italy and, occasionally, Belgium/Luxembourg (B/L), the Netherlands and Denmark.

Among the CEECs, Czechoslovakia is an obvious leader with respect to the similarity of her export structure to that of the EU member states. Even back in 1984–85 the similarity indices for Czechoslovakia are comparable to those among the EU member states. It should also be noted that the similarity indices of Czechoslovakia and Hungary in 1991–92 in general increased as compared to 1984–85, whereas in the other three countries for the most part they decreased (especially with regard to the higher-income EU member states). The latter can be considered as an indication of a different type of specialization which is taking place in these three countries, similar to the process observed in the lower-income EU member states.

REVEALED COMPARATIVE ADVANTAGE AND PATTERNS OF EXPORT SPECIALIZATION

Specialization and Competition among CEECs

The notion of RCA was introduced in order to make it possible to quantify and measure the specialization of countries in exporting certain commodities which is asserted to 'reveal' their comparative advantage/disadvantage over other countries with respect to these commodities.

As already noted, there may be important links between the level of concentration of exports of a country and its export specialization. To analyse them I have used the export specialization indices (ESI) of the CEECs and the EU member states.[7] Besides static measures of RCA such as the ESI dynamic measures can also be used, such as $\Delta ESI = ESI(t) - ESI(t-1)$.

In practical application, in the static case ESI values greater than 1 are usually accepted as an indication of RCA of the country with respect to the commodity under consideration. In the dynamic case one has to take into account both the current and the past level of the ESI. Commodities with positive values of ΔESI obviously improve their relative position over time. However this alone does not give sufficient information about the actual standing of the commodity in the export structure. Such a situation can be referred to as the case of 'weak' dynamic RCA. The 'weak' dynamic RCA indicates a situation when a commodity improves its relative standing over time but does not necessarily indicate static RCA.

Let us now consider the case when at the same time $ESI > 1$ *and* $\Delta ESI > 0$. Such a combination indicates a situation when a commodity displays static RCA in period *t* and at the same time has improved its relative standing over the previous period. I shall refer to such a situation as the case of 'strong' dynamic RCA, or simply dynamic RCA.

The static ESIs for the CEECs and for the EU member states have been calculated for the two points: 1984–85 and 1991–92; the dynamic indicator ΔESI was evaluated for 1991–92 over 1984–85. All computations were performed on the NACE 3-digit level (108 sectors). Further, the computed ESIs on the sectoral structure of exports of CEECs can be superimposed on those for the EU member states in order to analyse the composition of exports from the point of view of export performance (RCA) in individual sectors.

The level of concentration of exports in sectors with RCA (Table 6.4 and Table 6.5)[8] can be interpreted as an indication of the importance of comparative advantage as a determinant of exports in the individual countries. In general these results seem to confirm the hypothesis that comparative advantage plays a more important role as a determinant of trade for lower-income countries whereas for high-income industrialized countries its importance diminishes.

To take just one indicator – the cumulative export share of the ten sectors with highest ESI within the EU-12 in 1991–92 – it ranges from 17.9 per cent in France to 52.9 per cent in Greece (Table 6.4). High levels of this indicator exhibit a tendency for the country to specialize in exporting a limited number of commodities. On the neo-factor proportions hypothesis it is presumed that it enjoys comparative advantage in these commodities. However it should be mentioned that smaller economies also tend to be more specialized (e.g. Ireland) than large economies.

On the other hand, the identification of sectoral export specialization *per se* is not an argument against the neo-technological hypothesis, because such a specialization may be the result of economies of scale or of imperfect markets. Moreover, judging from another measure of concentration – the cumulative export share in sectors with RCA (Table 6.5) – in all EU member states this concentration is high, in the range of 60 to 80 per cent of total exports. This means that, whatever the driving forces (the neo-factor proportions, or the neo-technological hypothesis), the tendency for country export specialization is overwhelming.

In four of the CEECs (Bulgaria, Czechoslovakia, Hungary and Poland) the concentration of exports in sectors with high ESIs declined substantially in 1991–92 as compared to 1984–85 (Table 6.4). This can be interpreted as the outcome of the already outlined tendency for a diversification of trade of these countries with the EU as well as of the emergence of new trade since the start of the transition. Romania again was an outlier, manifesting the reverse trend (Table 6.4).

As to the general tendency of export specialization (as measured by the cumulative share of exports in sectors with RCA), it was very well manifested

Table 6.4 *CEE and EU exports in sectors with highest export specialization indices, %*

	Exports to the EU						Total exports										
	Bul	Cze	Hun	Pol	Rom	CEE	B/L	Dk	Fra	Ger	Gre	Irl	Ita	Nl	Pt	Spa	UK
Sectors																	
1984–85																	
10 highest	52.1	25.5	40.6	29.7	53.3	23.0	21.7	31.4	7.4	24.6	52.6	44.0	19.0	12.0	46.0	14.2	25.2
20 highest	75.0	52.9	64.3	49.5	65.7	45.2	39.7	38.5	18.5	32.4	67.6	58.1	32.0	37.6	59.3	29.6	46.5
30 highest	84.3	65.7	75.9	72.1	79.3	62.3	63.7	56.1	29.8	53.6	81.8	74.2	45.2	48.5	69.4	51.0	56.3
1991–92																	
10 highest	27.6	11.4	23.7	17.0	59.9	11.9	19.4	25.4	17.9	25.1	52.9	50.0	19.9	15.9	47.6	30.9	24.9
20 highest	53.3	28.6	47.4	46.1	74.9	24.4	46.4	37.3	26.0	32.9	66.0	65.6	35.8	33.0	57.9	38.3	42.1
30 highest	66.7	44.0	61.3	62.1	85.6	47.3	56.0	53.2	34.6	50.3	73.1	75.0	51.2	48.7	69.9	50.0	58.4

Source: Own calculations based on Eurostat COMEXT.

Table 6.5 *CEE and EU exports in sectors with revealed comparative advantage (RCA) (cumulative export shares, %)*

	CEECs *vis-à-vis* the EU						EU member states *vis-à-vis* the world										
	Bul	Cze	Hun	Pol	Rom	CEE	B/L	Dk	Fra	Ger	Gre	Irl	Ita	Nl	Pt	Spa	UK
Exports in sectors with static RCA[a]																	
1984–85	85.1	82.4	77.2	81.5	79.7	75.0	71.0	74.6	58.8	67.1	82.5	75.7	59.7	66.4	69.4	67.5	64.3
1991–92	76.6	74.8	77.0	79.9	81.1	80.0	72.3	71.7	58.4	69.0	78.9	71.8	64.7	64.1	69.8	61.9	59.4
Exports in sectors with dynamic RCA[b]																	
1991–92	25.1	11.7	9.4	19.7	11.2	8.8	7.2	1.4	11.9	0.0	30.8	11.3	0.0	1.3	28.4	1.6	0.0

Notes:
[a] Sectors with export specialization index > 1.0.
[b] Sectors with export specialization index > 1.0 and positive increment over previous period.

Source: Own calculations based on Eurostat COMEXT.

Table 6.6 CEE exports to the EU in sectors of absolute competition among CEECs[a] *(export shares, %)*

		Bulgaria	Czechoslovakia	Hungary	Poland	Romania	CEE
NACE 3-digit sectors							
	1984–85						
221	Iron and steel industry	19.28	11.44	4.32	4.49	5.48	7.09
253	Industrial chemicals (except petrochemicals)	2.59	2.10	3.81	10.16	4.73	5.31
347	Manufacture of electric lighting equipment	0.22	0.35	2.07	0.35	0.32	0.71
412	Preparing and preserving of meat	3.04	3.69	20.13	6.88	2.81	7.95
436	Knitting industry	4.77	1.86	3.10	1.60	6.06	3.04
451	Manufacture of footwear	1.21	1.74	3.12	2.61	4.06	2.73
453	Manufacture of ready-made clothing	9.82	4.11	10.67	8.41	17.83	9.80
455	Manufacture of household textiles	0.54	1.23	0.69	0.46	0.57	0.73
465	Wood manufactures (except furniture)	0.42	1.02	0.65	0.38	0.81	0.69
467	Manufacture of wooden furniture	3.16	2.16	1.60	2.47	14.05	4.58
	Subtotal	45.04	29.70	50.16	37.81	56.71	42.64

	1991–92						
221	Iron and steel industry	6.82	7.14	2.42	3.49	5.35	4.62
222	Manufacture of steel tubes	0.47	1.75	0.83	0.85	1.42	1.14
247	Manufacture of glass and glassware	0.87	3.83	1.68	1.57	2.09	2.26
248	Manufacture of ceramic goods	0.85	1.13	0.76	0.49	1.11	0.80
311	Foundries	0.45	0.41	0.46	0.57	0.18	0.46
346	Manufacture of domestic electric appliances	1.04	0.87	1.99	1.00	0.85	1.17
352	Manufacture of bodies for motor vehicles	0.12	0.33	0.90	0.36	0.24	0.45
451	Manufacture of footwear	4.37	2.25	4.48	2.02	4.80	2.97
453	Manufacture of ready-made clothing	12.87	5.71	11.49	13.71	24.59	11.78
455	Manufacture of household textiles	1.85	1.11	0.95	0.80	0.74	0.97
456	Manufacture of furs and fur goods	0.13	0.12	0.21	0.09	0.16	0.13
464	Manufacture of wooden containers	0.12	0.09	0.06	0.11	0.17	0.10
465	Wood manufactures (except furniture)	0.28	1.12	0.62	2.00	0.48	1.24
467	Manufacture of wooden furniture	1.64	2.42	2.31	5.29	17.08	4.63
	Subtotal	31.88	28.27	29.16	32.36	59.26	32.71

Note: [a] Sectors in which all CEECs display static RCA *vis-à-vis* the EU (export specialization index > 1.0).

Source: Own calculations based on Eurostat COMEXT.

in the exports of CEECs to the EU in 1991–92 (although dropping down slightly from 1984–85): in all the countries this share was in the range of 75–80 per cent (Table 6.5).

Turning to dynamic RCA, it could be pointed out that a high concentration of exports in sectors with dynamic RCA (as defined above) is an indicator of a process of internal restructuring and repositioning of the sectoral composition of a country's exports. This means that relatively larger shares of the country's exports tend to be located in sectors which improve their relative standing in the export structure (*vis-à-vis* the corresponding market). In this sense it can be interpreted as an indicator of export specialization dynamics in the narrow sense of shifting more exports to sectors which improve their ESI. Hence, such sectors increase their weight in the sectoral composition of exports. The higher the concentration of exports in sectors with dynamic RCA, the more pronounced the tendency of a country for such export specialization over time.

This should not be confused with the static export specialization, as discussed above, which is measured over all sectors with static RCA, although the standing of some of the latter may deteriorate over time.

Within the group of CEECs Bulgaria appears as the country of highest concentration of exports in sectors with dynamic RCA, followed by Poland (Table 6.5). Within the EU-12 it is again Greece and Portugal that manifest highest dynamic export specialization. These results make it possible to look at the already noted peculiarities of these two countries' export performance from one more angle. The somewhat unusually high level of dynamic export specialization of France (Table 6.5) is due to dynamic RCA in one single sector – aerospace equipment (NACE 364) – in this period.

The computed ESIs for the CEECs enable us to address one more trade performance issue concerning these countries. If all the countries within this group display RCA *vis-à-vis* the EU in a given sector (measured by a static ESI > 1.0), this can be interpreted as a sign of strong competition among all of them for a portion of the EU market. I shall refer to such sectors as 'sectors of absolute competition among the CEECs'.

It is important to note that a significant share of the exports of CEECs is concentrated in sectors in which they compete fiercely with one another on the EU market (Table 6.6). Although the tendency over time was for the share of such exports to decline in 1991–92 as compared to 1984–85, the number of sectors falling into the category of absolute competition increased. Again Romania is an extreme case with almost 60 per cent of exports included in this category (double the other countries' shares).

It is also important to note that a number of sectors from the list of 'sectors of absolute competition among the CEECs' at the same time fall into the category of highly protected on the part of the EU ('sensitive') manufacturing sectors (iron and steel industry (NACE 221), steel tubes (NACE 222), textiles and clothing (NACE 453 and 455)). All this results in the following picture: in a number of sectors in which each CEE country enjoys comparative advantage and specializes *vis-à-vis* the EU, it faces strong competition on the part of the other CEECs and protectionist measures on the part of the EU.

Factor Endowments and Factor Content of Trade Flows

The role of factor endowments as determinants of international trade is widely recognized regardless of the underlying explanatory framework. Different hypotheses of the determination of international trade imply different initial assumptions. Thus the neo-factor hypothesis is equivalent to the assumption that for any good the same production function holds in all countries, whereas according to the neo-technology hypothesis there are inter-country differences in the mode of production (Hulsman-Vejsova and Koekkoek, 1980).

A proper test of these hypotheses would necessarily require detailed country-specific data on factor endowments which, in practical terms, sets definite limits to the possible level of analysis, at least regarding the CEECs. For this reason I have chosen a simplified approach to the study of the impact of factor endowments, namely a comparative structural analysis of the factor content of exports in the countries under consideration. For this purpose five factor endowments have been specified, for which it was possible to specify quantifiable indicators, namely:

Factor	*Definition of quantifiable indicator*
Capital intensity	Cumulative investment/number of employees
Labour intensity	Number of employees/output
R&D content	R&D expenditure/output
Skill content	Non-manual labour/total employment
Energy intensity	Energy costs/output

For the actual measurement of the sectoral factor intensities (on the NACE 3-digit level) I have used the average of the four largest EU member states (as a proxy for the EU average): Germany, France, Italy and the UK (see European Commission, 1995).[9] Then the values of the indicators of factor intensities were superimposed on the structure of exports of the countries and the factor intensities were juxtaposed with other indicators of export performance.

The main emphasis in this exercise is the quantification and analysis of the factor content of the trade flows (and, in particular, exports) of different

Table 6.7 Relative factor intensity of CEE and EU exports in selected groups of sectors (unweighted average factor intensity of all sectors = 1.0)

	Exports to the EU						Total exports											
	Bul	Cze	Hun	Pol	Rom	CEE	B/L	Dk	Fra	Ger	Gre	Irl	Ita	Nl	Pt	Spa	UK	EU
10 largest exporting sectors																		
1984–85																		
Capital	0.91	1.08	0.84	0.92	1.16	0.92	1.16	0.87	1.20	1.20	1.10	1.09	0.86	1.31	1.12	1.20	1.09	1.23
Labour	0.93	0.94	1.03	0.97	0.93	0.96	0.77	0.97	0.87	0.87	0.98	0.86	1.03	0.71	1.03	0.84	0.87	0.81
R&D	0.25	0.40	0.94	0.39	0.37	0.35	0.92	1.22	2.42	2.42	0.44	1.76	0.82	1.22	0.91	0.85	1.65	1.59
Skill	0.90	0.86	0.92	0.84	0.88	0.80	1.01	1.06	1.16	1.16	0.86	1.21	0.98	1.17	0.93	1.06	1.15	1.13
Energy	1.10	1.32	1.08	1.09	1.51	1.07	1.30	0.63	1.15	1.15	1.84	0.54	0.77	1.18	0.85	1.17	0.81	1.15
1991–92																		
Capital	0.79	1.09	0.85	0.97	1.03	0.90	1.16	0.87	1.15	1.09	1.13	1.20	0.82	1.18	0.92	1.14	1.11	1.16
Labour	1.04	1.02	1.00	0.92	1.01	0.98	0.77	0.97	0.90	0.94	1.00	0.77	1.10	0.82	1.14	0.89	0.88	0.90
R&D	1.04	0.39	0.57	0.38	0.23	0.37	1.23	1.22	2.57	2.68	0.25	2.10	0.83	1.80	1.09	1.02	2.29	2.44
Skill	0.90	0.82	0.86	0.81	0.79	0.81	1.01	1.06	1.15	1.24	0.82	1.27	0.95	1.20	0.89	1.00	1.17	1.16
Energy	1.07	1.52	1.12	1.10	1.94	1.08	1.29	0.63	1.03	0.61	1.99	0.60	0.50	0.65	0.76	1.15	0.70	1.07

10 sectors with highest export specialization index

1984–85

Capital	1.05	1.31	0.59	1.08	0.81	1.25	1.29	1.11	1.11	0.88	1.12	1.18	0.82	1.67	0.96	1.13	0.91	–
Labour	0.90	0.90	1.21	0.92	1.22	0.94	0.70	0.85	0.97	1.09	0.96	0.85	1.09	0.57	1.15	1.02	1.14	–
R&D	0.22	0.29	1.06	0.22	0.17	0.21	0.64	0.18	0.76	1.05	0.37	0.76	0.65	0.36	0.12	0.22	1.92	–
Skill	0.89	0.83	0.95	0.86	0.75	0.79	0.92	0.89	0.98	1.01	0.81	1.09	0.87	1.04	0.78	0.83	1.24	–
Energy	1.12	1.92	0.69	1.68	1.32	1.87	1.28	0.74	1.15	0.65	1.66	0.67	0.92	0.72	1.07	1.98	0.51	–

1991–92

Capital	1.18	1.21	0.63	0.95	0.89	1.22	1.35	1.13	0.98	0.89	1.15	1.44	0.82	1.66	0.98	0.90	1.05	–
Labour	0.95	1.02	1.09	0.95	1.15	1.00	0.79	0.87	1.02	1.06	0.95	0.69	1.09	0.59	1.13	1.12	0.97	–
R&D	0.18	0.32	1.21	0.40	0.26	0.26	0.49	0.21	0.71	1.72	0.59	2.03	0.65	0.36	0.51	0.41	2.47	–
Skill	0.82	0.82	0.92	0.79	0.78	0.77	0.91	0.91	0.97	1.13	0.83	1.26	0.87	1.04	0.81	0.84	1.29	–
Energy	1.92	1.97	0.60	1.33	1.84	1.95	1.92	0.76	0.85	0.72	1.85	0.76	0.92	0.76	1.08	1.40	0.48	–

Source: Own calculations based on Eurostat COMEXT and European Commission Services.

countries.[10] This approach also makes it possible to trace some relations between export specialization and factor content of exports. To do this I have computed for each country the factor intensities of some subsets of sectors which are assumed to represent their export specialization (Table 6.7). The subsets of the ten largest exporting sectors for the individual countries are assumed to reflect their 'absolute' export specialization whereas the subsets of the ten sectors with highest export performance ratios are selected as representing their 'relative' export specialization in terms of RCA.

In terms of absolute specialization in their exports to the EU all CEECs appear to be specialized in products of high energy content, low skill content and very low R&D content (see the upper part of Table 6.7). The only exception – the relatively high R&D content for Bulgaria in 1991–92 – is due to the shift of one single sector of high R&D intensity (electrical machinery – NACE 342) to the top ten exporting sectors. The obvious specialization of the CEECs in the exports of highly energy-intensive products has undoubtedly resulted from the access to energy resources from the former USSR at below world market prices. The production structure of the East European countries has

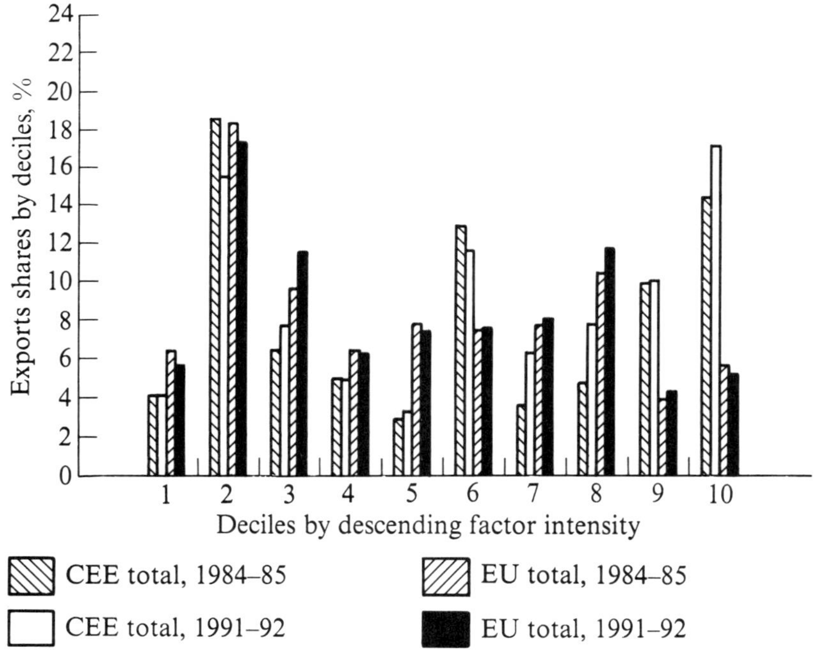

Figure 6.1 Breakdown of exports by capital intensity (CEE exports to the EU; EU total exports)

developed in such 'greenhouse' conditions and due to inertia it will take time until it readjusts. Such a specialization cannot be considered as economically viable and it is not an indication of 'healthy' comparative advantage.

As regards capital and labour intensity the picture is mixed: some countries tend to be specialized in more capital- or labour-intensive products, and some countries are less so. In terms of dynamics the situation did not change substantially in 1991–92 as compared to 1984–85. Perhaps one interesting development is that in this period three countries (Bulgaria, Czechoslovakia and Romania) switched to specialization in relatively more labour-intensive products whereas the reverse occurred in Hungary and Poland.

As for the EU member states, the picture is almost a mirror image of that in the CEECs. In 1991–92 most of these countries were assessed to display an absolute export specialization (of their total exports) in R&D-intensive (with the exception of Greece and Italy), skill-intensive (except Greece, Italy and Portugal) and capital-intensive goods (except Denmark, Italy and Portugal). The R&D content of the largest exporting sectors is especially high in France, Germany, Ireland and the UK. Only a few countries manifest an

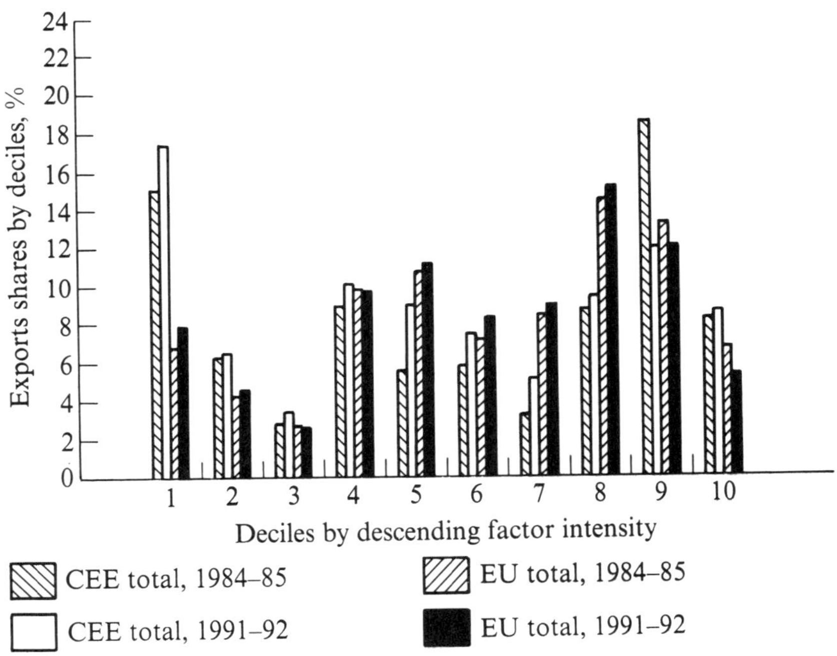

Figure 6.2 Breakdown of exports by labour intensity (CEE exports to the EU; EU total exports)

absolute export specialization in labour-intensive and energy-intensive products. As compared to 1984–85 the energy intensity of the largest exporting sectors in most countries declined, which can be regarded as an echo effect of the process of industrial restructuring induced by the oil shocks.

Turning now to the relative export specialization of the countries as displayed by the sectors with higher export performance ratios (the lower part of Table 6.7), one can see that the picture for the factor intensities of these exports is similar, with some important exceptions.

In the group of the CEECs Hungary is a very interesting case. On average the sectors with highest ESI in this country (i.e. the sectors in which it enjoys highest RCA) are sectors of relatively high R&D content and relatively low energy content as well as low capital intensity. This can already be seen in 1984–85 and is reinforced in 1991–92. This indicates a process of successful industrial restructuring in prospective manufacturing branches (for example in electrical engineering industries and, lately, in components for motor vehicles), which Hungary had started quite a few years ago. Although these sectors are not the leading exporters yet, their future prospects seem to be good.

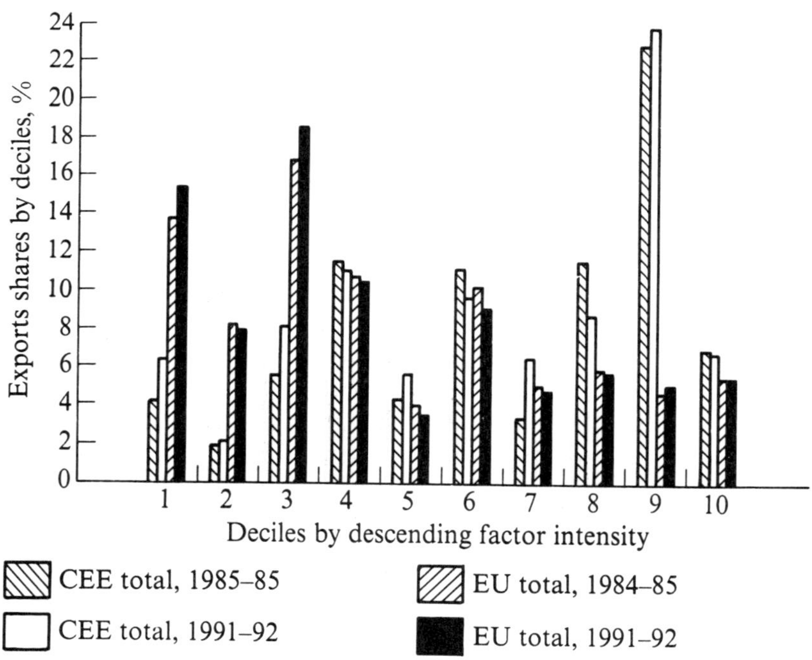

Figure 6.3 Breakdown of exports by R&D intensity (CEE exports to the EU; EU total exports)

For the other CEECs the quantitative assessment of the factor intensity of the sectors with highest ESI makes the picture even more gloomy, especially regarding the energy intensity. The illusory 'cheap' energy appears as the major determinant of RCA in these countries, and this is especially manifested in the 1991–92 figures. Most probably this also reflects the process of reorientation of some ex-CMEA exports to the West which the CEECs attempted after the collapse of the CMEA. Since the transition economies of Eastern Europe no longer have access to 'cheap' energy such a specialization will hardly be sustainable in the future (unless subsidized by the states).

At the same time it can be pointed out that in all the 'newcomers' to the EU from the 1980s (Greece, Portugal and Spain) RCA seems to be related to high energy content (Table 6.7). Among the other EU member states such a situation is observed only in Belgium/Luxembourg.

In the group of the EU member states it is worth mentioning that only for three countries (Germany, Ireland and the UK) are the R&D content and the skill content assessed as determinants of RCA and, hence, of their relative

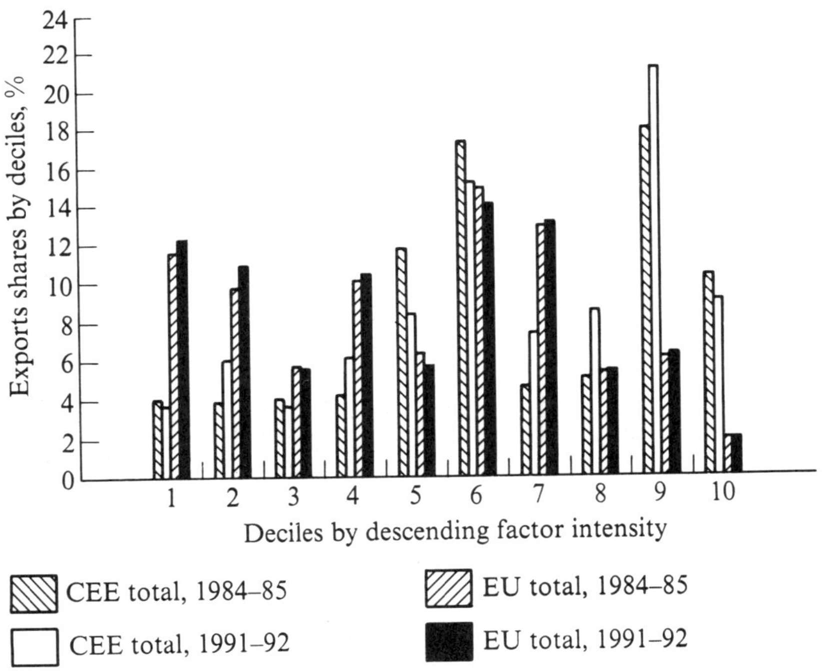

Figure 6.4 Breakdown of exports by skill intensity (CEE exports to the EU; EU total exports)

export specialization (Table 6.7). For a number of EU member states the high capital intensity seems to be a more important driving force of RCA.

It is interesting to note that according to these results in 1991–92 two highly industrialized and high-income countries – France and Germany (the latter also in 1984–85) – display a phenomenon which is similar to the 'Leontief paradox' (Leontief, 1953). In the case described here the 'paradox' is in a weaker form: it only refers to the relative export specialization. According to the results given in Table 6.7 France and Germany display RCA *vis-à-vis* the rest of the EU in sectors which are relatively less capital-intensive and relatively more labour-intensive.[11] An attempt at further insight into the underlying causes of this phenomenon[12] gives a relatively clear interpretation of the situation in Germany, where these are industries which are at the same time labour-intensive and skill-intensive (such as the mechanical engineering branches). The interpretation of the French 'paradox' obviously needs deeper investigation. One more technical point is that French exports are in general much less concentrated (see Tables 6.1 and 6.4), which makes their indicators more vulnerable to changes which are not driven by fundamental economic factors.

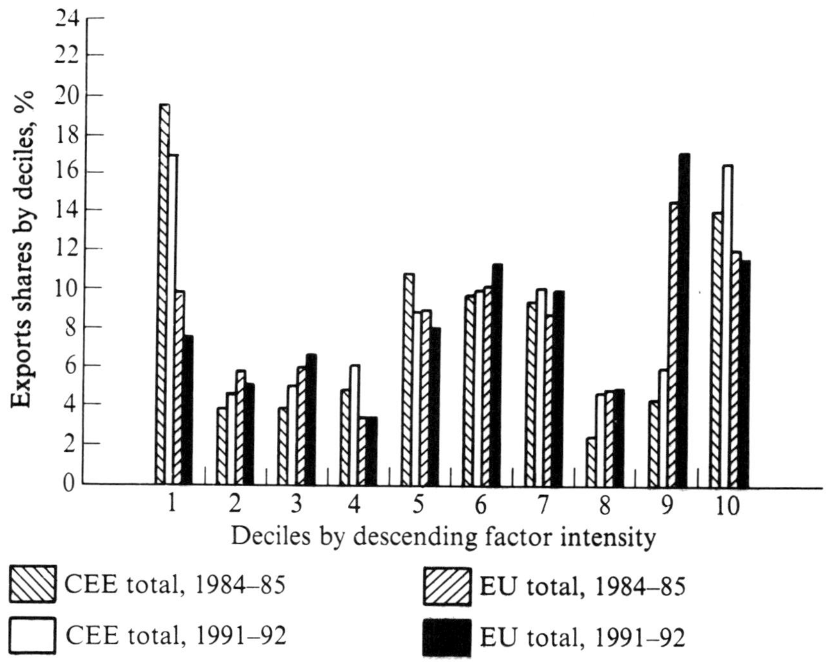

Figure 6.5 *Breakdown of exports by energy intensity (CEE exports to the EU; EU total exports)*

The analysis of export specialization-*cum*-factor content which has been performed on the basis of the subsets of the specialized sectors presents only one, albeit important, side of the whole picture. For a more detailed analysis I have assessed the full export structure[13] of the countries under consideration with respect to the factor endowment content. To do that all export sectors for each country were ranked by each of the factors (in descending order of factor intensities), then the set of sectors was divided into deciles and the cumulative export shares by deciles were calculated. The aggregate results for CEE and the EU as a whole are displayed in Figures 6.1 to 6.5.[14]

In a way, such an approach can be regarded as a test of Michaely's (1981) proposition that countries of different income level are positioned differently in terms of the factor intensity of their trade flows.[15] In general the results reported here seem to confirm this proposition, although they also indicate that the income differentiation is not the only determinant of structural differences in the factor intensity of the exports.

The differences in the breakdown of exports in CEECs and EU member states by factor intensities are noticeable. They are most pronounced in the initial and in the final deciles within each of the five breakdowns. In the group of the CEECs there is massive concentration of exports in sectors of low capital intensity, low R&D intensity and low skill intensity. With respect to labour intensity there is some concentration of exports both in the sectors of highest and in the sectors of lowest factor intensity. The picture is the same in the breakdown by energy intensity. In the group of the EU member states in general there is marked concentration of exports in high capital intensity, low labour intensity and low energy intensity decile zones.

All in all this latest comparison indicates that with respect to the factor contents of exports the differences in the export structures between the CEECs and the EU member states are much more pronounced than the similarities. In spite of the changes after the start of the transition the gap still remains, though it has decreased moderately.

CONCLUSIONS

The process of economic transformation in the former centrally planned economies is having a profound impact on all aspects of their economic life. However the fundamental economic structures which, in turn, determine their trade performance, require much more time to adjust in accordance with market principles.

The study reported in this chapter is an attempt to analyse some aspects of the evolution and change in the commodity composition of trade of the CEECs with the EU. The analysis is performed in parallel (though not in direct comparison) with a review of the trade performance of EU member states, using a similar methodological approach. The differences stem from the data available for the study which covers trade of CEECs with the EU.

The results of the study indicate that the process of economic transformation has brought about important changes in the commodity composition of trade of CEECs. Progress, however, is uneven both across countries and in different directions of change. Regarding exports and export structures, which was the focus of the study, as a whole there is still a significant gap between CEECs and EU member states, as shown by a number of quantitative indicators of export performance, computed and analysed in the study.

The most important cause for these differences appears to be the difference in the level of economic development, that is, in the level of income, between these two groups of countries. Such a conclusion is confirmed by the revealed analogous differences between the export structures of the high-income and lower-income EU member states. One conclusion from the results of this study (which supports some theoretical propositions) is that comparative advantage plays a more important role as determinant of trade in the lower-income countries (such as the CEECs, but also some EU member states) whereas in high-income countries the main driving forces of trade (especially of trade among themselves) appear to be of a different nature.

Although the export structures of the CEECs are quite similar in many aspects, this group is not homogeneous with respect to their trade performance *vis-à-vis* the EU. The results show that Hungary and Czechoslovakia appear most advanced in the process of their trade restructuring. By different measures of trade performance they display changes which bring their export structure somewhat closer to that of West European countries.

On the other end of the scale is Romania where the recent changes have increased the gap with respect to the export structures of EU member states. However the results of the study indicate that a similar increase of the existing gap also occurred in Greece and Portugal after joining the EU.

It is not realistic to expect that the trade structures of the CEECs will change fundamentally while the income gap with respect to West European countries remains in the current range. As long as the income gap remains (which is certain to be so in the foreseeable future), the principal driving forces of trade are likely to remain different in the Eastern and in the Western parts of Europe.

NOTES

1. The most comprehensive study of this type was performed by UNIDO covering 47 countries and 129 commodity groups (UNIDO, 1982).

2. For the actual quantitative assessments I have composed an 'average' 1984–85 and an 'average' 1991–92 from the yearly figures to level out the yearly fluctuations.
3. The Gini–Hirschman coefficient (see Hirschman, 1945) is defined (in our case for country i) as:

$$GHC_i = [\Sigma_j (x_{ij} / X_i)^2]^{1/2},$$

where x_{ij} is country i's exports of commodity j; X_i is country i's total exports.
4. Various specifications of this index have been suggested in the literature listed. Reviewing and analysing the properties of these indices Vona (1991) convincingly argues that the original formulation used by Grubel and Lloyd is superior regarding the proper measurement of intra-industry trade. For this reason, I have stayed with the original specification namely,

$$GL = 1 - \frac{\Sigma_j \mid x_{ij} - m_{ij} \mid}{\Sigma_j (x_{ij} + m_{ij})}$$

where x_{ij} and m_{ij} are country i's exports and imports of commodity j, respectively.
5. Unfortunately the data which were available at the time of preparing this study refer only to the already non-existing state of Czechoslovakia and no distinction can be made with respect to the Czech and the Slovak Republics.
6. In the course of the study several specifications of such indices were tested including the most commonly used similarity index:

$$1 - \Sigma_j (s_{ij} - s_{kj})^2,$$

where (in the case of exports) $s_{ij} = x_{ij}/X_i$ and $s_{kj} = x_{kj}/X_k$ are the export shares for countries i and k, respectively. It can be analogously specified for imports.

The higher the value of the similarity index (these values are in the interval (0,1) by definition), the closer the two commodity structures resemble each other. A drawback of this index is that with the growth of the number of commodities in the breakdown of trade its values tend to shift to the upper range of the interval (0,1) and so it becomes more difficult to analyse them.

For this reason another specification was chosen, namely an integrated similarity index, defined as:

$$1 - \frac{\Sigma_j (s_{ij} - s_{kj})^2}{\Sigma_j s_{ij}^2 + \Sigma_j s_{kj}^2}$$

This specification is superior in the sense that the distribution of its values does not depend on the level of disaggregation but solely on the degree of resemblance of the two structures.

Apart from the similarity indices an evaluation of the rank correlations of the commodity structures was also performed. However the latter did not produce any significantly different results.
7. The ESI definition which was used for the CEECs is the same as the one given in Chapter 5; however, in my case the calculations were performed on the NACE 3-digit level. The ESIs for the EU member states were defined *vis-à-vis* 'the world', that is, relative to their total manufacturing exports. It should be borne in mind that as the ESIs for the CEECs and those for the EU member states are based on different specifications the results do not allow for a direct comparison between the two groups of countries.
8. In order to assess this concentration all sectors in the individual countries were ranked by the value of the computed static ESIs (in descending order). Accordingly the cumulative export shares of the 10, the 20 and the 30 sectors with highest ESI in each country were evaluated (Table 6.4). As another measure of this concentration, the cumulative export shares in sectors with static or dynamic RCA were calculated (Table 6.5).

9. It must be pointed out that the available factor intensity data cover only 89 of the total 108 NACE 3-digit sectors. Differing from country to country, these sectors comprise between 80 and 85 per cent of the total exports.
10. It should be mentioned that such an approach is also equivalent to the assumption that for any manufacturing sector (on the NACE 3-digit level) the same production function holds for all countries under consideration. This assumption might be quite strong, especially in view of the differences between East and West European economies, but it does not go beyond the traditional factor proportions assumption.
11. The same is also valid, for example, in the cases of Portugal and Spain, but for these countries this would not be a 'paradox' as their level of income is lower.
12. The relatively highly labour-intensive sectors within the ten sectors with highest ESI of the two countries in 1991–92 were: France – NACE 247, 361, 374, 442, 461, 464, 481; Germany – NACE 322, 323, 324, 326, 327, 342, 362, 374.
13. In this case, according to the available data, 89 out of 108 NACE 3-digit sectors.
14. Detailed results for individual countries are available from the author on request.
15. Besides, this exercise is limited to the exports only.

REFERENCES

Balassa, B. (1965), 'Trade liberalization and "revealed" comparative advantage', *The Manchester School of Economic and Social Studies*, **33**(2), 99–123.

Balassa, B. (1966), 'Tariff reductions and trade in manufactures among industrial countries', *American Economic Review*, **56**(3), 466–73.

Balassa, B. (1979), 'The changing pattern of comparative advantage in manufactured goods', *The Review of Economics and Statistics*, **61**(2), 259–66.

Balassa, B. (1986), 'Comparative advantage in manufactured goods: a reappraisal', *The Review of Economics and Statistics*, **68**(2), 315–19.

Balassa, B. and Bauwens, L. (1988), 'Inter-industry and intra-industry specialization in manufactured goods', *Weltwirtschaftliches Archiv*, **124**(1), 1–13.

Dobrinsky, R. (1993), 'The economic interpenetration between the EC and Eastern Europe: a country study on Bulgaria', paper presented at the IV Workshop on the Economic Interpenetration Between the EC and Eastern Europe, Brussels, 13–14 December 1993.

Ellsworth, P.T. and Clark Leith, J. (1984), *The International Economy*, New York: Macmillan.

European Commission (1995), 'Economic interpenetration between the EC and Eastern Europe', *European Economy*, Brussels: European Commission, Directorate-General for Economic and Financial Affairs.

Gray, H.P. (1973), 'Two-way trade in manufactures: a theoretical underpinning', *Weltwirtschaftliches Archiv*, **109**(1), 19–39.

Gray, H.P. (1980), 'The theory of international trade among industrial nations', *Weltwirtschaftliches Archiv*, **116**(3), 447–70.

Grubel, H.G. and Lloyd, P.J. (1971), 'The empirical measurement of intra-industry trade', *The Economic Record*, **47**, 494–517.

Grubel, H.G. and Lloyd, P.J. (1975), *Intra-Industry Trade. The Theory of Measurement of International Trade in Differentiated Products*, London: Macmillan.

Hartigan, J.C. (1981), 'The U.S. tariff and comparative advantage: a survey of methods', *Weltwirtschaftliches Archiv*, **117**(1), 65–109.

Hirschman, A.O. (1945), *National Power and the Structure of Foreign Trade*, Berkeley: University of California Press.

Hufbauer, G.C. (1970), 'The impact of national characteristics and technology on the commodity composition of trade in manufactured goods', in Vernon, R. (ed.), *The Technology Effect in International Trade*, New York: Columbia University Press, 145–231.

Hulsman-Vejsova, M. and Koekkoek, K.A. (1980), 'Factor proportions, technology and Dutch industry's international trade patterns', *Weltwirtschaftliches Archiv*, **116**(1), 162–177.

Johns, R.A. (1985), *International Trade Theories and the Evolving International Economy*, New York: St Martin's Press.

Leontief, W. (1953), 'Domestic production and foreign trade: the American capital position re-examined', *Proceedings of the American Philosophical Society*, 97 (Sept.).

Michaely, M. (1981), 'Income levels and the structure of trade', in Grassman, S. and Lundberg, E. (eds), *The World Economic Order: Past and Prospects*, London: Macmillan, 121–61.

Nolle, D.E. (1990), 'The determinants of intra-industry trade for developing economies', *Rivista Internazionale di Scienze Economiche e Commerciali*, **37**(4–5), 409–23.

Preusse, H.G. (1985), 'Inter- and intra-industrial division of labour and the gains from trade', *Aussenwirtschaft*, **40**(4), 389–405.

Rosati, D. (1993), 'The economic interpenetration between the EC and Eastern Europe: the case of Poland', paper presented at the IV Workshop on the Economic Interpenetration Between the EC and Eastern Europe, Brussels, 13–14 December 1993.

Sapir, A. (1993), 'Regionalism and the new theory of international trade: do the bells toll for the GATT? A European outlook', *The World Economy*, **16**(4), 423–38.

UNIDO (1982), *Changing Patterns of Trade in World Industry: An Empirical Study on Revealed Comparative Advantage*, New York: United Nations Industrial Development Organization.

Vollrath, T.L. (1991), 'A theoretical evaluation of alternative trade intensity measures of revealed comparative advantages', *Weltwirtschaftliches Archiv*, **127**(2), 265–79.

Vona, S. (1991), 'On the measurement of intra-industry trade: some further thoughts', *Weltwirtschaftliches Archiv*, **127**(4), 678–700.

Wolter, F. (1977), 'Factor proportions, technology and West German industry's international trade pattern', *Weltwirtschaftliches Archiv*, **113**(2), 250–67.

Yeats, A.J. (1989), 'Developing countries' exports of manufactures: past and future implications of shifting patterns of comparative advantage', *The Developing Economies*, **27**(2), 109–45.

7. The pattern of East–West European integration: catching up or falling behind?

Michael Landesmann

INTRODUCTION

Economic theory suggests that industrial and trade specialization increases as countries, which have attained different levels of economic development, liberalize their trade relationships with each other. Countries which are rather similar in their overall levels of economic development, on the other hand, will increase the volume of intra-industry trade, but not necessarily their pattern of inter-industry specialization.

The problem which the integration of East European economies into the European economy poses is that the underlying level of economic development of the different Central and East European (CEE) economies is difficult to evaluate and hence the pattern of trade and industrial specialization over the medium run (the next five to ten years) is difficult to predict.[1] In the light of this uncertainty it is difficult to arrive at straightforward answers to the question: will there be a more pronounced pattern of inter-industry specialization based on different factor endowments and technological abilities or will there be rapid expansion of intra-industry trade and a rapid closure of a currently existing technological and developmental gap? And, even if the tendencies towards more inter-industry specialization were to be realized in the period immediately following the breakdown of the CMEA and the rapid process towards liberalization with the West, will these tendencies persist? And for how long?

Recent growth-theoretical literature has addressed the issue of convergence or divergence of growth patterns and levels of economic development (see the classic paper by Abramovitz, 1986; see also the empirical tests and further analysis contained in the papers by Baumol, 1986; Ben-David, 1994; Levine and Renelt, 1992; Dollar and Wolff, 1993; Verspagen, 1991; Fagerberg, Verspagen and von Tunzelman, 1994). One conjecture which emerges from this literature is the likelihood of a bifurcation in development patterns which leads to some less developed countries embarking upon a process of (sometimes rapid) catching up while other economies are unable to close the gap to more advanced economies or fall even further behind. A number of factors are responsible for determining on which side of the bifurcation point countries or regions find themselves. Abramovitz's concept of 'social capability' seems to be crucial in this respect (see Abramovitz, 1991). The evidence for postwar Western Europe is in favour of convergence (see e.g. Ben-David, 1994) and the relatively successful process of West European integration has been cited as one of the crucial factors behind that picture of convergence. Nonetheless, strong regional disparities also remain in Western Europe, and there is no clear evidence that these are declining. Recent literature on economics and geography (see particularly Krugman, 1991; Rotemberg and Saloner, 1990; and Krugman and Venables, 1990) has shown in a number of theoretical models why regional disparities might persist or be reinforced.

In this chapter, we would like to pick up the theme of convergence or divergence in the context of East–West European integration and bring to bear some empirical evidence on the process of integration so far.

In the next section we shall review current patterns of specialization in trade relationships between West and East European economies. We shall attempt to examine whether there is evidence of clear inter-industry specialization and/or whether there is a tendency towards more intra-industry trade. We shall be interested in detecting any evidence of differentiation amongst East European economies in this respect.

CURRENT PATTERNS OF EAST–WEST EUROPEAN TRADE INTEGRATION

We shall first review the current process of overall reorientation of trade towards the West and the European Union (EU) in particular and show that, largely because of geographical location, there are important differences between the different CEE economies. Second, we shall present some evidence for very pronounced patterns of export specialization with repect to the EU which, indeed, reveals a pattern of specialization quite distinct from the structure of EU imports in general and in comparison with the advanced West European economies, such as the EFTA countries, Austria, Sweden and Switzerland. This complements Dobrinsky's analysis in Chapter 6 which contained comparisons with EU economies and the less developed Southern European economies of Portugal, Spain and Greece in particular. We shall show that important changes in the structure of exports of CEE economies to the EU have taken place over the period 1989 to 1993 which, in some ways, confirm prior beliefs based on Heckscher–Ohlin (HO) theoretical conjectures

Table 7.1a Percentage of exports and imports which go to/come from Western industrial countries

	1989	1990	1991	1992	1993
Czech Rep.					
Exports	37.0	43.6	55.2	67.5	69.9
Imports	37.3	47.3	57.5	69.8	73.1
Hungary					
Exports	44.1	54.1	67.9	71.3	67.6
Imports	49.6	53.1	66.6	69.7	64.9
Poland					
Exports	49.1	63.4	74.0	77.8	75.1
Imports	53.0	66.4	68.9	75.8	76.2
Slovenia					
Exports	67.6	73.0	79.0	66.8	69.6
Imports	77.6	80.8	82.2	67.0	73.4
Bulgaria					
Exports	8.0	9.0	26.3	42.2	43.1
Imports	17.1	14.9	32.8	43.8	42.6
Romania					
Exports	39.3	46.2	47.4	48.0	–
Imports	11.5	31.4	40.7	54.0	–

Source: WIIW database; shares (in %) calculated from data in national currencies.

about trade specialization and, in other ways, contradict them. Third, we shall examine in some detail evidence for more intra-industry trade between CEE economies and the EU and the characteristics of such trade.

Tables 7.1a and b show the degree of trade exposure to Western and EU markets over the period 1989 to 1993 for the five CEE economies with which we shall be concerned in this chapter.[2] Apart from the rather well-known dramatic process of trade reorientation from intra-CMEA trade towards trade with Western economies, it shows the importance of the geographical factor in determining the degree of trade integration between CEE economies and the EU. While the Czech Republic, Hungary, Poland and Slovenia which all have common borders with the EU export 70–75 per cent of their manufacturing exports to the Western industrial economies, and in the range of 50–64 per cent to the EU, Bulgaria and Romania export a significantly smaller proportion to the West and the EU (about 43–50 per cent to the West and 28–35 per cent to the EU).

The importance of this geographical factor is also supported by projections made by R. Baldwin in his book *Towards an Integrated Europe* (Baldwin,

Table 7.1b Percentage of exports and imports which go to/come from the EU

	1989	1990	1991	1992	1993
Czech Rep.					
Exports	26.3	31.4	43.3	52.8	54.6
Imports	26.5	31.9	39.8	47.7	51.4
Hungary					
Exports	24.8	32.2	45.7	49.8	46.5
Imports	29.0	31.0	41.1	42.7	40.1
Poland					
Exports	32.1	45.1	55.6	59.1	63.2
Imports	33.8	43.5	49.9	55.6	57.2
Slovenia					
Exports	51.3	57.9	63.8	54.9	57.4
Imports	56.9	58.3	60.2	50.1	55.7
Bulgaria					
Exports	5.5	5.0	15.7	29.4	28.1
Imports	10.3	9.6	20.7	31.1	30.2
Romania					
Exports	25.2	31.5	34.2	32.6	–
Imports	5.7	19.7	27.4	37.5	–

Source: WIIW database; shares (in %) calculated from data in national currencies.

1994) where he estimates two scenarios of East–West European trade integration using a gravity model. The results show a long-run equilibrium trade pattern based on (a) the GDP per capita levels of 1989 and (b) a catching-up process in which Romania and Bulgaria are assumed to catch up with the average of Ireland, Greece and Portugal by the year 2010, and the other economies with Spain. In Tables 7.2a and b we calculate the geographical trade patterns which emerge from Baldwin's two scenarios. Again, we can see that the geographical distance to EU markets will continue to be an important factor determining the extent of trade integration of CEE economies and Western Europe.[3]

Next we come to an analysis of patterns of trade specialization. We examined trade flows between the EU and the different CEE economies at the NACE 3-digit level over the period 1989–93. This amounts to distinguishing between 108 manufacturing sectors. At times this sample of industries shrank to 89 industries since other measures, such as the factor intensity measures which were used to examine the nature of commodity trade specialization

Table 7.2a Shares of exports to geographical areas, 1989 income level scenario

Table 7.2b Shares of exports to geographical areas, income catch-up scenario

	Table 7.2a				Table 7.2b			
	E. Eur.	Visegr.	W. Eur.	EU-12	E. Eur.	Visegr.	W. Eur.	EU-12
Austria	21.74	13.18	78.26	66.33	54.72	34.59	45.28	38.38
Finland	21.66	3.90	78.34	55.44	54.10	10.59	45.90	32.48
Iceland	10.62	2.90	89.38	72.71	33.83	9.86	66.17	53.83
Norway	11.30	3.34	88.70	66.74	35.47	11.16	64.53	48.56
Sweden	15.05	4.10	84.95	63.12	43.38	12.62	56.62	42.07
Switzerland	6.38	2.37	93.62	84.05	22.69	8.83	77.31	69.40
Albania	22.43	6.40	77.57	64.47	90.89	27.78	9.11	7.57
Bulgaria	26.32	7.34	73.68	59.81	70.44	18.90	29.56	23.99
Croatia	23.52	9.47	76.48	58.09	58.90	25.46	41.10	31.22
Czech Rep.	17.59	7.22	82.41	63.38	56.78	25.43	43.22	33.24
Estonia	24.96	3.39	75.04	42.35	73.99	16.07	26.01	14.68
Hungary	26.67	10.01	73.33	52.38	75.41	28.76	24.59	17.56
Latvia	32.50	7.04	67.50	47.23	87.85	10.25	12.15	8.50
Lithuania	37.12	10.25	62.88	46.57	83.60	25.70	16.40	12.15
Poland	28.49	6.67	71.51	55.69	73.56	18.97	26.44	20.59
Romania	31.12	8.30	68.88	55.02	82.81	24.12	17.19	13.73
Slovakia	22.91	11.55	77.09	43.23	68.29	36.43	31.71	17.78
Slovenia	19.84	7.46	80.16	62.60	56.50	23.31	43.50	33.97
Belarus	40.84	9.27	59.16	44.36	79.88	19.39	20.12	15.09
Russia	25.17	7.03	74.83	55.59	67.75	18.94	32.25	23.96
Ukraine	37.53	9.61	62.47	48.26	81.47	23.17	18.53	14.31
Moladova	36.54	7.55	63.46	49.91	85.18	17.96	14.82	11.66
Belgium/Lux.	3.60	1.31	96.40	90.76	13.89	5.29	86.11	81.08
Germany	7.25	3.18	92.75	67.89	25.18	11.38	74.82	54.76
Denmark	10.87	3.91	89.13	70.09	34.62	13.07	65.38	51.42
Spain	7.90	2.44	92.10	78.29	27.14	8.85	72.86	61.93
France	5.38	1.87	94.62	74.54	19.75	7.20	80.25	63.23
Greece	15.99	4.11	84.01	68.71	46.54	12.17	53.46	43.73
Ireland	6.63	2.08	93.37	79.98	23.48	7.78	76.52	65.55
Italy	13.13	4.16	86.87	65.35	39.66	13.29	60.34	45.39
Netherlands	4.59	1.67	95.41	78.53	17.21	6.54	82.79	68.14
Portugal	7.32	2.19	92.68	80.60	25.54	8.07	74.46	64.76
UK	6.41	2.16	93.59	76.68	22.71	8.06	77.29	63.43

Source: Calculated from Baldwin (1994), Appendix 3.1.

were only available for that sample. We start with an examination of factor intensity biases in the different economies' exports to the EU over the period 1989–93. The measures used to analyse factor intensities of commodity trade flows were uniformly those obtained for EU economies (see also the recent studies in Buigues et al., 1994, which first used these measures; they were subsequently used in a number of further contributions including Dobrinsky's chapter in this book).[4] The advantage of using these measures is that the patterns of trade are examined with respect to a common ranking of industries in terms of capital, labour, energy, R&D and skill intensities; this common ranking has been extracted from the production statistics for EU economies. The drawback is that we are not analysing actual factor intensities of CEE's trade flows with the EU since individual countries' actual factor contents might (and most probably will) deviate from this common measure; however, as long as the rankings of industries across countries in terms of relative factor intensities do not differ very much – even if the absolute levels do – the following analysis will not be much affected (for further discussion of the pros and cons of their use in this type of exercise, see Buigues et al., 1994).

Table 7.3 compares the shares in total exports to the EU of the 10, 20, 30 most capital-, labour-, energy-, R&D- and skill-intensive industries (out of 89) of the five East European countries (CEE-5) and the shares of these industries in total EU imports (excluding intra-EU trade). We can see that the most capital-intensive industries accounted for a significantly lower share of CEE-5 exports than of total EU imports in 1989 and their shares declined further significantly over the period 1989–93. The opposite was true for the shares of the most labour-intensive industries in CEE-5 exports to the EU: they were significantly higher than in total EU imports and their shares increased rather strongly after 1989. The most dramatic differences are with respect to the most R&D- and skill-intensive industries which account for much lower shares of CEE-5 exports to the EU than in total EU imports, although there was a slight closure of this wide gap over the period 1989–93. As regards the shares of the most energy-intensive industries, these were over-represented in the CEE-5 exports to the EU as compared to total EU imports, but their share declined considerably over the period 1989–93 and now the gap is no longer very wide.

Although the general pattern is rather similar in the different CEE economies, there are significant differences in the degree to which capital-, labour-, energy-, R&D- and skill-intensive industries are under- or over-represented. In Figure 7.1 we plot the percentage differences in the representation of the different categories of industries in the CEE economies' exports to the EU compared to total EU imports. We can see that the degree of under- or over representation of the different categories of industries differs widely. Thus by standard definitions of levels of economic development in terms of industrial specialization, there is a definite ranking in that the CSFR and Hungary have the smallest gap in the representation of capital-, labour-, R&D- and skill-intensive branches in their exports to the

Table 7.3 *Difference in the representation of 10, 20 and 30 most x factor-intensive industries in CEE manufacturing exports to the EU compared with their representation in total EU imports*

		CSFR					Hungary					Poland				
		1989	1990	1991	1992	1993	1989	1990	1991	1992	1993	1989	1990	1991	1992	1993
NACE	Intensity															
10		1.3	2.2	–2.1	–1.9	–3.2	–8.8	–8.4	–9.7	–9.5	–10.1	–8.3	–8.0	–8.2	–8.4	–9.4
20	Capital	–5.7	–5.6	–6.5	–6.4	–7.9	–14.1	–13.7	–15.2	–15.4	–14.7	0.8	–2.8	–4.2	–3.3	–5.3
30		–6.0	–6.0	–8.5	–8.7	–9.8	–19.7	–19.0	–20.3	–20.4	–18.9	–5.3	–9.3	–11.0	–10.3	–12.0
10		1.4	1.7	1.8	3.1	2.6	10.3	9.8	9.3	11.1	9.8	6.6	6.9	8.8	9.7	10.1
20	Labour	–0.7	–0.6	0.7	1.0	1.2	8.3	8.6	8.0	9.5	9.2	5.0	5.1	6.7	7.2	9.9
30		–3.4	–2.8	–1.4	–0.4	1.5	7.2	7.5	6.8	8.7	9.1	1.0	1.9	3.5	4.5	7.6
10		–20.4	–20.6	–20.7	–18.5	–16.4	–16.0	–15.4	–15.7	–12.7	–10.0	–19.0	–18.8	–21.7	–20.9	–18.7
20	R&D	–25.1	–25.4	–23.8	–21.6	–19.6	–24.4	–24.3	–23.9	–19.7	–15.0	–23.5	–25.7	–29.6	–26.8	–21.2
30		–23.9	–24.0	–20.3	–19.5	–16.8	–25.4	–24.3	–22.6	–19.5	–14.8	–25.3	–27.6	–31.5	–29.1	–23.0
10		–8.6	–9.0	–9.9	–9.4	–9.0	–13.2	–12.9	–11.3	–9.8	–8.0	–12.1	–11.8	–12.6	–12.9	–12.0
20	Skill	–20.6	–20.8	–21.5	–20.4	–18.4	–21.4	–20.7	–19.5	–16.8	–13.9	–23.9	–23.8	–25.3	–25.1	–24.0
30		–22.5	–23.4	–22.8	–22.6	–20.3	–26.5	–25.4	–24.0	–21.6	–18.3	–28.5	–28.9	–30.8	–29.8	–26.1
10		10.1	11.5	8.6	9.1	6.7	–1.9	0.1	–2.5	–2.6	–2.9	5.2	5.5	6.8	7.0	1.9
20	Energy	12.7	14.0	10.7	11.8	9.6	–1.4	0.1	–2.6	–3.3	–3.6	6.4	6.5	7.8	7.4	2.0
30		11.4	12.5	10.5	10.9	9.0	–0.2	2.3	0.9	–0.2	–0.1	11.0	11.9	11.2	10.3	6.5
10	ECT	15.5	17.1	12.7	12.1	12.4	17.0	16.9	15.9	16.5	15.8	15.7	15.8	15.9	15.6	15.1
20	Barriers	13.5	14.3	11.1	10.7	10.1	32.6	31.0	27.6	25.5	24.3	25.6	24.1	24.0	22.6	17.6
30	1991	9.8	10.4	6.8	7.3	7.4	27.1	26.7	23.9	21.7	21.6	20.5	19.2	17.2	14.8	10.2

		Romania					Bulgaria					CEE-5				
		1989	1990	1991	1992	1993	1989	1990	1991	1992	1993	1989	1990	1991	1992	1993
NACE	Intensity															
10		–6.8	–7.5	–8.7	–7.1	–8.7	5.1	4.2	–0.2	–4.4	–8.5	–5.3	–5.2	–6.6	–6.3	–7.5
20	Capital	–9.5	–16.4	–19.1	–19.5	–19.8	2.5	3.0	1.8	–3.2	–5.0	–6.0	–7.3	–8.5	–8.1	–9.2
30		–16.5	–23.8	–26.7	–26.7	–27.9	–5.3	–4.9	–6.4	–10.5	–12.8	–10.9	–12.3	–13.7	–13.2	–14.1
10		14.9	20.6	19.4	26.3	32.1	4.7	6.2	7.4	15.0	15.3	7.6	7.9	7.9	9.5	9.9
20	Labour	16.7	24.5	22.4	29.1	35.1	4.0	6.6	10.2	15.8	16.5	6.4	6.9	7.0	7.9	9.6
30		12.0	19.8	17.5	23.6	29.8	2.2	4.0	7.2	12.9	13.7	3.4	4.2	4.3	5.8	8.2
10		–20.8	–20.6	–21.1	–21.6	–21.3	–17.0	–18.9	–18.7	–19.0	–17.1	–18.9	–18.6	–19.8	–18.4	–16.4
20	R&D	–29.0	–29.7	–30.6	–31.5	–30.8	–23.6	–27.2	–27.4	–27.8	–25.7	–25.1	–25.8	–26.7	–24.1	–20.5
30		–31.2	–31.5	–32.0	–33.4	–32.9	–20.8	–25.2	–27.0	–28.4	–26.4	–25.8	–26.3	–26.3	–24.4	–20.5
10		–14.3	–14.8	–14.9	–15.2	–14.3	–7.4	–10.8	–10.6	–10.9	–10.2	–11.7	–11.7	–11.7	–11.3	–10.4
20	Skill	–26.7	–27.1	–26.9	–28.2	–27.5	–17.5	–22.3	–21.5	–22.3	–21.3	–22.7	–22.7	–22.9	–22.0	–20.5
30		–32.0	–33.2	–32.6	–32.7	–32.0	–22.3	–27.0	–24.0	–27.2	–25.9	–26.9	–27.2	–27.0	–25.9	–23.3
10		7.1	3.0	0.4	0.9	–0.5	6.7	7.4	6.8	7.3	6.5	5.1	5.3	4.6	5.1	2.4
20	Energy	6.7	1.5	–1.8	–1.0	–2.2	7.9	8.9	7.2	7.7	6.2	6.2	6.2	5.3	5.8	3.0
30		4.8	0.6	–3.4	–2.6	–4.0	9.5	10.5	12.0	8.0	5.8	7.3	8.4	7.4	7.1	5.0
10	EU Trade	21.5	26.8	24.3	32.4	36.7	18.5	22.9	20.9	23.2	19.7	17.1	17.9	16.0	16.4	16.5
20	Barriers	29.9	29.5	28.2	34.3	38.6	24.1	30.5	29.2	33.1	32.7	25.0	24.4	21.9	21.0	19.1
30	1991	24.0	24.0	21.1	26.2	30.7	18.3	24.0	21.9	26.1	27.0	20.0	19.7	16.5	15.4	14.1

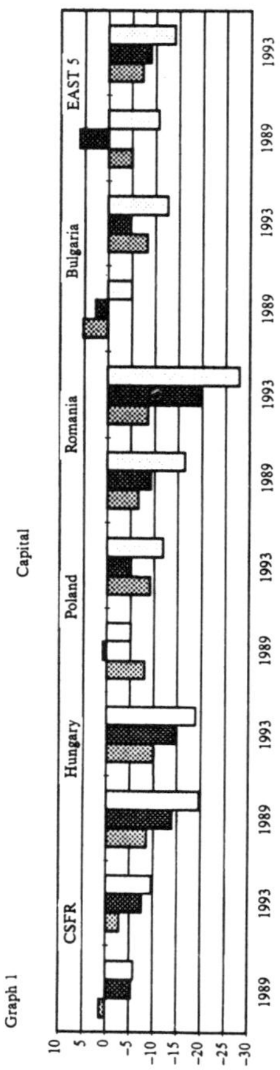
Graph 1
Capital
CSFR
Hungary
Poland
Romania
Bulgaria
EAST 5
1989
1993
10
5
0
-5
-10
-15
-20
-25
-30

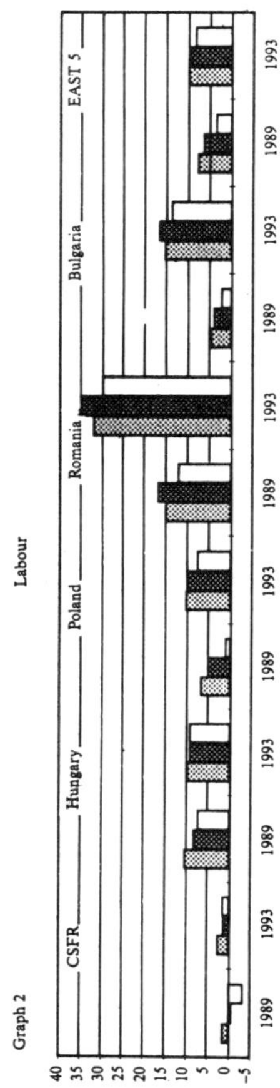
Graph 2
Labour
CSFR
Hungary
Poland
Romania
Bulgaria
EAST 5
1989
1993
40
35
30
25
20
15
10
5
0
-5

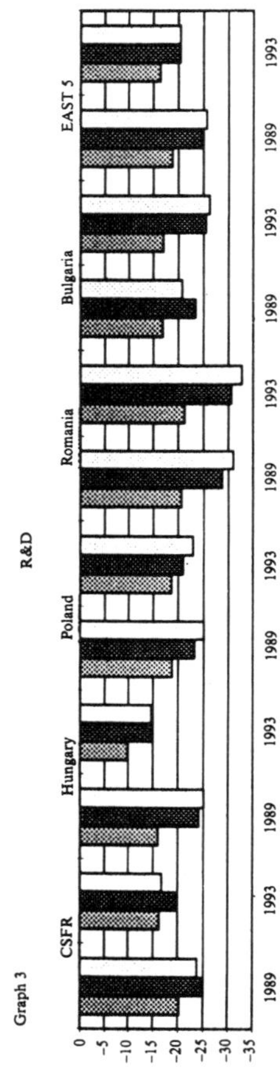
Graph 3
R&D
CSFR
Hungary
Poland
Romania
Bulgaria
EAST 5
1989
1993
0
-5
-10
-15
-20
-25
-30
-35

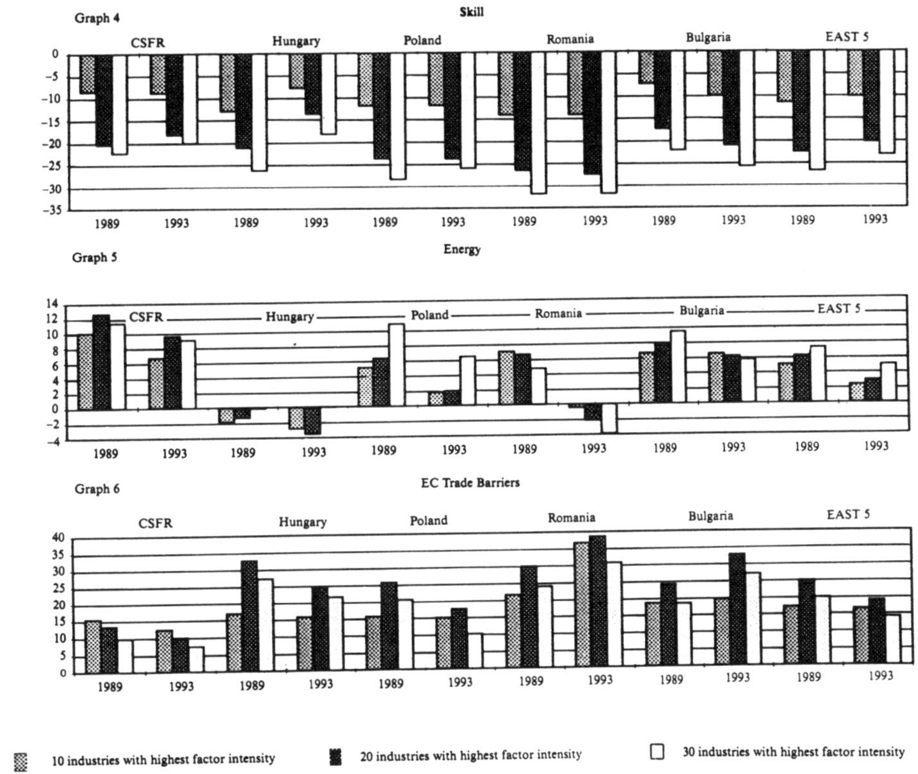

Figure 7.1 *Difference in the representation of 10, 20 and 30 most* x *factor-intensive industries in CEE*

Table 7.4 Changes in export structures = f (factor intensitites)

	K/L	L/Y	R&D	Skill	Energy	EU-TB 91
CSFR						
89–93	–.1529	.0709	.0726	–	–.1507	–
	(2.96)	(2.55)	(1.77)		(3.07)	
89–91	–.0955	.0397	.0305	–	–.0866	–
	(2.60)	(2.01)	(1.04)		(2.47)	
91–93	–.0575	.0311	.0422	–	–.064	–
	(2.45)	(2.50)	(2.32)		(2.90)	
Hungary						
89–93	–.0750	.0650	.0856	–	–.1100	–.0669
	(1.39)	(2.31)	(2.08)		(2.17)	(1.20)
89–91	–.0471	.0344	.0222	–	–.0616	–.0476
	(1.62)	(2.26)	(.98)		(2.25)	(1.58)
91–93	–.0280	.0305	.0634	–	–.0483	–.0193
	(.86)	(1.79)	(2.62)		(1.58)	(.57)
Poland						
89–93	–.1451	.1081	–	–.0182	–.1401	–.0658
	(2.70)	(3.96)		(1.43)	(2.74)	(1.15)
89–91	–.0852	.0625	–	–.0093	–.0211	–.0221
	(2.71)	(3.89)		(1.24)	(.67)	(.65)
91–93	–.0599	.0456	–	–.0089	–.1190	–.0438
	(1.28)	(1.86)		(.83)	(2.76)	(.90)
Romania						
89–93	–.2494	.1639	–	–	–.2138	.1591
	(2.79)	(3.53)			(2.48)	(1.67)
89–91	–.1471	.0807	–	–	–.1467	.0074
	(3.72)	(3.84)			(3.91)	(1.67)
91–93	–.1017	.0832	–	–	–.0670	.1518
	(1.59)	(2.49)			(1.09)	(2.33)
Bulgaria						
89–93	–.2242	.1217	–	–.0343	–.1570	.1090
	(2.44)	(2.49)		(1.59)	(1.76)	(1.12)
89–91	–.1124	.0559	–	–.0178	–.0662	.0715
	(2.51)	(2.34)		(1.69)	(1.51)	(1.51)
91–93	–.1118	.0657	–	–.0166	–.0908	.0374
	(1.77)	(1.97)		(1.13)	(1.50)	(.57)

Note: Number of observations 89; *t*-statistics in brackets underneath the coefficients; coefficients with very low significance not reported.

EU compared with total EU imports, then comes Poland, then Bulgaria and finally, Romania. The last item in Table 7.3 and in Figure 7.1 refers to the representation of those industrial branches in a country's exports to the EU in which EU trade barriers (EU-TB) are the highest.[5] Again we can see important differences across the different CEE economies, this time with the CSFR in the best position, followed by Poland, then Hungary and then Bulgaria and Romania.

We now report a number of econometric estimates on changes in export structures (to EU markets) and export specialization, over the period 1989–1993, across the whole sample of 89 industries which complements the picture obtained in Table 7.3 and Figure 7.1. Table 7.4 gives the results of an econometric analysis, showing whether there were significant shifts in the CEE's export structures to the EU over the periods 1989–91, 1991–93 and 1989–93. As there was evidence for significant multicollinearity between the different factor intensity measures, we report here estimates of the impact of one regressor at a time upon changing export structures; only significant estimates are reported.[6] We can see that the previous picture is confirmed. There was a significant movement away from capital- and energy-intensive exports and towards labour-intensive exports. Furthermore, there is some evidence of a shift towards more R&D-intensive exports in the case of Czechoslovakia and Hungary and away from skill-intensive exports in the case of Bulgaria. This, together with significant differences in the size of the coefficients (compare particularly the differences between Bulgaria and Romania, on the one hand, and the other three economies on the other hand) supports our view of significant inter-country differences in developments since 1989. The move away from capital-intensive exports and towards labour-intensive exports was much more dramatic in the case of Bulgaria and Romania than in the case of the other CEE economies. Also, while these shifts became somewhat weaker over the period 1991–93 compared to the period 1989–91 in the case of the 'more Western' CEE economies, this was not the case in Bulgaria and Romania. In these two economies we also have a shift in the direction of exports which encountered high EU trade barriers in 1991 (while the signs on these – albeit insignificant – parameters in the case of the other three economies were negative).

To summarize the analysis so far, we have evidence of significant specialization structures in trade relationships between the EU and the CEE economies. The specialization pattern inherited from the pre-1989 period was significantly affected (partly strengthened, partly changed) by developments after 1989. There is evidence of a strong 'developmental gap' between CEE economies and the EU. This gap shows up in biases in specialization patterns of CEE economies away from capital-, R&D- and skill-intensive industries and towards labour-intensive industries. The original bias towards energy-intensive exports based on the supply of cheap oil from the Soviet Union has been declining rapidly. As mentioned in the introduction, one would expect that liberalization of trade between countries which have attained different levels of economic development would strengthen this pattern of inter-industry specialization; and this is exactly what has happened. However, the strength by which such specialization patterns were reinforced since 1989 differed across the different CEE economies; the more Western CEE economies experienced less reinforcement of this pattern of specialization (and, in the case of the CSFR and Hungary, there was even evidence of some closure of the gap in R&D- and skill-intensive areas) than was the case with Romania and Bulgaria. This is a process of differentiation which one would again expect, reflecting differences in the developmental gaps between the different CEE economies and the EU and/or the dynamic processes of differential widening or narrowing of such gaps.

We now move on to discuss, in some detail, evidence for intra-industry trade developing between CEE economies and the EU and we shall further analyse what the characteristics of this intra-industry trade are. Table 7.5 reports the Grubel–Lloyd (GL) indices for the different CEE economies' trade with the EU over the period 1989–93.[7] We can see that while the GL indices are lower in the case of the CEE countries than for total EU trade with non-EU economies (see column EU ext. in Table 7.5) and significantly lower if all EU trade including intra-EU trade is considered (see column EU total), there were considerable increases in the GL indices, and thus of intra-industry trade, for most of the CEE economies since 1989. The increases in GL indices were considerable for the CSFR and Hungary and persisted after 1991, while they stagnated for Poland after 1991, declined again after the initial jump in 1991 for Romania, and also declined first and then increased again to the 1990 level for Bulgaria. Hence, in so far as this aggregated measure of intra-industry trade is concerned, we can again perceive a process of differentiation taking place across the CEE economies with continued

Table 7.5 Aggregated Grubel–Lloyd index

	CSFR	Hungary	Poland	Romania	Bulgaria	CEE-5	EU ext.	EU total
1989	0.448	0.484	0.419	0.243	0.605	0.500	0.675	0.868
1990	0.464	0.492	0.384	0.295	0.525	0.486	0.675	0.869
1991	0.513	0.521	0.458	0.367	0.427	0.505	0.684	0.871
1992	0.480	0.542	0.456	0.346	0.441	0.507	0.683	0.870
1993	0.617	0.589	0.458	0.341	0.525	0.547	0.682	–

Note: See text for method of calculation; calculated from export and import data to/from EU for 108 manufacturing industries, then aggregated using export shares as weights.

Table 7.6 Characteristics of the 30 industries with highest export shares

		1989	1991	1993
CSFR				
exp. shs%		83.30	79.50	76.03
spec. ind.		3.47	3.50	3.05
GL		0.444	0.500	0.622
gr 89–93		13.30	23.40	30.20
gr agg 89–93	22.6			
Hungary				
exp. shs%		84.20	82.34	83.72
spec. ind.		4.20	3.90	3.42
GL		0.484	0.510	0.604
gr 89–93		6.75	10.97	18.29
gr agg 89–93	12.0			
Poland				
exp. shs%		84.80	82.41	81.90
spec. ind.		3.21	3.23	3.22
GL		0.405	0.448	0.438
gr 89–93		14.34	18.27	26.19
gr agg 89–93	20.9			
Bulgaria				
exp. shs%		87.10	87.60	84.94
spec. ind.		3.47	3.23	2.79
GL		0.640	0.420	0.532
gr 89–93		5.08	13.68	27.20
gr agg 89–93	17.1			
Romania				
exp. shs%		93.33	91.34	91.07
spec. ind.		8.56	10.12	6.71
GL		0.236	0.347	0.337
gr 89–93		–8.56	0.33	7.21
gr agg 89–93	–1.05			

Notes: exp. shs% refer to shares in total manufacturing exports to the EU; spec. ind. to the export specialization indices (see text); GL to the Grubel–Lloyd measures of intra-industry trade (see Table 7.5); gr 89–93 to the per annum (exponential) growth rates of exports to the EU over the period 1989–93 calculated from current price ECU data); gr agg 89–93 are the aggregated export growth rates of total manufacturing exports to the EU. All indicators have been calculated for each of the 30 individual industries and then aggregated using export shares within the group as weights.

moves towards more intra-industry trade in the case of the CSFR and Hungary and stagnation or reversal of initial increases in the case of the other CEE economies. A similar picture emerges from Table 7.6 in which the analysis restricts itself to the 30 industries (out of 108) which accounted for the highest export shares of trade with the EU in the years 1989, 1991 and 1993 respectively and in which four different indicators are presented. The four indicators refer in turn to the shares of the 30 most important industries in total exports to the EU (shs %) which shows that these industries accounted in all cases for more than 75 per cent of total exports to the EU; it gives the aggregated specialization index for this group of industries (Sp^x);[8] next it again calculates the aggregated Grubel–Lloyd (GL) indices for this group of industries; and, finally, it shows the aggregated growth rates of exports to the EU for that group of industries over the period 1989–93 (gr 89–93); for comparison the growth rates for total manufacturing exports over the period 1989–93 are also given (gr agg 89–93).

We can see from the information in Table 7.6 that there was considerable compositional change in the group of industries which represented the industries with the highest shares of exports to the EU in 1989, 1991 and 1993 respectively. This can be seen, for example, in the fact that the aggregated growth rates of the industries which formed that group in 1989, 1991, and 1993 respectively differed considerably and, as one would expect for simple arithmetic reasons if there is uneven growth across industries, increased dramatically. This is evidence for considerable differential growth of industries' exports to the EU. Second, confirming our discussion about the tendencies in the Grubel–Lloyd indices above, there was also an increase in GL indices for this more restricted group of industries across most of the CEE economies over the period 1989–93 with the exception of Bulgaria with its distinct U-shaped pattern, and with slight declines for Poland and Romania after 1991. The increase/decrease in GL indices is quite compatible with the decline/increase in the export specialization indices which show whether a country's composition of exports to the EU differs markedly from the composition of EU imports in total (excluding intra-EU imports). This, indeed, is the case again for Czechoslovakia and Hungary, while there is no movement in the degree of export specialization in the case of Poland over the period 1989–93, and there is some reduction for Bulgaria specifically after 1991. Romania has reduced its degree of export specialization but the index remains at a much higher level than in the case of the other CEE economies.

To summarize the analysis on intra-industry trade, there is evidence of a general increase in such trade between the CEE economies and the EU after 1989 with the exception of Bulgaria. However, the increase is much more marked for the CSFR and Hungary where there is a continuing trend after 1989, and the other economies in which initial jumps occurred but the trend towards increased intra-industry trade then stagnated or even (slightly) reversed. Similar tendencies are revealed with the aggregated measure of export specialization which, over the period 1989–93, declined for the CSFR and Hungary, stagnated for Poland and declined for Romania but remained at a very high level; it also strongly declined for Bulgaria over the latest period. The movements towards more intra-industry trade and less export specialization confirm the picture of considerable differentiation across the CEE economies, roughly reflecting differences in their respective 'developmental gaps' *vis-à-vis* Western Europe and each other.

Finally, I would like to report some evidence on the characteristics of intra-industry trade between the CEE economies and the EU. In particular, we would like to point out that while there is some evidence for reduced inter-industry specialization between the more advanced CEE economies and the EU, there is also evidence for strong intra-industry specialization and also for a very significant 'quality gap' which is likely to persist for a long time.

As regards the degree of intra-industry specialization, Figures 7.2a and b show the relative over- or under-representation of NACE 3-digit industries' exports to the EU of three of the CEE economies and of Austria relative to the structure of total EU imports in the respective NACE 2-digit industries.

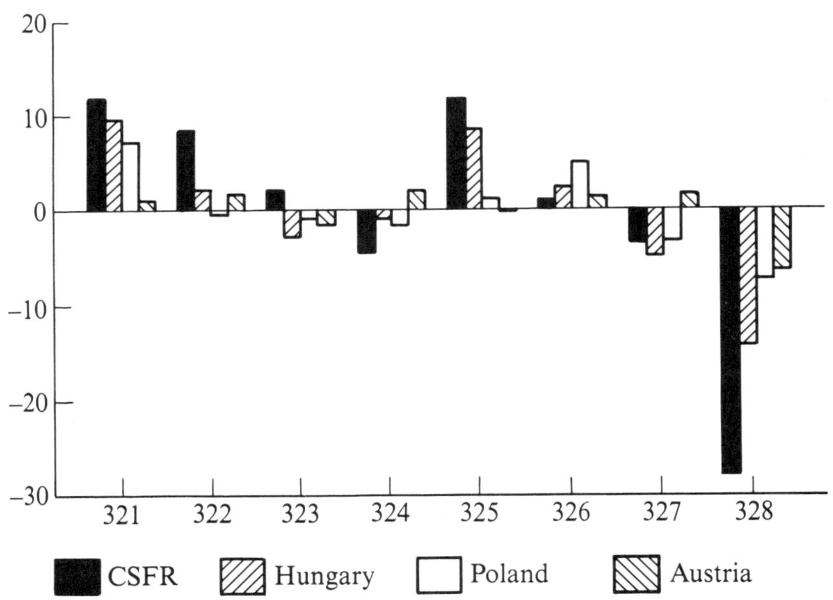

Figure 7.2a Intra-industry specialization – mechanical engineering, 1992: export structure to EU relative to EU import structure

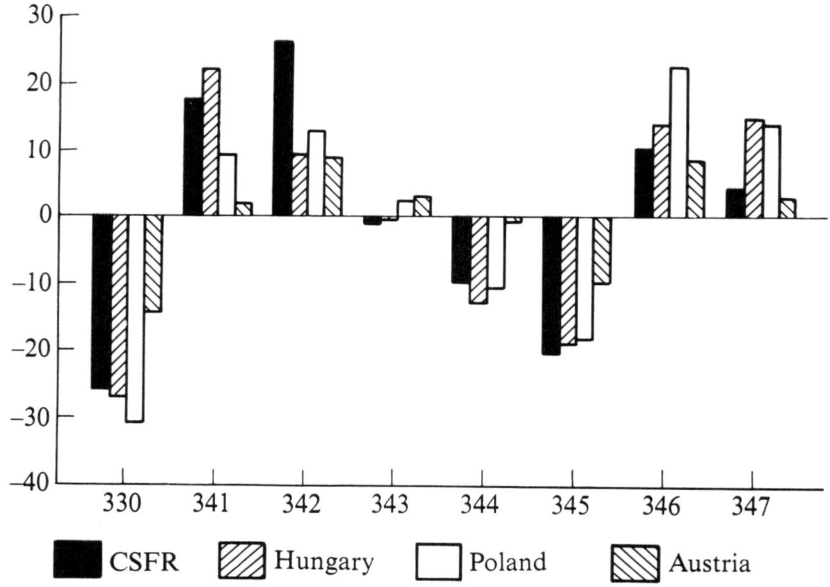

Figure 7.2b Intra-industry specialization – electrical engineering, 1992: export structure to EU relative to EU import structure

We can see that the export profile within the NACE 2-digit engineering industries depicted in the figures of the CEE economies deviates from the general structure of EU imports much more than does the Austrian export profile to the EU in the same two industries. Table 7.7 presents a numerical aggregate measure for the degree of intra-industry specialization (focusing, as in Figures 7.2a and b, on exports only) in a wider range of engineering industries. We can see that, for this sample of industries, the degree of intra-industry specialization is considerably higher for the CEE industrial exports to the EU than for most of Austria's engineering exports. Thus, while there is evidence for increased overall intra-industry trade for most of the CEE economies over the period 1989–93, there are also very distinct export profiles – and hence specialization – at the sub-industry or commodity level. Such a high degree of intra-industry specialization could be taken as evidence for the existence of substantial 'developmental gaps' at the industrial level as could be the 'price/quality gaps' to which we now turn.

In Table 7.8 we present evidence for substantial 'quality gaps' between CEE exporters to the EU and their competitors in EU markets. The indicators we use to measure these 'quality gaps' are price per kg comparisons which were calculated at a detailed commodity level. For each commodity a CEE

Table 7.7 Intra-industry trade specialization in engineering industries

	CSFR	Hungary	Poland	Austria
NACE				
	7.04	6.99	10.86	2.36
31	8.99	5.75	3.39	3.69
32	14.51	14.99	15.08	12.99
33+34	9.21	13.86	8.81	13.58
35+36	13.49	15.52	24.95	7.17
37	13.49	15.52	24.95	7.17

Note: The measure calculated here compares the share of each 3-digit industry within a 2-digit industry's exports to the EU with the share of that 3-digit industry in NACE 2-digit imports of the EU. If $n(j)$ refers to the number of 3-digit industries identified within a NACE 2-digit group, we have

$$\frac{1}{n(j)}\sum_{i=1}^{n(j)} | x_i^c / x_j^c - m_i^{EU} / m_j^{EU} |$$

where x and m refer respectively to exports to the EU and total imports of the EU and subscript i to the 3-digit industry and j to the 2-digit industry.

industry's export prices to the EU were compared with the 'price leader' (which could be any other country exporting to EU markets including another EU country) in that specific commodity trade. These price per kg comparisons at the detailed commodity level were then aggregated for each industry, using the shares of each commodity's exports to the EU within the industry's exports as weights.[9] In Table 7.8 we report the quality indicators for three of the CEE economies scaled (divided) by the quality indicator calculated for the six core EU economies (Germany, France, Italy, Belgium, Netherlands and the United Kingdom); on the other half of the table are the market shares in EU markets (including intra-EU trade) as they evolved over the period 1988–91.

From Table 7.8 we can see that while there were major improvements in the EU market share positions of the three CEE economies in EU markets over the period 1988–91, there were no clear and pervasive trends in the 'price/quality gap' indicators. Although the figures are affected by exchange rate movements and the particular conditions under which CEE economies attempted to expand their exports to the EU in the early 1990s, it is nonetheless clear that there are very significant 'quality gaps' between CEE economies and competitors in the EU and that these gaps have persisted over the recent period of transformation.

Table 7.8 Quality (price) gaps and market shares in EU markets (incl. intra-EU trade)

		Quality indicators					Market shares in EC markets			
		EU-6	Poland	Czechoslovakia	Hungary		EU-6	Poland	Czechoslovakia	Hungary
NACE	310	(Metal products)				310				
	1988	1	0.490	0.539	0.598	1988	69.75	0.40	0.23	0.30
	1989	1	0.506	0.561	0.566	1989	69.76	0.43	0.24	0.27
	1990	1	0.464	0.547	0.589	1990	69.99	0.67	0.29	0.39
	1991	1	0.492	0.512	0.546	1991	68.49	0.91	0.64	0.45
NACE	320	(Mechanical engineering)				320				
	1988	1	0.385	0.489	0.564	1988	64.42	0.13	0.18	0.11
	1989	1	0.515	0.478	0.566	1989	63.65	0.14	0.17	0.13
	1990	1	0.366	0.477	0.497	1990	63.81	0.21	0.19	0.18
	1991	1	0.384	0.447	0.533	1991	63.30	0.25	0.26	0.26
NACE	330	(Office machinery and computing)				330				
	1988	1	0.263		0.193	1988	46.23	0	0	0.01
	1989	1	0.596	0.274	0.435	1989	47.30	0	0.01	0.01
	1990	1	0.540	0.375	0.326	1990	48.81	0	0	0.01
	1991	1	0.616	0.306	0.207	1991	48.27	0	0.01	0.01

NACE	340	(Electrical engineering)				340				
	1988	1	0.382	0.442	0.514	1988	51.43	0.15	0.09	0.13
	1989	1	0.431	0.473	0.517	1989	51.07	0.17	0.08	0.14
	1990	1	0.458	0.399	0.607	1990	52.71	0.26	0.09	0.19
	1991	1	0.565	0.587	0.653	1991	50.91	0.19	0.14	0.24
NACE	350	(Motor vehicles)				350				
	1988	1	0.495	0.413	0.445	1988	73.45	0.18	0.10	0.01
	1989	1	0.513	0.468	0.522	1989	72.15	0.14	0.11	0.01
	1990	1	0.512	0.477	0.461	1990	72.17	0.09	0.11	0.02
	1991	1	0.470	0.523	0.524	1991	69.74	0.07	0.25	0.03
NACE	370	(Instrument engineering)				370				
	1988	1	0.451	0.427	0.433	1988	46.03	0.05	0.05	0.04
	1989	1	0.355	0.527	0.354	1989	45.80	0.05	0.05	0.03
	1990	1	0.350	0.334	0.462	1990	46.79	0.07	0.04	0.03
	1991	1	0.484	0.397	0.620	1991	46.33	0.08	0.07	0.06

Source: Eurostat, Detailed Trade Data; see text for method of calculation of quality (price) gap indicator; market shares refer to shares in total EU imports including intra-EU imports (in %).

CONCLUSIONS

This chapter has addressed a rather ambitious question: is there evidence for a process of 'catching up' or of 'falling behind' of CEE economies in relation to the countries of Western Europe?[10]

We have attempted to answer this question solely from the standpoint of international trade theory which predicts that countries which are at different levels of economic development would experience an increase in the degree of industrial and trade specialization if they liberalized trade with each other, while countries which are at rather similar levels of economic development would experience an increase in intra-industry trade without a clearly discernible pattern of inter-industry specialization.

Following the liberalization of trade relations, it is thus likely that a catching-up process first initiates a process of increasing inter-industry specialization to be followed by the next phase in which intra-industry trade becomes the dominant pattern. The timing of these phases will differ across industrial branches depending upon the speed by and the extent to which the developmental gap can be reduced. However, *a priori* there are possibilities that such a 'developmental gap' might widen rather than shrink (the reasons for both these possibilities have been extensively discussed in the literature; see Abramovitz, 1986 and 1991; Verspagen, 1991; and much earlier Gerschenkron, 1952). In that case the second type of process will not occur – or only occur with much delay. Of course, in the context of the East European transition, the transformation process itself together with the sudden act of fundamental trade liberalization and trade reorientation could initiate processes which could accelerate the dynamics of either catching up or falling behind.[11]

As regards the results of our empirical investigation which restricted itself to examining features of trade relations, one might conclude that it is probably premature to seriously address the question of 'catching up' or 'falling behind' of CEE economies, given the scant evidence of the few years' developments since 1989. Nonetheless, we have found a number of interesting tendencies.

First of all, the evidence for a marked pattern of inter-industry specialization is rather strong and follows, broadly, an HO pattern: CEE economies' exports to the EU are strongly biased away from capital-, R&D- and skill-intensive branches and towards energy-intensive (a legacy of cheap oil supplies from the Soviet Union) and labour-intensive branches. In some respects these specialization patterns have been strengthened since 1989, but only in some respects. There is evidence that export structures have moved further away from capital-intensive branches and towards labour-intensive branches and also away from energy-intensive branches (after the loss of cheap Soviet oil). However, the extent of these moves was quite different across the different CEE economies. They were most considerable in the cases of Romania and Bulgaria, with Poland coming third; the size of the estimated coefficients of such shifts was considerably lower for the CSFR and Hungary. Also, for these last two economies, there is some evidence for significant shifts towards more R&D-intensive exports after 1989 which are not discernible for the other three economies. This picture is reinforced by significant differences across the CEE economies in their respective expansions of intra-industry trade with the EU. Such trends seem to be continuous in the case of the CSFR and Hungary, while developments in the other three economies are more irregular and less persistent.

Nonetheless, we have also pointed out that the developmental gaps even of the most advanced of the CEE economies in relation to the EU are very significant, showing up in patterns of intra-industry specialization and also in very considerable 'quality gaps' in the products sold on EU markets.[12]

In summary, we conclude that there is some evidence that some countries of CEE have embarked on a process which is typical of catching up (at least, as regards the limited trade-related measures we have used in this study), but that this process has, first, a long way to go and, second, is not yet discernible across the whole set of CEE economies studied here. Hence, the problem identified in the theoretical literature and discussed in the introduction: there may be a bifurcation such that conditions in some countries develop in a way that facilitates catching up while in other countries there is no closure of an existing gap; in the latter countries/regions relative stagnation or a process of further falling behind might be a distinct possibility.

NOTES

1. Views diverge as to the level of economic development CEE economies have reached. The use simply of GDP per capita as an indicator of economic development seems to be insufficient; some authors point to the high educational levels attained in the CEE economies (see e.g. CEPR, 1990; Hamilton and Winters, 1992); furthermore, should unusually high levels of industrialization and even the experience with high-tech industries which resulted from past planning ambitions and past specialization patterns within the CMEA be completely discarded when discussing the future potential of CEE economies?
2. These countries comprise Bulgaria, the CSFR, Hungary, Poland and Romania. We will continue to refer in this chapter to the unified CSFR even after the split in January 1993 since the EU trade statistics for 1993 still ignore this historical rupture.
3. Of course, the use of a gravity model in Baldwin's exercise implies that one attaches importance to the geographical distance factor, but the weight of this factor in explaining trade patterns is the result of rather robust econometric estimates (see also Wang and Winters, 1991).
4. The factor intensity measures used have been derived from information about the four largest EU member states (Germany, France, Italy, the UK). They refer to the following indicators:

Capital intensity	Cumulative investment/number of employees
Labour intensity	Number of employees/output
R&D content	R&D expenditure/output
Skill content	Non-manual labour/total employment
Energy intensity	Energy costs/output

5. The measure of EC trade barriers used here refers to a compound measure of tariff and non-tariff barriers which CEE economies on EC markets encountered in 1991. This measure has been developed in a number of detailed studies by Schumacher and Möbius (1992, 1993). As is well known, within manufacturing, tariff and non-tariff barriers are particularly high in so-called 'sensitive industries', such as steel, textiles, clothing and footwear, etc. For details, see the Schumacher and Möbius studies cited above.
6. We report some insignificant parameter estimates if the estimates were significant for other sub-periods to allow comparison.
7. The Grubel–Lloyd (GL) indices reported here are derived from detailed GL indices calculated for each of the 108 NACE 3-digit manufacturing industries in our trade data set; they have then been weighted together by the shares of the different commodities in the CEE's exports to the EU for the respective year. The following specification of the GL index has been used:

$$GL = 1 - \frac{\Sigma_j \mid x_{ij} - m_{ij} \mid}{\Sigma_j (x_{ij} + m_{ij})}$$

where x_{ij} and m_{ij} are country i's exports and imports of commodity j, respectively.
8. The export specialization index Sp^x is calculated as sh_i^C/sh_i^{EU} where sh_i^C refers to the share of industry i in country C's total manufacturing exports to the EU and sh_i^{EU} to the share of that industry in total EU manufacturing imports. We shall later also refer to an import specialization index Sp^m in which exports have to be substituted for imports in the above definitions and vice versa. The notions 'aggregated' index for a group of industries (see also the notions aggregated GL index and aggregated growth rate) refers to the fact that the indices or growth rates have first been calculated for each of the industries separately and then weighted together to arrive at group indices using the shares of the different industries i in the group's total exports to the EU as weights.
9. Formally, the 'quality' indicator of a country C's exports in industry j was the following:

$$QP_j^c = \Sigma_{i \subset \{i(j)\}} (p_i^c / p_i^L).sh_i^c$$

where $\{i(j)\}$ refers to the set of commodities identified in industry j's trade (6-digit trade data within the Combined Nomenclature (CN) classification were used in the calculations); p_i^C and p_i^L refer, respectively, to the prices charged by country C's exporters of commodity i and the 'price leaders' on EU markets (where price leader could be any other exporter of that commodity to EU markets including exporters from other EU economies; notice that price leaders were sought for each commodity separately) and sh_i^C is the share of commodity i in C's exports to the EU ($\Sigma_{i \subset \{i(j)\}} sh_i^c = 1$).
10. There is of course also a possibility that a country is catching up with Western Europe but is falling behind in the general process of catching up, i.e. that the speed of catching up of different CEE economies would differ.
11. Numerous instances could be given for either type of process. In the positive direction could be institutional and legal innovations which lead to a better utilization of existing developmental resources (better use of manpower, reduction of x-inefficiencies of both corporate and state-level organizational structures through competitive pressures, etc.). On the negative side, longer-term under-utilization of manpower resources, deterioration of infrastructure through budgetary restrictions, chaos in the financial allocation mechanism, etc. in the wake of the 'transformational recession' (Kornai, 1995) could all lead to a contraction of some of the stocks which represent the developmental capabilities of a country or region.

12. There are numerous other measures of the existence of such a 'developmental gap' which we have not referred to in this chapter and which would give a more complete picture, such as relative productivity levels, wage gaps etc. (see e.g. Peneder, 1993).

REFERENCES

Abramovitz, M. (1986), 'Catching Up, Forging Ahead and Falling Behind', *Journal of Economic History*, **46**, 385–406.

Abramovitz, M. (1991), 'The Elements of Social Capability', paper presented for the International Conference on the Economic Development of LDCs During the Five Decades, 1940s to 1980s, Korea Development Institute, Seoul, July 1–2, 1981, mimeo.

Baldwin, R. (1994), *Towards an Integrated Europe*, London: Centre for Economic Policy.

Baumol, W. (1986), 'Productivity Growth, Convergence and Welfare: What the Long-run Data Show', *American Economic Review*, **76**(5), 1072–83.

Ben-David, D. (1994), 'Income Disparity Among Countries and the Effects of Freer Trade', in Pasinetti, L. L. and Solow, R. M. (eds), *Economic Growth and the Structure of Long-Term Development*, London: Macmillan.

Buigues, P. et al. (1994) 'The Economic Interpenetration between the EU and Eastern Europe', *European Economy*, no. 6.

CEPR (1990), 'Monitoring European Integration. The Impact of Eastern Europe', London: CEPR Annual Report.

Dollar, D. and Wolff, E.N. (1993), *Competitiveness, Convergence and International Specialization*, Boston, Mass.: MIT Press.

Fagerberg, J., Verspagen, B. and von Tunzelman, N. (1994), *The Dynamics of Technology, Trade and Growth*, Aldershot: Edward Elgar.

Gerschenkron, A. (1952), 'Economic Backwardness in Historical Perspective', in Hoselitz, B.F. (ed.), *The Progress of Underdeveloped Areas*, Chicago: University of Chicago Press.

Hamilton, C. and A. Winters (1992), 'Opening up International Trade in Eastern Europe', *Economic Policy*; **14**, 77–116.

Kornai, J. (1995), 'Transformational Recession: The Example of Hungary', Chap. 2 in Saunders, C.T. (ed.), *Eastern Europe in Crisis and the Way Out*, London and Basingstoke: Macmillan; previously published in *Economie Appliqué*, 1993, no. 2.

Krugman, P. (1991), *Geography and Trade*, Cambridge, Mass.: MIT Press.

Krugman, P. and Venables, A. (1990), 'Integration and Competitiveness of Peripheral Industry', in Bliss, C.J. and Macedo, B. de (eds), *Unity with Diversity in the European Community*, Cambridge: Cambridge University Press.

Levine, R. and Renelt, D. (1992), 'A Sensitivity Analysis of Cross-Country Growth Regressions', *American Economic Review*, **82**(4), 942–63.

Peneder, M. (1993), 'Kosten- und Produktionsstruktur der Industrie in den Ländern Ost-Mitteleuropas', in Aiginger, K. (ed.), *Chancen und Gefährdungspotentiale der Ostöffnung: Konsequenzen für die österreichische Wirtschaft*, Wien: WIFO.

Rotemberg, J. and Saloner, G. (1990), 'Competition and Human Capital Accumulation; a Theory of Interregional Specialisation and Trade', National Bureau of Economic Research, Working Paper 3228.

Schumacher, D. and Möbius, U. (1992), 'Analysis of Current Community Trade

Barriers to Central and East European Countries', paper prepared for the II Workshop on the Economic Interpenetration Between the EC and Eastern Europe, Brussels, August.

Schumacher, D. and Möbius, U. (1993), 'Community Trade Barriers Facing Central and East European Countries (CEEC), Impact of the Europe Agreements; supplementary and updated results', paper prepared for the IV Workshop on the Economic Interpenetration Between the EC and Eastern Europe, Brussels, December.

Verspagen, B. (1991), 'A New Empirical Approach to Catching Up or Falling Behind', *Structural Change and Economic Dynamics*, **2**(2), 359–80.

Wang, Z.K. and Winters, L.A. (1991), 'The Trading Potential of Eastern Europe', Centre for Economic Policy Research, Discussion Paper 610, London.

8. Trade reorientation and competitiveness in CEECs

Peter Havlik

INTRODUCTION

This chapter deals with some aspects of the process of trade reorientation in three CEECs (the focus of analysis is on Czechoslovakia, Hungary and Poland)[1] in the transition period. After the collapse of communist rule in 1989, the subsequent dissolution of the CMEA and the start of radical economic reforms, the foreign trade of the reforming CEECs underwent sweeping changes. One of the most conspicuous features has been the reorientation of trade from the former CMEA markets to markets in the West, in particular in the EU. This has been facilitated by important Western trade liberalization measures, notably by unilateral suspension of most quotas, inclusion of the CEECs in the General System of Preferences (GSP) and by tariff concessions on industrial products contained in the Europe Agreements (in their trade part, basically in force since March 1992).[2]

As a result, the regional trade composition of Czechoslovakia, Hungary and Poland changed radically between 1989 and 1992. In 1989 the EU accounted for only 18 per cent of Czechoslovak exports, 25 per cent of Hungarian exports and 32 per cent of Polish exports. But already in 1991 the share of the EU in Czechoslovak exports jumped to almost 40 per cent, in Hungarian exports to 47 per cent and in Polish exports to a high of 56 per cent. Similar changes occurred in the imports of these countries: the share of the EU in Czechoslovak imports rose from 18 per cent in 1989 to 35 per cent in 1991, in Hungarian imports from 29 per cent to 43 per cent and in Polish imports from 34 per cent to 50 per cent of the total.[3]

By 1992 this trend had become even more pronounced and the share of the EU in the reforming countries' trade increased further: 49.4 per cent of Czechoslovak exports went to the EU and 42.1 per cent of imports originated there in 1992; the respective shares for Hungary were 49.7 per cent and 42.7 per cent, for Poland 58 per cent and 53.2 per cent (in comparison, Austria conducted about two-thirds of its foreign trade with the EU in 1992).

No doubt the rapid expansion of exports to the West, especially to the EU, has helped the CEECs to soften the adverse effects created by reduced domestic demand and the loss of traditional markets in the East. Below, we look at the adjustment patterns of the CEECs' export and import structures in manufacturing trade with the EU and try to identify those CEECs' industries which were most successful on EU markets until 1992. A similar exercise for CEECs' imports from the EU is performed as well.

STRUCTURAL ADJUSTMENT OF CEECS' MANUFACTURING TRADE WITH THE EU

Recent studies confirm a dramatic asymmetry in the adjustment processes regarding import and export structures of CEECs' trade with the EU.[4] Obviously, after trade liberalization, adjusting the structure of imports was much easier for the CEECs than in the case of their exports. Compared with total EU imports, the imports from the CEECs (i.e. CEECs' exports to the EU) traditionally contained relatively less engineering products whereas metals, minerals, metal products and food were over-represented. The adjustment of the CEECs' export structure until 1992 was, however, not very dramatic: except for declining specialization in food (Hungary and Poland) and beer (Czechoslovakia), the 'traditional' CEECs' export specialization on low-processed goods such as metals and minerals or low-tech manufactures like textiles and furniture even strengthened.

The situation was quite different in the case of imports: in 1989 the CEECs' imports from the EU were concentrated in chemicals, mechanical engineering and textiles whereas transport equipment, office machinery and a whole range of consumer goods were relatively under-represented as compared to what the world generally imported from the EU. By 1992, however, the import shares of chemicals and engineering products dropped, whereas those of cars, other transport equipment and consumer goods increased and the structure of CEECs' imports approached the average pattern of the EU export structure.

As pointed out in Chapter 5, this export/import asymmetry was one of the characteristic features of the process of CEEC trade adjustment after the start of the transition. Such a development is also confirmed by other studies. By using distance measures, Landesmann and Székely (1994) have shown that a much stronger adjustment has taken place on the CEECs' import side as compared to their exports.[5]

This analysis can be extended further by taking another reference point – Austria – which appears relevant for the three CEECs under consideration. A similar exercise based on the distance measure for Austria (Havlik, 1994) shows that its export structure has been much more similar to that of EU imports than in the case of CEECs (though the export distance widened somewhat between 1989 and 1992). As regards imports, the structure of Austrian imports from the EU differed more strongly from the average EU export structure than in the case of any of the three CEECs.

Table 8.1 Correlation of market shares of CEECs in their trade with the EU, 1980–92

	Correlation coefficients with the market shares of 1980				Correlation coefficients with the market shares of 1989			
	Czecho-slovakia	Hungary	Poland	Austria	Czecho-slovakia	Hungary	Poland	Austria
Exports to the EU								
1981	0.990	0.957	0.881	0.972				
1982	0.989	0.971	0.920	0.931				
1983	0.987	0.929	0.845	0.931				
1984	0.984	0.883	0.600	0.901				
1985	0.976	0.860	0.834	0.856				
1986	0.981	0.871	0.789	0.849				
1987	0.968	0.817	0.775	0.832				
1988	0.952	0.826	0.782	0.784				
1989	0.936	0.723	0.757	0.745				
1990	0.951	0.771	0.631	0.774	0.994	0.930	0.895	0.979
1991	0.848	0.728	0.672	0.711	0.783	0.849	0.850	0.941
1992	0.670	0.568	0.641	0.714	0.594	0.645	0.769	0.965
Imports from the EU								
1981	0.838	0.933	0.618	0.933				
1982	0.897	0.924	0.364	0.882				
1983	0.868	0.922	0.528	0.933				
1984	0.832	0.850	0.497	0.899				
1985	0.830	0.660	0.467	0.855				
1986	0.796	0.681	0.553	0.781				
1987	0.761	0.635	0.599	0.824				
1988	0.781	0.823	0.482	0.652				
1989	0.711	0.791	0.163	0.615				
1990	0.687	0.714	0.034	0.493	0.912	0.855	0.886	0.909
1991	0.015	0.506	0.052	0.659	0.041	0.716	0.584	0.909
1992	0.124	0.489	0.154	0.599	0.199	0.631	0.239	0.894

Note: All correlation coefficients have been calculated on the basis of 106 NACE categories.

Source: Own calculations based on Eurostat COMEXT database.

An even more striking adjustment asymmetry in CEECs' trade with the EU during recent years is revealed by the correlation analysis of CEECs' market shares in EU imports and exports.[6] Table 8.1 shows that, despite declining trends, the correlation between CEECs' market shares in the EU in 1980 with those in subsequent years is rather high for all CEECs (and, for that matter, Austria as well). After 1989, the structure of CEECs' market shares changed and the correlation declined (especially for Czechoslovak exports), though all correlation coefficients remain highly positive and statistically significant. In comparison, the structure of Austrian market shares in the EU over the years has been much more stable, especially in the period after 1989.

On the other hand, adjustment on the import side has been quite dramatic (Table 8.1). Comparing the correlation of the structure of CEECs' imports from the EU in 1980 with that in subsequent years we see significant drops in the values of the correlation coefficients and therefore a growing dissimilarity in the composition of CEECs' imports from the EU (especially in Poland). Notably, compared with the import structure of 1989, there has been a striking fall in the correlation coefficients for Czechoslovakia and Poland after the trade liberalization. In 1991, as measured by the EU market shares, the structure of Czechoslovak imports from the EU was completely different from that in the preceding year (almost no correlation between the market shares in the two years). In Poland, and even more so in Hungary, import adjustments have been more gradual. The huge dissimilarity of CEECs' import structures in 1989 and 1992 becomes even more apparent when compared with the relative stability of Austrian imports indicated by high correlation coefficients.

CEECS' EXPORT COMPETITIVENESS ON EU MARKETS

The expansion of trade with the West has been one of the success stories of CEECs' reforms after 1989. EU manufacturing imports from the three CEECs more than doubled between 1989 and 1992 (all calculations are in terms of current ECU – see Table 8.2). EU imports from Czechoslovakia jumped by 131 per cent; imports from Poland by 111 per cent; those from Hungary grew by 64 per cent. At the same time, total EU imports from outside the Community increased by only 12.2 per cent during the same period. As a result, CEECs' market shares in the EU rose dramatically, though still remaining rather low (see Chapter 5). Austria, a small country highly integrated with the EU (and a member of the EU in the near future), had a much higher EU market share (5.77 per cent) than the three CEECs combined.

In order to get a better understanding of the factors contributing to this development we perform a simple *shift and share analysis* with the same

Table 8.2 CEECs' manufacturing exports to the EU and competitive gains, 1989–92

	Total exports (m ECU)		Export increment 1992/1989		Competitive gains 1989–92	
	1989	1992	(%)	(m ECU)	(m ECU)	(% of export increment)
Czechoslovakia	2152	4974	131.1	2822	2573	91.2
Hungary	2136	3513	64.4	1377	1095	79.5
Poland	2814	5926	110.6	3112	2556	82.1
CEE-3, total	7102	14413	102.9	7311	6224	85.1
Austria	17820	21808	22.4	3988	1251	31.4

Source: Eurostat COMEXT database and own calculations.

NACE 3-digit data on EU trade as used above.[7] The *shift and share analysis* makes it possible to decompose the total increment in the CEECs' exports to the EU into three hypothetical components:

1. a *general demand component*, showing how a given country's exports would develop if growing at the same rate as total EU imports;
2. a component measuring the *structural effect*, showing whether the country's exports are centred on commodities that are in above-average demand in the EU (that is, grew at above-average rates as compared with total EU imports); and
3. a component measuring the *competition effect*, namely, whether the country has exported more in certain commodities to the EU than its competitors outside the EU (this decomposition refers only to 'extra-EU' trade).[8]

The shift and share analysis reveals that 85 per cent of the total increment in EU imports from the three CEECs during 1989–92 can be attributed to improved competitiveness of CEECs' industries on the EU markets (component 3). The biggest competitive gains were recorded by Czechoslovakia and Poland (Table 8.2). More specifically, the three CEECs' competitive gains have materialized especially in the following industries: iron and steel, non-ferrous metals, chemicals (including petrochemicals), tools and finished metal goods, motor vehicles, knitting industry and clothing.

On the other hand, the three CEECs were not so competitive (their exports to the EU grew less than total EU imports from 'extra-EU' in that particular industry) for example in meat, dairy and wood products. With respect to all three CEECs, the structural effect in exports to the EU (component 2) was negligible (or even slightly negative in the case of Czechoslovakia) which means that there were only few CEECs' industries which could expand their exports to the EU at a time when demand for these particular products was shrinking in the EU.

The factor of general demand (component 1) has contributed only to a negligible extent – total EU imports grew only 12.2 per cent during the period – to the overall growth of EU imports from the CEECs as well.

A similar exercise for Austria reveals a distinctly lower share of competitive gains in the total export increment – only 31 per cent as compared with 80–90 per cent in the case of the three CEECs – with the general demand component playing a decisive role. Besides, the export growth patterns of individual industries have also been different (see below).

I shall now turn to a more detailed analysis of the industries which were most competitive on the EU markets in each of the three CEECs. As mentioned above, growing market shares of CEECs in the EU (from 2.11 per cent in 1989 to 3.82 per cent in 1992, without intra-EU trade) resulted largely from improved competitiveness of selected CEECs' industries on EU markets (component 3).

Despite similar general patterns and increasingly correlated export structure (see below), the industries reporting the largest competitive gains on EU markets differed among the individual CEECs (see Tables 8.3 to 8.5 for the detailed quantitative results): iron, steel and non-ferrous metals (Czechoslovakia and Poland), cement (Czechoslovakia), petrochemicals (Hungary and Poland), other basic chemicals (Czechoslovakia), metal structures (Czechoslovakia), manufacture of tools and finished metal goods (all three CEECs), plants for mines, iron and steel (Czechoslovakia), other machinery and equipment (Hungary), insulated wires and cables (Hungary), electrical machinery (Czechoslovakia and Hungary), motor vehicles (all three CEECs), knitting industry (Hungary and Poland), footwear (Hungary), clothing (all three CEECs) as well as wood products and furniture (Poland) were the main winners.

In comparison Austria has also recorded large competitive gains in some of these industries – manufacture of iron and steel, plants for mines, iron and steel, manufacture of other machinery and especially motor vehicles (see Table 8.6).[9]

Several industries, even those that have not recorded any spectacular competitive gains during the last few years, have already achieved quite impressive market shares in EU imports from 'extra-EU'. The individual CEECs' industries with the biggest market shares on the EU market in 1992 were the following:

- Czechoslovakia: clay, cement and concrete (32.5 per cent, 31 per cent and 14.7 per cent market share, respectively), brewing and malting

Table 8.3 *Czechoslovakia: gaining and losing industries in exports to the EU, 1989–92*

NACE 3-digit sectors		Exports to the EU in 1992 (m ECU)	Rate of growth 1992/89 (%)	Competitive gain (m ECU)	Share in EU market 1992[a] (%)
	10 biggest winners				
351	Manufacture & assembly of motor vehicles & engines	315.74	235.75	195.68	1.58
453	Manufacture of ready-made clothing & accessories	296.52	244.51	176.88	1.79
221	Iron & steel industry (as def. in ECSC Treaty)	358.88	51.21	148.91	7.42
224	Production & prel. processing of non-ferrous metals	157.40	539.06	135.00	0.74
316	Manuf. of tools & finished met. goods (exc. electr. equipt.)	162.66	410.86	121.37	2.80
242	Manufacture of cement, lime & plaster	114.52	1795.98	101.88	31.03
314	Manuf. of structural met. prod. (incl. integr. assembly)	94.34	2109.30	86.64	8.85
325	Manuf. of plant for mines, iron & steel ind. & foundries	106.64	499.76	85.66	2.26
253	Manufacture of other basic chemicals	131.50	181.57	84.66	2.30
342	Manuf. of electrical mach. (compris. electr. motors, etc.)	117.95	275.39	80.48	1.39
	Sum of 10 biggest winners	1856.12	219.96	1217.16	
	Sum of 10 biggest winners as % of total	37.32		47.31	
	5 biggest losers				
412	Slaughtering, preparing & preserving of meat	38.48	–50.90	–34.35	0.95
461	Sawing & processing of wood	82.80	–31.58	–23.74	1.45
413	Manufacture of dairy products	8.43	–73.29	–18.79	1.11
212	Extraction & preparation of non-ferrous metal ores	3.49	–56.59	–1.81	0.14
414	Processing & preserving of fruit and vegetables	17.02	9.99	–1.57	0.47

Note: [a] Share in EU imports from 'extra-EU'.

Source: Eurostat COMEXT database and own calculations.

Table 8.4 Hungary: gaining and losing industries in exports to the EU, 1989–92

	NACE 3-digit sectors	Exports to the EU in 1992 (m ECU)	Rate of growth 1992/89 (%)	Competitive gain (m ECU)	Share in EU market 1992[a] (%)
	10 biggest winners				
252	Manufacture of petrochemicals	291.41	63.99	106.33	2.10
436	Knitting industry	142.60	154.95	93.88	1.44
453	Manufacture of ready-made clothing & accessories	424.66	74.92	87.21	2.56
341	Manufacture of insulated wires & cables	100.35	830.88	85.13	6.05
451	Manufacture of mass-prod. footwear (excl. wood, rubber)	168.36	121.96	56.40	3.77
316	Manuf. of tools & finished met. goods (exc. electr. equip.)	93.86	136.78	42.46	1.62
342	Manuf. of electrical mach. (compris. electr. motors, etc.)	85.50	124.46	40.08	1.00
351	Manufacture & assembly of motor vehicles & engines	41.81	657.37	34.76	0.21
352	Manufacture of bodies for motor vehicles	41.29	657.60	33.96	11.26
328	Manufacture of other machinery & equipment	78.47	111.29	32.24	0.54
	Sum of 10 biggest winners	1468.29	113.14	612.46	
	Sum of 10 biggest winners as % of total	41.80		55.93	
	5 biggest losers				
253	Manufacture of other basic chemicals	27.89	–45.84	–23.75	0.49
418	Manufacture of starch & starch products	1.77	–74.62	–5.51	0.25
413	Manufacture of dairy products	4.11	–62.92	–5.45	0.54
221	Iron & steel industry (as def. in ECSC Treaty)	85.67	–15.47	–3.99	1.77
465	Other wood manufactures (except furniture)	18.86	24.51	–3.51	2.54

Note: [a] Share in EU imports from 'extra-EU'.

Source: Eurostat COMEXT database and own calculations.

Table 8.5 Poland: gaining and losing industries in exports to the EU, 1989–92

NACE 3-digit sectors		Exports to the EU in 1992 (m ECU)	Rate of growth 1992/89 (%)	Competitive gain (m ECU)	Share in EU market 1992[a] (%)
	10 biggest winners				
453	Manufacture of ready-made clothing & accessories	850.17	189.41	441.84	5.12
224	Production & prel. processing of non-ferrous metals	654.45	107.34	367.43	3.09
467	Manufacture of wooden furniture	326.34	197.03	168.32	11.77
252	Manufacture of petrochemicals	224.15	100.01	107.43	1.61
465	Other wood manufactures (except furniture)	121.48	526.18	92.83	16.34
221	Iron & steel industry (as def. in ECSC Treaty)	212.91	48.80	86.32	4.40
316	Manuf. of tools & finished met. goods (exc. electr. equip.)	134.86	258.47	86.08	2.32
495	Miscellaneous manufacturing industries	106.26	170.92	68.38	1.58
351	Manufacture & assembly of motor vehicles & engines	213.73	86.57	67.48	1.07
436	Knitting industry	139.69	212.43	64.61	1.41
	Sum of 10 biggest winners	2984.04	142.62	1550.71	
	Sum of 10 biggest winners as % of total	50.35		58.38	
	5 biggest losers				
341	Manufacture of insulated wires & cables	27.92	–43.54	–41.89	1.68
413	Manufacture of dairy products	39.43	–55.75	–37.44	5.20
421	Manufacture of cocoa, chocolate & sugar confect.	5.57	–65.19	–12.17	1.02
438	Manuf. of carpets, linoleum & other floor coverings	5.11	–14.64	–1.63	0.32
345	Manuf. of radio, TV receiving sets, sound reprod. equipt.	22.28	5.27	–1.24	0.11

Note: [a] Share in EU imports from 'extra-EU'.

Source: Eurostat COMEXT database and own calculations.

Table 8.6 Austria: gaining and losing industries in exports to the EU, 1989–92

NACE 3-digit sectors		Exports to the EU in 1992 (m ECU)	Rate of growth 1992/89 (%)	Competitive gain (m ECU)	Share in EU market 1992[a] (%)
	10 biggest winners				
351	Manufacture & assembly of motor vehicles & engines	2024.99	77.93	568.23	10.16
325	Manuf. of plant for mines, iron & steel ind. & foundries	675.32	66.21	195.89	14.34
328	Manufacture of other machinery & equipment	939.33	54.03	183.13	6.49
471	Manufacture of pulp, paper & board	1093.66	0.52	136.23	7.53
495	Miscellaneous manufacturing industries	447.01	22.05	91.74	6.63
353	Manufacture of parts & access. for motor vehicles	512.88	49.24	86.73	15.06
221	Iron & steel industry (as def. in ECSC Treaty)	719.85	–3.52	63.25	14.89
322	Manufacture of machine-tools for working metal	304.70	18.99	61.44	8.75
327	Manuf. of other mach. & equipt. for use in spec. ind. branches	274.39	29.72	60.75	10.75
462	Manufacture of semi-finished wood products	277.66	31.31	59.86	13.50
	Sum of 10 biggest winners	7269.79	35.19	1507.25	
	Sum of 10 biggest winners as % of total	33.34		120.52	
	5 biggest losers				
345	Manuf. of radio, TV receivers, sound reprod. equipt.	1123.52	–0.79	–133.46	5.44
453	Manufacture of ready-made clothing and accessories	371.76	7.97	–106.85	2.24
494	Manufacture of toys & sports goods	196.94	20.11	–88.37	3.19
451	Manufacture of mass-prod. footwear (excl. wood, rubber)	233.67	8.01	–86.50	5.23
224	Production & prel. processing of non-ferrous metals	704.27	–18.23	–79.46	3.32

Note: [a] Share in EU imports from 'extra-EU'.

Source: Eurostat COMEXT database and own calculations.

(28.5 per cent), wooden containers and other wood manufactures (10.8 per cent and 7.3 per cent), glass and glassware (10 per cent), structural metal products and boilers (8.8 per cent each), iron and steel, steel tubes, rolling products (about 7 per cent each);

- Hungary: manufacture of bodies for motor vehicles (11.3 per cent), slaughtering and preparing of meat (9 per cent), asbestos (7.7 per cent), electric lamps and lighting (6.2 per cent), insulated wires and cable (6 per cent), structural metal products and boilers (3.8 per cent and 4.4 per cent, respectively);
- Poland: cement (20.7 per cent), wooden containers and other wood manufactures (12.1 per cent and 16.3 per cent, respectively), structural metal products and boilers (10.8 per cent and 14.4 per cent), wooden furniture (11.8 per cent) and salt extraction (10.4 per cent).

Further, it is interesting to note that the combined market share of the three CEECs in some of these industries is extremely high. Thus, for instance, the combined market share in cement and lime is almost 52 per cent, in clay it is 37.2 per cent, in boilers 27.5 per cent, in other wood manufactures 26.2 per cent, in wooden containers 24.9 per cent, in structural metal products 23.5 per cent. This means that the three CEECs have become important EU suppliers of selected industrial products.

Austria, with its global market share in the EU substantially higher than that of any CEEC, has many industries with quite large market shares in the EU as well (concrete and cement 34.1 per cent, standard and narrow gauges 34.1 per cent, soft drinks 46.9 per cent, retreading of rubber tyres 30.8 per cent).

Another characteristic feature is that the export structure of the CEECs is quite similar and they are apparently competing on EU markets with very similar products. The evidence that the CEECs have recently been more and more competing on EU markets with similar products, already discussed in Chapter 6, is supported by the results of a correlation analysis of export structures specially performed for this purpose.

While in 1989 there was a strong correlation only between the Hungarian and Polish export structures, by 1992 the structure of all three CEECs' exports became more similar: the already strong correlation between Hungarian and Polish exports increased further and also Czechoslovak exports became strongly correlated with those of Poland (Table 8.7). A rather weak correlation between the Hungarian, Polish and Austrian export structures suggests that these two CEECs do not represent Austrian competitors on EU markets. However, Czechoslovakia is emerging as a potential Austrian competitor as the structure of Czechoslovak exports to the EU becomes strongly correlated with that of Austrian exports. Nevertheless, all three CEECs still

Table 8.7 Correlation matrix of EU imports from Czechoslovakia, Hungary, Poland and Austria, 1989 and 1992

EU imports from:	Czechoslovakia	Hungary	Poland	Austria	Extra-EU total
Czechoslovakia	–	0.603	0.678	0.667	0.504
Hungary	0.544	–	0.717	0.303	0.410
Poland	0.533	0.703	–	0.367	0.509
Austria	0.593	0.294	0.474	–	0.701
Extra-EU total	0.390	0.333	0.524	0.747	–

Note: Year 1989 below diagonal, year 1992 above diagonal. Correlation coefficients calculated for 106 NACE 3-digit categories.

Source: Eurostat COMEXT database and own calculations.

have an export structure which is more different from what is demanded on average on EU markets; in this respect Austrian exports are much more adjusted to EU import demand (Table 8.7).

Many of the successful CEECs' industries mentioned above are among the 'sensitive sectors' affected by various protectionist barriers, and the prospects for their further export growth are uncertain.[10] It is also too early to say whether the CEECs' industries which were assessed as most competitive really possess a long-term comparative advantage, or whether their recent export success (at least until 1992) has been the result of some special factors (e.g. exporting without due regard to profitability, one-time effect of liberalization measures, and so on) in the initial stage of economic reforms. There is, for instance, some evidence that CEECs' export prices are not only much lower than those of their competitors, but, moreover, that they might even have declined after trade liberalization (see Danielewski, 1993; Exportní výkony, 1994; Stankovsky, 1993b). The preliminary results for 1993 (a marked drop in Hungarian and Slovak exports but a strong increase in the Czech export performance) also suggest that no definite conclusions can be drawn at this stage.

I shall now turn to those industries which lost their competitive edge on EU markets during the first years of transition. The industries suffering the biggest competitive losses between 1989 and 1992, revealed by the shift and share analysis, were the following:

- Czechoslovakia: extraction and preparation of non-ferrous metals, slaughtering, preparing and preservation of meat, manufacture of dairy

products, processing and preserving of fruit, sawing and processing of wood (Table 8.3);
- Hungary: iron and steel, manufacture of other basic chemicals, dairy products, starch and starch products and other wood manufactures (Table 8.4);
- Poland: manufacture of insulated wires and cables, radio and TV sets, dairy products, cocoa, chocolate and manufacture of carpets, linoleum (Table 8.5).

Some of the 'gaining' and 'losing' industries are common to all three CEECs – for example motor vehicles (with expanding exports) and insulated wires and cables (losing market shares) which is another indication of growing competition among the CEECs on EU markets.

In Austria, too, there were many industries that incurred competitive losses. The biggest losers were: production and processing of non-ferrous metals, radio and TV sets, footwear, clothing (Table 8.6). At least some of these export losses (for instance in footwear, clothing, knitting industry) may have resulted from increased competition on the part of the CEECs.

CEECS AS MARKETS FOR EU MANUFACTURING EXPORTS

EU manufacturing exports to the three CEECs have approximately doubled between 1989 and 1992. This impressive growth should be seen against the meagre 7.4 per cent growth of total EU exports to 'extra-EU' during the same period. The fastest export growth, reflecting the CEECs' import liberalization measures introduced after 1989, occurred in relation to former Czechoslovakia (161 per cent) and Poland (106 per cent). In Hungary, where trade liberalization had already been implemented gradually during the 1980s, the growth of imports from the EU was far less pronounced (39 per cent).

The importance of the CEECs as an outlet for EU manufacturing industries should not be over-rated as starting trade levels were very low (less than 2 per cent of EU exports in 1989 went to the three CEECs – see Table 8.8 and Table 5.1 in Chapter 5). Despite impressive growth, exports to the three CEECs in 1992 still accounted for only 3.65 per cent of EU exports to 'extra-EU'. For illustration, the importance of the Austrian market for the EU was nearly twice as high.

The asymmetry regarding the importance of mutual trade between the CEECs and the EU is striking: as mentioned above, imports from the EU accounted for some 42 per cent of Czechoslovak and Hungarian imports in 1992 and even more in the case of Poland (53 per cent). Another feature

Table 8.8 EU manufacturing exports to the CEECs and competitive gains, 1989–92

	Total exports (m ECU)		Export increment 1992/1989		Competitive gains 1989–92	
	1989	1992	(%)	(m ECU)	(m ECU)	(% of export increment)
Czechoslovakia	2079	5435	161.4	3356	3242	96.6
Hungary	2505	3478	38.9	974	824	84.6
Poland	3109	6400	105.8	3291	3089	93.8
CEE-3, total	7693	15311	99.1	7620	7155	93.9
Austria	23090	27320	18.3	4231	2829	66.9

Source: Eurostat COMEXT database and own calculations.

worth mentioning is the growing EU trade surplus with the CEECs (from 590 m ECU in 1989 to 900 m ECU in 1992), implying that the CEECs' trade opening was at least as beneficial for the EU as it was for the CEECs.

Applying the shift and share analysis to data on EU exports to the CEECs we have to bear in mind that the results must be interpreted somewhat differently than in the case of imports.[11] Rather than measuring components of general demand, structural effects and competitiveness of EU industries on CEECs' markets, it is the changing importance of the CEECs as outlets for individual EU manufacturing industries (relative to other trading partners) which is compared by the available data.

The results reveal that for the period 1989–92 the 'general demand' component was slightly positive whereas the 'structural effect' was negative. Thus almost the whole increment in EU exports to the CEECs during 1989–92 can be attributed to the effect of the 'competitiveness factor'. A negative 'structural effect' means that EU exports to the CEECs (and, by the way, even more so to Austria) centred on industries whose exports to the rest of the world grew less than the average. The highly positive 'competitiveness factor' reflects the rapid expansion of EU exports to the CEECs in virtually every industry resulting from overall CEECs' import liberalization.

CEECs' markets were especially promising and expanding (industries with the biggest 'competitive gains') for the following EU industries: tools and finished metal goods, machinery for food and chemical industry, office machinery, telecommunications equipment and processing of plastics, etc. (Tables 8.9 to 8.11). Given the above-mentioned large expansion of total manufacturing exports to the CEECs and the impressive structural changes (see also Table 8.1), it is perhaps more interesting to show which EU industries

Table 8.9 Gaining and losing industries in EU exports to Czechoslovakia, 1989–92

NACE 3-digit sectors		EU exports 1992 (m ECU)	Rate of growth 1992/89 (%)	Competitive gain (m ECU)	Share in total EU exp. 1992[a] (%)
	10 biggest winners				
351	Manufacture & assembly of motor vehicles & engines	387.91	1243.64	360.11	1.52
328	Manufacture of other machinery and equipment	431.39	155.05	236.17	1.64
342	Manuf. of electrical mach. (compris. electr. motors, etc.)	221.69	450.92	173.62	1.92
324	Manuf. of mach. for the food, chem. & related industries	301.34	137.37	159.76	3.42
344	Manufacture of telecommunications equipment	251.64	160.96	135.10	1.88
330	Manuf. office mach. & data-processing machinery	208.95	177.56	128.36	2.09
325	Manuf. of plant for mines, iron & steel ind. & foundries	215.86	167.85	127.35	2.21
483	Processing of plastics	137.31	314.96	100.37	1.81
316	Manuf. of tools & finished met. goods (exc. electr. equip.)	120.90	400.62	94.90	1.57
327	Manuf. of other mach. & equipt. for use in spec. ind. branches	149.68	102.60	74.20	2.48
	Sum of 10 biggest winners	2426.67	224.15	1589.94	
	Sum of 10 biggest winners as % of total	44.65		49.04	
	5 biggest EU losers				
412	Slaughtering, preparing & preserving of meat	19.59	−64.13	−36.87	0.52
252	Manufacture of petrochemicals	165.75	−17.11	−27.86	1.03
420	Sugar manufacturing & refining	2.58	−89.95	−20.47	0.21
212	Extraction & preparation of non-ferrous metal ores	2.64	−72.09	−3.94	0.89
239	Other mineral extraction	3.24	−40.98	−0.80	1.45

Note: [a] Share in EU exports to 'extra-EU'.

Source: Eurostat COMEXT database and own calculations.

Table 8.10 Gaining and losing industries in EU exports to Hungary, 1989–92

NACE 3-digit sectors		EU exports 1992 (m ECU)	Rate of growth 1992/89 (%)	Competitive gain (m ECU)	Share in total EU exp. 1992[a] (%)
	10 biggest winners				
351	Manufacture & assembly of motor vehicles & engines	262.67	159.58	165.22	1.03
436	Knitting industry	111.75	142.88	62.11	2.50
316	Manuf. of tools & finished met. goods (excl. electr. equipt.)	98.25	130.47	52.36	1.28
453	Manufacture of ready-made clothing & accessories	78.93	168.29	46.51	1.15
451	Manufacture of mass-prod. footwear (excl. wood, rubber)	70.19	212.93	46.32	1.68
257	Manufacture of pharmaceutical products	109.25	136.47	45.24	1.04
330	Manuf. office mach. & data-processing machinery	91.22	109.51	44.61	0.91
322	Manufacture of machine-tools for working metal	93.11	68.83	43.72	1.58
483	Processing of plastics	105.88	88.90	43.31	1.40
344	Manufacture of telecommunications equipment	125.10	71.09	36.73	0.94
	Sum of 10 biggest winners	1146.35	122.27	586.12	
	Sum of 10 biggest winners as % of total	32.96		71.09	
	5 biggest EU losers				
252	Manufacture of petrochemicals	155.59	–27.35	–51.77	0.97
253	Manufacture of other basic chemicals	27.89	–45.06	–21.60	0.58
364	Aerospace equipment manufacturing & repairing	2.28	–80.14	–13.42	0.01
345	Manuf. of radio, TV receiving sets, sound reprod. equipt.	75.67	2.35	–13.14	0.85
422	Manuf. of animal & poultry foods (incl. fish meal)	23.90	–17.53	–12.92	2.28

Note: [a] Share in EU exports to 'extra-EU'.

Source: Eurostat COMEXT database and own calculations.

Table 8.11 *Gaining and losing industries in EU exports to Poland, 1989–92*

NACE 3-digit sectors		EU exports 1992 (m ECU)	Rate of growth 1992/89 (%)	Competitive gain (m ECU)	Share in total EU exp. 1992[a] (%)
	10 biggest winners				
351	Manufacture & assembly of motor vehicles & engines	305.44	365.82	242.49	1.20
483	Processing of plastics	274.34	303.14	198.12	3.62
324	Manuf. of mach. for the food, chem. & related industries	310.16	133.38	161.31	3.52
258	Manufacture of soap, synthetic detergents, perfume	182.41	709.63	152.90	4.41
344	Manufacture of telecommunications equipment	249.75	189.73	145.45	1.87
328	Manufacture of other machinery & equipment	412.74	68.78	131.52	1.57
345	Manuf. of radio, TV receiving sets, sound reprod. equipt.	173.27	304.84	121.91	1.95
330	Manuf. office mach. & data-processing machinery	168.87	267.59	119.71	1.69
316	Manuf. of tools & finished met.goods (excl. electr. equipt.)	157.66	326.45	117.73	2.05
472	Processing of paper & board	135.35	362.89	101.14	4.02
	Sum of 10 biggest winners	2369.99	205.91	1492.28	
	Sum of 10 biggest winners as % of total	37.03		48.31	
	5 biggest EU losers				
412	Slaughtering, preparing & preserving of meat	74.73	–39.00	–51.45	1.98
323	Manufacture of textile machinery and accessories	54.48	–46.00	–51.44	1.04
424	Distilling of ethyl alcohol from fermented materials	5.35	–84.26	–35.79	0.15
322	Manufacture of machine-tools for working metal	83.80	–25.50	–17.43	1.42
223	Drawing, cold rolling & cold folding of steel	33.65	–45.85	–16.06	1.67

Note: [a] Share in EU exports to 'extra-EU'.

Source: Eurostat COMEXT database and own calculations.

Table 8.12 Gaining and losing industries in EU exports to Austria, 1989–92

NACE 3-digit sectors		EU exports 1992 (m ECU)	Rate of growth 1992/89 (%)	Competitive gain (m ECU)	Share in total EU exp. 1992[a] (%)
	10 biggest winners				
351	Manufacture & assembly of motor vehicles & engines	3136.46	38.99	970.15	12.28
322	Manufacture of machine-tools for working metal	522.91	33.14	169.43	8.87
495	Miscellaneous manufacturing industries	645.94	52.90	168.55	4.41
224	Production & prel. processing of non-ferrous metals	755.84	-4.31	155.55	11.27
316	Manuf. of tools & finished met. goods (excl. electr. equipt.)	864.45	25.85	122.62	11.23
353	Manufacture of parts and access. for motor vehicles	457.47	32.92	120.18	8.19
483	Processing of plastics	883.44	29.36	118.56	11.66
481	Manufacture of rubber products	416.46	34.68	116.51	11.51
467	Manufacture of wooden furniture	548.17	24.69	108.55	15.45
325	Manuf.of plant for mines, iron & steel ind. & foundries	599.41	30.84	95.48	6.14
	Sum of 10 biggest winners	8830.54	30.19	2145.59	
	Sum of 10 biggest winners as % of total	37.87		75.84	
	5 biggest EU losers				
345	Manuf. of radio, TV receiving sets, sound reprod. equipt.	684.64	–6.05	–189.80	7.70
362	Manufacture of standard & narrow-gauge railway	54.01	45.10	–88.18	3.45
330	Manuf. office mach. & data-processing machinery	700.38	–2.09	–65.06	7.02
346	Manufacture of domestic type electric appliances	467.46	24.12	–44.76	12.35
344	Manufacture of telecommunications equipment	601.54	14.03	–36.75	4.50

Note: [a] Share in EU exports to 'extra-EU'.

Source: Eurostat COMEXT database and own calculations.

suffered 'competitive losses' (that is, their exports to the CEECs increased less than total EU exports of the particular product).

This can be demonstrated by the example of the five biggest 'loser industries' in each of the countries compared:

- Czechoslovakia: non-ferrous metal ores, other mineral extraction, petrochemicals, slaughtering, preparing of meat, sugar manufactures (Table 8.9);
- Hungary: petrochemicals, other basic chemicals, radio and TV sets, aerospace equipment, animal and poultry foods (Table 8.10);
- Poland: drawing and rolling of steel, machine tools for working metal, textile machinery, slaughtering and preparing of meat, distilling of ethyl alcohol (Table 8.11).

The EU industries with shrinking export markets in Austria were different: partly those which gained considerably in the CEECs (such as office machinery, telecommunications equipment, radio and TV sets, domestic electric appliances, rolling stocks – Table 8.12). It is also interesting to note that there was no apparent demand for imports from the EU to replace reduced CEECs' imports from the former USSR (such as ores and petrochemicals).

Finally, the correlation analysis of the structure of EU exports to the CEECs (and to Austria) reveals that, on the one hand, the structure of the individual CEECs' markets in 1989 was very similar for EU exports but, on the other hand, quite different from what the EU exported on average both to Austria and to the rest of the world. The Czechoslovak and Polish markets

Table 8.13 Correlation matrix of EU exports to Czechoslovakia, Hungary, Poland and Austria, 1989 and 1992

EU exports to:	Czechoslovakia	Hungary	Poland	Austria	Extra-EU total
Czechoslovakia	–	0.899	0.882	0.824	0.860
Hungary	0.833	–	0.892	0.899	0.848
Poland	0.906	0.892	–	0.776	0.817
Austria	0.526	0.727	0.581	–	0.831
Extra-EU total	0.665	0.806	0.715	0.878	–

Note: Year 1989 below diagonal, year 1992 above diagonal. Correlation coefficients calculated for 106 NACE 3-digit categories.

Source: Eurostat COMEXT database and own calculations.

showed the greatest dissimilarities (low correlation with the average EU export structure) before trade liberalization (Table 8.13). In 1992 the correlation between the EU export structures to each country of the region increased across the board.

The above-noted asymmetry in the speed and degree of structural adjustment in CEECs' exports (Tables 8.1 and 8.7) and imports (Tables 8.1 and 8.13) is again clearly visible. It will be interesting to see whether future industrial restructuring in the CEECs will lead to stronger adjustments on their export side as well or whether the CEECs will maintain their distinct export specialization patterns of residual suppliers.

CONCLUDING REMARKS

The trade reorientation from former CMEA markets to markets in the West, especially in the EU, has been one of the most outstanding features of the process of economic transition in CEE. Between 1989 and 1992 a dramatic structural change took place in both CEECs' exports and imports – much more pronounced than in Austria, which is used as a point of reference in this chapter.

The analysis of the changes in trade structures on the basis of 'shift and share analysis' reveals that more than 80 per cent of the total increment in CEEC manufacturing exports during 1989–92 can be ascribed to 'competitive gains' of CEECs' industries on EU markets. In contrast to the CEECs' remarkable import adjustment, by 1992, the structure of CEECs' exports remained quite different from what the EU imported from the rest of the world and the structural adjustment was much less pronounced. Moreover, the export structure of the individual CEECs is becoming increasingly correlated and all three CEECs have been competing on EU markets with similar products.

On the import side, the CEECs have represented expanding markets for most EU industries as well, but their importance remains marginal. The correlation analysis of the structure of EU exports to the CEECs reveals that after trade liberalization the structure of these exports has lost its distinctive character and now resembles closely the average structure of EU exports in general.

NOTES

1. The acronym CEEC (CEECs) as well as the term 'reforming countries' in this chapter refer only to these three countries.

2. See, for example, Stankovsky (1993a) and Messerlin (1993). More recently, protectionist tendencies reappeared both in the East and in the West; see Messerlin (1993) and Richter (1993).
3. The shifts have also been affected by German unification. The former GDR was naturally not part of the EU in 1989 (and, accordingly, is not included in the EU data in this year). At the same time, it used to be an important trading partner for the reforming countries: in 1989, the GDR accounted for 6.5 per cent of Czechoslovak exports and for 7.8 per cent of imports. The respective data for Hungary were 5.4 per cent (exports) and 6.2 per cent (imports), for Poland 4.2 per cent and 4.5 per cent, respectively; see Foreign Trade Data (1992).
4. See Landesmann and Székely (1994) and Rosati (1994) as well as Chapters 6 and 9 of this volume.
5. That study is based on a comparison of CEECs' export structures with the average EU import structure and, conversely, of CEECs' import structures with the average EU export structure.
6. Correlation coefficients between the individual CEECs' market shares on the EU market (CEEC's exports in EU total imports from 'extra-EU' and CEEC's imports in EU total exports to 'extra-EU') in 1980 and subsequent years. The same was done again for 1989 and subsequent years. Computation was performed at the NACE 3-digit level for 106 individual categories (see Annex).
7. Pertaining to our case, the shift and share analysis can be applied to decompose the increment of country i's (a given CEEC's) total exports to another country (in our case the EU) ΔX_i as follows:

$$\Delta X_i = \Sigma_i \Delta x_{ij} = \Sigma_i x_{ij}\,(\Delta M/M) + \Sigma_i x_{ij}\,[(\Delta M_j/M_j) - (\Delta M/M)] + \Sigma_i x_{ij}\,[(\Delta x_{ij}/x_{ij}) - (\Delta M_j/M_j)],$$

where x_{ij} is country i's exports of commodity/sector j; M_j denotes EU's total imports of commodity/sector j (in our case total imports from 'extra-EU', that is, from non-EU member states); M denotes EU's total imports (from 'extra-EU') and 'Δ' stands for increment.

$\Sigma_i x_{ij}\,(\Delta M/M)$ can be interpreted as a general demand component; $\Sigma_i x_{ij}\,[(\Delta M_j/M_j) - (\Delta M/M)]$ is a structural effect component and $\Sigma_i x_{ij}\,[(\Delta x_{ij}/x_{ij}) - (\Delta M_j/M_j)]$ is a component measuring the competition effect.
8. The third component does not measure competitiveness in a strict sense since different factors (e.g. preferential treatment or non-tariff barriers) could have affected gains in market shares (I owe this insight to G. Graziani). Strictly speaking, the third component is a sum of market-share gains weighted by exports of a particular commodity in the base year.
9. Detailed computation results for all NACE 3-digit industries are available from the author on request.
10. For an assessment of the impact of EU protectionist measures on imports from CEE see Schumacher and Möbius (1992).
11. In this case the interpretation of the shift and share analysis is a mirror image of the interpretation suggested in the analysis of CEECs' exports to the EU. However, as the COMEXT data do not cover the total trade of the CEECs, the interpretation of the three components is somewhat truncated.

REFERENCES

Danielewski, J. (1993), 'Ceny towarow w Polskim eksporcie do krajow uprzemyslowionych w 1992 r.', Warszawa: Instytut koniunktur i cen handlu zagranicznego.

Exportní výkony (1994), 'Exportní výkony vybraných odvetví zpracovatelského prumyslu Ceské republiky v mezinárodním srovnání', Praha: Centrum vnejsích ekonomických vztahu.

Foreign Trade Data (1992), *Foreign Trade Data of Countries in Transition, 1980–1991*, Vienna: WIIW, Orac-Verlag.

Havlik, P. (1994), 'Trade reorientation in Central and Eastern Europe', paper presented at the Conference on 'Transforming Economies and European Integration', Sofia, 27–28 May 1994.

Landesmann, M. and Székely, I.P. (1994), 'Industrial structural change in Central and Eastern European economies and patterns of East–West trade integration', mimeo.

Messerlin, P.A. (1993), 'The trade relations of the Central and Eastern European countries', paper presented at the WIIW Workshop on 'Transformation of the East European Economies, 1989–1993: Critical Assessments and Ways Out of the Crisis', Vienna, 21–25 November 1993.

Richter, S. (1993), 'East–West trade under growing Western protectionism', WIIW Research Report 198, June, Vienna: The Vienna Institute for Comparative Economic Studies.

Rosati, D. (1994), 'Changes in the structure of manufactured trade between Poland and the EC', Working Paper No. 49, February, Warsaw: Foreign Trade Research Institute.

Schumacher, D. and Möbius, U. (1992), 'Analysis of current Community trade barriers to Central and East European countries (CEEC)', Berlin: DIW, mimeo.

Stankovsky, J. (1993a), 'OECD-Handel mit Ost-Mitteleuropa kräftig gewachsen', *WIFO Monatsberichte*, **9**, 463–71.

Stankovsky, J. (1993b), 'Österreichische Importe aus Ost-Mitteleuropa 1989/1992', *WIFO Monatsberichte*, **9**, 459–62.

Discussion of Chapter 8

Lubomir Mitov

The excellent chapter 'Trade Reorientation and Competitiveness in CEECs' provides a thorough and sound empirical analysis of the shifts in the external trade of three CEECs – Czechoslovakia, Poland and Hungary. Despite the somewhat limited scope (only three of the former CMEA countries) and the time frame (with 1992 being the last year covered, thus limiting the observations to only two 'full' reform years), the chapter highlights a number of important issues which should be a matter of concern for policy makers both in the East and in the West:

- the rising asymmetry in export and import adjustments in the trade of the CEECs with the EU;
- the lack of significant structural shifts;
- the dominance of resource-intensive, low value-added commodities in the export structure of the CEECs.

In these discussion notes, on the basis of empirical research performed by the World Bank and its Resident Mission in Bulgaria, I would like to focus on the following points:

1. What was the 'engine' of the post-liberalization export recovery?
2. Is the improvement of export competitiveness 'real', or is it only a temporary phenomenon of transition?
3. What are the impediments to structural changes in CEEC exports?
4. Is the CEEC export expansion sustainable?

Given the limited space and the purpose of these discussion notes, I shall only raise the issues rather than try to provide a simple and easy answer. Obviously, further detailed research (both on the macro- and on the micro-level) is necessary in order to come up with comprehensive conclusions concerning these issues.

First it is beyond doubt that all CEECs experienced an export 'boom' towards Western markets immediately after the start of the market reforms.

This export surge was especially pronounced in their exports to the EU. Two questions can be raised in this respect: was the export 'boom' so impressive just compared to previous years, and what triggered this export expansion?

The increase of CEEC exports to the EU after the collapse of the CMEA is significant, compared to the late 1980s. However it should be noted that the share of the CEECs in total OECD imports had been declining throughout most of the previous decade. This was partly caused by the recession in the early 1980s, but mostly it was due to the failing economies and the structural weaknesses of all these countries towards the end of the CMEA era. For example, in 1989 the share of Czechoslovakia in total OECD imports of manufactured goods declined by 27.0 per cent compared to 1980; the share of Hungary by 28.3 per cent; that of Poland by 40.2 per cent; Romania by 41.0 per cent and Bulgaria by 55.3 per cent. Thus, in a sense, the export 'boom' of the early 1990s was to a certain extent simply a recovery to levels previously achieved in the trade with the OECD countries.

The reversal of the CEEC export performance cannot be attributed to a sudden upsurge in OECD import demand; neither to a better match between their investment strategies and the OECD demand structure, as the exports were generated by the already existing production capacities. On the other hand, the improvement cannot be attributed to successful structural reforms in the CEECs, as their impact could not have been experienced so soon; or to private sector development, as there was no large-scale privatization at the outset of the reforms, and most of the export surge was generated by state-owned enterprises (SOEs). This implies that the source of this export expansion could be either some reorientation of trade from CMEA to OECD, or the response to macroeconomic reforms at the micro-level.

While it is often argued that a massive reorientation of exports from CMEA to hard currency areas is impossible, given the low quality of most manufactured goods exported to the ex-CMEA market and due to the low technological level in CEECs, the available data clearly indicate that some trade reorientation of this type has taken place in virtually all countries. Some of this shift could be explained by the reorientation of generally competitive commodities, which were previously destined for the CMEA market in order to pay for vital imports, or in line with the CMEA specialization schemes. Other factors, such as low wages, better quality control and subsidies (direct or indirect, for example through subsidized energy prices) also played a significant role.

The other important factor contributing to the export surge is the impact of market reforms and, especially, the shift from a supply- to a demand-constrained economy. The restrictive monetary and fiscal policies, the reduction in budgetary spending and in real incomes in all CEECs resulted in declining domestic demand which shifted the economies from chronic shortages to oversupply and left more resources available for export.

Trade liberalization also played a very important role in this respect. However, this was a necessary but not a sufficient condition. As indicated by the examples of Bulgaria in 1990 and Romania in 1990–92, if trade liberalization is not an element of a coherent reform package together with macroeconomic stabilization, currency convertibility and price liberalization, this may result in chaos and deepening of the external imbalances. Trade liberalization would only produce positive results if it worked on a par with currency convertibility (at least partial) and within the framework of market-based relative prices. The initial devaluation of the national currencies was also beneficial as it made CEEC exports more competitive and amplified the impact of the low labour costs.

In this respect, it could be noted that the opening of the EU markets was of limited significance and its impact could be expected only in the medium term, with the gradual implementation of the Europe Agreements.

Second, as the history of transition is still very short, it is difficult to give a definite answer to the question whether the improved competitiveness was 'real' or whether it was only a temporary phenomenon. Long-term competitiveness depends mostly on the investment activity in the economy and its technological development. In all CEECs, investment is declining and the existing technological base is in poor condition. Thus, apart from the cases of significant foreign investment, involving transfer of technology and know-how, there seems to be little optimism in the longer run.

In the short term, though, there is enough scope for improving competitiveness. Thus the currency devaluation temporarily reduced domestic costs of exports and made them more competitive. However with the gradual real appreciation of the national currencies this competitive edge will be eroded. Subsidies are also an important factor. In most CEECs, there are few or no export subsidies at all, but the continuing support of low utility prices (energy, in the first instance) results in implicit subsidies to the energy-intensive industries. It is easy to check that the latter were among those which exhibited highest 'competitive' gains. This could hardly be considered as a sustainable development.

Another source of trouble is the fact that the increase in exports does not necessarily result in higher profitability for producers. SOEs, which are still the main generators of exports, report high and rising losses both in Hungary and in Poland. The situation in Bulgaria is almost out of control, with SOEs' cash losses running at around 20 per cent of GDP, despite improving export performance. This indicates that most probably profit maximization was not the top determinant of SOEs' exports, suggesting either a transfer of the surplus in current spending (wages) or exports at prices below costs. In both cases, while such a policy may result in short-term gains, it cannot be sustained in the longer run.

All this suggests that the observed improvement of competitiveness is most probably of a transitional nature and is likely to be eroded soon (the worsening of the export performance in all CEECs in 1993 might already reflect their declining competitive advantage).

Third, the CEECs are small economies, heavily dependent on trade, and they cannot become more efficient and competitive without major structural change fostering their export performance. There is no evidence yet of such a process of restructuring. With few exceptions, mostly related to successful large privatization deals or massive foreign investment, the CEEC export structure has not changed substantially since the communist era. These countries still remain suppliers of low value-added, resource-intensive and technologically unsophisticated commodities. In my opinion, this can be explained by the following factors:

- Shortage of investment capital, especially for technological development. The traditional supplier of such funds – the state budget – is now unable to provide them, and capital markets capable of supporting market-based development are still non-existent. In this respect, the assistance of the developed market economies (both official and through the private sector) is indispensable.
- Inappropriate pricing policy. The low prices of utilities (and, in some countries, of some other key inputs as well) create disincentives to restructure or rationalize the resource allocation which conserves the existing trade patterns. While it may be beneficial in the short term, such a strategy is disastrous in the longer run.
- Foreign investment is still limited in size and concentrated mostly in the traditional areas. To some extent this reflects the delays in privatization (with the notable exception of Czechoslovakia, and now, of the Czech Republic) but also the reluctance of Western investors to breed competition in their backyard.
- The general delay in the structural reforms in all CEECs. This is reflected in the slow pace of privatization and in the tedious process of shifting resources from the old failing industries to the sectors with comparative advantages for the future, as this requires painful decisions like closure of hopeless SOEs and substantial redundancies. Even in the more advanced reforming countries, the restructuring of the already privatized companies by the new owners has not taken place yet.

Fourth, the answer to the question, whether the export drive is sustainable, is extremely tentative, as the existing evidence is quite ambiguous. On the one hand, it is questionable whether the CEECs have already revealed their full export potential in the course of the implementation of the market reforms so far: first, because the transition is far from completed; and, second, because of the existence of a number of institutional constraints, the most important of them being the still underdeveloped private sector.

One could expect that, with the growth of the private sector, export performance is likely to improve. The absence of appropriate export promotion and export credit schemes, the deficiency of marketing and information infrastructure, the lack of adequate business contacts and experience are also a substantial impediment to CEEC exporters. With the progress in these areas, it is likely that CEEC export performance will improve in the medium term.

On the other hand, the inadequate investment, coupled with the financial squeeze on most enterprises, the lack of long-term capital and the generally inadequate own technological base of these countries provide less optimism with respect to their future chances on world markets. Besides, the fast catching up of local wages in US dollar terms and the imminent future adjustments in energy prices are likely to undermine their main current competitive advantages – low labour and input costs. Finally, it is not yet clear whether foreign investment will have a positive impact on exports, or vice versa.

In this respect it would be useful to explore what are the likely comparative advantages of these countries and how they compare with their current export structure. It is difficult to assume that energy-intensive industries or low-value-added products, based on imported inputs, could be competitive under normal market conditions.

Indisputably, the role of the OECD and of the EU is very crucial. It is time to understand that most of the CEECs do not need any more grants or technical assistance but a real opening of the Western markets for their products and substantial inflow of private investment capital. If the CEECs have adequate access to the OECD markets and capital, they will be able to take care of themselves.

9. Threats and opportunities for West European industry deriving from trade liberalization with Central and Eastern Europe

Giovanni Graziani

INTRODUCTION

The rapid increase of EU trade with the CEECs over the period 1989–92 has been at the core of widespread apprehension by many EU entrepreneurs and governments, which seem to feel threatened by the enhanced competition of CEEC products engendered by trade liberalization, both on EU and other international markets. Many firms, especially in the 'sensitive' sectors, have raised complaints over alleged unfair competition by CEEC products on EU markets. A host of restrictive practices have been mushrooming over the past few years, with a more frequent resort to contingent protectionist measures and to the safeguard clauses of the Europe Agreements (EAs).

As in the case of trade liberalization, closer links between the CEE and the EU are not going to have a uniform effect on all sectors and countries: some industries and/or countries are likely to be hurt, others may receive some benefits; still others may obtain contrasting results. A precise quantitative appraisal of the impact of trade opening on the individual sectors of industry is an almost impossible task due to the great uncertainty overshadowing the transition period of the CEECs combined with the difficulty of forecasting the EU economies' future growth. I shall therefore rather try to present some reasonable predictions on the potential losing and winning industrial sectors in the EU as a whole. A pilot study on one of the EU countries (Italy) has recently been conducted by the author (Graziani, 1995).

The analysis is mainly based on trade and production data at the NACE 3-digit level and runs up to 1992.[1] After 1 January 1993 intra-EU trade data are based on a new system of trade data compilation (Intrastat), which makes data for 1993 and the following years not fully comparable with those of previous years.

CHANGING TRADE PATTERNS BETWEEN CEE AND THE EU

A basic fact which has been stressed often in this volume is that the EU is much more important to the CEECs than the CEECs are to the EU, and this difference has increased considerably since the mid-1980s. In 1992, the EU share of the CEECs' exports ranged between 38 per cent for Romania and 58 per cent for Poland, the other CEECs coming in between with shares close to 50 per cent (Table 9.1). A similar picture emerges on the import side.

Table 9.1 Share of EU in CEECs' total exports and imports, %

	1985	1988	1989	1990	1991	1992
EU share in exports of:						
Bulgaria	17.1	18.1	19.2	29.7	39.3	47.1
Czechoslovakia	22.8	24.2	25.7	32.0	40.6	50.6
Hungary	16.0	22.5	24.7	33.5	39.6	48.7
Poland	22.6	29.4	30.1	38.1	47.3	58.2
Romania	24.1	24.0	25.2	31.4	34.2	37.8
EU share in imports from:						
Bulgaria	33.5	33.8	36.0	42.8	45.0	47.7
Czechoslovakia	22.6	26.5	26.0	31.1	32.1	44.5
Hungary	21.6	25.2	28.5	30.9	41.9	40.7
Poland	19.5	27.9	27.2	59.9	62.8	56.0
Romania	10.2	6.2	5.6	19.6	26.7	35.5

Source: Calculated from IMF DOTS.

Again, there is a profound structural asymmetry in reciprocal importance (Graziani, 1993). Altogether, CEE accounts for 1.89 per cent and 1.57 per cent of EU world exports and imports, respectively, with a marked rise since 1989 (Table 9.2). Growth rates of trade on both sides have been particularly impressive in the last two years under consideration, except for Romanian exports. All in all, however, in 1992 the CEECs' total market share in total EU imports was still six times smaller than that of the less developed countries (LDCs) and more than four times lower than EFTA's.

This pattern also holds true for manufacturing, which is the object of our study and has the largest share in reciprocal trade. As shown in Table 9.3,

Table 9.2 Directions of EU total trade (shares of regions/countries, %)

	1985	1988	1989	1990	1991	1992
EU exports to:						
Intra-EU	52.53	59.56	59.98	60.98	61.63	61.29
Extra-EU	46.91	40.03	39.59	38.58	37.94	38.33
EFTA	10.53	10.64	10.35	10.33	9.76	9.48
Other industrialized	17.47	13.85	13.49	12.96	11.96	11.63
LDCs	15.17	12.53	12.58	12.47	12.78	13.45
CEE	1.17	1.03	1.10	1.11	1.57	1.89
Bulgaria	0.19	0.16	0.14	0.08	0.09	0.10
Czechoslovakia	0.23	0.24	0.23	0.24	0.34	0.55
Hungary	0.29	0.26	0.29	0.27	0.31	0.36
Poland	0.32	0.30	0.38	0.41	0.71	0.72
Romania	0.14	0.07	0.07	0.11	0.12	0.16
EU imports from:						
Intra-EU	50.82	58.11	58.17	58.84	58.61	59.31
Extra-EU	49.01	41.69	41.61	40.93	41.17	40.40
EFTA	9.94	9.73	9.56	9.62	9.23	9.25
Other industrialized	16.85	15.94	15.68	14.88	15.22	14.59
LDCs	17.82	12.54	12.77	12.76	12.53	12.07
CEE	1.30	1.12	1.13	1.15	1.34	1.57
Bulgaria	0.07	0.05	0.05	0.05	0.06	0.07
Czechoslovakia	0.26	0.24	0.24	0.24	0.34	0.46
Hungary	0.23	0.23	0.24	0.26	0.30	0.33
Poland	0.41	0.36	0.36	0.46	0.52	0.59
Romania	0.33	0.24	0.24	0.14	0.12	0.12

Source: Calculated from EU trade files. Totals may not add up to 100.

manufacturing accounts for 84–92 per cent of EU exports and 84–95 per cent of EU imports from CEE. The latter share has experienced a continuous and particularly rapid increase since 1985, when it represented just 53–83 per cent. This is particularly true for Romania, Poland and Bulgaria, which started from a relatively lower level. The growth rates of exports of manufactures in the last two years have been particularly impressive in all CEECs, but they stayed behind the respective import growth rates.

Table 9.3 Share of manufacturing in CEE trade with the EU, %

	1985	1988	1989	1990	1991	1992
CEE exports to the EU						
Bulgaria	61.7	75.8	75.0	75.6	79.7	84.9
Czechoslovakia	82.6	88.2	87.1	89.3	90.6	92.2
Hungary	80.3	84.1	84.3	86.8	86.6	89.2
Poland	60.1	76.0	73.7	76.8	80.1	84.5
Romania	52.6	69.6	64.9	73.2	82.4	95.1
CEE imports from the EU						
Bulgaria	84.0	92.5	89.6	90.8	86.6	87.9
Czechoslovakia	88.3	90.7	89.8	89.8	89.8	89.9
Hungary	90.6	90.2	89.5	91.3	90.0	92.2
Poland	85.0	89.3	83.6	84.6	84.6	85.5
Romania	83.2	91.0	93.2	83.2	82.0	84.0

Source: Calculated from EU trade files.

Given such quantitative importance, any policy affecting manufacturing trade should in principle have an impact on the partners involved. However, if we consider total EU imports of manufactures, none of the individual CEECs represents even 1 per cent of the total: altogether, the five CEECs account for a mere 1.6 per cent, as against 8.4 per cent of the LDCs and 9 per cent of EFTA. EU manufacturing imports from CEE are rather concentrated and the concentration ratio tends to be more or less inversely correlated with the degree of industrialization of different CEECs. The top five NACE 2-digit and the top ten NACE 3-digit industries represent 76 per cent and 74 per cent, respectively, of total manufacturing imports from Romania, 67 per cent and 57 per cent from Bulgaria, 63 per cent and 54 per cent from Poland, 63 per cent and 53 per cent from Hungary and finally 49 per cent and 43 per cent from Czechoslovakia (Table 9.4).

There are three broad (NACE 2-digit) groups of industries which appear among the top five of all CEECs. The first is the footwear and clothing industry (mostly clothing). Its share in EU imports has been increasing recently in all cases, and particularly so from Romania, Bulgaria, Hungary and Poland, where it holds by far the top position (with 33 per cent, 23 per cent, 18 per cent and 17 per cent, respectively). Clothing by itself ranks first among the NACE 3-digit industries in the same four CEECs (Romania 27 per

Table 9.4 *Main components of EU manufacturing imports from CEECs, 1992 (% of total CEECs' manufacturing exports to the EU)*

Bulgaria		Czechoslovakia		Hungary		Poland		Romania	
Five largest NACE 2-digit EU import categories									
Sector	(%)	Sector	(%)	Sector	(%)	Sector	(%)	Sector	(%)
Footwear & clothing	22.63	Production of metals	13.75	Footwear & clothing	17.82	Footwear & clothing	16.96	Footwear & clothing	33.49
Production of metals	15.31	Chemicals	9.62	Food, drink, tobacco	15.54	Production of metals	15.88	Timber, furniture	18.85
Chemicals	11.19	Footwear & clothing	9.47	Electr. engineering	11.12	Timber, furniture	11.55	Production of metals	9.04
Food, drink, tobacco	9.69	Mineral products	7.95	Chemicals	10.76	Food, drink, tobacco	10.45	Textiles	8.35
Textiles	8.57	Mechan. engineering	7.92	Mechan. engineering	7.28	Chemicals	8.48	Chemicals	5.85
Total above	67.38	Total above	48.71	Total above	62.52	Total above	63.32	Total above	75.59
Five largest NACE 3-digit EU import categories									
Ready-made clothing	14.63	Iron and steel ind.	7.03	Ready-made clothing	11.95	Ready-made clothing	14.21	Ready-made clothing	27.54
Non-ferrous metals	8.77	Motor vehicles	6.19	Slaughtering	10.21	Non-ferrous metals	10.94	Wooden furniture	15.98
Other ind. chemicals	5.85	Petrochemicals	5.85	Petrochemicals	8.20	Wooden furniture	5.45	Knitting	7.08
Footwear	5.78	Ready-made clothing	5.81	Footwear	4.74	Proc. fruit & veget.	4.04	Iron and steel ind.	6.19
Knitting	5.45	Glass and glassware	3.44	Knitting	4.01	Petrochemicals	3.75	Footwear	5.12
Total above	40.48	Total above	28.32	Total above	39.11	Total above	38.39	Total above	61.92

Source: Calculated from EU trade files.

cent, Bulgaria 15 per cent, Poland 14 per cent and Hungary 12 per cent). As will be shown later, the practice of 'outward processing traffic' (OPT) is one of the main determinants of this boom.

The other NACE 2-digit category always present among the top five is the production of metals. Its share, however, has been decreasing in all cases. It still ranks first for Czechoslovakia (14 per cent), half of it being iron and steel (7 per cent).

The third important NACE 2-digit industry is chemicals, mainly represented by petrochemicals and other industrial chemicals. Food and beverages ranks second for Hungary (the majority of which is slaughtering and meat preparations) and fourth for Bulgaria and Poland. Textiles are particularly important for Romania and Bulgaria, timber and furniture for Romania and Poland, mechanical engineering for Czechoslovakia and Hungary, and electrical engineering again for Hungary.

A very important feature of such flows is that they still seem to be concentrated on sensitive products (food, chemicals, steel, textiles, clothing and footwear), which represent more than half of Bulgarian and Hungarian exports, more than 40 per cent of Polish and Romanian products and 40 per cent of Czechoslovakia's exports. Altogether, resource-based products or, among the non-resource-based ones, too many capital- and energy-intensive products, prevail in CEECs' export structure, compared with that of their competitors. Skill-intensive sectors are, on average, either marginal or else losing ground. This seems to confirm that the upgrading of the CEECs' export structure with the EU seems to be rather slow (Graziani, 1994).

CEE IMPORT PENETRATION AND EXPORT SPECIALIZATION ON THE EU MARKET

Enhanced competition due to trade liberalization can take place both on the external and on the internal EU market. Only the latter will be considered here, as it is by far the most important for all the competitors under examination. Trade liberalization may provoke both a certain trade stimulation on the EU market, i.e. new export flows from the partners, possibly causing a displacement (and, consequently, contraction) of local production, and trade diversion, i.e. a displacement of other countries' exports to the EU by imports from the now preferred CEE sources. Only the first aspect will be dealt with here in more detail.

An insight into the likely threat to EU industrial sectors and the possible displacement of domestic production can be derived from the index most widely used to indicate the significance of foreign competition: the import

Table 9.5 Import penetration ratios (IPR)[a] of total manufacturing imports into the EU

	1985	1988	1989	1990	1991	1992
Imports from:						
World	32.03	35.49	36.71	36.62	37.83	32.57
Extra-EU	12.89	13.12	13.52	13.17	13.88	11.82
EFTA	3.44	3.43	3.48	3.47	3.43	2.94
Other industrialized	6.02	5.74	5.88	5.60	5.98	4.89
LDCs	2.64	3.06	3.15	3.06	3.19	2.73
CEE	0.39	0.37	0.37	0.40	0.50	0.52

Note: [a] Share of imports in domestic apparent consumption (production + imports – exports).

Source: Own calculations from EU trade files and EUROSTAT estimates on production values.

penetration ratio (IPR), i.e. the share of imports in apparent domestic consumption.[2]

The estimations presented in Table 9.5 clearly show that the share of EU domestic consumption of manufactures accounted for by imports from the world is roughly one-third and shows a generally ascending trend up to 1989, followed by a slight fall in 1990 and a substantial one in 1992.

The second notable feature highlighted by the same table is the rather marginal role of CEE: the IPR from the CEE was only 0.52 per cent, compared with 2.73 per cent from the developing countries, 2.94 per cent from EFTA and 4.89 per cent from the other industrialized countries. However, the IPR from the CEECs has been growing since 1990 at a faster rate than the IPR from other sources and was the only increasing one in 1992. EFTA's IPR has been constantly declining since 1989. At first glance, then, trade liberalization with the CEECs seems to have been one of the factors affecting their competitiveness *vis-à-vis* EFTA more than *vis-à-vis* the developing countries.

A small IPR indicator for manufacturing as a whole may, however, conceal important events taking place at a more disaggregated level. Table 9.6 shows calculations for EU manufacturing IPRs for the five CEECs taken together at the NACE 3-digit level in 1992. Only the 21 categories hypothetically most at risk, with a value greater than 1 per cent, are shown in the table. Due to incompatibility between production and trade data at our disposal, the IPRs for textile yarn and woven fabrics could not be calculated.

Table 9.6 *Import penetration ratios (IPR), indices of intra-industry trade (IIT)*[a] *and export specialization (ESI)*[b] *of CEECs' manufactured products exported to the EU, 1992 (NACE 3-digit categories with IPR > 1%, ranked by IPR)*

		CEE	Bulgaria		Czechoslovakia		Hungary		Poland		Romania	
NACE 3-digit sectors		IPR (%)	IIT	ESI	IIT	ESI	IIT	ESI	IIT	ESI	IIT	ESI
465	Other wood manufactures	4.54	0.11	1.62	0.15	7.36	0.21	3.65	0.08	13.98	0.13	2.82
456	Furs and fur goods	4.21	0.84	1.93	0.97	1.64	0.85	2.57	0.96	1.53	0.63	2.03
453	Ready-made clothing	4.19	0.22	5.25	0.31	2.09	0.31	4.29	0.18	5.10	0.18	9.88
455	Household textiles	3.31	0.07	6.38	0.26	3.27	0.34	2.90	0.46	2.25	0.41	2.09
451	Footwear	3.29	0.70	5.53	0.56	2.36	0.59	4.53	0.53	1.83	0.53	4.90
436	Knitting	2.60	0.65	2.66	0.70	1.19	0.88	1.96	0.89	1.14	0.61	3.45
442	Leather products	2.57	0.28	4.62	0.48	2.16	0.42	2.86	0.61	0.93	0.66	1.15
224	Prod. of non-ferrous metals	2.19	0.18	2.45	0.77	0.86	0.51	0.82	0.16	3.06	0.79	0.29
467	Wooden furniture	1.95	0.45	1.73	0.45	2.80	0.61	2.59	0.25	5.81	0.03	17.04
414	Proc. of fruit and vegetables	1.93	0.18	3.66	0.86	0.35	0.10	3.19	0.23	4.20	0.88	0.56
222	Steel tubes	1.74	0.74	0.96	0.41	4.01	0.76	1.61	0.94	1.70	0.41	3.33
247	Glass and glassware	1.54	0.65	1.48	0.23	4.98	0.55	2.32	0.88	1.99	0.27	3.13
466	Articles of cork, straw, etc.	1.51	0.22	0.39	0.96	0.89	0.96	1.39	0.90	1.50	0.15	7.11
347	Electric lamps and lighting	1.49	0.97	0.54	1.00	0.94	0.40	5.03	0.74	1.68	0.34	1.25
221	Iron and steel industry	1.46	0.24	2.56	0.22	3.45	0.58	1.18	0.55	1.75	0.28	3.04
242	Cement, lime and paper	1.39	0.26	2.22	0.04	19.16	0.21	0.06	0.05	10.91	0.00	16.77
461	Sawing and processing of wood	1.30	0.01	1.41	0.08	2.53	0.14	1.19	0.04	3.62	0.14	0.89
441	Tanning and dressing of leather	1.22	0.65	1.50	0.78	1.46	0.29	1.38	0.91	2.31	0.09	0.34
494	Toys and sport goods	1.22	0.86	0.70	0.75	0.75	0.56	0.49	0.71	0.38	0.77	0.26
223	Cold rolling of steel	1.07	0.85	1.74	0.42	3.45	0.83	0.82	1.00	1.15	0.66	0.47
248	Ceramic goods	1.02	0.78	2.17	0.73	2.38	0.91	1.46	0.77	0.92	0.93	2.11

Notes:

[a] Calculated as $1 - (|x_{ij} - m_{ij}|)/(x_{ij} + m_{ij})$, where x_{ij} and m_{ij} are coutry *i*'s exports and imports of commodity *j*, respectively.

[b] For definition see text.

Source: Own calculations from EU trade files and EUROSTAT estimates on production values.

It is immediately apparent that: no NACE 3-digit 'product' had even reached the threshold of 5 per cent of apparent EU domestic consumption by 1992. The highest IPRs appear to be, in descending order, those for other wood manufactures (4.5 per cent), furs and clothing (4.2 per cent each), household textiles (3.3 per cent), footwear (3.3 per cent), knitting and leather products (2.6 per cent each), non-ferrous metals (2.2 per cent), furniture (2 per cent), processing of fruit and vegetables (1.9 per cent), steel tubes (1.7 per cent), glass and glassware, as well as articles of cork and straw (1.5 per cent each). Leather products, footwear, clothing, household textiles, other wood manufactures and steel tubes had the fastest increasing IPRs over the last three years. Thus, altogether, import penetration from the CEECs was still at very manageable levels in 1992.

This pattern seems to be confirmed by both import shares and growth rates of individual imports. In general, a real threat could only materialize if the quantities involved and the growth rates of CEECs' exports were substantial. If we compare the shares in the EU import structure and the respective growth rates, the products where CEEC competition could be threatening in principle are reduced to a handful.

First and foremost, clothing. As already recalled, this category by itself accounts for almost 28 per cent of Romanian exports on the EU market, for 15 per cent of Bulgarian and Polish exports, 12 per cent of Hungary's and 7 per cent of Czechoslovakia's exports. In the last three years, on average, it has roughly grown by 60 per cent for Bulgaria, more than 40 per cent for Poland and Czechoslovakia, 20 per cent for Hungary, and decreased in the first two years but more than recovered (by 42 per cent) in 1992 for Romania.

Household textiles, semi-finished wood products, carpentry, other wood manufactures and foundries, while never separately representing more than 2 per cent of individual CEECs' exports, have maintained sustained growth rates in most cases and are present in the better performing exports of four or five CEECs.

Finally, there are other products whose share in at least one CEEC's exports is equal to or greater than 3 per cent. These are: processing and preservation of fruit and vegetables (4 per cent in Polish and Bulgarian exports and 3 per cent in the case of Hungary), with a recent negative growth; wooden furniture (16 per cent for Romania, 5 per cent for Poland, 3 per cent for Czechoslovakia, 2 per cent for Hungary and Bulgaria, all showing high and positive growth, except Romania); glass and glassware (3 per cent for Czechoslovakia and between 1 and 2 per cent for each of the other CEECs, with generally positive and high growth rates); footwear (6 per cent for Bulgaria, 5 per cent for Hungary and Romania, 2 per cent for Czechoslovakia and Poland, characterized by high growth rates in 1992); knitting (7 per cent for Romania, 5 per cent for Bulgaria, 4 per cent for Hungary, 2 per cent for

Poland and Czechoslovakia, showing average growth rates above 20 per cent, except for Romania).

Of what quality are the products exported by the CEECs to the EU market? A very rough and imperfect indicator is the import and export unit values. Here conclusions should be drawn very cautiously since: the unit values are taken as a proxy for prices; the latter are assumed to be an indication of relative quality; finally, the level of aggregation is too high. Be that as it may, in many cases EU import unit values in trade with CEE tend to be lower than their export counterparts, suggesting that the CEECs tend to export lower-quality goods than their EU partners, although a certain upgrading seems to be taking place.

The previous findings receive further confirmation by the CEEC specialization pattern on the EU market, as shown by the CEECs' export specialization indices for the EU market relative to world exports to the same market (or normalized relative export performance ratios, see Balassa, 1989), calculated for the same 21 products which show the highest import penetration ratios (Table 9.6).[3] A value higher (lower) than one will denote relative specialization (despecialization) on the EU market compared to the world.

With only one exception (toys and sports goods), the CEECs generally specialize in all goods under consideration. The indices obtained by other wood manufactures, clothing, household textiles, footwear, furniture and cement are particularly impressive.

This confirms some previous findings that the CEECs seem to be specialized on the EU market mostly in the metal processing and manufacturing industries, the wood industry, as well as in leather, footwear and clothing (Graziani, 1993; 1994). These are all products which obtain a greater weight in the CEECs' export structure than in average world exports to the EU market. This is also the area of possible competition among individual CEECs on the EU market.

Summing up, competition and a possible threat to EU industry seem to materialize mostly in very specific traditional sectors, like the wood industry, clothing, footwear, leather, steel tubes and non-ferrous metals. However, the amounts involved still appear to be relatively modest in the majority of cases.

INTRA-INDUSTRY TRADE AND STRUCTURAL ADJUSTMENT

Even admitting that some of these products could exert heavy competitive pressure, let us examine to what extent this would involve painful structural adjustments. To consider such a matter in detail, one would need a thorough analysis of each of the domestic industries involved. This is beyond the scope of the present study, centred as it is mainly on trade issues. However, just considering the latter, the nature of trade flows may have relevant implications for structural adjustment to trade liberalization.

As has often been argued, the degree of intra-industry trade (IIT), as opposed to inter-industry trade, may be seen as an important indication of the costs involved in such trade expansion. Adjustment costs are supposed to be lower in industries characterized by high levels of IIT (and when the major part of new trade is of the IIT type), because it should cost less to transfer resources within industries than to switch them from one industry to another, as would be the case if inter-industry trade prevailed. In other words, resources are seen to be more mobile within industrial sectors than across sectors. If firms primarily compete on the basis of product differentiation – the realm of IIT – trade liberalization is more likely to lead to the rationalization of production within domestic industries, where labour reallocation is relatively less painful (Greenaway and Milner, 1986; Hamilton and Kniest, 1991).

IIT indicators have rapidly grown over the last three years, and especially so in 1991–92, suggesting considerable amounts of two-way trade, including intermediate products and intra-firm transactions. In 1992 the number of products for which the IIT index between the EU and individual CEECs was higher than 0.5 was greater than in EU–LDC trade, with the exception of Romania. Hungary showed the largest number (64) of products exhibiting a value higher than 0.5.

Table 9.6 presents the IIT indices for the same NACE 3-digit industries for which the import penetration ratios were previously shown. Although a more disaggregated level would in principle be more appropriate for measuring intra-industry trade for specific commodities, for the purpose of our study the NACE 3-digit aggregation appears to be a reasonable approximation for 'industry'. The IIT index measures the share of two-way trade in global reciprocal trade for each of the categories involved. It varies between 0 (all inter-industry trade) and 1 (all intra-industry trade).

If we concentrate our attention on the industries where import penetration on the EU market is relatively higher, we notice immediately that clothing, household textiles, various wood products and cement exhibit low values in all the five CEECs, and furniture and leather do so in four of them. These are then the industries that might incur structural adjustment problems, should a very rapid surge of imports materialize.

Some other industries present a low IIT value in three CEECs only (iron and steel, and processing of fruit and vegetables) or in two CEECs (steel tubes, glass and non-ferrous metals), and are therefore no reason for great concern. All the other industries considered show, on the contrary, rather high

IIT values, suggesting lower adjustment costs, through the possibility of switching resources within the sectors involved and specializing in different segments and quality levels.

Summing up, an analysis of the indicators presented above tends to show that on the whole intra-industry trade as a share of total trade is on the increase between the EU and CEE. By sectors, the brunt of adjustment is likely to be borne by those industries where the products of the CEECs compete more directly with EU products and the level of IIT is relatively low and/or stagnant. Cases in point appear to be clothing, household textiles, various wood products, cement, furniture, leather and leather products, plus possibly some steel products. In other sectors liberalization will encourage production to concentrate even more on high-value-added commodities.

It should be recalled, however, that in some of these industries the import surge is specifically tied to EU policies and practice (see Chapter 5). Such is the case, for instance, of the clothing industry. The upsurge of imports and import penetration ratios has in fact to be seen against the growing practice of OPT. This means that EU producers export fabrics to the CEECs and then import the finished clothing product under a special tariff regime. OPT seems to have played a central role in stimulating clothing imports from these countries. At the beginning of the 1990s OPT accounted for almost three-quarters of EU clothing imports from Hungary and Poland, 44 per cent from Czechoslovakia and Romania, and one-third from Bulgaria. Moreover, EU entrepreneurs seem to show a definite tendency to increase this share.

Import penetration of the EU market therefore appears to be more the result of some redeployment strategy applied by EU producers than an independent new threat to displace local production. Clothing being a highly labour-intensive industry, most of its productive phases tend to be relocated where labour costs are far below those of the EU and transport costs far lower than from other distant, albeit cheap-labour regions (Wang and Winters, 1993). This also seems to be the path increasingly taken by the footwear industry. In this respect, growing import penetration by CEE of the EU's clothing and other similar industries should rather be considered as the counterpart of increased exports of intermediate products.

THE LIKELY IMPACT OF TRADE LIBERALIZATION ON EU EXPORTS TO CEE

The likely effects on EU manufacturing industry production and employment deriving from growing import penetration into the domestic market and increased competition on foreign markets should be balanced against the possible benefits of trade liberalization for EU exports to CEE.

Table 9.7 *Main components of EU manufacturing exports to CEECs, 1992 (% of CEECs' total manufacturing imports from the EU)*

Bulgaria		Czechoslovakia		Hungary		Poland		Romania	
Five largest NACE 2-digit EU export categories									
Sector	(%)	Sector	(%)	Sector	(%)	Sector	(%)	Sector	(%)
Mechan. engineering	14.46	Mechan. engineering	25.66	Mechan. engineering	16.59	Mechan. engineering	16.91	Textiles	17.96
Chemicals	12.93	Electr. engineering	14.08	Chemicals	13.60	Chemicals	14.13	Mechan. engineering	16.98
Food, drink, tobacco	10.59	Chemicals	10.54	Textiles	11.74	Textiles	11.62	Food, drink, tobacco	11.51
Textiles	10.29	Motor vehicles, parts	8.68	Electr. engineering	11.22	Electr. engineering	10.56	Other means transp.	9.18
Motor vehicles, parts	9.36	Textiles	5.70	Motor vehicles, parts	9.43	Food, drink, tobacco	9.30	Chemicals	7.90
Total above	57.64	Total above	64.65	Total above	62.58	Total above	62.53	Total above	63.54
Ten largest NACE 3-digit EU export categories									
Aerospace equipment	8.99	Other machinery	7.66	Motor vehicles	7.01	Woven fabrics	7.48	Woven fabrics	12.00
Motor vehicles	7.89	Motor vehicles	6.89	Woven fabrics	6.53	Other machinery	5.92	Aerospace equipment	8.35
Woven fabrics	6.09	Mach. food, chem. ind.	5.35	Other machinery	6.06	Mach. food, chem. ind.	4.45	Other machinery	3.96
Other machinery	5.16	Telecom. equipment	4.47	Petrochemicals	4.15	Motor vehicles	4.38	Telecom. equipment	3.59
Petrochemicals	3.76	Electrical machinery	3.94	Telecom. equipment	3.34	Process. of plastics	3.94	Motor vehicles	3.33
Mach. food, chem. ind.	3.51	Mach. iron & steel ind.	3.84	Knitting	2.98	Telecom. equipment	3.58	Mach. food, chem. ind.	3.33
Industrial chemicals	3.30	Office machinery	3.71	Pharmaceutical prod.	2.92	Petrochemicals	3.05	Mach. f. specific ind.	3.28
Footwear	2.43	Machine tools	2.98	Mach. food, chem. ind.	2.85	Pharmaceutical prod.	2.95	Tobacco products	2.98
Distil. ethyl, spirit	2.34	Petrochemicals	2.95	Industrial chemicals	2.85	Miscellaneous manuf.	2.78	Textile machinery	2.95
Miscellaneous manuf.	2.27	Mach. f. specific ind.	2.66	Process. of plastics	2.83	Soap, deterg., perfum.	2.62	Knitting	2.67
Total above	45.74	Total above	44.45	Total above	41.52	Total above	41.15	Total above	46.43
Memo item: High-tech industries (NACE 32 to 37)	44.20	Memo item: High-tech industries (NACE 32 to 37)	56.00	Memo item: High-tech industries (NACE 32 to 37)	42.20	Memo item: High-tech industries (NACE 32 to 37)	39.10	Memo item: High-tech industries (NACE 32 to 37)	40.90

Source: Calculated from EU trade files.

As already pointed out, the CEECs are not important markets for EU exporters. As a consequence, trade liberalization should not initially have a very strong impact on EU exports. If this is true on the whole, however, the analysis of the different export sectors reveals interesting insights.

Table 9.7 lists the major sectors in the EU manufacturing industry's export structure with each of the five CEECs. Some general features are visible immediately. First, the EU export structure is much less concentrated than its import structure, except for trade with Czechoslovakia, where its degree of concentration is considerably higher in the export flows. The share of the first ten NACE 3-digit export products varies between 41 per cent in Poland and 46 per cent in Romania.

Second, as expected, high-tech industries are much more important in the EU export structure than in its import structure. The share of the NACE 32–37 groups is well over one-half of exports to Czechoslovakia and between 39 per cent and 44 per cent of exports to the other four countries.

At the NACE 2-digit level, mechanical engineering represents the largest exporting category in the case of four out of the five countries (although it has been slightly decreasing since 1990), varying from a low of 14 per cent in Bulgaria to a peak of 26 per cent in Czechoslovakia. As is also the case with EU trade *vis-à-vis* the world, this sector shows the highest trade surplus for the EU, but growing only with Czechoslovakia and Romania. Machinery for the food and chemical industries and other machinery always figure among the first ten NACE 3-digit industries. Machinery for special industries, textile machinery, machine tools and machinery for mines and iron and steel industry follow suit.

Electrical engineering is also present in three cases among the top five NACE 2-digit sectors. Although its share is lower than the one pertaining to mechanical engineering (it ranges between 11 per cent and 14 per cent), its surplus tends mostly to grow very rapidly. Different NACE 3-digit products prevail here in the structure, such as telecom equipment, electrical apparatus, radio and TV receivers. They never figure however among the top three sectors. The motor vehicles category is always present among the top ten NACE 3-digit exports, from 3 per cent to 8 per cent of the total in different countries. Other means of transport (mainly aerospace equipment) and office and data-processing machinery are sometimes present too among the top export sectors.

The nature of trade is however not the same in all cases. For instance, more than half of the Italian exports to Poland in this category are represented by parts of motor vehicles, with a growing surplus, while the rest is mostly motor vehicles, with a growing deficit, which more than offsets the first. This is an indirect sign of a great deal of intra-firm trade going on with this country, as also confirmed by the presence of FIAT local production. Similar features should be detected in German trade with the Czech Republic, due to Volkswagen involvement in Skoda production. On the contrary, most of the Italian exports to Czechoslovakia and Bulgaria in this sector are represented by motor vehicles (Graziani, 1995).

Chemicals always rank among the first five NACE 2-digit categories too. It is relatively important in the cases of Poland and Hungary (14 per cent), while never representing less than 8 per cent in the other countries. The balances of the various chemical products reveal interesting features. Almost invariably, the EU runs a deficit in petrochemicals and other industrial chemicals, while it obtains a surplus in more value-added and refined products, like paints, pharmaceutical products, soap and detergents, and the like.

The last sector which is always among the top five is textiles. As a mostly growing EU export category, it represents 18 per cent of total manufacturing exports to Romania, 12 per cent to Hungary and Poland, 10 per cent to Bulgaria and 6 per cent to Czechoslovakia. The EU runs a growing surplus in this category. Woven fabrics, yarns and knitting represent the bulk of EU exports. Woven fabrics are the top NACE 3-digit product in Polish and Romanian imports from the EU, and the second- and third-ranking in Hungarian and Bulgarian imports, respectively.

The reason for the importance of EU textile exports and their surplus can only be understood in conjunction with the situation in the clothing industry. Here EU trade with CEE shows considerable deficits. Apart from intra-industry trade going on among different types of the same products, much inter-industry trade is materializing between the textile and clothing sectors, mostly in the form of OPT. A large quantity of EU imports of clothing could be thus due to a contract relocation of production to the CEECs, where labour costs tend to be far lower than in the EU. This has implications for EU textile exports as well, in so far as their outlets are positively correlated with production in CEE destined for re-export. In such a situation, growing import penetration ratios in the clothing industry would represent the pay-off for the increased exports of textiles.

THE EXPORT ORIENTATION OF THE EU MANUFACTURING SECTOR

Any sizeable beneficial impact on the EU industry deriving from trade liberalization with CEE depends upon the particular export propensity of EU industrial sectors towards the CEECs. Table 9.8 presents various ways to derive it from recent past trends of 25 products present among the top fifteen EU products at the NACE 3-digit level exported to each of the five CEECs. Next to the more common export growth rates and trade balances, I calculated the ratio between exports, both to extra-EU countries and to the five CEECs, and domestic production (export propensity index). Finally, I divided the two export propensity ratios, one for exports towards the CEECs, the other for exports towards the world as a whole, to derive the relative export propensity index.

Almost all of the 25 products performed very well in the period 1989–92. Only two of them showed an absolute decline – petrochemicals and other industrial chemicals, where surplus turned into deficit, and textile machinery, where the surplus diminished. Broadly speaking, there are three large groups of products which have performed very well in the recent period.

First, there is the group of high-tech industries. The most rapid export growth was reached by aerospace equipment, which increased sixteen-fold, followed by motor vehicles (almost eight-fold), office machinery, telecom equipment, electrical machinery, wires and cables, and radio and TV receivers. All these products more than doubled their exports. Sizeable export performance was also achieved in categories such as machinery for mines, food, the chemical industry and other machinery.

It will be noted that machine tools form a relatively stagnant category. It is quite apparent that this is the one higher-tech group of products where the CEECs' production is relatively closer to international standards and more able to satisfy local demand. The only high-tech sector recording an export decline was textile machinery. For all but two of these sectors the EU trade surplus in the high-tech industries increased rapidly; machine tools and textile machinery experienced a reduction of their trade surplus.

How did the export propensity to the CEECs vary for this first group of products? As can be seen from Table 9.8, the absolute indices in 1992 are still rather low. Exports to the CEECs represent between 0.5 per cent and 3 per cent of EU domestic production. What is more interesting, however, is that in all cases but one (textile machinery) there was an increase in both the absolute and the relative export propensity index. The latter trend materialized even in the light of declining domestic EU production, as in the case of machinery for specific industries and radio and TV receivers. In the other cases, a greater relative export orientation to the CEECs has gone hand in hand with growing production levels.

Machinery for the food and chemical industry reached the first rank in its relative export propensity to the CEEC by 1992: 9 per cent of the propensity to export to extra-EU which, however, has decreased slightly over the period. Then came machine tools, machinery for specific industries and telecom equipment, and the other industries are following suit. On the other hand, motor vehicles, office machinery, telecom equipment and electrical machinery, in this order, gained most in their relative export propensity index.

Table 9.8 *Growth rates, trade balances and propensity to export of the most important NACE 3-digit products exported from the EU to the CEECs*[a] *(values in % unless otherwise indicated)*

		Growth rate of EU exports	EU trade balance (mn US $)		Export propensity index to extra-EU[b]		Export propensity index to the CEECs[b]		Relative export propensity ind. to the CEECs[c]	
NACE 3-digit sectors		1992/1989	1992	1989	1992	1989	1992	1989	1992	1989
252+253	Petrochem. & ind. chemicals	–19.9	–607.7	106.4	18.37	17.45	0.68	0.78	3.69	4.47
255+256	Paints & other chemicals	26.8	570.0	474.0	17.09	17.40	1.11	0.97	6.52	5.56
257	Pharmaceutical products	138.5	387.2	157.0	15.06	13.92	0.61	0.33	4.06	2.36
258	Soap, detergents, perfume	456.4	292.1	49.5	10.85	10.02	0.78	0.17	7.23	1.70
316	Tools, finished metal goods	217.8	100.6	–4.5	10.49	11.82	0.57	0.22	5.45	1.85
322	Machine tools	5.6	179.3	253.1	27.73	27.77	1.70	1.45	6.15	5.21
323	Textile machinery	–14.6	211.1	274.5	62.00	53.44	2.96	3.13	4.77	5.86
324	Mach. for food, chemical ind.	72.2	750.9	450.5	28.79	30.40	2.63	1.80	9.12	5.91
325	Mach. f. mines, iron & steel ind.	83.5	305.2	186.7	22.23	22.72	1.13	0.69	5.10	3.05
327	Other mach., mach. f. specif. ind.	47.4	314.1	216.4	40.90	36.90	2.38	1.49	5.81	4.03
328	Other machinery	66.0	949.3	626.3	34.71	32.66	1.56	1.02	4.50	3.13
330	Office machinery & data	182.8	482.0	167.1	20.18	20.67	1.01	0.39	5.03	1.90
341–343	Wires, cables, electr. machinery	124.1	440.2	196.8	19.29	18.23	0.92	0.44	4.75	2.43
344	Telecommunications equipment	138.3	667.1	276.5	15.87	15.14	0.84	0.40	5.27	2.67
345	Radio and TV receivers	138.6	289.5	101.0	24.88	19.31	1.03	0.40	4.13	2.08
351	Motor vehicles	381.6	820.7	–4.1	11.41	13.73	0.48	0.12	4.25	0.85
364	Aerospace equipment	803.5	279.3	29.5	37.42	29.99	0.63	0.08	1.69	0.26
429	Tobacco products	642.0	124.4	16.7	3.55	2.29	0.31	0.05	8.74	2.27
436	Knitting	147.6	–60.3	–80.8	21.90	22.09	1.73	0.76	7.89	3.44
441	Tanning and dress. of leather	117.1	149.8	81.5	23.95	23.41	3.11	1.24	13.00	5.29

451	Footwear	212.8	–171.0	–121.4	26.68	25.92	1.33	0.44	5.00	1.70
453	Ready-made clothing	212.9	–1252.6	–750.5	14.20	14.56	0.56	0.20	3.93	1.38
483	Processing of plastics	194.1	436.5	126.0	8.92	9.80	0.67	0.28	7.51	2.85
Memo:										
431	Yarns[d]	45.1	102.7	68.3	–	–	–	–	–	–
432	Woven fabrics[d]	143.3	986.5	333.3	–	–	–	–	–	–

Notes:

[a] Products which appear among the top fifteen export categories in EU exports to each of the CEECs; in three cases reaggregation of 3-digit products has been performed because of lack of corresponding production data.

[b] Calculated as the ratio between exports and domestic production.

[c] Calculated as the index towards the CEECs divided by the index towards the extra-EU.

[d] Production data for these two sectors are not available.

Source: Calculated from EU trade files and EUROSTAT estimates on production values.

The second large well-performing group of exports is represented by various high-value-added chemical products, textiles, tanning and dressing of leather and plastics. The first and the last of these subgroups are generally characterized by high export growth rates and growing surpluses and export propensity indices, although the absolute values of the latter are still minimal. Of special interest are finally the two remaining subgroups. Textiles (woven fabrics, yarns, knitting) and leather more than doubled their exports, increasing their surplus at the same time, except knitting which decreased its deficit. Although it was not possible to calculate the propensity ratios for fabrics and yarns (due to lack of compatible production data), a reasonable guess would be for them to be at roughly the same level as those of knitting and leather, which are among the best of the well-performing sectors.

This particular orientation towards the CEECs mostly confirms previous findings about the clothing and the footwear industries, for which these items represent some kind of intermediate products. Increasing EU exports in these sectors are deeply tied to the relocation and OPT to CEE going on in the two industries mentioned above.

The third and last well-performing group of exports is represented by two different types of products: tobacco products, with a growing surplus, and footwear and clothing, with a rapidly mounting deficit. The growing absolute and relative values of the propensity indices for the two latter products show that there is still room for increasing EU exports in some of the sensitive industries, by specializing in different, mostly up-market segments of production.

All in all, if we put together the data on the EU export structure and growth rates, the trade balances and trade propensity ratios, the products which stand to gain in a relatively substantial way from more liberal trade mostly belong to mechanical engineering (machinery for food, chemical, mining, as well as steel and iron industries, plus other machinery); office machinery; electrical engineering (wires and cables, telecom equipment, radio and TV receivers); motor vehicles; aerospace equipment; plastics; textiles; tanning and dressing of leather; and finally two of the sectors most at risk because of the CEECs' competition: footwear and clothing.

CONCLUSIONS AND PERSPECTIVES

The analysis reported in this chapter has tried to show that the likely negative impact of trade liberalization with CEE on some EU industrial sectors is far less important than is sometimes indicated. In particular, it might be tempered by the following factors.

First, restructuring in some of the EU sectors involved has already been a practice over the past few years. In this respect, among the sectors more at risk, clothing and, less so, footwear seem to be further ahead in the process of restructuring. The main strategy followed appears to be redeployment abroad, along with quality upgrading and, whenever possible, technical innovation. As for clothing, redeployment without investment under the OPT scheme is very likely to increase, due to the lifting of duties on reimported value-added as from 1994.[4]

Data up to 1992 do not fully capture a recent acceleration of redeployment taking place in some of these industrial sectors. However, as noted, large segments of the productive phases in footwear and clothing are more and more rapidly being relocated in low-labour-cost countries, including CEE. Since this will generate much greater flows of imports than exports in the short term, IIT indices might soon start to fall both in industries where they are relatively high (footwear) and in sectors where they are lower. Moreover, the increasing use of contractual arrangements, like franchising operations, in the case of commodities with a strong brand identity, may also limit the extent of intra-industry (here intra-firm) trade.

In the car industry, some of the large investments in Poland and Czechoslovakia are bound to enhance intra-firm trade (for instance, EU motors against CEEC cars) showing up as intra-industry trade, but the production of all components may in the not too distant future be located closer to the assembly lines in the CEECs.

It should be stressed, however, that the fast redeployment occurring in these sectors is not so much a result of trade liberalization with CEE, but a consequence of international competition and structural transformation of the industries involved.

Second, in some sensitive sectors the actual process of trade liberalization with the CEECs could be much slower than is officially forecasted (Rollo and Smith, 1993, Wenyon, 1993). There is some evidence already that the escape clause included in the EAs may well be used to obtain new import quotas or anti-dumping proceedings, as the cases cited at the beginning of the chapter show; it is not unthinkable that similar 'grey measures' will be adopted in other sectors, like footwear (Winters and Wang, 1992).

Third, the impact on trade balances and employment may not be so drastic due to the fact that many Asian products are still much cheaper and of higher quality than those in CEE. Moreover, a peak might already have been reached in the rate of growth of CEE exports during the first two years of the 1990s under the desperate necessity to reorient part of their exports previously destined for the CMEA countries. This might also explain one of the factors behind the slump in the CEECs' exports in 1993.

Fourth, threats and opportunities for individual EU countries may be rather different. Although a comparison among EU members is beyond the scope of this study, let us just recall the example of Italy, where some of the most penetrated industries also showed a relatively high and often growing IIT index with at least three of the CEECs. Such is the case, for instance, with footwear, knitting, clothing, and leather products (Graziani, 1995). Evidence from Italian production and exports all over the world seems to suggest that Italian firms tend to specialize in upper-stage niches in some of these industries, while increasing imports of lower-quality or lower-value-added products. Besides footwear, the textile and clothing sector seems to be a case in point (Graziani, 1991). A comparison between Italian export and import unit values with the CEECs, taken again as imperfect proxies of quality levels, appears to confirm these remarks.

Fifth, trade diversion might occur at the expense of other competitors. To the extent that the CEECs' products replace those of other competitors outside the EU, like the developing countries, in the imports of particular commodities, the problem of adjustment of EU industry arising from trade liberalization with the CEECs may not materialize. It is for instance likely that the competitive advantage of the Mediterranean countries will be eroded by new preferences for the CEECs. But the size of this type of trade diversion can only be gauged *ex post*.

Finally, any likely negative impact should be balanced against a possible expansion of EU exports, both in the same and in other sectors. EU export growth of clothing and footwear seems to be evidence of the possibility of EU industries finding new niches or enlarging the existing ones, by switching exports to higher-quality types of the goods that are increasingly imported. The reasonably good performance in the export of mechanical and electrical engineering, as well as in other higher-tech industries, shows where the best perspectives for EU producers lie, given also the necessity for CEE to import these kinds of goods. While the prospective gains in the first two sectors should be viewed against their possible losses due to increased import penetration, the rest of the gains would accrue to industrial sectors other than those likely to be hit, calling for a general policy of welfare redistribution at the EU level.

Summing up, the analysis of IPRs and the preceding remarks tend to show that there is still considerable scope for an expansion of most imports of manufactured goods from the CEECs. However they appear to put pressure on EU industry not just by themselves, but combined with the concurrent increasing competitive challenge by the developing countries in the same range of products.

All in all one could safely say that the real threat to EU production and employment would come more from the disappearance of international protection in some sectors (i.e. from the elimination of the Multi Fibre Agreement – MFA – for the textile and clothing industries over a period of ten years, as foreseen by the recent Uruguay Round) than from the expansion of the CEECs' exports. Although admittedly the timespan is too short, this would suggest that it is inappropriate to think that the EAs will necessarily lead to much greater structural adjustments than has been the case because of trade liberalization agreements with developing countries or agreements concerning the Single Market. Lastly, internal causes may also be at the root of the structural problems of some EU import-competing industries.

Policy responses by the EU should start from the recognition that the actual threat to EU industry seems to be much lower than is usually thought and limited to very specific sectors. For most of the sectors concerned, competitive pressure by the CEECs is only a supplementary factor to a challenge already taking place on the world market.

At the same time, any new non-tariff barriers in EU trade with CEE would inevitably restrict the CEECs' export access and consequently diminish the chances of economic transition in these countries, which are extremely dependent on export revenues. In addition, there could also be a serious negative impact on future EU export expansion towards those markets. If at all, the additional competitive pressure exerted by the CEECs' exports on EU industries, building up gradually, can only help to develop an industrial policy centred on promoting new, more dynamic sectors, phasing out non-competitive EU production lines and actively retraining the labour force expelled from them.

NOTES

1. For a definition of the NACE categories see the Annex.
2. Domestic absorption equals the sum of domestic production plus the balance of imports and exports.
3. For a definition of the export specialization index (ESI), see Chapter 5. Note, however, that in my case I have calculated the CEECs' specialization indices for the EU market relative to total EU imports (and not only relative to EU imports from 'extra-EU', as is done in Chapter 5).
4. See also Cline (1987).

REFERENCES

Balassa, B. (1989), *Comparative Advantage, Trade Policy and Economic Development*, London: Harvester Wheatsheaf.

Cline, W. (1987), 'The future of world trade in textile and apparel', Washington, DC: Institute of International Economics.

Graziani, G. (1991), 'Il mercato mondiale del tessile-abbigliamento e la competitività dei prodotti italiani', Università di Brescia, mimeo.

Graziani, G. (1993), 'Specialization for Eastern Europe and access to EC markets', in Brabant, J.M. van (ed.), *The New Eastern Europe and the World Economy*, Boulder, Col.: Westview Press.

Graziani, G. (1994), 'Trade patterns and comparative advantages of Central Eastern Europe with EC countries', in Gacs, J. and Winckler, G. (eds), *International Trade and Restructuring in Eastern Europe*, Heidelberg/Wien: Physica-Verlag.

Graziani, G. (1995), 'Italy's manufacturing trade with Eastern Europe. Specialization patterns and possible impact of liberalization on Italian industry', in 'Economic interpenetration between the EU and Central and Eastern Europe', *European Economy*, Brussels: European Commission, Directorate-General for Economic and Financial Affairs (forthcoming).

Greenaway, D. and Milner, C. (1986), *The Economics of Intra-Industry Trade*, London: Basil Blackwell.

Hamilton, C. and Kniest, P. (1991), 'Trade liberalisation, structural adjustment and intra-industry trade: a note', *Weltwirtschaftliches Archiv*, **127** (2).

Rollo, J. and Smith, A. (1993), 'The political economy of Eastern European trade with the European Community: why so sensitive?', Economic Policy, **16**.

Schumacher, D. and Möbius, U. (1993), 'Community trade barriers and East European countries. Impact of the Europe Agreements: supplementary and updated results', paper presented at the IV Workshop on Economic Interpenetration Between the EC and Eastern Europe, Brussels, 13–14 December 1993.

Wang, Z.K. and Winters, L.A. (1993), 'Liberalising EC imports of clothing from Eastern Europe', University of Birmingham, mimeo.

Wenyon, S. (1993), 'The Association Agreements. Additional trade access granted and impact on future export growth. The Polish case', London: Department of Trade and Industry, mimeo.

Winters, L.A. and Wang, Z.K. (1992), 'Liberalising EC imports of footwear from Eastern Europe', University of Birmingham, mimeo.

Discussion of Chapter 9

Françoise Lemoine

Chapter 9 provides an in-depth analysis of the recent trends and most probable prospects of trade between the EU and the CEECs. It brings interesting insights into the general adaptation process of EU industries to international competition.

The general conclusion of the chapter is that increased imports from CEE would have a relatively mild impact on EU industry. This plays down the threat of competition from the CEECs to EU industries in the context of trade liberalization. This conclusion is grounded on well-documented facts and two sets of reasons support the assertion that competition from the CEECs should have a marginal impact.

First, trade flows with the CEECs represent relatively small amounts in the overall trade of the EU, and CEE exports account for a tiny share of EU domestic consumption. As these exports are highly concentrated on a limited number of products, the real threat to EU producers concerns a handful of well-identified sectors.

Second, the detailed analysis of the trade flows support the conclusion that EU industries have already begun to adapt to international competition, whether from CEECs or from third countries, and that their adjustment is well under way.

The chapter draws evidence of this adaptation from several indicators: the level of intra-industry trade which has increased, and is especially high in a number of the sectors where the penetration of CEE products in the EU markets is large. In these industries, the EU producers tend to specialize in upper-range goods and CEE producers in lower value-added products. For example, the relocation of segments of production into CEE in the footwear and clothing industries has been going on at an accelerating pace since 1990, and this explains to a large extent the high import penetration ratio of CEE products in EU markets in these sectors. Export and import flows are thus closely connected through outward processing traffic (OPT). The chapter convincingly argues that the adjustment costs are to be felt mostly in the few sectors that have not yet begun to adapt to worldwide competition but could not expect to avoid it in the long run.

These findings are in line with the conclusions of other studies that also underline the moderate impact that trade liberalization with the CEECs would have on EU economies (see, for example, Rollo and Smith, 1993). This and other studies, carried out with different methods, stressed that, even in the so-called sensitive industrial sectors, an increased flow of goods from CEE would have a marginally detrimental effect on West European producers.

The recent trends in CEE exports to the EU seem, to a certain extent, to confirm that the fears of a possible disruption of the European markets by eastern European exporters are not appropriate. In 1993, their exports to the EU slowed down markedly. Partial data for the first eight months of 1993 (Eurostat-COMEXT) indicate that their exports to the EU lost ground in several sectors: agricultural products, food, non-ferrous metallurgy, iron and steel products. In these sectors, the CEE performance undoubtedly suffered from the protective measures taken by the EU.

The chapter foresees that these restrictive measures could proliferate in the future, but in this case it turns clearly to a scenario of non-liberalized trade. It should be emphasized that the partial results for 1993 also indicate that the CEECs as a whole achieved relatively good performances in traditional labour-intensive industries, such as clothing and furniture, as well as in more skills-intensive sectors, such as transport equipment and electrical engineering.

The 1993 results seem to confirm an increasing differentiation in the commodity composition of exports between the transforming countries of Central Europe (the Visegrad-4) and those of South-Eastern Europe (Bulgaria, Romania). To a large extent, the CEE export drive to the West since 1989 had relied on the same industries and so their mutual competition in the same labour-intensive sectors was bound to affect their export performances. Nevertheless, some differentiation also emerged: now the Visegrad-4 have a relatively important share of their exports (between one-fifth and one-fourth) made up by the products of engineering industries, whereas, for example, Romania relies mainly on the competitiveness of its labour-intensive industries, such as clothing and footwear. The upgrading of the commodity exports of the Visegrad-4 has been boosted by foreign direct investments.

The differentiation in national export specialization should improve the export prospects of the CEECs as a whole. It should also alter the competitive pressure felt by the EU countries. For instance, how to assess the medium- and long-run impact of the development of automobile production in CEE. The differentiation between the Central and the Southern parts of Eastern Europe may also confront the different countries of the EU with different competitive pressures, depending on the relative intensity of their bilateral trade flows with CEE.

The chapter mentions a crucial question, however, without elaborating on it. It foresees that CEE exports may progress on the EU markets at the expense of other foreign competitors, so that trade liberalization with the CEECs would entail no additional costs for EU industries. It seems doubtful that this could occur at the expense of the industrializing countries in Asia (the second generation of newly industrializing countries such as China and Thailand) which have proved their competitiveness and their capacity to take advantage of the liberalization of international trade and capital flows. They have increased their market shares considerably in Europe in the last ten years. The CEECs would be able to compete only if they benefit from substantial capital inflows and foreign direct investment.

The chapter mentions the Mediterranean countries as the most probable losers in the competition from the CEECs on the EU markets. This is certainly what the developing countries from North Africa and from the Middle East (Turkey and Egypt) fear most. Until 1992 these fears did not materialize and these countries managed to increase their share in the industrial imports of the EU. But their textile industries, for instance, display a similar productive integration with European firms as do those of the CEECs, and they would be vulnerable to decisions of West European producers to relocate in Eastern Europe. A pervasive competition between these areas for European markets and investments would raise problems if it were to result in displacing Mediterranean producers and exporters, in the context of a zero-sum game.

Another important point is the impact on domestic employment of trade liberalization. As Graziani states, the gains and losses will occur in different sectors. The relocation of industries and the direct investment by EU firms in CEE will increase the need for inter-sectoral and intra-sectoral adjustments in employment. Moreover the increase in trade with CEE may have a more detrimental impact on employment in the EU than on the level of production.

In developed countries, the labour content of exports to less-developed countries is generally lower than the labour content of the parts of domestic production that disappear under the pressure of competitors with low labour costs. Even if the EU achieved a trade surplus with the CEECs, as with developing countries, the net impact on jobs could turn out to be negative.

A related and also controversial point is that the unemployment which results from such competition tends to be concentrated in the unskilled labour force and this adds to the difficulties of labour adjustment policies. The discussion on this point is beyond the scope of the chapter but I think it should be mentioned when analysing the impact of trade liberalization with CEE as a part of the general process of world trade liberalization. I think this should help to assess the needs for adjustment in EU industries and, consequently (I agree with this conclusion of the chapter), the EU has to adapt to international competition to which the CEECs only bring an additional pressure.

REFERENCES

Rollo, J. and Smith, A. (1993), 'The political economy of Eastern European trade with the European Community: why so sensitive?', *Economic Policy*, **16**, April, 139–81.

Marek Belka

It is a pleasure to discuss the excellent chapter written by Giovanni Graziani. At the same time, it is difficult to discuss something with which one is in broad agreement.

The author tries to analyse the grounds behind the fears in the EU that the growing import penetration from the CEECs might displace domestic production and employment, especially in the most sensitive sectors, and demonstrates that these fears are greatly exaggerated, at least at present. As far as the near future is concerned, these fears may be even less substantiated, as a further rapid growth of CEECs' exports to the EU does not, in my opinion, seem very likely. The spectacular growth which was observed in 1989–92, may well be a one-time phenomenon driven by a combination of factors which will not be replicated in the future.

First, the introduction of the radical economic reform policies eliminated shortage – the eminent feature of the centrally planned economies. This resulted in firms beginning to search for outlets, also in the West. Contrary to some casual observations, exports to the convertible currency markets under socialism were supply-constrained, with governments trying to install intricate incentives to stimulate SOE's interest in selling to the demanding Western markets.

Second, stabilization policies initiated in some of the CEECs in the early 1990s brought about a significant contraction of domestic demand. With the collapse of the formerly state-owned wholesale trade and increasing import competition, domestic markets proved in many cases to be equally, or even more, difficult than foreign markets. A large upfront currency devaluation, which was an element of the new economic policy, facilitated the export expansion to the West.

Third, the disintegration of the CMEA and the total collapse of the Soviet market forced a one-time geographical reorientation of trade.

Fourth, CEE exports were stimulated in 1990 by the still cheap energy imports from the USSR, a factor which is gradually fading with the process of phasing out of subsidies to domestic prices of energy and fuels in CEECs.

In summing up, the surprising dynamics of CEECs' exports to the West in the early 1990s is the outcome of a unique concurrence of circumstances which, most probably, will never occur again. It is true that the export potential of these countries is still not fully utilized but the future growth of exports entails a further restructuring and adjustment of their economies and it will take place much more gradually.

The real problem in EU–CEECs relations is not that the latter will flood the Western markets but rather the opposite, that they may remain marginalized in the intra-European trade. I have the impression that Giovanni Graziani is sympathetic to that concern and tries to soothe the fears of some West Europeans by his quantitative measures of the impact of the Eastern trade 'expansion'.

PART THREE

Opening up of Eastern Markets

10. Financial reforms and economic integration

István P. Székely

INTRODUCTION

Two or more national economies are fully integrated when the impact of country borders on the decision-making processes of economic agents is insignificant. For the country borders to be insignificant in this regard means that the flow of goods and capital and the movement of labour across national borders is not hindered by institutional imperfections and regulations (such as, for example, customs duties or quotas, legal provisions, restrictions on forex transactions), unbridgeable gaps in business culture (managerial culture, industrial relations, business ethics), market imperfections other than those due to institutional or regulatory factors (market concentration leading to local monopolies, information asymmetries and so on) and significant differences in risk components that are related to national policies. That is, countries are economically integrated when their markets are integrated, their institutional and regulatory frameworks are harmonized, their economic policies are coordinated, and their business cultures and their levels of economic development are sufficiently similar.

Integration among national economies presumes economic integration within national borders. This is especially important for the CEECs. CEE economies, in particular their financial systems, were highly segmented. The essence of central planning was market segmentation: segmentation of goods, labour and capital markets, segmentation of markets for different products (including financial products) and segmentation of regional markets. That is, the starting positions of the CEECs, even those of the leading reforming countries such as Hungary and Poland, were very unfavourable as far as economic integration within and across national borders was concerned. Furthermore, financial markets were probably the most segmented of all markets. Wholesale financial markets and a wide range of financial products playing a vital role for the internal integration of financial markets in developed economies were simply non-existent in CEE economies. The degree of market concentration and market distortion was the highest in financial markets, again even in leading reforming countries.

While from certain aspects the CMEA was a fairly tightly integrated institution, as far as the vital elements of economic integration pointed out above (the integration of markets, similarity of institutional and regulatory frameworks and policy coordinations) are concerned, member countries were hardly integrated at all. That is why CMEA collapsed immediately after abolishing central planning, introducing the basic elements of a market economy and opening up of goods markets.

Thus one of the goals of economic transformation is to achieve the sufficient level of economic integration *within* the national borders of the CEECs and to create an institutional and regulatory framework as well as a business culture that are sufficiently similar to the European ones. The integration of CEE economies into the European economy, and through this into the world economy, will take place through the integration of their markets, the harmonization of their institutional and legal structures and the coordination of their economic policies.

In this chapter, I shall concentrate on the integration of financial systems. If we accept the fact that money and capital markets play a vital role in the efficient functioning of a modern market economy, we also have to accept the fact that integrating CEE financial markets into the European and the world financial markets is a vital component of the process of economic integration of CEE economies.

THE ROLE OF THE FINANCIAL SECTOR IN ECONOMIC TRANSFORMATION AND INTEGRATION

Due to the very nature of central planning, the financial system was perhaps the point where market-based economies differed most from centrally planned economies. Strictly speaking, the financial services industry in the Western sense simply did not exist in centrally planned economies.[1] The whole financial sector was very rudimentary, and almost perfectly monopolized. The system, widely termed in the literature as a *monobank* system, technically consisted of several banks, but at product level and locally, competition was virtually eliminated. This was true even for Hungary and Poland, where other elements of central planning underwent some important reforms, attaching more weight to market forces in resource allocation (Tardos, 1987; Wyczański, 1993). Moreover, the tight and direct central control over financial institutions was kept intact, again even in countries where control over other enterprises was largely relaxed and made indirect.

The first country to launch reform measures in this area was Hungary, first introducing bond finance for state-owned enterprises (SOEs) in 1984. Later, in 1987, a major reform of the banking system was carried out leading to the establishing of a Western-type two-tier banking system and a relatively liberal licensing policy for new entrants (Bácskai, 1989). The next country to follow the Hungarian example was Poland which established a similar two-tier banking system in 1989[2] (Wyczański, 1993). That is, even in these countries reforms touched the financial system only in the very last phase of central planning. Moreover, even in this phase the financial system, unlike other industries, remained almost completely protected from foreign competition of any sort and financial liberalization was unheard of in the CEECs until 1990.

Therefore – though this kind of institution building was indeed very important and countries introducing reforms in this regard earlier than others did enjoy an advantage – in terms of increased competition and (allocative and operational) efficiency these reform steps achieved very limited results (Székely, 1990; Várhegyi, 1993). In other countries, reforms in the financial systems started after the collapse of the previous socioeconomic and political system and were implemented simultaneously with other reform measures (Kemme and Rudka, 1992).

This means that in all aspects of reform the CEECs had the longest way to go and the most drastic measures to implement in the financial system. On the other hand, many characteristics of economic transition imposed very high demands on the financial system, in particular on merchant banking.

First, as a result of liberalization and opening up of these economies, in each CEEC there was an explosive increase in the number of enterprises. This generated an enormous demand for new corporate accounts and payment services. On the other hand, the importance to enterprises of timely payment increased substantially. Due to the liberalization of foreign trade transactions and the consequent process of integration of product markets, a fast growing proportion of the rapidly increasing number of enterprises started to engage in foreign trade, generating an even faster increase in the demand for foreign payment services, forex transactions and related derivative instruments (such as currency options).

The newly created state-owned commercial banks (SOCBs) that were carved out of the commercial section of the previous central monobank were neither technically equipped to meet this increased demand nor had they the necessary know-how and experience in any of the areas mentioned above. Foreign-owned and joint venture banks, though playing a very important role in providing foreign payment services and in introducing innovative financial instruments, had very limited capacity and perhaps even willingness to enter these markets on any large scale, at least in the first phase of economic transformation.

Compared to their starting positions, the financial systems of the CEECs underwent major changes and achieved significant progress towards Western-type financial systems (Bonin and Székely, 1994; Kemme, 1994; Daianu, 1994). A two-tier banking system and the core of the necessary banking regulations were established in each CEE transition economy. The number of banks increased substantially and foreign participation in the banking industry became significant. This led to a decrease in market concentration and a subsequent increase in competitiveness, though the extent to which it took place varied significantly across CEECs, being the largest in Hungary, Poland, and the Czech Republic (Ábel and Székely, 1994; Hrnčíř, 1994; Kokoszczyński, 1994).

Nonetheless – partly because of the explosive increase in demand and partly because of domestic factors hindering faster development – this progress turned out to be less than adequate. Regarding the factors hindering faster development, first one should mention the bad corporate loans in the portfolios of commercial banks. Bad loans not only increased the costs of bank loans substantially but also seriously hindered the privatization of SOCBs and their ability to cater for the newly emerging and fast growing private enterprises.

Many analysts (e.g. Wijnbergen, 1994) regard commercial banks as the best candidates to be the agents of change, that is, the type of institution that could foster a relatively fast restructuring of non-bank SOEs by imposing the much needed tight corporate governance on them. If, however, banks themselves are lacking proper corporate governance, remain state-owned, and do not undergo major restructuring, it is very difficult to believe that they can fulfil these expectations. Thus, not surprisingly, the price and quality of financial and in particular banking services and the access to and cost of short- and long-term finance remained a factor hindering rather than supporting economic transformation, at least so far.

The speed and nature of further financial reforms and the extent of progress with strengthening financial institutions will be critical factors in determining future developments in the region. Several of the CEECs have either already started to enjoy economic recovery or are on the verge of it. Whether this will be a short-term phenomenon or the beginning of a long period of sustained high growth depends very much on the cost and availability of investment finance and on the quality and cost of financial services. To provide this, the efficiency of financial institutions will have to be improved significantly.

While foreign intermediated finance and FDI will undoubtedly be important sources of investment finance, the major part of the demand for such finance will have to be secured from domestic sources. For the CEECs which aim at EU membership in the foreseeable future, the pressure to strengthen and make their financial institutions more competitive will be enormous. In this respect, the experience of the new EU members, even though their financial systems are at present much more developed, will be very instructive and should therefore be closely followed by these countries.

Regarding the role of the financial sector in economic transformation, the debate in the literature has two main aspects: the role of financial institutions during economic transformation in general, on the one hand, and the relative importance of the different types of financial institutions and instruments, on the other. The latter is also known as the 'model issue', as it was mainly brought up as a choice between the 'Anglo-Saxon' and the 'German' (universal banking based) models (Corbett and Mayer, 1991). Regarding legislation and regulations, the CEECs started practically from scratch and this gave the impression that legislators and policy makers in CEE had almost complete freedom to choose any model they regarded suitable.

However, the debate regarding the role of commercial banks was a highly political one. The fear many analysts and policy makers had was that large commercial banks might gain too much economic and thus political power concentrated in the hands of few bank managers. Therefore, mainly based on political considerations and past experience with state-run businesses, they suggested set-ups that were nearer to the Anglo-Saxon model than to the German one. Some, mainly Western researchers (McKinnon, 1991) seriously questioned the SOCBs' ability to properly allocate financial resources and impose financial discipline and corporate governance on enterprises. Thus, they suggested opting for narrow banking, a system that keeps banks as far away from enterprise businesses as possible.

Conversely, other researchers (Ábel and Bonin, 1994; Wijnbergen, 1994) and in the course of time an increasing number of policy makers in the leading reforming countries emphasized the positive role commercial banks in general, and SOCBs in particular, could play in the restructuring of CEE economies and enterprises. Their main argument was the insider knowledge these banks possess about enterprises, stemming from their credit links. This line of argument naturally leads to policy measure proposals that bring the actual financial systems in CEE nearer to a universal banking based (German) model.

However, as anywhere else, real-world development is usually an outcome of a series of compromises and corrections that embody the learning processes of policy makers and legislators. Thus, not surprisingly, legislation and regulations on the financial system were changed and amended several times in the CEECs since the beginning of economic transformation.[3] Moreover, the actual implementation of laws already passed and the practices adopted by regulative authorities (such as banking and securities supervision, central banks) also mirrored this evolutionary process. Thus, the original debate and the first decisions of policy makers in this regard now turn out to have influenced only the starting positions of the process.

The major factor shaping this process was that in reality there were hardly any non-bank financial institutions, especially at the beginning, which could have assumed the role of collecting and allocating domestic savings and foreign financial resources to productive uses. Banking finance had an overwhelming share and importance whereas other instruments (such as corporate bonds or equity shares) and institutions supporting them (such as stock exchanges or investment banks) were just too embryonic to assume this role. Consequently the role of financial institutions other than commercial and savings banks was also very limited. The limited capacities of supervisory bodies also pointed towards a more commercial bank based system as, in spite of all related problems, prudential regulations for banks were much more elaborate and the authorities had much more experience with enforcing them than for any other type of financial institution.

The intention to join the EU also had practical consequences, in that any legislation or regulations different from the European ones (which are based on the universal banking model) were bound to create obstacles to future EU membership. Thus the actual practice and the modifications implemented since the beginning of economic transformation gradually pushed the financial systems of the CEECs toward a universal bank based model.

In what follows, I shall try to give an overview of the different functions financial institutions are thought or expected to fulfil during economic transformation and also the possible consequences of having different kinds of models of the financial system.

Financing Economic Restructuring

The success of economic transformation depends to a very large extent on the success and speed of economic restructuring. This entails the restructuring of existing SOEs and the nurturing and financing of newly emerging enterprises. Both need massive new investments that can be financed from several channels. As will be discussed below, intermediated finance, in particular bank loans, have to play a large role in this respect. Restructuring is necessary to make CEE enterprises produce products which are marketable on world markets

There are, however, a number of factors that make this process very difficult. In the past, the cost of capital was hardly a factor influencing enterprises' investment decisions. At present, due to the gradually hardening budget constraints, tightening bankruptcy regulations (mainly in Hungary, so far) and prudential regulations, the cost of capital and, more precisely, the capacity of enterprises to service bank loans became an imperative factor in the process of credit allocation. At the same time, rates on bank deposits became an important factor influencing the portfolio allocation and, to some extent, the savings decisions of financial investors (mainly households). Thus, banks had to gradually offer sufficient (though not necessarily always positive) levels of real (after-tax) interest rates on deposits, where real rates were calculated mainly on the basis of consumer prices.

On the other hand, corporate borrowers calculated their real interest rates by using the price index relevant for them, namely the producer price index. The problem was, and still is, that due to several reasons, in almost every country, there was (at least so far) a sizeable gap between consumer and producer price increases, the former growing faster for most of the time. Moreover, in some countries (such as Hungary) there was a withhold tax on deposit rates. The outcome was that even disregarding the pressure imposed by banks for wide spreads, it was impossible to find an interest rate that could have satisfied both sides. What was a too low (real, after-tax) rate for depositors was an intolerably high rate for corporate borrowers. The eventual outcome was that only the state could pay rates that satisfied financial investors.

This already difficult situation was made worse by the bad loan problems of the SOCBs, the financial institutions providing the lion's share of long-term investment credits. SOCBs burdened with bad loans had to resort to charging very wide margins between lending and deposit rates (Ábel and Székely, 1994; Dittus, 1993; Dobrinsky, 1994; Hrnčíř, 1994). Other banks not burdened with bad loans charged similar spreads, showing clearly the lack of competition (Ábel and Székely, 1994; Dobrinsky, 1994). The high reserve requirements and low rates on mandatory reserve balances kept with the central bank, embodying the appetite of the state for seigniorage, further added to the problem. The outcome was real lending rates and interest rate spreads much higher than in developed market economies and comparable only to levels observed in the highly repressed financial systems of developing countries.[4]

Another equally serious problem of financing economic restructuring was the very strongly emerging 'short-termism' in CEE economies. The share of long-term loans[5] in new loans and the average maturity of bank loans decreased rapidly, while the share of short-term assets in banks' asset portfolios increased enormously. In general, with very few exceptions, the share of long-term financial instruments declined radically. Equity finance, another natural and sizeable source of long-term finance, was also not significant due to reasons discussed later. The only sizeable source of long-term funds was borrowing abroad. This was however available only to the best enterprises in the leading reforming countries and only very recently when financial liberalization had progressed to an extent that allows such borrowing.

Financial Institutions and the Restructuring of Ailing State-Owned Enterprises

While there is wide agreement that the lack of proper corporate governance is the main factor explaining why the process of restructuring SOEs is so painfully slow (Dittus, 1993; Mayhew and Seabright, 1992; Phelps et al., 1993; Wijnbergen, 1994), the views regarding the question of which are the most efficient and fastest ways to impose a tight corporate governance on large SOEs, or put differently, who should be the 'agent of change' (Wijnbergen, 1994), are rather diverse. As Wijnbergen (1994) points out, 'governments throughout Eastern Europe have been singularly unsuccessful in dealing with large loss-making SOEs'. For the very same reason, governments were also unsuccessful in privatizing these enterprises through outright sales. That is, privatization, which is thought to be the ultimate solution for the corporate governance problem, is hardly a solution for the vast majority of large (loss-making, or low-profit-making) SOEs.

As in many other instances, the exception is Czechoslovakia (and now, the Czech Republic) where policy makers embarked upon a wholesale voucher privatization of a large number of SOEs at a very early stage. In the Czech case, the main question is whether the investment funds created in the course of voucher privatization will be successful in imposing tight corporate governance on the privatized enterprises.

The other peculiar aspect of the Czech voucher scheme is that the enterprises involved in the scheme were not made subject to any serious bankruptcy regulation before privatization. That is, their real financial situation – and that of the commercial banks also involved in the voucher scheme – might have been left unrevealed. By now, policy makers in Hungary and Poland are also hastily implementing similar schemes aiming to involve small investors in large numbers, but the major difference is that in these countries, with few exceptions, firms to be involved will have to be chosen from among those that are not attractive to large (foreign) investors on the basis of the conventional forms of privatization.

Many researchers find commercial banks the best-positioned institutions to impose the needed corporate governance on large SOEs (Ábel and Bonin, 1994; Hrnčíř, 1994; Wijnbergen, 1994). The main argument is that banks possess the necessary insider information about the enterprises through their credit links. The problem is that these commercial banks themselves lack the necessary corporate governance due to the fact that they themselves are (again with the exception of the Czech ones) state-owned and loss-making. Moreover, they are overburdened with bad loans, partly inherited from central planning, partly made by themselves due to the lack of proper internal organization, corporate governance, and credit appraisal procedures (Golden,

1994; Montias, 1994; Wyczański, 1994). The privatization of large SOCBs, which still dominate the banking system, is a very slow process. This being the case, why should these state-owned, so far rather poorly performing banks suddenly be able and motivated to deal efficiently with the ailing SOEs? Not surprisingly, thus, analysts are rather sceptical as to the capacity and willingness of large, loss-making SOCBs to perform this function (Phelps et al., 1993; Montias, 1994).

The conclusion that can be drawn is that even if some of the commercial banks were willing and able to act as 'agent of change' the overall impact of this would most likely be rather limited and delayed in time.

Financing and Servicing the Emerging Private Sector

One of the most important roles the financial system, in particular the banking system, is expected to play in the process of economic transformation is the financing of the newly emerging private sector. By now, it is becoming clear that the newly emerging enterprises will have an equally important, if not more important role in the economic revival than the restructuring of existing enterprises. Even though foreign capital plays a dominant role in privatization, an increasing proportion of FDI is connected to new ventures. In choosing the location of an FDI project, the quality and price of financial services as well as the availability and price of local finance is a factor of increasing importance.

In spite of the remarkable development reported here and elsewhere, the capacity of the financial system, in particular banks to finance and service the newly emerging private sector, remained severely impaired in CEE for several reasons. First, due to the lack of a proper track record and a fairly unstable macroeconomic environment, new ventures were just too risky for the weak banks to finance. For the same reason, equity finance through the stock exchange and bond finance were also practically unavailable for newly emerging private firms. The uncertainties of legislation regarding collateral and the mediocre system of title registration has put great obstacles to collateralization in the banks' practice. Second, banks themselves had very little experience with and expertise in credit appraisal, especially in the case of small ventures. Third, very high real lending rates made it extremely risky and thus almost impossible for newly emerging private firms to rely on bank loans to any larger extent. Actually, a prudent banker would (and should) be very reluctant to give loans, in particular long-term loans to a start-up or relatively young firm at a real rate of around 15 per cent per annum.

For several reasons, a major part of the newly emerging private sector consists of small enterprises. Unfortunately this segment of the market, even in developed market economies with well-established and competitive financial systems, is one of the least competitive. Like retail banking, servicing small enterprises is very costly, hardly producing sufficient profit to finance the massive investments for the development of the necessary branch network. Thus this segment remained (and probably will remain for quite some time) underdeveloped even in the capital cities of CEE, where banking is mostly concentrated. In the countryside, in particular in regions most severely hit by the recession, also due to the lack of a modern communications network, the situation is much worse.

Financing the State Budget

The financing of central government (in Hungary, local government as well) was also a large task for the financial system to cope with. This involved not only financing the current budget deficit, which in itself was sizeable in each CEEC except for Czechoslovakia (and now, the Czech Republic), but also the refinancing of the already existing stock of public debts.

Due to central bank legislation and changing attitudes, both parts were increasingly financed by issuing government securities of several kinds. These were almost entirely new instruments even in the CEECs with more developed financial systems like Hungary and Poland. Introducing government securities with a sufficiently large variety of maturities and making liquid markets for them was also vital to the conduct of monetary policies. Without these instruments, more fine-tuned policies were simply impossible to carry out, in many cases forcing the monetary authorities to resort to very rudimentary and costly methods, such as credit ceilings.[6] Besides the apparent costs, the lack of these instruments also deprived policy makers of vital signals from the market regarding the supply and demand of capital and price expectations for the short and long run. Due to tax reforms, the decline of SOEs and the slow growth of the private sector, short-term, seasonal fluctuations in government revenues became much more pronounced than before. This created a further strong need for a sufficiently wide range of highly liquid short-term securities.

Because of the high level of inflation and the uncertain macro-environment, government securities met hardly any competition on the market. Recently, a few of the best corporate borrowers in the leading reforming countries issued commercial papers but, at least so far, the impact of this was negligible. Moreover, it was only after quite a while that the central authorities in these countries (central bank and ministry of finance) could rely on the collaboration of financial firms in producing these products and making the markets for them.

Monetary Policy and the Independence of the Central Bank

An important element of financial reforms in CEE is the status of the central bank and the conduct of monetary policy. The establishment of two-tier banking systems in CEE not only created commercial banks, but also Western-type (classical) central banks, previously non-existent in the region.

Legislators and policy makers appeared to have a choice among a variety of existing models that were different in the extent to which the central bank is independent in devising and conducting monetary policy. As achieving reasonably low rates of inflation was a major problem and policy target for virtually all CEE governments and because economic literature[7] tends to suggest that, at least on the average and in the longer run, more independent central banks deliver less inflation, central bank independence had to be given serious consideration. And indeed it was. The newly established central banks in CEE were given fairly high degrees of independence and relatively clear-cut orientations on policy targets (Dobrinsky, 1994; Daianu, 1994; Siklos, 1994).[8]

On the other hand, fiscal deficits and economic decline turned out to be much more severe problems than originally anticipated. Due to the soaring budget deficits (reflecting not only cyclical but also structural problems) and some other factors discussed below, real interest rates for enterprises reached much higher levels than envisioned.[9] Naturally, this built up political pressure on governments to relax monetary policy, even if the price to be paid was higher inflation.

As Western experience clearly suggests, the actual practice regarding central bank independence can be quite different from what is legislated in central bank laws (Cukierman, 1992). Probably the same is true for the CEECs. In spite of the relatively high degree of independence given in the laws to central banks, governments have several ways to exert pressure on central bankers to relax monetary policy when they think it is politically important. On the other hand, whatever the law says, central bankers also have to take into account the economic and political consequences of their policies. Thus, though they may enjoy a large degree of freedom in principle, their room for manoeuvre may be extremely small in reality.

One should not forget that though the costs of monetary instability and large and erratic rates of inflation may be rather high, the costs of alternative options may also be high, in certain cases even higher. Thus, as in the case of banking reforms, the reality can best be interpreted as a compromise between competing interests and claims and central bankers have to play along with governments.[10] After all, their legitimacy stems not only from laws but also from their actions and the way these are perceived by people. Moreover, though sometimes not that easily, laws are also subject to changes.

COMPETITION IN FINANCIAL MARKETS

As pointed out earlier, the traditional financial systems of the centrally planned economies were kept intact until the political changes took place, even in countries where major reform steps had been taken in earlier phases. Put differently, the almost complete financial repression remained an inherent characteristic of these economies until the very end of their existence. This meant a very rudimentary institutional structure providing no alternative to bank finance, a handful of financial products available for financial investors and borrowers, almost completely monopolized markets and, consequently, highly distorted product pricing. Thus, as far as competition is concerned, CEE economies had virtually no experience with any kind of competition, foreign or domestic, when embarking on economic transformation. Though previously CEE economies were in general highly protected from foreign competition and domestic competition was also very weak, other sectors of the economy, unlike the financial sector, had at least some experience of competition.

Therefore, in spite of the fact that the CEECs made remarkable progress in financial deregulation in a very short time (Sándor, 1994; Hrnčíř, 1994), it is not at all surprising that financial sectors in CEE need considerable time to develop a more competitive environment and that they are lagging behind other sectors in this regard. The lack of full convertibility, and especially the restrictions on cross-border capital movements, certainly hinder competition from abroad, which is a major driving force in other sectors of the economy. Moreover, the privatization of SOCBs takes place very slowly in CEE, the Czech Republic being the only notable exception. Though the pace of privatization in general is widely regarded as slower than desirable, the progress achieved so far in other sectors is much more significant.

Alternative Sources of (Enterprise) Finance

In what follows, we shall investigate four main sources of corporate finance: banking (intermediated) finance, direct (bond and equity) finance, foreign direct finance, and retained earnings.

Bank (intermediated) finance for investment

During the economic transformation, the availability of long-term (investment) bank finance to industrial firms has been rather limited, first, because of the limited supply of long-term loanable funds. Private financial investors have been reluctant to hold long-term financial assets in large amounts, even in those countries where stabilization polices have been relatively successful and private saving has increased (Ábel and Székely, 1993; Wyczański, 1993).

Moreover, commercial banks have fairly limited capacities to carry out maturity conversion (converting shorter-term deposits into longer-term loans) due to the newly introduced Western-type prudential regulations. Furthermore, banks have little experience with and knowledge of commercial lending, especially in granting longer-terms loans (Golden, 1994; Wyczański, 1994).

Regarding the actual development so far, the share of long-term loans in new loans and the average maturity of bank loans has decreased rapidly, while the share of short-term assets in banks' asset portfolios has increased substantially (Ábel and Székely, 1994; Kokoszczyński, 1994). In general, with very few exceptions, the share of long-term financial instruments declined radically. Inter-bank deposits also became very short-term (Dobrinsky, 1994; Kokoszczyński, 1994), long-term refinance credit from the central bank diminished (Ábel and Székely, 1994), and bonds other than government ones practically disappeared. Thus banks with a weak deposit base, in particular among households, had practically no access to long-term loanable funds.

Second, enterprises have to compete with the government for long-term funds. Massive budget deficits characterizing economic transformation and costly rescue operations carried out by governments (such as bad loan schemes discussed below) create a strong demand for long-term funds on the part of the government.

While this is true in general for CEE, the extent to which these factors are present varies across countries and over time. In countries where macroeconomic stabilization was relatively successful, such as the Czech Republic (before the split, Czechoslovakia), Hungary, and Poland (after 1991), private saving increased significantly. However, even in former Czechoslovakia, which is a very special case in this respect, a part of private saving was mopped up by the budget deficit. In Poland after 1990, the current budget deficit exceeded private saving, while in Hungary the positive gap between private saving and the current budget deficit narrowed rapidly.

The decline of investment credit is a very complex issue that can only be understood when one investigates a large number of factors. Dittus (1993) finds the conservative lending policies of commercial banks as the major factor explaining this development and, at the same time, rejects the crowding-out hypothesis. The introduction of new Western-type prudential regulations has undoubtedly contributed to the decline of lending to enterprises, especially in the longer run. The radical liberalization of goods and financial markets – leading to fast and substantial changes of relative prices, including interest rates – has indeed increased the risk attached to corporate lending.

A sizeable part of large SOEs, the core of the traditional clientele of large SOCBs, lost their foreign and domestic markets in an abrupt manner. This change deteriorated their creditworthiness and capacity to borrow under market conditions. Under such conditions, a prudent bank management would tend to reduce lending to these firms. On the other hand, the newly emerging private sector, consisting mainly of small and medium-sized firms, though hungry for bank loans, in particular for investment loans, cannot take the place of the ailing SOEs, because it has hardly any proper track record and has very little to offer as collateral.

Another explanation, frequently mentioned by bankers, is that enterprise demand for credit has declined dramatically. An important determinant of this change is the enormous increase in real borrowing rates for enterprises in the transition period. In Hungary, for example, real (*ex-post*) lending rates on investment loans increased from –3.1 per cent in 1989 to 16.8 per cent in 1992. It is extremely difficult to believe that any sound business can support such high real rates. That is, at these prices enterprises with reasonably hard budget constraints and a strong interest in maximizing the market value of the firm would undoubtedly decrease their demand for bank finance substantially.

But this is the point where one starts to question the outright rejection of the crowding-out hypothesis. If enterprise demand for bank finance was low and declining why did prices (interest rates) remain high, or in fact increase rapidly? One of the explanations is the high credit demand by the government. Government securities, which are a virtually risk-free form of investment, offered to banks yields comparable with if not higher (at least for certain periods) than the risky corporate loans. Thus the crowding out of corporate borrowers from credit markets by the governments was indeed an important factor explaining the dramatic decline in investment finance in CEE.

Direct (non-intermediated) finance for investment

Bond and equity finance will perhaps be even more scarce than long-term bank finance. With high and fluctuating rates of inflation characterizing CEE economies (with few exceptions), long-term fixed rate (bond) finance is just too risky for both parties. The lack of institutional investors with long planning horizons and wholesale financial markets (Király, 1993; Székely, 1994) makes this situation even more severe. For small investors, the costs of monitoring enterprises and gaining a reasonably good understanding of future macroeconomic development are just too high. The collapse of the Hungarian bond market in 1988, when inflation started to accelerate and government guarantees on new corporate bonds were terminated, was a clear example of the problems involved (Székely, 1990).

Equity finance faces similar problems. Without Western-type accounting and a proper track record, it is just too risky for private investors to hold equity directly. On the other hand, for the same reason, the supply of tradeable shares is also rather limited (Járai, 1993). The underdeveloped financial system is a further stumbling-block, because if industry analysts and finance houses do not keep track of industries' performance, it is very expensive to gather information on specific firms or industries. Hedging is also very difficult, that is, portfolios are bound to be far from optimal. Also, the amounts of fresh enterprise capital generated at the CEECs' stock exchanges so far have been negligible. Most of the boom observed recently is related to underpriced shares floated in the course of privatization, rather than to new issues.

Direct investment and retained earnings

Foreign direct investment (FDI) is a very important source of finance, especially for larger projects. Besides finance, it is also expected to bring in know-how, expertise and access to distribution networks in the West. The problem is that FDI into the whole region is very limited and, in addition, it is highly concentrated in a few countries where the legal and financial infrastructure is relatively well developed (Gray et al., 1992; Sárközy, 1993), and which enjoy relative economic and social stability (former Czechoslovakia, now the Czech Republic, and Hungary). Much of the FDI at present is absorbed by the process of privatization, that is by the purchase of existing capacities. It is hoped that this will generate future investment, but its extent is still rather uncertain.

Domestic direct investment (private placement), though rather neglected and not fully recorded by official statistics, is perhaps the most dynamic source of finance. The advantage of this form, as is the case with any other direct investment, is that moral hazard is less of a problem. However this process is almost exclusively confined to small private ventures, at least in the first years of economic transformation. The lack of collateral and track record, as well as of competition and experience in the financial sector, makes it very difficult for these firms to rely on banking finance. Therefore, new firms created by this process will go through the natural life cycle of firms mainly relying on retained earnings and direct investment, like many firms in postwar Western Europe. The successful ones will increasingly be able to attract direct and banking finance, but this process is bound to be slow, and not at all a solution for large existing SOEs in dire need of restructuring.

The most important source of finance for large SOEs during economic transformation will thus be retained earnings (McKinnon, 1991). Though retained earnings are the major source for corporate finance in market economies as well (Stiglitz, 1992), in CEE this will have a rather different impact on the pattern of industrial restructuring. Due to the lack of other sources of finance and, in general, of government assistance to the process, the SOEs which most badly need restructuring will simply have neither access to the necessary external finance nor the necessary internal funds. FDI, as pointed out earlier, can be a way out for a handful of large SOEs (for firms like Skoda, or TUNSGRAM); for the vast majority it is just too risky a venture for foreign investors. Unemployment, especially in certain regions, may turn out to be a reason for governments to keep some large SOEs alive in the short to medium run. However, without a major restructuring they have very little, if any, hope of survival.

Market Structures and Product Pricing

While in each CEEC there was a spectacular increase in the number of banks and some consequent increase in the degree of competition, the extent of the latter remained limited. The markets for banking products are still highly concentrated and dominated by the large SOCBs.[11] While in general this is true for all CEECs, the differences in the extent to which markets are uncompetitive, concentrated and dominated by large SOCBs are significant, being lower in the leading reforming countries (Hungary being the leader in this respect) and higher in the late reformers (such as Bulgaria, after the bank consolidation, and Romania).

Moreover there is a wide variation across different markets. With few exceptions, the more short-term the product, the lower the risk involved; the smaller the amount of up-front investment needed to enter that specific market (entry barrier), the lower the degree of concentration and the more competitive the market. Thus, in foreign trade finance as well as in certain groups of fee-based services and derivative products related to forex transactions (in general the upper ends of markets – see below), the markets are much more competitive. On the other hand, in retail banking, long-term (investment) loans, and in general at the lower ends of markets, there is very little competition, market structures are highly concentrated and pricing is seriously distorted.[12]

The lack of an adequate degree of competition is confirmed by the wide interest rate spreads mentioned above. More precisely, what is an indication of the lack of competition is not so much the fact that spreads are wide in general, but that banks which were free from bad loans gradually started to follow the pricing policies of the banks burdened by bad loans and forced to finance their heavy provisioning needs from wide spreads (Dobrinsky, 1994; Ábel and Székely, 1994).

Balanced market structures and adequate levels of competitive pressure (including that coming from the contestability of markets) are important prerequisites of a well-functioning and efficient financial system which, in turn, is one of the most important prerequisites of a successful economic transformation. Thus, policy makers will have to pay proper attention to this aspect and will have to adequately lower entry barriers and foster healthy competition in the banking system.

Foreign Banks and Competition

In the leading reforming countries of CEE, foreign participation in the financial system became significant, in particular in banking. In the Czech Republic in 1993, there were 19 banks with foreign participation and 6 branches of foreign banks (out of 50 banks in total), in Hungary in 1992, 13 banks with foreign participation (out of 38); and in Poland in 1992, 11 banks with foreign participation (out of 94). In the other countries, foreign participation is very moderate (Dobrinsky, 1994; Daianu, 1994).

But even in the leading reforming countries, the nature of the business strategies of foreign and joint venture banks turned out to be quite different from what policy makers expected at the beginning of economic transformation. Foreign banks, in particular major international banks with adequately large capital strength, international network, access to international financial markets, and expertise have shown, at least so far, very moderate interest in exactly those areas where they would be most desperately needed. Thus, the interest in buying into large SOCBs or moving into the least competitive (but also most costly or risky) segments such as retail banking or servicing small enterprises has been rather moderate.

On the other hand, in those segments where foreign banks have huge competitive advantages (such as foreign payment services and related primary and derivative products), where the risk is limited, the capital and staff requirement is relatively small, and there is no need for a large branch network, foreign and joint venture banks captured significant market shares. Put differently, they concentrated their business activities in areas where the profit–risk ratio is the highest and where activities can be expanded rapidly. Moreover in each segment where they have significant market share they concentrate on the upper end of the market by taking only the best clients. Thus in handling corporate accounts and financing corporate units, they attract the foreign and joint venture firms by offering Western standards of service.

While some researchers (e.g. Várhegyi, 1994) and policy makers appear to be somewhat irritated by this attitude of foreign and joint venture banks, from the viewpoint of economic theory it is a very rational approach and not that much different from the experiences of some Western countries (see Savela and Herrala, 1992 for the Finnish experience). CEE financial markets are highly volatile and risky for several reasons related to the nature of economic transition. The macroeconomic environment is rather unstable by Western standards even in the most successful countries. Due to the rapid changes in relative prices, the sudden trade reorientation, and the consequent massive changes in the market values of enterprise assets, the real financial situation of the firms, as well as their economic viability in the future, is extremely difficult to judge. This is further made difficult by the continuous changes in corporate law and other legislation (including accounting and taxation). Regulations regarding financial institutions are new, in many cases hardly tested in courts, and also changing; supervisory agencies are inexperienced.

On the other hand, domestic banks and financial institutions are inexperienced and ill equipped to provide certain services and make markets for sophisticated products (such as options or commercial papers). They also lack the necessary infrastructure to meet the existing demand of foreign and joint venture firms for Western standards in some traditional banking services. Therefore, it is just natural for foreign banks to concentrate their activities and resources on these markets and clients.

Also, major banks cannot afford to miss new emerging markets, especially those of the size of Poland's. Thus, it is again rational to put their feet in as early as possible, be present and accumulate local experience. Doing so, they will position themselves for the time when it will be rational to move in on a large scale and they will be able to attract FDI from other strategic and portfolio investors, probably much more than domestic banks.

State Influence in the Financial Sector

State (government) influence is widely reported as one of the main obstacles to competition in the financial sector in CEE (Várhegyi, 1993, 1994; Wyczański, 1993). The influence of the state is not confined to equity holding, but includes a variety of forms, stretching from prudential regulations and supervision to the overwhelming weight of the state (represented by the central bank) in money and capital markets (Sándor, 1994). As privatization is not likely to be a rapid process, it is of utmost importance to find solutions to shield banks from political influence and in general from the volatility typical of the political scenes of many CEECs.

Prudent Operation

Even in developed economies with highly sophisticated financial systems and well-established and experienced supervisory agencies, there is a trade-off between competition and efficiency, on the one hand, and prudent operation (safety and soundness) of the financial system, on the other. The general experience is that excessive risk is coming from either new products (such as options) not yet properly covered by existing regulations, or from products where the market is suddenly liberalized (such as mortgage products or pension funds), changing some of the characteristics of the product and thus introducing new elements of risk with which financial firms have had little experience.

In most cases the origin of the problem is the inadequate pricing of the new type of risk and the inadequate assessment of financial firms' ability (capital strength) to assume the new type of risk. The general belief is that the strong drive and competition for market shares in new or newly expanding markets leads to excessive risk taking and underpricing of the products. That is, there is a very fine line to draw between healthy and excessive competition and between over- and under-regulation.

Though at present the financial systems of the CEECs are simply incomparable to those of developed Western market economies, the origins of the trade-off between competition and prudential operation are not that different. Since, as pointed out above, CEE economies started from a highly monopolized and distorted financial system with a small number of players, there was a high priority attached to increasing the number of players. By now, it is widely recognized that this might have been overdone. Licensing policies were fairly liberal (Ábel and Székely, 1994; Wyczański, 1993) resulting in a fast increase in the number of banks, but at the same time also in a large number of banks with a weak capital base and, in some cases, suspicious owners and management.[13]

The very fragile credibility of the banking system was shaken by the collapse of banks and, in some cases, the subsequent run on banks (Wyczański, 1993). The failure to establish adequate deposit insurance schemes covering all banks and saving cooperatives further added to the problem. The banks, including the SOCBs, were unprepared to properly evaluate and price the risk involved in products which were new to them, even if those were the most classical bank loans. This is clearly shown by the fact that a considerable part of so-called bad loans was not related to loans inherited from the monobank, but made afterwards, in many cases to newly emerging private enterprises.

Policy makers and authorities in CEECs are increasingly realizing that licensing policies and regulations were perhaps too liberal (for the sake of increasing competition) and that in the future the ability of financial institutions to assume risk should be strengthened. Moreover, more regulation, control and monitoring is needed over owners and management in order to be able to single out suspicious business (such as money laundering). The strengthening of the credibility of the financial system and the goal of EU membership are the major reasons for doing so.

UNRESOLVED ISSUES HINDERING TRANSFORMATION AND INTEGRATION

Privatization and Corporate Governance in the Financial Sector

Privatization of SOCBs has been much slower than expected and also significantly slower than privatization in other sectors. The main form of private sector expansion was through new entries and relatively fast growth of the new banks. While this process was a very important factor in increasing competition and decreasing market concentration, it also meant that the expansion of the private sector in the financial system was less than sufficient.

With the exception of Czechoslovakia (and now, the Czech Republic) where the generally adopted wholesale privatization involved the large SOCBs as well, governments decided to separate the privatization of SOCBs from that of SOEs, and deal with the banks on a case-by-case basis. With the exception of early sell-off of a few relatively small SOCBs, this resulted in major delays in the privatization of SOCBs.[14]

Regarding the privatized SOCBs, it is important to note the outcome of the process. Though the Czech voucher privatization led to the sale of a major part of the equity shares of the large SOCBs (the Consolidation Bank, which is the Czech 'hospital bank', remaining the only fully SOCB), the state retained a substantial equity stake in the large banks (on average some 42 per cent). It remains to be seen whether any of the investment funds will be able to impose the much needed tight corporate governance on these banks and attract foreign strategic partners. These two elements are thought to be vital to the eventual success of these banks.

In Poland, the two privatization deals completed so far raise similar concerns. While the participation of EBRD is indeed important in attracting foreign strategic partners, it alone will probably do little to improve the efficiency of a bank. The example of Wielkopolski Bank Kredytowy, which was publicly offered in the first half of 1993, clearly attests to this view (Kokoszczyński, 1994). The case of Bank Śląski, which was privatized in 1994, is much more exciting and promising, since this is the first case when a relatively large SOCB was privatized with the participation of a strategic investor with the relevant expertise, know-how and access to foreign capital markets. The success or failure of this bank will most likely have a strong bearing on the process of bank privatization in the whole region.

'Bad Loans' in the Portfolios of Commercial Banks

When SOCBs were established in CEE, their portfolios were created by transferring the existing enterprise loans (assets side) and deposits (liability side) from the portfolio of the central bank or, in some cases, from those of specialized state financial institutions. That is, the newly created SOCBs inherited the loans previously made by the monobank. Needless to say, these loans were not granted on the basis of any prudent practice of loan appraisal and therefore in most cases did not even reflect the enterprises' capacity to repay them under the previously existing conditions (market shares and relative prices). Moreover, economic transformation very quickly led to major liberalization measures significantly changing the financial positions of enterprises and consequently rapidly reducing the quality of banks' loan portfolios.

Since this was a wholesale transfer operation based on bureaucratic and political consideration rather than on any kind of business principle, it is not at all surprising that the composition of the asset portfolios of the newly created banks was far from optimal. The new SOCBs were exposed to dangerously high degrees to either certain industries or geographical regions. This seriously hindered competition and would have necessitated massive bank rescue operations even if the effect of the external shocks was not that strong.

Bad loans were difficult to identify because of the lack of proper accounting standards and bankruptcy regulations (Mizsei, 1994). Moreover banks may have strong incentives to either over- or underestimate the precise amounts of bad loans in their portfolios, depending on which way is more favourable for them under the acting regulations. Thus it was (and in many countries it still is) difficult to estimate the amount of bad loans at any given point in time. Nonetheless, the widely known estimates suggest that at least 20–30 per cent of loans in the portfolios of the commercial banks may turn out to be bad loans (Dittus, 1993). Moreover, these loans are highly concentrated mainly in the portfolios of large SOCBs (or their own 'hospital banks').

The literature hints at several different ways to deal with bad loans.[15] Begg and Portes (1992) suggest removing these loans from the portfolios of commercial banks and replacing them at face value with government bonds, providing the banks with an adequate yield to become and remain profitable. The advantage of this scheme is that it lifts the pressure on commercial banks to build up large provisions against bad loans financed from wide interest rate spreads. The problem with this solution is that it ignores the insider information banks possess about the enterprises involved and thus gives no incentive to the banks to reveal the information they have on the liquidation values or the viability of the enterprises involved.

Székely (1994) suggests a scheme in which loans would be sold in a special type of auctioning process. During this process the sale of the loans would be subsidized in order to bridge the gap between what the banks originally holding the loan can afford to lose on a loan (as compared to the face value) and what the purchaser can afford to pay for it (given its expectation about the actual value of the loan contract). The advantage of this scheme is that it gives some incentives to the banks to reveal their information on individual loan contracts and enterprises. The disadvantage is that it takes a long time to implement and relies on agents and information that may simply not exist in some CEECs.

Gurgenidze (1993), while still opting for a market-based solution, points to the problems involved in trying to market non-standardized individual loan contracts and to the fact that this is very rarely done even in developed market economies. Instead, he suggests a scheme based on the securitization of the bad loans involved. The problem with this solution is that it relies on even more sophisticated instruments that do not exist in any of the CEECs. Ábel and Bonin (1994) question the feasibility of a market-based solution and the merits of a wholesale transfer of bad loans to a government-run 'hospital bank' at face value. They suggest a system of incentive contracts for 'lead' banks that would give a strong incentive to the commercial banks to work out the acquired bad loans and collect as much as possible. Finally, Várhegyi (1994) argues in favour of the recapitalization of the commercial banks involved.

Naturally, the decision on how to deal with substandard loans has a profound impact on the interest margins of commercial banks (Begg and Portes, 1992; Dittus, 1993), and through this, on lending rates. However, as noted, crowding out is at least as important as commercial banks' interest spreads in producing high lending rates. Thus even the most generous solutions will take away only part of the pressure on interest rate spreads. Moreover if the costs of cleaning up the loan portfolios of banks is assumed by the state budget and not financed by borrowing from capital markets, it results either in a budget deficit monetized by the central bank, or in an increase of the tax burden on successful firms and individuals. In the former case, as pointed out, the impact on portfolio allocation is immediate and unfavourable (a shift towards more liquid short-term assets), pushing up lending rates again. In the latter case, retained earnings are further taxed, reducing the available enterprise finance for new investments.

The CEECs have so far implemented several bad loan schemes aimed at cleaning up the loan portfolios of commercial banks and including certain elements of the solutions mentioned above. However the results are, at least so far, disappointing (Dobrinsky, 1994; Hrnčíř, 1994; Várhegyi, 1994). This apparent lack of success was mainly due to the fact that the implemented schemes did too little, too late. The solutions were partial and the amounts involved were inadequate. On the other hand, they paid very little attention to the problem whether the financial institutions involved ('hospital' agencies or commercial banks) were able to assume the task of working out the bad loans (Kruse, 1994), and whether the proper incentives had been created for them to do so.

Though the recently implemented Polish scheme may deliver more promising results (Wijnbergen, 1994), the time that has elapsed since its launching in April 1994 is too short to draw any firm conclusion in this respect.

CONCLUSIONS: FUTURE REFORMS AND INTEGRATION

The internal integration of CEE economies, that is the integration of different markets within national borders, is an essential prerequisite and component of their external integration. Moreover internal integration is an important component of economic transformation which is supposed to create previously non-existent markets, and other institutions of a market economy which are not too different from those of developed market economies.

As the discussion in this chapter has shown, the reform of the financial system is an essential element of economic transformation and, thus, of the internal integration of CEECs. Financial markets and institutions play a central role in the integration of different markets within and across national borders. Moreover the role of the financial system is critical in providing the necessary means for new investments and restructuring of ailing enterprises and production in general. Without a successful restructuring CEE economies will hardly be able to achieve faster growth which is essential if they are to catch up and be fully integrated into the European Union. Financial reforms are also expected to create the new instruments policy makers need to devise economic policy, in particular monetary policy in a market economy.

The financial reforms and the consequent changes in the behaviour of financial institutions have been very important components of economic transformation. Though the financial systems of CEECs have changed radically, developments so far have been largely inadequate as compared to the enormous needs of transition economies. Financial institutions could play only a very limited role in providing the necessary finance for old enterprises to restructure and for new enterprises to expand. Though the SOCBs, mainly as the result of increased competitive pressures, have improved their operations and the newly emerging (mainly private and partly or fully foreign-owned) banks have increased their market shares, the efficiency of financial systems, in particular that of the banking systems, has remained low and inadequate.

The main reason for the slow improvement in the efficiency and in the degree of competition has been the slow privatization. SOCBs have been left paralysed by vast amounts of low-quality assets ('bad loans') for much too long and have been given wrong signals by partial and inadequate bad loan schemes. This not only kept them inefficient and paralysed but also largely diminished their attractiveness for strategic investors. The rather unstable macroeconomic environment, partly due to the collapse of the Eastern export markets, which has undermined the financial positions of the large SOEs, still the major corporate bank clients, and the fast changing legal and institutional environment were other important factors in this respect.

While the lack of more aggressive policies to privatize large SOCBs was perhaps the single most important policy failure, the present situation of the leading transition economies provides a second chance for policy makers in this respect. Poland has already started to enjoy a strong recovery and the Czech Republic and Hungary are on the verge of it. Corporate clients are becoming stronger and more willing and able to expand their activities by embarking on new investment projects. There is an almost uniform expectation that at least these three countries are facing a strong investment boom and pick-up of industrial production, generating not only more profits for enterprises but also more income for households. The recent explosive increase in stock exchange indices in these countries, partly due to increased interest on the part of foreign portfolio investors, clearly reflects this new mood. The real estate market will no doubt follow suit. The improving financial situation will in turn improve the position of banks, including large SOCBs.

All this will make the banking markets of these countries much more attractive than previously, which in turn will undoubtedly generate more interest in the large SOCBs up for privatization on the part of foreign strategic and portfolio investors. Whether this interest will translate into big privatization deals will to a large extent depend on how decisive the governments' policies will be on bad loans and other problems raised above. If policies are ambiguous and policy makers remain captive to old lobbies, this second chance may well slip away. It is now the governments' turn and responsibility to do their best to grab these opportunities. The strong performance of stock exchanges, though carrying the danger of speculative bubbles, will greatly increase the degree of competition in the financial system, especially if new issues become significant.

The privatization of large SOCBs by involving foreign strategic partners is an essential element of integration. Foreign ownership in these banks would not only speed up their restructuring but also accelerate the integration of CEE financial markets into the international ones through the parent banks and contribute greatly to the establishment of a modern business culture which is another important element of integration.

NOTES

1. For a detailed description of the financial system of a traditional centrally planned economy see Podolski (1973), Portes (1983), and Zwass (1979).
2. Though a new banking law was adopted in 1982 in Poland which, in principle, created the legal opportunity to set up new banks, only three new banks were actually set up in Poland between 1982 and 1989. For more detail, see Wyczanski (1993).
3. In Czechoslovakia, the first Law on Banks and Saving Banks came into force on 1 January 1990. A new Law on Banks was passed in 1992. In Hungary, the Act on Financial Institutions and Financial Institutional Activities was passed in 1991. A major amendment to this law was made at the end of 1993. In Poland, the first Banking Law was enacted in 1982. This was replaced by the new Banking Law in 1989, which was amended in 1992. The minimum capital requirement for banks was raised in 1990 and 1992. However, experts still suggest further major amendments and changes (see Wyczański, 1993).
4. There are conceptual and practical problems with calculating real interest rates, especially for longer-term products. Regarding *ex-post* real interest rates, the figures for CEECs reported by central banks or researchers, with very few exceptions (like Dittus, 1993), use the CPI or PPI index for the period ending at the time when the product was created, while the correct way would be to use the price index for the period covering the lifetime of the product involved, which is usually the period ahead. Since the rates of inflation in the region were highly volatile over time, this may lead to large differences. Bearing this problem and the possible distortion in mind, the reported real rates for most CEECs were in the range of 15–30 per cent, Hungary being near to the lower and Poland to the higher end of this range; Czechoslovakia (now the Czech Republic) was the only exception with real rates of the order of 5–10 per cent per annum (see Dittus, 1993; Dobrinsky, 1994). The situation in Romania is completely different. Due to the apparent lack of competition and financial liberalization and the symbiotic relationship between SOCBs and SOEs, lending and deposit rates were hugely negative (Daianu, 1994).

   Regarding interest rate spreads, when comparing figures across countries and over time it is important to bear in mind the differences in the rates of inflation. The reported spreads are in the range of 5–25 percentage points (pp), the lowest being in the Czech Republic (6–7 pp in 1991–92 and 7–8 pp in 1993), the highest in Poland (15–25 pp in 1991 and 15–20 in 1992) (for more details see Ábel and Székely, 1994; Dittus, 1993, Hrnčíř, 1994). For evidence of the pricing policies of CEE banks see Ábel and Székely (1994) and Dobrinsky (1994).
5. Long-term meaning maturity over one year. In developed market economies with a stable macroeconomic environment and strong banks, a loan with a maturity just over one year would hardly qualify as a long-term loan. In most CEE countries, however, even this seems to be too long at present.
6. A well-documented episode of this kind is given in Kokoszczyński (1994), p. 255.
7. One of the most comprehensive works in this field (among numerous publications) is that of Cukierman (1992).
8. The first preliminary attempt to construct a suitable composite index of central bank independence and investigate central bank independence through econometric analysis of observed behaviour for four CEE countries was presented by Siklos (1994). After investigating the issue for the Czech Republic, Hungary, Poland and Slovakia, he concluded that, as compared to market economies, newly enacted central bank laws gave a reasonably high degree of independence to central banks in these countries, the highest one in the Czech Republic and the lowest in Slovakia.
9. Regarding the impact and efficiency of such policies, widely termed 'credit crunch' in the literature, in CEE economies see Siklos and Ábel (1993).
10. For the details of such a situation in Romania, where (apart from Russia) the tension between government and central bank was perhaps the highest, see Daianu (1994). The eventual outcome was a reluctant partial 'accommodation' of the government's policy.
11. In the case of the Czech Republic, the large commercial banks, which were privatized via

voucher privatization. These banks, while the majority stakes of their equity shares were floated, remained under the heavy influence of the National Property Fund, which retained 40–45 per cent of the equity shares, while the floated stakes are not necessarily held in one hand.

12. For detailed information on market structures in Bulgaria see Dobrinsky (1994); in the Czech Republic Hrnčíř (1994); in Hungary Ábel and Székely (1994); in Poland Wyczański (1993); in Romania Daianu (1994); in general in CEE Dittus (1993).

A characteristic example for the differences across markets for banking products is given in Ábel and Székely (1994). Between 1987 and 1991, the market share of the large SOCBs as measured by the balance sheet total declined from 58.2 per cent in 1987 to 42.4 per cent in 1991. The corresponding figures for the corporate deposit market were 84 and 54.9 per cent, for the corporate loan market 91.6 and 62.9 per cent, while for the market for discounting of bills of exchange 90.3 and 20.3 per cent. Regarding long-term investment loans, the share of SOCBs in 1991 was around 74 per cent, which is much higher than for corporate loans in general. Though the new banks did enter the retail market, consumer and housing loans, as well as retail deposit markets, remained much more concentrated, dominated by the National Savings Bank.

The other end of the spectrum is probably occupied by Romania where the four biggest SOCBs accounted for 94 per cent of total credits in 1991 and for 80 per cent in June 1993 (Daianu, 1994). Concurrently, the State Saving Bank accounted for 95 per cent of sight deposits and 40 per cent of term deposits by individuals in June 1993.

Bulgaria is a very special case in this respect, because in the course of the initial break-up of the monobank system a large number of very small SOCBs were created. Nonetheless, at the local level, this created little competition, but rather weak banks. This was later realized by policy makers and a bank consolidation scheme was launched.

In spite of the increasing number of detailed studies on financial market structures in CEE, still very little is known about local market structures and the extent of differences in this respect across regions within countries.

13. An important aspect of this problem was money laundering. CEE is allegedly an attractive location for this business. Recognizing the damage such an image can do to a country, policy makers and legislators in CEE started to adopt internationally accepted regulations to attack money laundering.

14. In Bulgaria, a large-scale privatization is planned after completing the process of bank consolidation; until now, however, no such deals have been made. Spontaneous privatization was significant during the period 1990–91 mainly via new share issues. As a result, four regional banks went into private hands and by the end of 1992 the overall equity share of the private sector in state-owned banks reached 19.4 per cent. The development of the newly emerging private banks was even faster. Thus, the total equity share of the private owners reached 26.5 per cent by the end of 1992. For more details, see Dobrinsky (1994).

In Hungary, the SOCBs were created as joint stock companies; thus their commercialization was not an issue later. Besides the state (with an average equity share of 44.2 per cent), the major equity holders in the large SOCBs were SOEs (having equity shares of 30.7 per cent on average). The latter (termed in the literature 'indirect state' ownership) amounted to 28 per cent in the whole banking sector whereas the 'direct' state ownership was 38 per cent (all figures quoted refer to December 1991). Fifty per cent of the equity shares of one of the smaller SOCBs with no significant bad loans inherited from the monobank, the General Banking and Trust Ltd (ÁÉB) was directly sold to foreign (Canadian) investors in 1990. Since then no major privatization deal has been completed. In fact in the course of 1993, the state largely increased its equity holding in some banks through the bad loan consolidation scheme in which the participating banks were recapitalized. For more details see Várhegyi (1993 and 1994).

In Poland, SOCBs were commercialized (converted into joint stock companies) in late 1991. The first step towards privatization was the twinning arrangement with Western commercial banks that involved seven of the nine large SOCBs. Later two of the smaller SOCBs with no serious burden inherited from the past (Bank Inicjatyw Gospodarczych and Bank Rozwoju Eksportu) were privatized. The privatization of the large SOCBs however did not start until 1993. For more details on the Polish case, see Wyczański (1993).

In Romania, the newly created SOCBs were commercialized in March 1991. Twinning arrangements between Romanian and Western banks were made in 1993. Privatization of two major banks is planned for 1995. For more details, see Daianu (1994).

15. Due to the focus of this chapter, I do not attempt to give a complete overview of the existing proposals but concentrate only on those that have some relevance to the issues discussed here. For a more detailed overview of the existing proposals, see Dittus (1993).

REFERENCES

Ábel, I. and Bonin, J.P. (1994), 'Financial sector reform in the economies in transition: on the way to privatizing commercial banks', in Bonin, J. and Székely, I.P. (eds), *The Development and Reform of Financial Systems in Central and Eastern Europe*, Aldershot: Edward Elgar.

Ábel, I. and Székely, I. P. (1993), 'Changing structure of household portfolios in emerging market economies: the case of Hungary, 1970–1989', in Székely, I.P. and Newbery, D.M.G. (eds), *Hungary: An Economy in Transition*, Cambridge: Cambridge University Press, 163–80.

Ábel, I. and Székely, I.P. (1994), 'Market structures and competition in the Hungarian banking system', in Bonin, J.P. and Székely, I.P. (eds), *The Development and Reform of Financial Systems in Central and Eastern Europe*, Aldershot: Edward Elgar.

Bácskai, T. (1989), 'The reorganization of the banking system in Hungary', in Kessides, C., King, T., Nuti, M. and Sokil, C. (eds), *Financial Reform in Socialist Economies*, Washington, DC: The World Bank.

Begg, D. and Portes, R. (1992), 'Enterprise debt and economic transformation: financial restructuring in the state sector in Central and Eastern Europe', Discussion Paper Series No. 695, London: Centre for Economic Policy Research.

Bonin, J.P. and Székely, I.P. (eds) (1994), *The Development and Reform of Financial Systems in Central and Eastern Europe*, Aldershot: Edward Elgar.

Corbett, J. and Mayer, C. (1991), 'Financial reform in Eastern Europe: progress with the wrong model', *Oxford Review of Economic Policy*, **7**(4), 57–75.

Cukierman, A. (1992), *Central Bank Strategy, Credibility and Independence*, Cambridge, Mass.: The MIT Press.

Daianu, D. (1994), 'Banks in Romania today', paper presented at the conference on Banking Reform in the FSU and Eastern Europe: Lessons from Central Europe, Budapest, 14–15 January 1994.

Dittus, P. (1993), 'Corporate governance in Eastern Europe: the role of banks', Bank for International Settlement, Basle, mimeo.

Dobrinsky, R. (1994), 'Reform of the financial system in Bulgaria', in Bonin, J.P. and Székely, I.P. (eds), *The Development and Reform of Financial Systems in Central and Eastern Europe*, Aldershot: Edward Elgar.

Golden, R.A. (1994), 'Discussion of Chapter 5', in Bonin, J.P. and Székely, I.P. (eds), *The Development and Reform of Financial Systems in Central and Eastern Europe*, Aldershot: Edward Elgar.

Gray, C.W., Hanson, R. and Heller, M. (1992), 'Legal reform for Hungary's private sector', Working Papers WPS 983, Washington, DC: The World Bank.

Gurgenidze, L. (1993), 'Securitization of non-performing loans in transitional economies', Institute for EastWest Studies, New York, December, mimeo.
Hrnčíř, M. (1994), 'Reform of the banking sector in the Czech Republic', in Bonin, J.P. and Székely, I.P. (eds), *The Development and Reform of Financial Systems in Central and Eastern Europe*, Aldershot: Edward Elgar.
Járai, Z. (1993), 'Ten per cent already sold, privatization in Hungary', in Székely, I.P. and Newbery, D.M.G. (eds), *Hungary: An Economy in Transition*, Cambridge: Cambridge University Press, 77–83.
Kemme, D.M. (1994), *The Reform of the System of Money, Banking and Credit in Central Europe*, New York: Institute for EastWest Studies.
Kemme, D.M. and Rudka, A. (eds) (1992), *Monetary and Banking Reform in Postcommunist Economies*, New York: Institute for EastWest Studies.
Király, J (1993), 'A short run money market model of Hungary', in Székely, I.P. and Newbery, D.M.G. (eds), *Hungary: An Economy in Transition*, Cambridge: Cambridge University Press, 137–48.
Kokoszczyński, R. (1994), 'Money and Capital Market Reforms in Poland', in Bonin, J.P. and Székely, I.P. (eds), *The Development and Reform of Financial Systems in Central and Eastern Europe*, Aldershot: Edward Elgar.
Kruse, D. (1994), 'Discussion of Part One', in Bonin, J.P. and Székely, I.P. (eds), *The Development and Reform of Financial Systems in Central and Eastern Europe*, Aldershot: Edward Elgar.
Mayhew, K. and Seabright, P. (1992), 'Incentives and the management of enterprises in economic transition: Capital markets are not enough', *Oxford Review of Economic Policy*, **8**, 26–34.
McKinnon, R.I. (1991), *The Order of Economic Liberalization*, Baltimore: Johns Hopkins University Press.
Mizsei, K. (1994), 'Bankruptcy and banking reform in the transition economies of Central and Eastern Europe', in Bonin, J.P. and Székely, I.P. (eds), *The Development and Reform of Financial Systems in Central and Eastern Europe*, Aldershot: Edward Elgar.
Montias, J.M. (1994), 'Financial and fiscal aspects of system change in Eastern Europe' in Bonin, J.P. and Székely, I.P. (eds), *The Development and Reform of Financial Systems in Central and Eastern Europe*, Aldershot: Edward Elgar.
Phelps, E.S., Frydman, R., Rapaczynski, A. and Shleifer, A., (1993), 'Needed mechanism of corporate governance and finance in Eastern Europe', Working Paper No. 1, London: European Bank for Reconstruction and Development.
Podolski, T.M. (1973), *Socialist Banking and Monetary Control*, Cambridge: Cambridge University Press.
Portes, R. (1983), 'Central planning and monetarism: fellow travellers?', in Desai, P. (ed.), *Marxism, Central Planning, and the Soviet Economy. Essays in Honour of Alexander Erlich*, Cambridge, Mass.: MIT Press, 149–65.
Sándor, G. (1994), 'Financial liberalization in Central and Eastern Europe and its impact on exchange rate', in Bonin, J.P. and Székely, I.P. (eds), *The Development and Reform of Financial Systems in Central and Eastern Europe*, Aldershot: Edward Elgar.
Sárközy, T. (1993), 'Legal framework for the Hungarian transition 1989–1991', in Székely, I.P. and Newbery, D.M.G. (eds), *Hungary: An Economy in Transition*, Cambridge: Cambridge University Press, 239–48.
Savela, J. and Herrala, R. (1992), 'Foreign-owned banks in Finland', *Bank of Finland Bulletin*, **66**(4), 8–12.

Siklos, P.L. (1994), 'Central bank independence in the transitional economies: a preliminary investigation of Hungary, Poland, the Czech and Slovak Republics', in Bonin, J.P. and Székely, I.P. (eds), *The Development and Reform of Financial Systems in Central and Eastern Europe*, Aldershot: Edward Elgar.

Siklos, P.L. and Ábel, I. (1993), 'The credit crunch as a disinflation strategy: exchange rate and monetary policy in the transition to market in Hungary, Poland, and Czechoslovakia', Wilfrid Laurier University, mimeo.

Stiglitz, J. E. (1992), 'Interest rate puzzles, competitive theory, and capital constraints', invited paper presented at the tenth World Congress of the International Economic Association, Moscow, August 1992.

Székely, I.P. (1990), 'The reform of the Hungarian financial system', *European Economy*, **43**, March, 107–23.

Székely, I.P. (1994), 'Economic transformation and the reform of the financial system in Central and Eastern Europe', in Aganbegyan, A., Bogomolov, O. and Kaser, M. (eds), *Economics in a Changing World*, Vol. 1, Basingstoke and London: Macmillan.

Tardos, M. (1987), 'The role of money in Hungary', *European Economic Review*, **31**(1–2), 125–31.

Várhegyi, É. (1993), 'The modernization of the Hungarian banking sector', in Székely, I.P. and Newbery, D.M.G. (eds), *Hungary: An Economy in Transition*, Cambridge: Cambridge University Press.

Várhegyi, É. (1994), 'The "Second" Reform of the Hungarian Banking System', in Bonin, J.P. and Székely, I.P. (eds), *The Development and Reform of Financial Systems in Central and Eastern Europe*, Aldershot: Edward Elgar.

Wijnbergen, S. van (1994), 'On the role of banks in enterprise restructuring: the Polish example', Discussion Paper Series No. 898, London: Centre for Economic Policy Research.

Wyczański, P. (1993), 'Polish banking system 1990–1992', Economic and Social Policy Series No. 32, Friedrich Ebert Stiftung, Warsaw.

Wyczański, P. (1994), 'Discussion of Chapter 5', in Bonin, J.P. and Székely, I.P. (eds), *The Development and Reform of Financial Systems in Central and Eastern Europe*, Aldershot: Edward Elgar.

Zwass, A. (1979), *Money, Banking and Credit in the Soviet Union and Eastern Europe*, New York: M.E. Sharpe.

Discussion of Chapter 10

Garabed Minassian

The chapter written by István Székely is an objective, unbiased and professional dissection of financial (primarily banking) reforms in the CEECs. It provides analysis of the acquired experience and outlines the major problems observed in the process of economic transformation. Economic integration of the CEECs into Europe is seen as rather a distant, not an immediate goal. According to the author, international economic integration presumes attaining a certain degree of unification of the financial systems in order to achieve one-way effects.

As a matter of fact, the banking system, this exceptionally important element of economic activities in any country, can hardly be considered in isolation from the general government economic policy. The author himself repeatedly mentions this. The solution of problems is further complicated by the specific features of the transition in each country. Banks and the banking system (including the central bank) are not ordinary economic agents in a country's business life. Very often, in addition to their economic functions, they perform social ones. For instance, they can even play the role of a safety valve for accumulated steam. In Bulgaria, the Bulgarian National Bank (BNB) has frequently been held up as all but the main culprit for economic failures in the country by both prominent and not so prominent politicians.

Again, from the point of view of the Bulgarian experience, one could say that the central bank has been commissioned to perform too many and sometimes even contradictory functions. Thus, in accordance with the central bank law, it is in charge of:

- control and supervision of inflation;
- control and supervision of the exchange rate;
- control and supervision of interest rates;
- running the lending policy.

This has served as a pretext for numerous attacks regarding alleged faults in the central bank's performance:

- the central bank is frequently blamed for the high level of the budget deficit, as far as it is responsible for the government's due debts to the bank;
- it is blamed for the delayed recovery since it is keeping the nominal interest rates relatively high;
- it has also been blamed for unfair redistribution of the national wealth, by keeping real interest rates negative;
- it has been charged with irrational utilization of the country's foreign exchange reserves.

The central bank, in its turn, tries to meet these numerous, varied and contradictory demands, and is not always successful. As a result of the recurrent attacks on its policy, BNB's relative independence has become one of its most vulnerable attributes. Politicians and statesmen do not seem to like the relative independence in BNB's decision making; in the end their criticisms have had an impact on BNB's policy.

A problem of great importance is whether and to what extent the central bank's activities, in the framework of financial reforms in the CEECs, are in a position to stimulate economic recovery. Following the classical monetarist prescriptions, the central bank and the appropriate monetary policy should be able to create the conditions and help most actively to find the way out of the crisis. I think that, regardless of the frequent reservations in I. Székely's chapter, this seems to be the author's viewpoint too. At the same time, the enormous burden of the SOEs (still occupying weighty shares in the CEECs' economies), coupled with the unstable political situation, bring substantial distortions into the general picture, which cannot be neglected.

Bulgarian experience has so far shown that, in spite of the provisions of the law, the independence of the central bank's policy is only relative. Moreover its individual efforts towards enhancing economic recovery, left isolated and without the support of adequate fiscal measures and appropriate government economic policy, may even have adverse effects. Such an example is the abrupt depreciation of the exchange rate in the winter of 1993 and the spring of 1994, when the national currency lost half of its value.

One cannot neglect the issue of personnel in the banking system either. The commercial banks used to have almost entirely accounting functions in the centrally planned economy. At present, under the market economy, they have to perform decision-making functions. Comprehensive risk assessment by bank managers is still only wishful thinking. Bad debts paralyse the operation of commercial banks while the criteria for granting new credits are still fuzzy. In any case, in practice, these criteria are not always related either to the requirement of high returns, or to risk reduction. The very notion of risk for the lender, under the dominant position of state-owned commercial banks and unclear bankruptcy regulations, is quite vague.

In this case, the overall government macroeconomic policy, along with a combination of various alternative approaches to privatization of commercial banks, will likely prove to be of decisive importance. One has to admit that, regardless of written regulations and proclaimed wishes, the banking system in the transforming economies (at least in Bulgaria), cannot be called independent and reforms in this field alone are not in a condition to provide for a sufficient degree of internal as well as external integration. Thus banking reforms should be implemented in the context of a consistent framework of broader reform policies.

11. Dealing with a stagnant pool: policies for coping with long-term unemployment in Central and Eastern Europe

Tito Boeri and Stefano Scarpetta

INTRODUCTION[1]

A common prophecy made at the beginning of transition was that economic transformation would involve high and rising unemployment. It was also anticipated that large flows of workers from the state to the private sector would occur, involving some – albeit possibly short – spells of unemployment.

Evidence collected at the start of economic transition seemed to support this prediction. Unemployment was, indeed, rising everywhere, employment in state enterprises was rapidly declining, and the private sector was booming. However information more recently collected by the OECD suggests that a different process may be at work. A striking feature of labour market adjustment in CEECs is the low turnover in the unemployment pool (OECD, 1994). Rather than being led by large inflows from the state sector, the growth of unemployment is the byproduct of very small outflow rates.

The spread of long-term unemployment in CEE challenges the newly established labour market policies in these countries. These were conceived to cope with rising unemployment, not necessarily with unemployment of long and increasing duration. Also long-term unemployment may not only involve permanent falls in effective labour supply but also erode the social consensus on the scope of the reform.

Labour market policies in CEECs are reviewed in this chapter by evaluating their likely impact on the duration of unemployment. The first section provides evidence on the duration of unemployment in the CEECs. The second section reviews unemployment benefit (UB) systems, whereas the third section analyses active labour market policies targeted to those who have experienced long unemployment spells.

THE SPREAD OF LONG-TERM UNEMPLOYMENT IN CEE AND THE POLICY RESPONSE

In spite of the depth of structural change, notably of dramatic employment reductions in state enterprises, monthly inflows into unemployment seem to be relatively modest in the CEECs, even when compared to those prevailing in low-unemployment OECD countries. Under these conditions, the rise of unemployment is mainly driven by the low pace at which job seekers are reintegrated into the labour market, rather than by large flows from employment to unemployment.

Table 11.1a Hungary: labour market transitions[a] *(working age population, transition probability over one year, %: March to March)*

	Employed in state sector	Employed in private sector	Unemployed	Out-of-labour-force
1991–92				
Status in 1991			Status in 1992	
Employed in state sector	84.0	3.6	7.6	4.8
Employed in private sector	3.2	87.0	7.8	2.0
Unemployed	9.8	7.2	80.4	2.6
Out-of-the-labour-force	3.8	2.0	2.5	91.7
1992–93				
Status in 1992			Status in 1993	
Employed in state sector	82.9	3.8	7.6	5.7
Employed in private sector	4.3	82.3	8.5	4.9
Unemployed	13.5	11.2	54.8	20.5
Out-of-the-labour-force	3.8	2.0	3.8	90.5

Notes:
State sector employment includes only employed in fully state-owned enterprises. Private sector employment includes employed in both fully private and mixed enterprises. Out-of-the-labour-force includes students, pensioners in early retirement and receiving disability pensions and other inactive persons.

[a] Figures along the diagonal are the probabilities of remaining in the same status over the reference period; off-diagonal figures are probabilities of moving into another status over the reference period.

Source: Estimates on the basis of the results of the Household Panel Survey (1992 and 1993).

Some possible explanations for these characteristics of unemployment dynamics in the CEECs are discussed in Boeri (1994a). Basically three factors may have played an important role in containing flows from employment to unemployment. The first factor is that sizeable flows from employment to out-of-the-labour-force occurred, especially in the early stages of transition, where quite extensive use of 'soft' disemployment measures – such as early retirement and more liberal access to various kind of 'disabilities' – was made and most working pensioners were pushed out of the labour market.[2]

The second factor reducing employment–unemployment flows is the flow of direct job-to-job shifts which played an important role in the process of ownership change. In addition to the employees in firms being privatized, many workers coming from state enterprises appear to have moved directly

Table 11.1b *Hungary: labour market transitions for those who changed their status[a] (% distribution of destinations of those changing status in one year: March to March)*

	Employed in state sector	Employed in private sector	Unemployed	Out-of-labour-force
1991–92				
Status in 1991 before change		Status in 1992 after change		
Employed in state sector	21.4	17.6	37.6	23.4
Employed in private sector	17.1	30.7	41.4	10.8
Unemployed	46.9	34.4	6.3	12.4
Out-of-the-labour-force	36.1	19.4	23.6	20.8
1992–93				
Status in 1992 after change		Status in 1993 after change		
Employed in state sector	29.3	17.7	34.5	18.5
Employed in private sector	11.3	38.3	34.8	15.6
Unemployed	25.2	26.1	25.2	23.5
Out-of-the-labour-force	12.2	14.9	24.3	48.6

Note: [a] Figures on the diagonal report changes in enterprise for those previously employed in the state and private sector, and in the case of the unemployed, the occurrence of repeated spells; off-diagonal figures report the distribution of possible destinations for those who changed their status in the reference period.

Source: Estimates on the basis of the results of the Household Panel Survey (1992 and 1993).

to jobs in the private sector without any intervening unemployment spell. Tables 11.1a and 11.1b propose transition matrices for the periods 1991–92 and 1992–93 in Hungary.[3] The matrices show probabilities of changing status – employment, unemployment or out-of-the-labour-force – in the labour market over a period of one year. As shown in Table 11.1a, the majority of those leaving state sector jobs move directly to private sector jobs or to out-of-the-labour-force. Among those employed in the state sector who have changed their employment status during the period 1991–92 (Table 11.1b), more than 20 per cent moved to another job in the state sector, some 18 per cent moved into the private sector directly, and about one-third joined the unemployment pool. Similar trends occurred in the following year.

Moreover once a worker becomes unemployed, her/his likelihood of getting a new job in the private sector is very low, albeit slightly increasing in the last two years. This is confirmed by microeconomic evidence on labour market transitions in the various countries (as shown in Tables 11.1a and 11.1b for Hungary), pointing to small flows from unemployment to the private sector.[4] If anything, the private sector would indeed appear to be a net contributor to the unemployment pool (Köllő, 1993; Godfrey, 1993). Private employers do not seem to recruit from the unemployment ranks. They rather prefer to hire either new entrants in the labour force or those holding a job in the state sector.

The third factor reducing flows from state jobs to unemployment is the spread of informal activities that offer some sort of subsistence income to those losing their job in the restructuring process. Although the size and dynamics of the so-called 'parallel economy' are notoriously difficult to assess, anecdotal evidence and unofficial estimates of the growth of the informal sector would indeed suggest that unregistered small business activities have been a factor in smoothing the social costs of transition. Labour force surveys (LFS) – nowadays implemented in most CEECs – are not the best data source on employment in the informal sector.[5] Yet the increasing discrepancy observed between administrative and survey-based measures of employment points to a sizeable informal economy.[6] Moreover LFS data also suggest that involuntary part-time jobs are spreading. All in all, under-employment or hidden unemployment may have been important in absorbing labour shed in the course of the restructuring process.

Whatever the explanation for the low turnover of the unemployment pool in these countries may be, it is clearly associated with the spread of long-term unemployment. As shown by Figure 11.1, while in some cases – such as the Czech and Slovak Republics in 1992 – unemployment has been significantly declining and is on a rising trend or stationary elsewhere, the increasing proportion of job seekers who experienced unemployment spells longer than twelve months is common to all countries. In Hungary and Poland, in

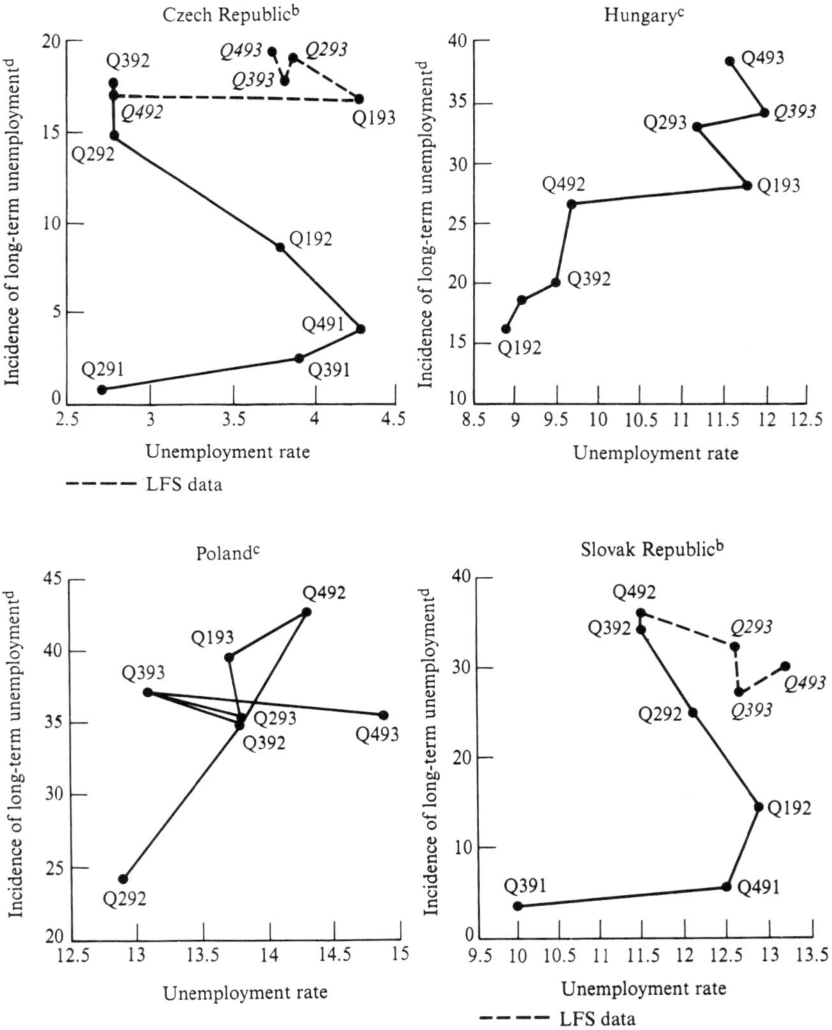

Notes:
[a] Persons unemployed 12 months and over as a percentage of total unemployment.
[b] Administrative data: Q1 93 data for the Slovak Republic are not available.
[c] Labour Force Survey data.
[d] Long-term unemployment as a percentage of total unemployment.

Source: OECD–CCET Labour Market database.

Figure 11.1 Incidence of long-term unemployment[a] and unemployment rate in CEECs (quarterly data, %)

particular, the incidence of long-term unemployment is close to 40 per cent, the level prevailing in OECD countries with a much longer history of open unemployment.

The first LFS was implemented in Bulgaria only in the autumn of 1993, and no information was available before that date on unemployment duration. Yet, survey data suggest that the share of long-term unemployment in total unemployment is not lower than 50 per cent.[7] No comparable information is available for Romania where no LFS has been carried out to date. However data from the unemployment register would suggest that the proportion of those with relatively long spells of joblessness is increasing. In particular, in 1993 almost 40 per cent of the registered job seekers were recipients of social assistance for those having exhausted the maximum duration of insurance-based benefits (nine months).

Who are the long-term unemployed? Table 11.2 summarizes available information on the characteristics of those having experienced unemployment spells longer than twelve months compared to the others in the unemployment pool. This gives an idea not only of the groups that are most at risk of experiencing long spells of unemployment but also of the factors behind the high incidence of long-term unemployment among these groups.

As shown by the first column of the table, long-term unemployment rates are increasing everywhere, except in the Slovak Republic where large inflows into the pool (and a significant increase in the overall unemployment rate) have occurred immediately after the split with the Czech Republic.[8] This increase has been associated in some countries – notably Poland and Hungary – with wider differences in long-term unemployment rates across various categories of unemployed, as can be seen by reading down the first column of Table 11.2. For example, in Poland, long-term unemployment rates for those with primary or lower levels of education were in 1993 twice as large as the country average, whilst in 1992 they were very close to the overall long-term unemployment rate. Long-term unemployment rates for the unskilled are also increasing faster than the country-wide long-term unemployment rate. It would therefore appear that the spread of long-term unemployment has been associated with greater dispersion in the incidence of spells of long duration across the different social groups.

Another striking fact highlighted by the first column of Table 11.2 is the spread of long-term unemployment among young people. Over one year, the long-term youth unemployment rate has almost doubled in Hungary, and increased by roughly 35 per cent in Poland and the Slovak Republic (20 per cent in Bulgaria). This has involved a larger concentration of long spells of joblessness among young people, similar to the situation prevailing in some Mediterranean OECD countries (for example Spain and Italy) with chronic and acute problems with youth unemployment.

Table 11.2 Characteristics of long-term unemployment in CEECs, 1992–93[a] (average yearly data)

	Long-term unemployment rate[b]		Share in long-term unemployment (%)		Share in total unemployment (%)	
	1992	1993	1992	1993	1992	1993
Bulgaria[c]	6.1	–				
Women	6.0	–	51.0	48.1	53.4	51.6
Youth[d]	5.4	–	32.0	25.2	45.1	41.4
Czech Republic	0.4	0.7				
Women	–	0.8	59.8	52.3	57.8	55.3
Youth[d]	–	0.8	–	18.8	31.8	31.1
Unskilled	–	–	–	–	–	18.3
Primary/low education[e]	–	4.1	–	83.9	35.5	30.4
Hungary	1.9	4.1				
Women	1.5	3.6	38.8	40.3	40.1	39.1
Youth[d]	2.5	4.9	20.4	17.5	27.0	27.2
Unskilled	7.3	7.1	49.6	45.2	41.5	34.4
Primary/low education[e]	2.7	5.6	69.8	70.9	44.2	41.7
Poland	4.8	5.3				
Women	4.5	6.1	52.2	52.9	50.3	51.2
Youth[d]	6.2	8.5	7.3	20.1	8.3	26.7
Unskilled[f]	6.2	5.9	8.0	13.0	7.3	12.1
Primary/low education[e]	5.3	10.6	23.3	27.6	23.3	24.9
Slovak Republic	4.1	3.8				
Women	4.9	4.2	51.5	47.7	43.6	43.9
Youth[d]	4.0	5.4	17.5	25.2	28.2	36.5
Unskilled	–	–	23.7	27.9	18.2	17.7
Primary/low education[e]	–	4.6	–	32.1	29.4	40.0

Notes:
– Data not available.
[a] All data come from Labour Force Surveys except for Bulgaria and the Czech and Slovak Republics in 1992.
[b] Long-term unemployed within each vulnerable group as a percentage of the group-specific labour force.
[c] 1992 data are drawn from the December 1992 population census; 1993 data come from the November 1993 LFS.
[d] The standard definition of youth refers to those under the age of 25. Exceptions: under 30 in Bulgaria, between 15 and 19 in Poland, under 22 in the Slovak Republic and under 24 in Hungary.
[e] Long-term unemployment data include vocational education.
[f] The 1993 long-term unemployment rate is based on an OECD estimate of unskilled labour force.

Sources: OECD–CCET Labour Market database; national submissions.

The share of women in long-term unemployment (column 2) tends to be lower than the share of women in total unemployment (column 3). This suggests that the driving force behind the spread of long-term unemployment among women may not be associated with relatively lower outflows from unemployment.[9] Rather asymmetries in the inflow side, that is, larger numbers of women becoming unemployed, seem to explain the dominance in countries like Poland and the Czech Republic of women in both total unemployment and long-term unemployment.

The strong role played by inflows – as opposed to outflows – in generating an uneven distribution of long-term unemployment across the different social groups is even more evident in the case of young people. The share of youth unemployment in total unemployment would indeed appear to be everywhere significantly higher than the corresponding share in long-term unemployment.

The case of the unskilled and those with primary and lower levels of education is just the opposite: their share in total unemployment is lower than the share in long-term unemployment, denoting greater difficulties for less educated and unqualified workers in being reintegrated into work. It should be stressed that differences between the share of total unemployment and the share of long-term unemployment for these two groups are widening over time. For instance, in Hungary, the incidence of unemployment for those with lower levels of education has decreased from 1992 to 1993, whilst the share of long-term unemployed with primary or lower levels of education has increased.

The effects of individual characteristics on exit-to-jobs probabilities can be better assessed by having access to individual data on the unemployed. Unfortunately such data are generally not available or come from the unemployment registers and, hence, are biased by frequent changes in regulations concerning the maximum duration of benefits (discussed below). Data gathered by OECD on the 1992 Hungarian quarterly LFS allow, however, some light to be shed on the effects of personal characteristics and duration on exit-to-jobs probabilities.

Table 11.3 displays conditional probabilities of leaving the unemployment pool towards jobs or the out-of-the-labour-force status for different categories of unemployed, and by duration of the past spells of unemployment in Hungary. As shown by the table, exit-to-job probabilities are rapidly decreasing with the length of the past unemployment spell, whereas exits from unemployment to out-of-the-labour-force are rather stable. Both probabilities however increase for spells longer than twelve months, probably because of the limited duration of UBs (twelve months at most) and the relatively short history of mass unemployment in Hungary, which reduces the reliability of data on persons having experienced spells longer than twelve months at the beginning of 1992.

Table 11.3 Exit probabilities for the unemployed in Hungary, 1992, %[a] *(different duration of the unemployment spell, first to second quarter of 1992)*

	Duration of the continuous spell			
	1–3 months	4–6 months	7–12 months	1–2 years
Number of cases	221	229	175	214
Total				
Out-of-the-labour-force	10.4	10.1	9.2	12.5
Unemployment	70.6	72.9	79.4	74.8
Employment	19.0	17.0	11.4	12.7
Women				
Out-of-the-labour-force	13.3	9.3	7.9	20.8
Unemployment	66.3	74.7	80.3	66.2
Employment	20.4	16.0	11.8	13.0
Youth				
Out-of-the-labour-force	2.4	7.3	9.4	12.5
Unemployment	69.0	80.5	87.5	67.5
Employment	28.6	12.2	3.1	20.0
Primary or less educational attainment				
Out-of-the-labour-force	12.4	10.6	8.4	14.9
Unemployment	69.7	70.2	83.3	76.3
Employment	18.0	19.2	8.3	8.8

Note: [a] Results are based on the probability of the unemployed at the time of the first survey (March 1992) remaining in the same status or moving in any of the three following months.

Source: Estimates on the basis of micro-data from the first and second quarters of the Labour Force Surveys in 1992.

A decline in exit-to-job probabilities may be typically a byproduct of heterogeneity effects, that is, the fact that in the pool of the long-term unemployed there may be more persons with characteristics acting against their quick reintegration into employment. However, as shown by Table 11.3, these negative effects of duration on exit probabilities hold also when the focus is only on women, the young or persons with primary or lower levels of

Table 11.4 Labour market expenditures in CEECs and in selected OECD countries

	Average unemployment rate[a]	Labour market expenditures as % of GDP[b]			Expenditure per one unemployed as % of output per worker[c]		
		Active	Passive	Total	Active[i]	Passive	Total
Bulgaria							
1990	1.0	0.14	0.06	0.20	–	–	–
1991	6.6	0.00	0.55	0.55	0.0	7.7	7.7
1992	13.2	0.04	0.59	0.64	0.3	3.9	4.2
1993[d]	16.6	0.09	0.67	0.76	0.4	3.4	3.8
Czech Republic							
1991	3.3	0.18	0.23	0.41	5.3	6.7	12.0
1992	4.1	0.32	0.19	0.51	7.5	4.4	11.9
1993	4.4	0.20	0.16	0.36	4.3	3.6	7.9
Hungary							
1990	0.9	0.24	0.14	0.37	27.3	15.9	43.2
1991	4.3	0.30	0.95	1.25	6.7	21.1	27.7
1992	10.8	0.39	2.39	2.78	3.2	19.8	23.0
1993	13.5	0.67	2.27	2.94	4.3	14.6	18.9
Poland							
1990	3.4	0.31	0.32	0.63	–	–	–
1991	9.5	0.29	1.35	1.64	2.8	12.8	15.6
1992	13.2	0.32	1.73	2.05	2.1	11.4	13.5
1993	15.5	0.36	1.82	2.18	2.3	9.9	12.2
Romania							
1991	1.8	0.02	0.30	0.32	1.1	16.1	17.1
1992	5.4	0.18	0.79	0.97	3.2	13.9	17.0
1993	–	–	–	–	–	–	–
Slovak Republic[e]							
1991	7.1	0.28	1.05	1.33	3.1	11.7	14.8
1992	12.0	1.30	0.82	2.12	9.0	5.6	14.6
1993	13.1	0.44	0.77	1.22	2.6	4.5	7.1
Austria							
1989	3.1	0.28	0.95	1.23	8.7	29.4	38.1
1992	3.6	0.30	1.16	1.46	8.1	31.1	39.2

Table 11.4 continued

	Average unemployment rate[a]	Labour market expenditures as % of GDP[b]			Expenditure per one unemployed as % of output per worker[c]		
		Active	Passive	Total	Active[i]	Passive	Total
France							
1989	9.6	0.67	1.90	2.57	6.3	17.8	24.1
1992	10.2	0.98	2.01	2.99	8.4	17.3	25.8
Germany[f]							
1991	5.5	1.35	1.63	2.98	22.8	27.5	50.3
1993	7.3	1.58	2.60	4.18	19.7	32.4	52.0
Spain							
1989	17.3	0.76	2.30	3.06	3.6	11.0	14.6
1992	18.4	0.54	3.07	3.61	2.4	13.6	16.0
Sweden							
1989[g]	1.3	1.75	0.68	2.43	128.1	49.8	177.9
1992	4.8	3.16	2.78	5.94	62.8	55.2	118.0
UK							
1989[g]	6.2	0.73	1.14	1.87	11.0	17.3	28.3
1992[h]	9.6	0.57	1.69	2.26	5.4	15.9	21.3

Notes:

– Data not available.

[a] For the CEECs the unemployment rate was calculated by taking the average number of registered unemployed divided by the labour force (defined as the average number of registered unemployed plus the average number of employed [first three quarters for 1993]). For the OECD countries, the unemployment rate was taken from the Quarterly Labour Force Statistics publication.

[b] For the CEECs 1993 GDPs were calculated by using estimated growth rates from the OECD Secretariat and are expressed in market prices.

[c] Calculated as the amount of labour market expenditure per unemployed as a percentage share of the output per worker.

[d] Employment data come from LFS; unemployment rate calculated using unemployment data as an average of January–October 1993.

[e] Employment data 1993 come from the Labour Force Survey.

[f] Data refer to unified Germany; 1993 GDP data represent an average of the first three quarters of 1993.

[g] Data for labour market expenditures come from 1989–90.

[h] Data for labour market expenditures come from 1992–93.

[i] Excluding expenditures on labour market training for employed adults.

Sources: OECD–CCET Labour Market database; OECD Quarterly Labour Force Statistics; OECD Main Economic Indicators; OECD Labour Force Statistics; OECD Short-term Economic Indicators; national submissions.

education. Moreover Table 11.3 seems to confirm our previous finding of the rather minor role exerted – especially at early stages of transition – by personal characteristics on exit rates. The pattern of exit-to-job probabilities is, in fact, quite similar across the different groups. The only noticeable differences concern the much higher exit-to-job rates experienced by the young unemployed and the relatively large flows of women to out-of-the-labour-force after the completion of the first year of joblessness. To summarize, long-term unemployment is spreading and it seems to be a self-fulfilling phenomenon: the more time spent unemployed, the more difficult it is to find a job. Under these conditions, unemployment may translate into permanent falls in effective labour supply. Finding appropriate ways to deal not only with mass unemployment but especially with unemployment of long duration is therefore a policy priority. Achieving a larger turnover of the pool is important not only to make sure that economic recovery can actually affect unemployment levels but also to reduce the social costs of transition.

High and persistent unemployment in CEE has fostered the rapid introduction of a battery of labour market policy measures to help the reintegration of jobless people into work. The range and scope of these policies are wide in all CEECs, especially when it is considered that similar policies have been developed in Western economies over a much longer timespan. Yet the effectiveness of these policies in providing income support to the long-term unemployed and in assisting their reintegration into work may be questioned. The analysis of the different types of support offered to the unemployed and long-term unemployed and, whenever possible, the assessment of the number of participants, provide some clues on how labour market policies are working in the CEECs.

Table 11.4 shows that the countries in CEE differ sharply in the amount of resources dedicated to labour market policies (columns 2 to 4). In the context of rapidly rising unemployment, all countries have devoted a growing percentage of their GDP to labour market policies and in some cases – Hungary and Poland – expenditures have already reached levels that are comparable with those often encountered in Western economies. It is important to note, however, that total expenditures have been mainly driven by unemployment compensation, while active measures have received only a marginal and often declining role.

The example of the Czech and Slovak Republics before and after the split is quite instructive in this context. In 1992, unemployment compensation expenditures in Czechoslovakia were considerably reduced and efforts were concentrated on active support to the unemployed. After the separation in 1993, the Czech Republic continued to face low unemployment and, despite reducing total expenditures, kept the previous order of priority between active and passive measures. On the contrary, the Slovak Republic was confronted with high and rising unemployment and fewer resources available for labour market policies and, in spite of inheriting a tight UB system, was forced to reverse the order of priority mainly by cutting active expenditures by almost two-thirds.

Since labour market expenditures and their composition are affected by unemployment levels, each country's commitment to labour market policies can be more properly measured in terms of expenditures per unemployed person. The estimate provided in Table 11.4 (last three columns) proposes this measure as a share of the output per worker. The degree of commitment varies less across countries than total expenditure figures would suggest but it diverges considerably from those generally encountered in West European countries. The table is also supportive of the idea that active expenditures are quite inelastic to changes in unemployment, which implies a decreasing share of active measures in the labour market budget as unemployment rises. In all but two countries – Poland and Romania – per capita expenditures were cut considerably from 1991 to 1993, with Bulgaria and the Slovak Republic spending in 1993 one-half and one-third, respectively, of what they spent in 1991.

The above suggests that the CEECs have rapidly expanded labour market policy expenditures, although differences persist, not least because of the different number of clients to be served. While UBs are taking the lion's share, active measures are mainly a residual which varies according to the budget available after paying unemployment compensation.

UNEMPLOYMENT BENEFIT SYSTEMS AND THE TRADE-OFF BETWEEN INCOME SUPPORT AND INCENTIVES TO JOB SEARCH

Economic theory suggests that the UB may be a factor in increasing the duration of joblessness and UB systems introduced in the CEECs have sometimes been challenged for being so 'generous'[10] as to create a disincentive to job search. A comparison of the benefit systems across CEECs and in a selected group of Western countries may shed some light on their potential effects (if any) on the high and persistent unemployment in the CEECs.[11]

Main Features of Unemployment Benefit Systems

All CEECs have developed unemployment compensation systems that can be reconciled for the most part with the principles of unemployment insurance benefits (UI) and unemployment assistance (UA), where the latter concept involves general welfare to a greater or lesser extent, depending on the country. Yet experiences differ among CEECs[12] in the way in which both insurance and assistance benefits are designed and operate.

The insurance-based systems in place in CEE share the characteristic that benefit is offered on the basis of an entitlement built up during periods of previous employment.[13] In all countries, benefits are financed to a greater or lesser extent via wage-based contributions. In Hungary employers' and employees' contributions actually provide the bulk of resources of the special fund administering UBs. In the other CEECs, employers' and employees' contributions are earmarked to extra-budgetary funds. These funds (which may also be financed via budgetary transfers) are used to finance all labour market programmes, including UBs.

There are two major features of any UB system which are important for the assessment of their potential effects on the unemployment duration, namely the relation of benefits to previous wage and the maximum period for which such benefits are available.[14] Both elements have undergone drastic changes in the CEECs, especially due to the need to contain expenditure in the face of rapidly rising numbers of unemployed claimants. The most striking case is Poland which started with an open-ended earnings-related UI system in December 1989 and then moved to a flat-rate system which provides benefits for a maximum of twelve months in January 1992. The other CEECs have maintained earnings-related benefits but have reduced their maximum duration: to twelve months in Bulgaria and Hungary (in this latter case from eighteen months in spring 1991), to nine months in Romania and finally to six months in the Czech and Slovak Republics (from twelve months before January 1992). At the same time, more stringent eligibility conditions have been introduced, together with smaller nominal replacement rates which steeply decline with the duration of the spell.

Another common feature of the UI systems in the CEECs is the redistribution towards low-wage groups. Since their first introduction, UI regulations have moved towards a compression of the spectrum of benefits obtained with a relatively low ceiling and a minimum which is generally close to the minimum wage. In Bulgaria, the range between minimum and maximum is extremely tight, as benefits should be between 90 and 140 per cent of the minimum wage (30 and 50 per cent of the average wage, respectively). In the Czech and Slovak Republics, benefit minima were removed and a maximum was introduced at 150–180 per cent of the minimum wage. However a minimum subsistence income is guaranteed and, hence, if UBs fall below the minimum and the unemployed do not have additional sources of support, social assistance benefits cover the difference between UB and the subsistence minimum. Finally, in Hungary, the range was reduced at the beginning of 1993 between one and two times the minimum wage.

The existence of a minimum level of benefits should, however, be carefully interpreted. In Hungary, this is offered only to those with a previous wage equal to or above the minimum level of benefit, that is to say, the replacement rate cannot exceed 100 per cent. In Bulgaria, on the contrary, the minimum level is considered a guaranteed minimum for all those fulfilling eligibility criteria, even if the initial replacement rate is above 100 per cent.

Another feature of UB systems which may affect incentives to job search is the opportunity to have a gainful activity while receiving benefits at the full rate. There is, in fact, a maximum admissible level of earnings above which the benefit claimant loses the right to benefits: it ranges from 50 per cent of the minimum wage in Poland and Romania, to 100 per cent in Hungary and 150 per cent in Bulgaria.[15] The rationale for allowing claimants to work and receive benefits is that benefits for many unemployed are very low and hence their integration with a 'small' wage may help prevent extreme poverty, especially in the case of large families with only one earner. However this regulation applies in a context where there is poor screening of the eligibility conditions of the claimants due to widespread under-reporting of wages and under-staffing of the labour offices. Therefore there are high risks that this regulation may translate into misallocation of scarce resources. We discuss this issue below.

Those who have exhausted their right to insurance benefits can have access to means-tested social assistance benefits (UA). As in Western Europe, there are two broad categories of UA benefits. In countries like Hungary, the social assistance benefit scheme is an extension of the insurance system available to the unemployed with a minimum employment record.[16] In the other countries, the long-term unemployed can benefit from social assistance schemes as can all people in need. However the unemployed receiving UA are required to continue reporting to the labour market institutions on their search activity, albeit less frequently than during the payment of UI benefits. In Romania, the social benefit ('support allowance' to UB exhaustees) is available only for a maximum duration of eighteen months while in all other CEECs social benefits are of unlimited duration for workers with previous work experience (the duration is generally limited only for school leavers).

In all CEECs, the level of social benefits is extremely low: it ranges from 40 per cent to 65 per cent of the minimum wage in Romania and Bulgaria, respectively, to 80 per cent of minimum pension in Hungary and one-quarter of the average wage in Poland.[17] In the Czech Republic, however, social assistance benefits can be even higher than the minimum wage. The means-test is also particularly severe, imposing a very low level of income per capita in the household of the claimant which, in practice, excludes a large share of long-term unemployed.

The Trade-off Between Income Support and Incentives to Job Search

How do UB systems of the CEECs cope with the twin task of providing income support while not discouraging job search? Given the brief history of the UB systems in CEE and the many changes they have undergone, it would be inappropriate to test empirically the effects of benefits on the choosiness of the unemployed and the intensity of their job search. There is, however, sufficient evidence to allow discussion on these issues.

Coverage rates of UI benefits in CEECs are close to the highest rates found in Western countries. At the end of 1993, coverage rates were in the range of 40–50 per cent. Bulgaria has the lowest percentage of registered unemployed receiving UI benefits but the highest share of unemployed covered by social insurance.[18] Coverage rates were in the order of 30–40 per cent in most West European countries at the beginning of the 1990s, with France and Austria having higher rates of about 53 per cent and 63 per cent, respectively (Scarpetta and Reutersward, 1994; Atkinson and Micklewright, 1991).

The share of benefit recipients over total registered unemployed is, however, falling in CEE as a result of the restrictions imposed on the maximum duration of benefits paralleled by the increasing average duration of unemployment spells. This is particularly evident in the Czech Republic and even more in the Slovak Republic where the maximum duration of benefits was halved in 1992, but it is also happening in the other CEECs. In Poland and Hungary, coverage rates were still high in 1992 but the restrictions imposed since then have already produced sharp declines in coverage rates. Further reductions are also foreseeable as the changes in regulations introduced in late 1992 and 1993 may not have yet fully displayed their effects due to the 'grandfathering' of entitlements achieved before regulatory changes.

Turning to the relationship between benefits and wages, Table 11.5 presents estimates of replacement rates for three earning groups (66 per cent, 100 per cent and 200 per cent of the average wage) and for different durations of the spell (up to 24 months). These estimates shed some light on the most relevant interactions between benefit levels, durations, and the often complicated operating of benefit minima and maxima. For long-duration groups, rough estimates are provided of the levels of social assistance benefits. The underlying assumptions used in our calculations are that: the three types of workers enter unemployment on 1 January 1992; they have a sufficiently long work history to allow them to receive UBs up to their maximum duration; they have no other sources of income that could lead to reductions in social assistance payments; and, finally, they have no dependent children.

Two measures of the relationship between benefits and past earnings are offered in Table 11.5. In the first measure (option A), benefits are divided by the reference wage corresponding, in general, to the average of wages received during a given reference period.[19] For comparative purposes, similar calculations are given for a selected group of West European countries.[20]

This way of calculating replacement rates, however, offers a very incomplete picture of the operating of UI and UA benefits in the real economic context of CEECs. In some of the countries, benefits, once calculated, are not adjusted to price changes. This would not be problematic in a context of low inflation, as it is in most parts of Western Europe nowadays. However, in most of the CEECs, inflation is running at double digits and in some of them is above 30 per cent. Thus the purchasing power of a certain level of benefits defined at the beginning of the spell tends to steadily decline in real terms throughout the duration of unemployment.

In order to take into account the effects of inflation, UBs have been divided in scenario B by the 'prospective' wage, that is, the market wage that the unemployed would have received if he or she had kept his or her job and maintained the same position in the earning distribution. Needless to say, this way of calculating replacement rates offers a better approximation of the perceived relation between UBs and previous and expected earnings in the labour market and, consequently, may be a more appropriate indicator of incentives to return to work related to the UB system. Scenario A suggests that the CEECs tend to offer relatively higher replacement rates for the lowest earning groups and lower rates to the higher earning groups (except Romania, where there is no maximum UI benefit as yet) than most West European countries. This seems to be consistent with the need to offer subsistence incomes to all those with previously low wages and, at the same time, to contain outlays; but is clearly at odds with UI principles. Moreover even the nominal replacement rates decline sharply for the long-term unemployed because of the generally shorter duration of UI benefits and the very low levels of UA benefits.

Once wage inflation is taken into account (scenario B), we observe that the CEECs have replacement rates well below most of the West European countries, especially for all those with medium/long spells of joblessness. The most striking case is Bulgaria. In this country, a sort of indexation of benefits to the minimum wage[21] has been introduced (in March 1993) but since this minimum has been kept constant for part of 1993 and inflation has been soaring, a replacement rate of 60 per cent in 'nominal' terms for an average earner in a medium spell of unemployment (four to six months) declined to around 44 per cent in 'real' terms and from the seventh month coincided with the minimum level of benefit, below the minimum wage. The real replacement rate for average earners approaching a year of continuous unemployment ranges from 44 per cent in Hungary to 32 per cent in Bulgaria.

The transition from insurance to social assistance benefits is synonymous with a large drop in the level of benefits. For instance, the replacement rate

Table 11.5 Replacement rates for different levels of previous earnings and lengths of the unemployment spell for CEECs and selected OECD countries, %

Level of previous earnings	2/3 of average monthly wage[a]				Average monthly wage				2 x average monthly wage			
Spells of continuous unemployment (months)[a]	0–3	4–6	7–12	13–24	0–3	4–6	7–12	13–24	0–3	4–6	7–12	13–24
CEECs												
Bulgaria												
A	64.4	64.4	65.9	67.5	60.0	60.0	52.5	45.0	33.4	33.4	27.9	22.5
B	51.9	47.1	39.2	33.1	48.4	43.9	31.6	22.1	26.9	24.4	16.9	11.0
Czech Republic												
A	60.0	59.2	59.2	59.2	60.0	50.0	39.4	39.4	34.8	34.8	19.7	19.7
B	58.7	55.3	48.6	44.3	58.7	46.8	32.4	29.6	34.1	32.5	16.2	14.8
Hungary												
A	75.0	64.1	64.1	38.1	75.0	60.0	60.0	25.4	39.0	37.2	37.2	12.7
B	65.6	52.7	47.1	27.0	65.6	49.3	44.1	18.0	34.1	30.6	27.3	9.0
Poland												
A	54.0	54.0	54.0	42.0	36.0	36.0	36.0	28.0	18.0	18.0	18.0	14.0
B	47.9	52.2	49.2	40.3	31.9	34.8	32.8	26.9	16.0	17.4	16.4	13.4

Romania												
A	65.4	65.4	53.2	40.9	60.0	60.0	43.6	27.3	60.0	60.0	36.8	13.6
B	59.8	55.7	40.7	26.3	47.6	47.6	32.1	17.5	47.6	47.6	28.0	8.8
Slovak Republic												
A	61.2	61.2	51.7	51.7	60.0	50.0	34.5	34.5	36.0	39.6	17.2	17.2
B	60.5	57.9	52.3	46.4	59.3	47.3	34.9	31.0	35.6	37.4	17.4	15.5
OECD countries[b]												
Austria	45.0	45.0	42.0	41.0	42.0	42.0	39.0	39.0	25.0	25.0	24.0	24.0
France	63.0	63.0	63.0	42.0	56.0	56.0	56.0	35.0	48.0	48.0	48.0	27.0
Germany	45.0	45.0	45.0	40.0	42.0	42.0	42.0	37.0	33.0	33.0	33.0	30.0
Spain	80.0	80.0	70.0	60.0	57.0	57.0	57.0	57.0	28.0	28.0	28.0	28.0
United Kingdom	23.0	23.0	23.0	21.0	15.0	15.0	15.0	14.0	8.0	8.0	8.0	7.0

Note:
Replacement rates refer to the period 1992–93. In scenario A they are calculated as the ratios between the unemployment benefit payments and the wage used for the calculation of these payments. In scenario B they are the ratios of benefit payments to the actual wage for each earning group. For details see text and Scarpetta and Reutersward (1994), Annex 1.

[a] Averages of the monthly replacement ratios for each period.

[b] The estimates of the replacement ratios for the OECD countries were made by the Task Force on Employment/Unemployment. These figures are provisional and refer to 1991.

Source: OECD.

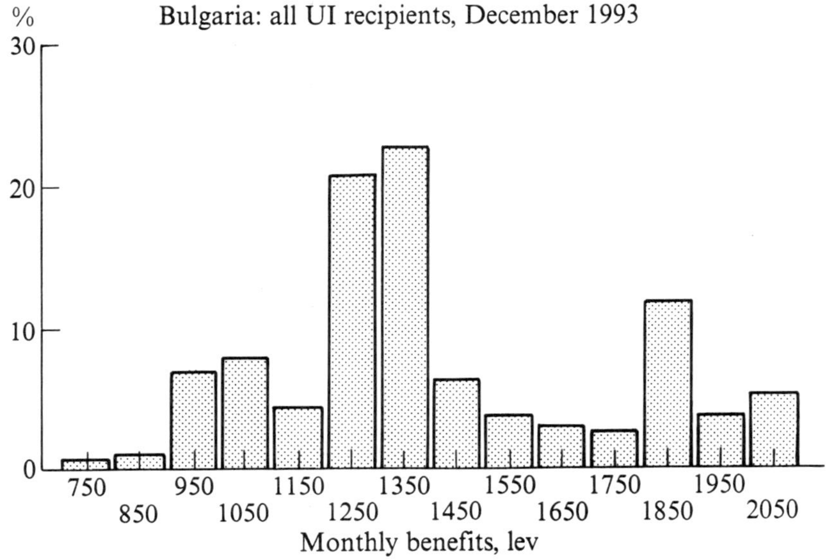

Source: Bulgarian unemployment register. Data from four local labour offices: Lovech, Mezdra, Pazardjik and Mladost (Sofia).

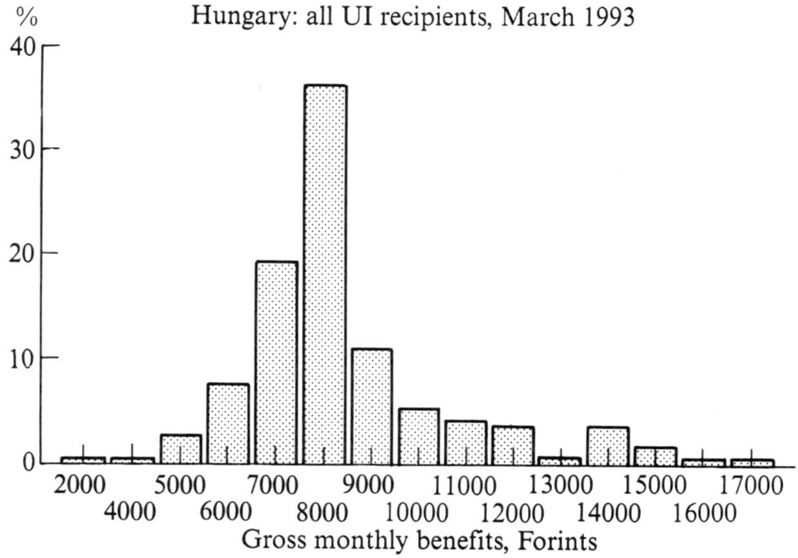

Source: Hungarian Household Panel, March 1993.

Figure 11.2 Distribution of monthly unemployment benefits, Bulgaria and Hungary

for the average earning group falls to 17 per cent in Romania, to 18 per cent in Hungary and to 22 per cent in Bulgaria. Poland is an exception since social benefits, like UBs, are calculated as a percentage of the average wage and, consequently, they are indirectly indexed to wage inflation. The lack of indexation of social benefits in the other countries is the corollary either of their functional dependence on the minimum wage (Bulgaria and Romania) and the minimum pension (Hungary) – which often results in the freezing of social benefits, as these minima are kept constant for long periods of time – or of the fact that benefit levels are set by regulations (the Czech and the Slovak Republics) which are amended only sporadically.

In addition to replacement rates, the absolute level of benefit is also important in assessing incentives to job search. In all but one country insurance benefits are earnings-related but a large majority of the claimants actually receive almost the same level of benefits, generally close to the minimum. This is clearly shown in Figure 11.2 which presents the distribution of a sample of benefit recipients in Hungary and Bulgaria according to their level of benefits in 1993.

In Hungary, in particular, more than 70 per cent of beneficiaries were receiving benefits ranging from 80 per cent to slightly above the minimum wage in March 1993. Such a compression of UB towards minima can be explained by the lack of indexation and the operating of benefit minima. As shown in Figure 11.3, benefits for an average wage earner (dotted line) rapidly converge to the legally binding benefit minima (thick lines) or to the level of minimum wages (the Czech and the Slovak Republics).[22] The convergence of benefits towards the minima is even more evident when it is considered that wages used to be very much compressed in these countries, and although a process of dispersion along the wage spectrum is taking place during the transition, most of the unemployed had earnings below the average wage.

Average UBs are also extremely low relative to the institutionally fixed poverty levels or subsistence minima. In Hungary both average UI benefits and minimum wage stood at about 70 per cent of the subsistence minimum in 1992 while in the former Czechoslovakia they were 75 per cent and 85 per cent, respectively, of the so-called minimum for life in the same year.[23] As a counterpoint, average UI benefits are also quite close to the minimum wage, that is, the wage that some unskilled unemployed may face in the labour market. Hence, on the one hand, benefits are – as a sole source of income – not sufficient to guarantee the minimum living costs but, on the other hand, may discourage some of those with low wage prospects from active job search. The situation is also complicated by the regulation allowing unemployed persons to earn a certain wage in the market and claim the full benefits. This possibility has been introduced with the aim of preventing

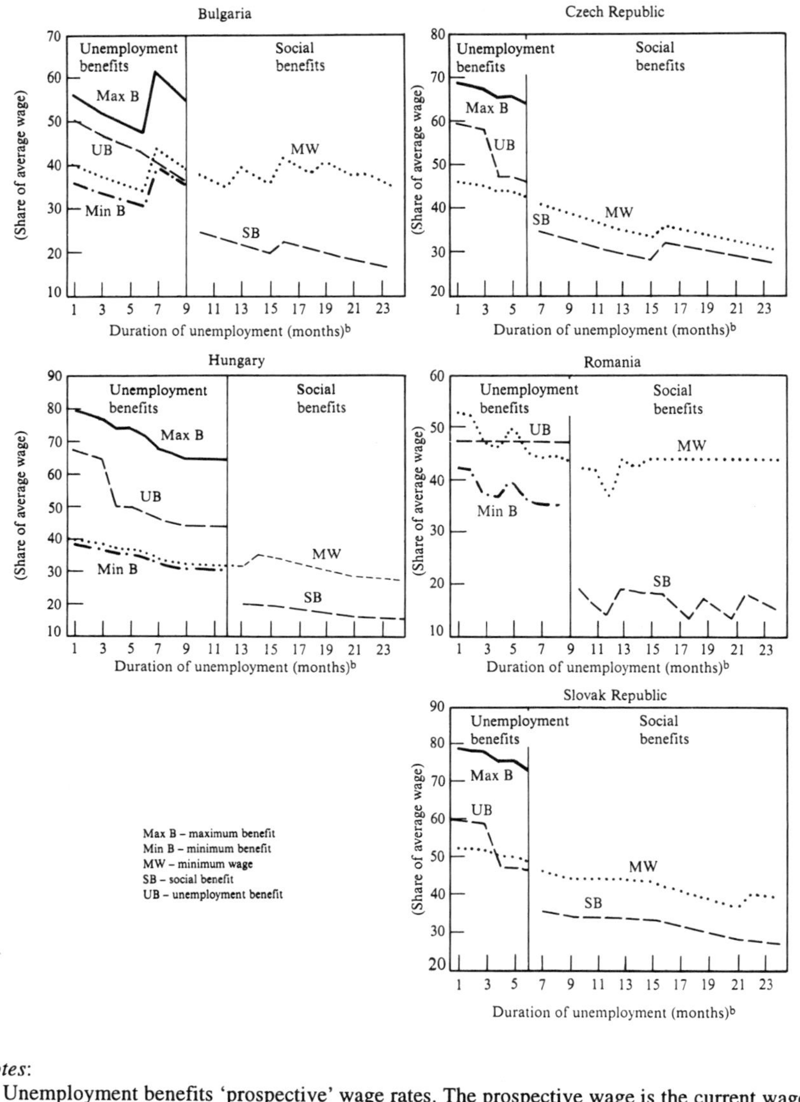

Notes:

[a] Unemployment benefits 'prospective' wage rates. The prospective wage is the current wage at the time of each payment of benefits. Gross replacement rates estimated beginning in January 1992 and ending 1993, based on available data for these two years.

[b] Figures refer to the 24 months from January 1992 to December 1993.

[c] Defined as reduced compensation.

Source: OECD–CCET Labour Market database; calculations based on Secretariat's estimations.

Figure 11.3 Unemployment and social benefits of an average wage earner during the spell of joblessness in CEECs[a]

cases of extreme poverty, but it may lead to poor allocation of the scarce resources available in the insurance fund, allowing some employed wage earners to receive benefits at the expense of those in greater need.

To sum up, UBs in the CEECs are characterized by a relatively low duration and a rapid decline in replacement rates during the spell of joblessness. This implies – together with the implementation of close benefit minima and maxima – that the systems work in practice as a redistributive tool offering to the large majority of claimants just a minimum income support.

Why then not move to a direct flat-rate system – as currently in Poland – instead of keeping such a fictitious earnings-related system? The advantage of such a choice would be a reduction in the administrative burden of UI benefit schemes and, perhaps, some financial savings that could be channelled towards more active programmes. Likewise, the regulation allowing the claimant to work for less than the minimum wage and collect the full amount of benefits should perhaps be reconsidered. If the objective is to offer an additional income support on the top of the flat-rate benefit, this should be carefully targeted to the most needy groups and not offered as an open possibility to all benefit claimants. Second, social benefits for long-term unemployed offer a very low level of income support (largely below subsistence minima), they are subject to extremely tight means-testing which practically exclude many long-term unemployed; and, finally, their linkage with UI benefits is not always fully developed.

Further evidence – especially from micro-data and over a sufficiently long period of time – would be required before any firm conclusion could be drawn on the effects of UBs in the CEECs. From the analysis presented above, however, one may be tempted to argue that the UI benefit systems currently in place in these countries may not exert a strong disincentive to job search and the acceptance of a job offer. This consideration seems also to be supported by estimates of matching functions in the CEECs showing that the tightening of UI regimes in 1992 and early 1993 have not exerted significant effects on outflows to jobs in CEE. Rather they seem to have increased drop-outs from the register after benefit exhaustion and in some cases a transition to inactivity.[24]

ACTIVE POLICIES FOR THE LONG-TERM UNEMPLOYED

In CEE, as in Western Europe, active labour market policies include a variety of measures ranging from training and retraining programmes to direct job creation and employment subsidies (see Figure 11.4). Most of these programmes are open to the unemployed registered at the labour offices, while only a few are tailored to the specific needs of the long-term unemployed.

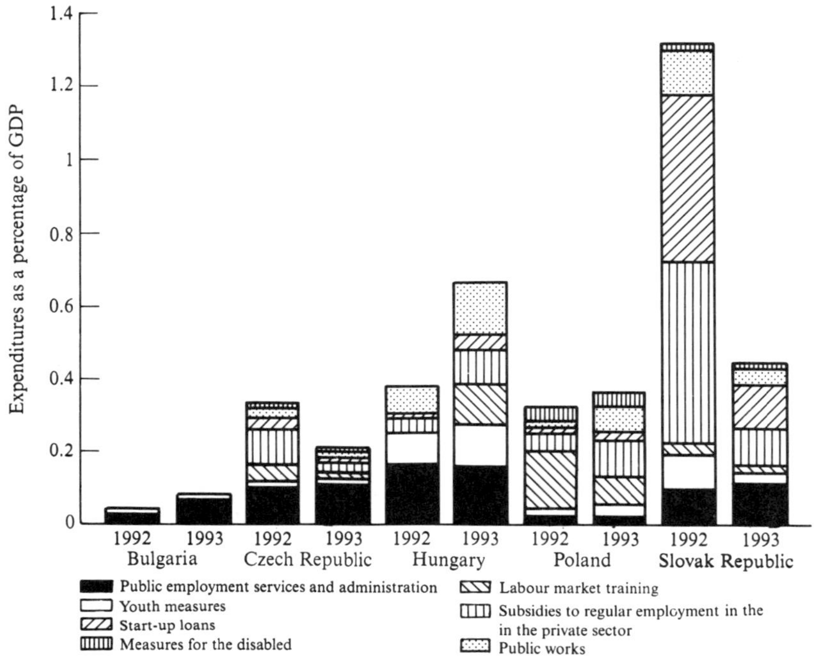

Sources: National submissions.

Figure 11.4 Public expenditure in active labour market policies in CEECs

In Poland and Hungary, there are specific employment subsidy schemes which are targeted to the long-term unemployed. Under these schemes, the Employment Fund (Labour Fund in the case of Poland) contributes to the wage of programme participants hired in firms which did not lay off workers in a similar line of work, in a certain period of time before the submission of the application. Subsidies are available only when the firm hires unemployed who have been without work for at least six months (three months in case of the Hungarian school leavers) and they cover half of the wage in Hungary or the level of UBs in Poland for a period ranging from twelve months to six months, in the two countries respectively. The number of unemployed involved in these schemes varies greatly between the two countries. In Hungary around 12,000 persons were involved in the employment subsidy scheme in 1992 and 1993, that is, 1.8 per cent of all unemployed persons. In Poland, there were 104,000 and 133,000 persons involved in 1992 and 1993 with an incidence on the total number of unemployed of about 4.4 and 4.8 per cent, respectively.

A general question can be raised as to the effectiveness of employment subsidies to help the reintegration of the long-term unemployed into work. The experience of most West European countries is not very supportive of the effectiveness of these schemes. The positive impact they have on employment is generally accompanied by high costs: 'deadweight' costs when participants in such schemes would have obtained a new job anyway; but also costs due to 'substitution effects' in all cases in which the genuine job impact (that is the impact for participants who would not have found employment without the help of these schemes) is obtained at the expense of other job seekers.[25]

In the CEECs, subsidized employment schemes have been introduced only recently and evaluations of the possible deadweight and substitution costs are scarce. However, as already indicated, the long-term unemployed in CEECs seem to have very little chance of being reintegrated into work and, consequently, deadweight losses are likely to be contained. Substitution effects may, on the contrary, be quite important when taking into account the limited number of vacancies available on the market.

Therefore the choice depends on whether one of the policy aims is to redistribute job opportunities in favour of the long-term unemployed who have particular problems of reinsertion. If, as we believe, this should indeed be considered as a policy objective in order to avoid the marginalization of a part of the labour force (which includes a large component of young persons), then it may be advisable to maintain such schemes amongst the priorities of active measures. Any further increase should, however, be based on the assumption that the staff of the labour offices can carefully screen participants and employers involved in the scheme in order to avoid abuses.

Public works, or works of public utility (PW)[26] have also been largely used in all CEECs to offer a way out, albeit temporary, from joblessness for the long-term unemployed (Figure 11.4). The main feature of this scheme is that the jobless are employed on special terms for activities of social interest. PW are generally offered on a temporary basis mostly in municipalities, including many kinds of local service, public building maintenance, and investments in infrastructure.

In Poland, the subsidy paid to the local bodies organizing PW cover up to 75 per cent of the wages with an average of about 55 per cent in 1992; in Hungary, the statutory amount is fixed at 70 per cent of wages, while in Bulgaria it covers up to the minimum wage. More generous provisions are offered in the Czech and in the Slovak Republics, where the entire cost is usually borne by the employment agency. There, PW have become one of the most important active programmes: in 1992, 16 per cent of the unemployed had been involved in such schemes in former Czechoslovakia. In 1993, however, participants decreased because of the overall reduction in total resources available for active programmes but also because PW have not always been popular among the unemployed who felt their chances of getting a 'normal' job afterwards were not enhanced after a period in PW. In principle, the main objective of PW is to mobilize labour supply. In particular in the most affected regions of the CEECs where there is a major need to renovate the existing infrastructure and where, at the same time, there is a need to keep the long-term unemployed in the labour market and avoid their marginalization, PW may prove to be an effective tool. However, PW may – like employment subsidies – produce deadweight and substitution effects in so far as they are used to finance ordinary municipal functions for which the same or other unemployed persons would have been hired in the absence of the scheme.

Moreover PW are designed to offer only temporary jobs. Available evidence suggests that so far only a few people involved in such programmes have afterwards received a job offer either from their PW employers or from other employers. The majority of PW participants usually return to unemployment and in some cases lose contact with the employment service.[27] One of the reasons behind this is that, as indicated, PW generally offer basic jobs which do not enhance the skills of participants and, consequently, their chance of getting a regular job in the market. Moreover, the jobs offered in the programme are often by nature seasonal or temporary, so that even the PW employer is not able or willing to take the participant into the permanent staff at the end of the programme.

In Western Europe, works of public utility had some popularity in the 1960s and 1970s but have become a minor item in the labour market policy agenda since then, mainly because of the same shortcomings they are displaying in the CEECs today. Notwithstanding this general orientation, there are exceptions like the Benelux countries and some of the North European countries, where PW have a significant role among labour market measures. The three Benelux countries employ large numbers of persons in permanent public make-work programmes.[28] In some of the North European countries, PW have a temporary nature, but they are integrated with training and job search assistance measures. For instance, in Norway, participants are invited to spend some time seeking permanent jobs while employed in PW. If, as we believe, the transformation of PW from temporary to permanent jobs is not a feasible option in the CEECs given their modest financial resources, they might follow the second approach, that is, combining PW with training and job search assistance in order to increase the chance of participants getting a real job.

The lack of an attentive targeting of active measures and the focus on the most needy people is a general problem in the CEECs. In Bulgaria, for instance, only UB recipients are eligible for free training, which clearly excludes the long-term unemployed. Targeting is particularly important in these countries because, on the one hand, active policies have quite a limited budget and, on the other (Scarpetta and Reutersward, 1994), labour market institutions are still under-staffed and further increases in resources would not necessarily lead to more effective actions.

During the last decade, in a number of West European countries, there has been a distinctive move towards selective measures focusing on the most disadvantaged unemployed (see OECD, 1990).[29] Skill-enhancing training courses, job-finding programmes and regular interviews with specialists have been particularly successful in reducing the incidence of long-term joblessness in these countries. Employment offices have adopted special procedures to make sure that the long-term unemployed are involved in these in-depth actions. Specific interviews are designed to orientate the unemployed towards an active approach in the labour market and in most cases these interviews are obligatory after a given duration of unemployment.[30] While not focusing on self-help, interviews with the long-term unemployed are used to identify specific training requirements and to adjust existing active labour market programmes to their specific needs.[31]

In the CEECs too, labour market policies could perhaps move towards a more selective approach, providing client-oriented services, if not for all unemployed, at least for the hard-to-place clients. Relatively inexpensive procedures could be implemented for those at earlier stages of unemployment and/or with fewer problems of reintegration into work, while in-depth forms of intervention could be reserved for the most disadvantaged unemployed persons, such as the long-term unemployed.

CONCLUDING REMARKS

According to search theory, the probability that an unemployed person finds a job depends on the probability of receiving a job offer times the probability of accepting that offer. Some of the early literature on labour market adjustment in the CEECs has stressed that the UB systems put in place at the beginning of transition may have been too generous. Too high benefits could have increased the reservation wage of individuals, thereby increasing their choosiness and reducing their search intensity. However evidence produced in this chapter does not lend support to this view. Rather than being too generous, UBs often fall below minimum subsistence levels due to the interplay of low wages, high inflation and little, if any, indexation of benefits. Under these conditions, UBs may well fail to provide the minimum income support required to devote enough time to job search activities.[32] In other words, if UBs have to bear the brunt of blame, this is perhaps because they are quite low, rather than because of their generosity.

While many unemployed remain without a job primarily because they receive too few job offers rather than because they reject too many, and demand factors play a major role in the spread of long-term unemployment, there is little that can be done by mobilizing labour market policy instruments. Yet active policies have a role to play in increasing the turnover of the unemployment pool, if not in increasing the stock of job offers.

This requires targeting of active measures on the long-term unemployed and especially so due to the low budget available for active policies, and the lack of qualified staff. Although there may be some scope for targeting the potentially hard-to-place unemployed, as they are likely to be more motivated to job search than those having already experienced long unemployment spells, this does not seem to be a viable option for the CEECs. Not only does the depth of restructuring make it difficult to identify those personal characteristics which may reduce re-employment probabilities, but also outflows to jobs do not seem to be highly differentiated in the CEECs across the various social groups. Moreover there is some evidence of positive forms of duration dependence suggesting that the length of past spells of joblessness is by itself a factor reducing the re-employability of the job seeker. Effective ways of targeting policies seem therefore to involve the screening of applicants on the basis of their past unemployment duration as well.

NOTES

1. We acknowledge the helpful comments of the participants in the conference on Transforming Economies and European Integration, Sofia, 27–28 May 1994, organized by the XXI Century Foundation. The views expressed in the chapter are those of the authors and do not necessarily reflect those of the OECD.
2. All these measures were clearly more socially acceptable than mass lay-offs. In the survey of 'Economic and sociological attitudes of the population' carried out in phases in former Czechoslovakia between 1990 and 1992, more than 65 per cent of the respondents in the Czech Lands and more than 70 per cent in Slovakia declared to be in favour of not allowing pensioners to be employed.
3. These transition matrices are based on the results of the Hungarian Household Panel Surveys conducted yearly since March 1992.
4. See Vecernik (1993) and Köllő (1993) for a description of two such surveys, in the Czech and Slovak Republics and in Hungary, respectively.
5. In particular the fear of legal sanctions (or the fact that some of these activities are not socially accepted) may discourage some of the respondents from fully declaring jobs held in the informal sector (ILO, 1993).
6. Another source of discrepancies between LFS data and figures reported by central statistical offices on the basis of establishment surveys and compulsory reporting from state enterprises is in the limited coverage of the small business sector (even when perfectly legal) provided by the latter statistical source.
7. This is roughly the same estimate for the incidence of long-term unemployment as could be made on the basis of the 1992 Population Census (Boeri, 1994a).
8. A larger number of starting spells involve a reduction in the average duration of unemployment. A better measure of duration would be provided, in this context, by the duration

of completed spells only, rather than of both unemployment spells that have been completed and spells that are still in progress. Unfortunately this information is not provided by the Slovak Statistical Office or the labour market administration.

9. This does not necessarily mean that women have better chances than men of being reintegrated into employment. Rather larger outflows from unemployment for women may reflect relatively large flows from unemployment to out-of-the-labour-force. Data on outflows from unemployment to jobs (which can be used to proxy flows from unemployment to employment) point to higher re-employment probabilities for men than for women.
10. Jackman and Layard (1990), analysing the UB systems in Hungary and Romania in 1990, concluded that they were 'relatively high' compared with those generally prevalent in Western countries. Layard (1990) arrived at a similar conclusion analysing the initial Polish unemployment compensation system. A more recent study by Burda (1992) suggests that Hungary still had a very generous UB scheme in 1992.
11. A comprehensive description of the unemployment insurance and assistance benefits introduced in CEECs since the beginning of the transition process can be found in Scarpetta and Reutersward (1994). A description of the main features which characterize unemployment insurance and unemployment assistance schemes in the OECD countries can be found in OECD (1988), OECD (1991) and Atkinson and Micklewright (1991).
12. For instance, the Romanian UB system contains a major departure from the usual insurance systems in so far as it includes a means-testing element: those unemployed who own an agricultural plot above a given size or those who have a personal income higher than half the minimum wage are not entitled to UBs. For more details, see Scarpetta and Reutersward (1994).
13. Also, school leavers generally receive UBs which are often close to or even below the minimum level of benefits offered to the unemployed with previous work experience and are offered for a shorter period of time. For details, see Scarpetta and Reutersward (1994).
14. The duration of benefits is generally extended for older workers. Furthermore in Poland and Hungary, there are different kinds of bridges between unemployment compensations and normal old-age pensions.
15. This holds only under the civil contracts, that is fixed-term contracts concluded under the Civil Code and generally not exceeding three months. These contracts do not involve payments of social contributions by the employer. As stressed by Bobeva (1994), in May 1993 some 68 per cent of the employees in the private sector were under civil contracts.
16. Social benefit for the long-term unemployed has been introduced by the new 'Social Law' of January 1993 which sets the formula for calculating the benefits and the eligibility conditions, including a tight means-testing and the requirement that the unemployment claimant reports to the labour office.
17. In the Czech and the Slovak Republics, social benefits available for the long-term unemployed are of two types: the first is related to each individual and depends on the age of claimants; the second is related to the size of the household.
18. This is also due to the fact that school leavers and young workers with insufficient contribution periods receive social benefits directly instead of UI benefits, see Shopov (1993).
19. The reference period ranges from the last quarter before the beginning of the spell in the Czech and the Slovak Republics and Romania, the average of the last two quarters in Bulgaria and, finally, the average of the last four quarters in Hungary.
20. For both CEECs and the West European countries reported in the table, the calculation of benefits under this scenario is based upon UI and UA formulae and the operating of minima and maxima, but does not consider changes in the economic variables undergone in the countries during the period under analysis, such as the minimum wage or the minimum pension.
21. In March 1993, both minimum wage and UBs were indexed by 90 per cent of the price increase in the previous quarter. After June 1993, however, indexation was to be negotiated for each quarter of the year.
22. Using micro-data drawn from administrative records of the Hungarian UI system, Micklewright and Nagy (1993) found out that the earnings-related system determines the

benefits of only a minority of claimants, while the majority had their benefits at the level of the minimum benefit or less. This is due to the fact that in Hungary the minimum is not guaranteed and those who had earnings below this value are entitled to their full wage but not the minimum.

23. The fact that UBs are sometimes even below subsistence minima can be explained by the role played by additional sources of income for the unemployed. For example, family benefit schemes are quite generous in these countries. In the case of Hungary, Micklewright (1992) reports that the monthly payment for a two-parent family with two children was 38 per cent of median gross monthly earnings in September 1990. Furthermore in Bulgaria, Hungary and Poland, a wage close to the minimum wage can be earned by the recipients of UI benefits, which means that the total income for the unemployed can be even twice as large as the benefits and close to the average wage.
24. Using unemployment flow data for a period from January 1991 to middle 1993, the stability of the 'matching function' – a function relating outflows to jobs to the stock of vacancies and the stock of unemployed – before and after the changes in the UI systems has been tested. The stability tests rejected the hypothesis that the tightening of the UI benefit regimes caused changes in the responsiveness of outflows to jobs to vacancies and unemployment (see Boeri, 1994b; Scarpetta and Reutersward, 1994).
25. An overview of studies is presented in OECD (1993), chapter 2, table 2.10. For example, a study of Ireland's Employment Incentive Programme put 'deadweight' at 70 per cent of total participation and 'substitution' (affecting other job seekers) at 21 per cent. The remaining 'net' effect of 9 per cent was further reduced, to around 5 per cent, when account was also taken of the additional indirect 'displacement' effects, such as those resulting from distortions in product markets (see Breen and Halpin, 1989).
26. Public works and public sector work are used in CEECs, as in most OECD countries, as synonymous with job creation in the public sector. The term 'public' should be considered in its broad sense, also including non-profit organizations.
27. The results of an ILO Survey on Hungary in 1992 suggests, for instance, that only 8 per cent of those who had been involved in PW had got a job offer afterwards, 13 per cent were out-of-the-labour-force, 39 per cent were registered unemployed and 40 per cent were unregistered unemployed (see Godfrey, 1993). Similar results emerge from another survey conducted by Frey (1993): in the two counties in which the survey was conducted, only 3 per cent of those completing PW participation in 1992 were taken into the staff of the WP employer and 1.7 per cent were employed in normal jobs elsewhere.
28. In Belgium these jobs are offered on special terms to long-term unemployed; Luxembourg has a scheme to employ former steel workers in PW and the Netherlands has a large sheltered workshop programme for the disabled and has also recently introduced a Belgian-type programme for long-term unemployed persons.
29. In some countries, after the first generic contact with staff of the offices, further interviews are organized with specialists. These interviews generally focus on counselling and advice ranging from how to improve job search, the definition of training needs and measures to overcome disability. These activities focus on self-help, like the 'job clubs' in Australia, France and the UK, or the 'job finding clubs' in Canada, or the 'help yourself groups' in Austria. In other countries, training centres provide short courses with a similar purpose, like in Ireland with 'job search courses' and in Denmark with 'labour market introduction' courses.
30. These interviews have different names: 'newstart' in Australia, 'restart' in the Netherlands and the UK or the '13th month interview' in France.
31. In France the government introduced a new scheme specifically designed to combat long-term unemployment in February 1992. Almost all long-term unemployed were interviewed in the course of 1992 with the aim of reviewing job prospects of each individual and defining specific training programmes or other active measures to her/his specific needs. After one year, many long-term unemployed were either placed into jobs or offered either a training course or a temporary job under the community work programme (see OECD, 1993).
32. Evidence from Western countries suggests that many unemployed remain without a job

primarily because they receive too few job offers rather than because they reject too many. The rate of job arrival may also depend on the search activity of the job seeker. Thus UB recipients may use their greater resources to finance search activity. They may, for instance, visit the job centre more often, may place advertisements or finance journeys to approach possible employers directly, all activities which they could not have afforded otherwise. For some empirical results of such a relationship in Western countries, see Wadsworth (1991) and an earlier study by Mortensen (1970). For a comprehensive review of evidence on the rates of job arrivals and rates of refusal of job offers see Layard et al. (1991). In particular, the authors of this study, using the results of the 1987 Manpower Services Commission, suggest that in 1987, within seven weeks of becoming unemployed, only 7 per cent of men had refused jobs and 29 per cent had obtained a job.

REFERENCES

Atkinson, A.B. and Micklewright, J. (1991), 'Unemployment compensation and labour market transitions: a critical review', *Journal of Economic Literature*, **29**(4), December, 1679–727.

Bobeva, D. (1994), 'Labour market policy in Bulgaria', in *Unemployment in Transition Countries: Transient or Persistent?*, Paris: OECD, 85–107.

Boeri, T. (1994a), 'Labour market flows and the persistence of unemployment in Central and Eastern Europe', in *Unemployment in Transition Countries: Transient or Persistent?*, Paris: OECD, 13–56.

Boeri, T. (1994b), 'Transitional unemployment', *Economics of Transition*, **2**(1), 1–25.

Breen, R. and Halpin, B. (1989), 'Subsidising jobs: an evaluation of the Employment Incentive Scheme', The Economic and Social Research Institute, Dublin.

Burda, M. (1992), 'Unemployment, labour market institutions, and structural change in Eastern Europe', Discussion Paper Series No. 746, London: Centre for Economic Policy Research.

Frey, M. (1993), 'Labour market impacts of direct job creation (in the public non-profit sector)', Labour Research Institute, Budapest, October.

Godfrey, M. (1993), 'Preliminary report on a survey of the unemployed and labour market programmes in Hungary, October/November 1992', Budapest, January, mimeo.

ILO (1993), 'Statistics of employment in the informal sector', paper presented at the 15th International Conference of Labour Statisticians, Geneva, 19–28 January 1993.

Jackman, R. and Layard, R. (1990), 'Social policy and unemployment', paper presented at the OECD/World Bank conference on the Transition to a Market Economy in Central and Eastern Europe, Paris.

Köllő, J. (1993), 'Unemployment and unemployment-related expenditures', paper presented to the Blue Ribbon Commission, Budapest, mimeo.

Layard R. (1990), 'Economic change in Poland', Discussion Paper No. 3, London: London School of Economics, Centre for Economic Performance.

Layard, R., Nickell, S. and Jackman, R. (1991), *Unemployment: Macroeconomic Performance and the Labour Market*, Oxford: Oxford University Press.

Micklewright, J. (1992), 'Income support for the unemployed in Hungary', Discussion Paper WPS/67, London: London School of Economics, Centre for Economic and Related Disciplines, February.

Micklewright, J. and Nagy, G. (1993), 'How does the Hungarian unemployment insurance system really work?', paper presented at the OECD Technical Workshop on the Persistence of Unemployment in Central and Eastern Europe, Paris, September.

Mortensen, D. (1970), 'Job search, the duration of unemployment and the Phillips curve', *American Economic Review*, **60**, 847–62.

OECD (1988), *Employment Outlook*, Paris: OECD.

OECD (1990), *Labour Market Policies for the 1990s*, Paris: OECD.

OECD (1991), *Employment Outlook*, Paris: OECD.

OECD (1993), *Employment Outlook*, Paris: OECD.

OECD (1994), *Unemployment in Transition Countries: Transient or Persistent?*, Paris: OECD.

Scarpetta, S. and Reutersward, A. (1994), 'Unemployment benefit systems and active labour market policies in Central and Eastern Europe: an overview', in *Unemployment in Transition Countries: Transient or Persistent?*, Paris: OECD, 255–307.

Shopov, G. (1993), 'Unemployment, poverty, social security: the Bulgarian experience', RRT Bulgarian Document No. 8, Sofia: Centre for the Study of Democracy.

Vecernik, J. (1993), 'Czechoslovakia and the Czech Republic in 1990–93', Institute of Sociology, Czech Academy of Sciences, Prague, mimeo.

Wadsworth, J. (1991), 'Unemployment benefits and search effort in the U.K. labour market', *Economica*, **58**, 17–34.

Discussion of Chapter 11

Fiorella Padoa Schioppa Kostoris

Chapter 11 by Boeri and Scarpetta presents the kind of study I much enjoy because it describes facts which I partially ignore. The chapter summarizes and updates the research which the authors have been conducting at the OECD for a long period of time.

The chapter is divided into two parts. The first part describes the basic problems of East European labour markets. The second part illustrates the labour policy responses provided in these countries. In the conclusions, some sketchy policy proposals are offered. In summarizing and commenting on the basic facts illustrated in the chapter, I shall try to provide some additional explanations for them and later I shall discuss some policy proposals.

The first important aspect of East European labour markets appears to be an unexpectedly low inflow into unemployment after the transition started. The chapter offers three explanations: movement from employment to out-of-the-labour-force; job-to-job movement; movement from open to underground employment in the so-called parallel economy. I would add as a separate explanation the movement from employment inside each country to labour force participation outside each country. In fact, from casual empiricism and from first available data, migration seems to be an important phenomenon particularly in some countries (Poland, FSU) and towards certain countries (USA, Germany, Austria, Israel). However, very little is known yet about individual characteristics of emigrants and about their participation in the labour markets of the countries of destination.

Another feature which is worth mentioning here is that in the first two years after the start of the transition, employment declined less than would have been expected in 1989 and less than GDP. This has resulted in an increase in presumably unwanted labour hoarding of the order of 2–3 per cent in former Czechoslovakia and Hungary, 7–8 per cent in Bulgaria and Poland and 12 per cent in Romania. Only in the last two years, a clear process of dishoarding started in some of these countries including Poland, Hungary and Bulgaria (in 1992 dishoarding has been of the order of 12 per cent in Poland, 16 per cent in Hungary and almost 6 per cent in Bulgaria). The most notable case from this viewpoint is Poland, where GDP started increasing, while employment kept decreasing in 1992 and 1993. The consequences in terms of unemployment inflows are, contrary to expectation, ambiguous, because, on the one hand, dishoarding should reduce mismatch unemployment, but, on the other hand, it should increase disequilibrium unemployment, as shown by Gora and Padoa Schioppa Kostoris (1994). I shall come back to this point at the end of my comment.

The second aspect of the labour market pointed out in the chapter is that outflows from unemployment were even lower than inflows in the East European countries (never higher than 5 per cent, according to Blanchard, Commander and Coricelli, 1994). As a consequence, long-term unemployment started rising with all the negative micro- and macro-effects. This is not only a very painful situation from the individual point of view, but it also has particularly severe implications for the labour market because it raises its rigidity and inhibits the market adjustment, in the sense that the long-term unemployed become discouraged, unable to adapt their human capital to new necessities, and incapable of playing a role in the downward flexibility of real wages.

The chapter further describes some passive and active labour market policy responses in the CEECs to cope with long-term unemployment. I share the view of the authors when they say that unemployment subsidies are not too generous in the CEECs, although they represent the most important policy action put forward against unemployment. Replacement rates, calculated as the ratio between unemployment benefits and wages which could be obtained (if the person had been working), are for average wage earners and for average unemployment spells of the order of 30–40 per cent.

If one compares these figures with the corresponding replacement rates existing in Italy, where unemployment benefits are provided to those temporarily laid off by the Wage Supplementation Fund (Cassa Integrazione Guadagni), one can understand why the former President of the Italian Republic, Mr Cossiga, has said that Italy represented the last country of 'real sozialismus'. Indeed, the unemployment benefit is 80 per cent of the gross wage which could be earned had the lay-off not occurred and its duration is in principle two years, but in fact it may last much longer. In CEECs, the duration of unemployment benefits is currently never longer than twelve months and is often much shorter.

As far as active labour market policies are concerned, I do not share the authors' enthusiasm for public works as a way to boost demand. It is true that outflows from unemployment could be increased by any form of expansionary demand management, but I consider the latter in general very dangerous for these countries, given its inflationary implications.

The only appropriate way to increase demand in the CEECs seems to me through exports. But this requires increasing competitiveness which in turn requires higher productivity for given (and possibly rising in the future) real wages. From this (and only this) point of view, public works may be desirable because they provide infrastructure capable of enlarging productivity as much as other instruments do, like training or retraining. In general, it is preferable to rely on supply management, tending to increase capital endowment, introduce technical progress and raise profitability. Higher work discipline induced by the threat of unemployment is also very useful, so that the existence of unemployment and its implications in terms of labour market flexibility and efficiency may be in the medium run a therapy of unemployment.

In conclusion, together with other economists, I believe that the current unemployment in CEE is essentially of a classical type, given that the mismatch is possibly declining due to dishoarding and that there exists excess demand for output except in the export component.

REFERENCES

Blanchard, O., Commander, S. and Coricelli, F. (1994), 'Unemployment and the labour market in Eastern Europe', in *Unemployment in Transition Countries: Transient or Persistent?*, Paris: OECD, 59–76.

Gora, M. and Padoa Schioppa Kostoris, F. (1994), 'Mismatch unemployment and labour hoarding in Eastern Europe: the case of Poland', mimeo.

Jan Švejnar

The chapter by Tito Boeri and Stefano Scarpetta is an important and very well written documentary of the unemployment problem in CEE. Open unemployment was basically an unknown phenomenon in the region some five years ago. Today, except for the Czech Republic and some countries of the FSU, unemployment has reached double digits in all these economies. This phenomenon occurred despite major declines in labour force participation, a fall in real consumption wages, reductions in the formerly generous unemployment benefits and introduction of active labour market policies. Moreover, as Boeri and Scarpetta show, the large pool of the unemployed is stagnant, characterized by limited inflows, very low outflows and rising long-term unemployment.

The resulting problem is obvious. The extent to which unemployment is detrimental to economic efficiency and sociopolitical stability depends very much on the length of time individuals spend in unemployment. A society where the unemployed are experiencing short spells of unemployment (while moving from low- to high-productivity jobs) is clearly better off than one having an identical unemployment rate but where the unemployed experience long spells without productivity-enhancing job mobility. Short unemployment spells are hence likely to be associated with less human suffering and more efficient reallocation of resources, while long spells induce social costs and impair efficiency by reducing the capacity of the unemployed to reintegrate into gainful employment.

As is evident from Table 11.2, different groups have different incidences of long-term unemployment. Moreover, comparing the share of a given group (for example, women) in long-term unemployment and in overall unemployment shows that there are different patterns across countries and over time. In Poland and in Slovakia in 1992 as well as in 1993, in the Czech Republic in 1992, and in Hungary in 1993, women's share in long-term unemployment was higher than their share in overall unemployment. The situation was just the opposite in Bulgaria in both 1992 and 1993, in the Czech Republic in 1993, and in Hungary in 1992.

To be able to draw policy conclusions, one clearly needs to know something about the flows rather than just the stock of the unemployed. For instance, in 1993, in a study of the dynamics of the unemployed (Ham, Švejnar and Terrell, 1993), we have found that during the first six months of unemployment, women in the Czech Republic have lower outflow rates than men. In contrast, in the Slovak Republic, the outflow rates are about the same both for men and for women.

In drawing conclusions about the incidence of long-term unemployment from stock data (that is, data collected at specific points in time either administratively or through surveys of individuals), one must bear in mind that these data suffer from what is called 'length biased sampling'. This means that between the points of two subsequent samplings, there might occur short unemployment spells, with duration shorter than the period between the sampling points, which will not be captured by either of the samplings. Due to the incidence of 'length biased sampling', there is a risk of underestimating the actual level of short unemployment spells. Thus, for example, in our study (Ham, Svejnar and Terrell, 1993), we find that the officially measured Czech long-term unemployment rate is halved when one corrects for length biased sampling.

In addition to documenting the evolution of unemployment, Boeri and Scarpetta also provide a very informative discussion of the policy responses to the problem. Perhaps most important is the sad fact that the share of active labour market policies in total expenditures decreased as unemployment rose and the share of passive unemployment policies (unemployment benefits) had to go up. This, of course, presents a dilemma for policy makers. Can higher expenditures for active labour market policies pre-empt higher payments for passive policies later? There is virtually no evidence on this in CEE.

In a recent study, Švejnar, Terrell and Munich (1994) use district-level data on outflows and other variables to examine the effectiveness of active labour market policies. Interestingly, controlling for other effects, it was found that expenditures on active labour market policies had a significant positive effect on outflow in the Czech Republic, but not in Slovakia. There is clearly a need to examine the effectiveness of different labour market policies in detail.

All in all, the chapter by Boeri and Scarpetta is an excellent exposé of the unemployment problem during the transition. It may serve as a reference for all scholars in this area.

REFERENCES

Ham, J., Švejnar, J. and Terrell, K. (1993), 'The emergence of unemployment in the Czech and Slovak Republics', *Comparative Economic Studies*, **35**(4), 121–34.

Švejnar, J., Terrell, K. and Munich, D. (1994), 'Explaining unemployment dynamics in the Czech and Slovak Republics', in Švejnar, J. (ed.), *From Planned to a Market Economy: Evidence from the Czech Republic*, San Diego: Academic Press, 1994.

12. Foreign direct investment in Eastern Europe: state-of-the-art and prospects

Klaus-Dieter Schmidt

INTRODUCTION[1]

Foreign direct investment (FDI) is rightly considered as an engine in transforming the countries of Central and Eastern Europe and the former Soviet Union (CEE–FSU countries) into Western-style market economies. It is hoped that it will perform a catalytic role in restructuring and privatizing the state industry and in integrating the CEE–FSU countries into the world economy. Without massive inflows of capital, technology and managerial know-how over many years to come, sustainable economic growth is unlikely.

Although FDI is still a hotly debated issue in CEE–FSU countries – the opposition stems not only from orthodox communists who reject foreign capital penetration for ideological reasons but also from ordinary people who are afraid that strangers could steal national property – governments make great efforts to create a favourable climate for foreign investment. By and large the basic legal and institutional framework for FDI has already been established (OECD, 1993; Alter and Wehrlé, 1993): in all CEE–FSU countries, joint ventures and fully foreign owned companies are permitted to operate; in some countries and in cases of large-scale investment, however, authorization by the government is still required, and in some sensitive sectors foreign participation is restricted. Is goes without saying that CEE–FSU countries are still far away from being an attractive harbour for international capital. There are still too many uncertainties surrounding the process of transformation which must be considered as an important impediment to attracting foreign capital (Donges and Wieners, 1993).

The international investors' community has responded hesitantly. FDI in CEE–FSU countries has expanded rapidly only with respect to the number of projects. At the end of 1992, 70,000 projects were registered in fourteen CEE–FSU countries – compared with only 2500 at the end of 1989. However the volume of capital invested (in value terms) was less impressive. In 1993, inflows into CEE–FSU countries were estimated to be nearly US$4 bn, and the stock did not exceed the total of US$15 bn at the end of the year. No doubt, foreign investors are still jealously 'tasting the water', but they are not rushing to jump. In particular, they are reluctant to realize large-scale investments. This is not surprising. Competition for international capital is keen and shifts in the flows of FDI can occur only gradually.

This chapter attempts to provide an overview of the current state and prospects of FDI in CEE–FSU countries. First, it briefly reviews the theoretical framework for understanding FDI. Then it focuses on the trends and patterns of FDI flows since 1989. Finally, it draws attention to the policy towards FDI. The discussion in the chapter is more descriptive than analytical. For the time being, it is too early for a comprehensive analysis: the database is poor and the period of time under consideration is short. Both trends and patterns are still influenced by accident, for example, by single large-scale projects of a few multinationals. Nevertheless the chapter may serve as a basis for discussing the large variety of issues related to FDI.

THEORETICAL CONSIDERATIONS

Economic Theory of FDI

Economists and policy makers in CEE–FSU countries often expect very much with respect to FDI. However investors are not in a hurry to invest their money there. They have several options to enter a foreign market: they can do it in the conventional way by producing at home and then going for trade in goods and services or they can build up a foreign production base either through greenfield investment, or through a joint venture or by acquiring an existing company. They can also opt for an intermediate mode of market entry: they can conclude a contractual arrangement with a foreign producer in the form of licensing or offshore processing (Schmidt and Naujoks, 1993).

Although there is an enormous literature on FDI, a generally accepted theory is still lacking.[2] Even the most popular approach, the 'eclectic theory of international production' developed by Dunning (1980) and others, is far from a generalization (Parry, 1985, Rugman, 1985). Notwithstanding the reservations, it postulates the conditions under which FDI is undertaken at all (Sander and Schmidt, 1993).

According to the 'eclectic approach' three conditions are necessary for FDI (OLI-paradigm):

- a company must have ownership advantages in operating in foreign markets that allow it to successfully compete with other, in particular domestic, companies;

- it must perceive some locational attraction of the foreign (as compared to its domestic) production base in manufacturing all or part of its products;
- it must believe that these advantages can be best exploited internally rather than by means of non-equity arrangements such as licensing agreements or management contracts.

Ownership advantages are to be conceived as specific competitive advantages a company has *vis-à-vis* its foreign competitors. They originate from intangible assets such as superior knowledge in terms of production technologies, managerial know-how or marketing skills as well as from brand names or access to cheap funds. If ownership advantages are large enough to compensate for the additional cost of operating in a foreign market, then the company may be tempted to become internationally active – either by trade, by licensing or by FDI.

Locational advantages may originate, first, from different relative factor endowments on which traditional trade theories are based. The traditional approaches to international trade, as discussed in Chapter 6, are: the Heckscher–Ohlin–Samuelson model, the product cycle model and the models explaining intra-industry trade. In the Heckscher–Ohlin–Samuelson model, the choice between domestic or foreign production is determined by the geographical distribution of immobile factors, such as cheap labour, plentiful natural resources or favourable climate. Second, locational advantages may originate from:

- a country's economic system and legal framework which predetermine the degree of political and economic stability as well as the structure of incentives and constraints which economic agents are facing;
- a country's trade regime (its 'openness') which is an important determinant of sales perspectives;
- a country's quality of infrastructure or agglomerational advantages which are important determinants of production costs.

Internalization advantages mainly originate from economizing transaction costs, especially with respect to the cost of internationally transferring and using intangible assets such as technological knowledge. It is well known that international licensing is often inefficient because the costs of enforcing property rights to intangible goods are prohibitively high. Mostly this is the case for non-standardized production technologies, for advanced technological knowledge, managerial know-how and other skills to which property rights are not codified but incorporated in an enterprise's employees. Intangible assets to which property rights cannot be enforced are public goods.

Private costs diverge from social costs such that the market mechanism fails to set prices efficiently. This market failure translates into high transaction costs. Companies which operate internationally can avoid incurring them by establishing or acquiring subsidiaries abroad. In this way they can use and transfer intangible assets on markets which are internal to their organization.

The initial theoretical approach to FDI was based on the proposition that the existence of each ownership, locational or internationalization advantage is a necessary condition, and their simultaneous existence is a sufficient condition for FDI to occur (OLI-paradigm). More recently it has been argued that the locational advantages of a potential recipient country can be both a necessary and sufficient condition for FDI (Stehn, 1992). FDI may be undertaken even without firm-specific advantages on the part of the foreign investor if the potential recipient country's locational advantages are large enough to compensate for the small or even non-existent firm-specific advantages. This argument has important implications for economic policy towards FDI as within the OLI-paradigm locational attractiveness is the variable which is most perceptible to economic policy.

Motives for FDI

The difficulties in establishing a general theory of FDI stem also from the observation that the motives differ considerably between the different markets in which foreign investors are engaged (Agarwal, Gubitz and Nunnenkamp, 1991). The traditional literature has focused on market access as the main motive for FDI. It states that there is an optimal timing for starting FDI: a company should have reached a certain market share in a foreign market by means of exporting before becoming an investor there. Actually, most multinationals start with exports and follow with FDI – as far as they are able to gain from specific ownership, locational and internalization advantages. Incidentally, the argument of market access is only convincing if foreign markets are closed; otherwise it may still be more profitable to serve them by exports. Thus, the motives for FDI are expected to be more on the supply side than on the demand side: in the primary commodity sector investors are mainly interested in finding access to the deposits of raw materials while in the manufacturing sector they mainly look for cheap labour or qualified staff.

The relative importance of labour costs for FDI decisions, however, is not as straightforward as it might appear (Agarwal, 1989). Low labour costs are a necessary, though not a sufficient condition. One factor which is reducing the importance of cheap labour as a locational advantage is the increasing degree of automation in most manufacturing industries. FDI is more important in industries producing sophisticated products (such as automotive, electrical, machinery and transport equipment) than in industries producing standardized products. For example, in the footwear and clothing industries, as discussed in Chapter 9, foreign investors prefer subcontracting rather than FDI as these industries are not characterized by firm-specific advantages which might induce equity arrangements.

Forms of FDI

The 'traditional' forms of FDI can be described as a package in which foreign investors provide capital, technology and management at the same time. Normally investors prefer to establish joint ventures in which they are the majority shareholder. The joint venture approach provides some advantages for them: above all, they can benefit from their partner's country-specific knowledge, yet still have full say in running the company. In CEE–FSU, this also conveniently meets the host government's desire to find foreign partners for restructuring ailing state-owned companies.

However, frequently the existing companies in CEE–FSU countries are in a deplorable state – suffering badly from technological backwardness and overstaffing. Restructuring them is risky and expensive. Foreign investors may therefore refrain from the traditional forms of FDI. Indeed, in recent years new forms of FDI have gained importance round the world (Hill, 1985).

1. There is a greater 'un-packing' of FDI, that is foreign firms separately 'sell' either technologies (mainly by licensing) or capital (by buying shares).
2. There is an increasing number of joint ventures in which the foreign partner is the minority shareholder.

Both forms have become common in developed market economies as well as in some (Asian) developing economies; they are now emerging in CEE–FSU countries as well. An outstanding example is the Skoda–Volkswagen deal, where at present VW holds only a minority stake of 31 per cent (though with an option to acquire the controlling interest) – although actually VW is running Skoda as its own company.

As theory suggests that investors may have different objectives when investing abroad – short- or long-term profit maximization, risk diversification and widening of the product cycle – there are different forms of FDI for realizing these objectives. It is controversially debated whether there are country-specific 'styles' of FDI. There are no definite answers (Caves, 1993); hence, there exists a great variety of FDI strategies applied by investors from the main donor countries such as the USA, Japan or Germany in the main recipient regions such as North and Latin America or Europe. It seems though that, for instance, German investors have a longer time horizon than investors from the USA and therefore also show a stronger engagement in politically and economically unstable countries. To some extent this kind of behaviour may explain why German companies are the leaders in FDI in most of the CEE–FSU countries.

Transformation and FDI

Embarking on the process of economic transformation exposes the CEE–FSU countries to major external and internal shocks. This inevitably forces these economies towards alleviation of the distortions resulting from former politically determined specialization. The CEE–FSU countries' new position in the world economy will depend upon:

- the specific quality of their resources and natural endowments, namely locational characteristics, natural resources, labour force and capital stock;
- the specific design of the institutional framework and the kind of economic policy they pursue (Sander and Schmidt, 1993).

Transformation by its very nature is a dynamic process. The beginning of this process is usually characterized by a large depreciation of the stock of fixed capital while labour force and natural resources do not have to undergo depreciation to the same extent. This makes the transforming economies relatively richly endowed with labour and natural resources while relatively poorly endowed with capital. With respect to resource endowment and, consequently, with respect to comparative advantages these economies now resemble the economies of less developed countries. In CEE–FSU countries, this is often perceived as a 'downgrading' and as a loss of economic prestige.

However, the underlying assumption of the 'eclectic approach' is that each type of international economic activity goes along with a specific level or stage of economic development (Dunning, 1991). Accordingly a transformation economy which is actually experiencing a major drawback with respect to development sees itself invaded by foreign investments which rather seem to fit a less developed country than its own until recently relatively highly industrialized economy. This 'downgrading', though, is not caused by FDI and the specific form in which it occurs. Rather causality runs in reverse: the types and forms of FDI which presently occur are indicating the very stage of development to which the transformation crisis has thrown the economy back. There should be no question which type of FDI the CEE–FSU countries need first: what they need is a rough Jeep, not a luxurious sports car. This can come later.

Hypotheses of FDI

Some hypotheses can be derived from the theoretical considerations discussed above: one should expect a high concentration of FDI in those recipient countries which:

- are leading in the transformation process, in particular in establishing a sound institutional framework of FDI, especially in privatizing state-owned enterprises; and
- are able to offer a promising economic environment, in particular growing markets, qualified labour and low production costs.

One can also expect that FDI will concentrate in certain sectors, according to the recipient country's level of development, pattern of specialization and factor endowment (Dunning, 1991). It is likely that FDI is more important in sophisticated industries than in industries producing standardized goods as these industries hardly allow ownership and internalization advantages to be realized.

SCOPE AND LIMITATION OF THE FDI DATABASE

An obstacle to analysing FDI in CEE–FSU is the poor database. Only a few CEE–FSU countries have made available FDI data and even these statistics report on different subjects. Therefore data collected by international organizations are incomplete and inconsistent so that it is hard to analyse them.

The main inconsistencies stem from differences in the methods of FDI registration and in the reporting of the capital inflows. Further problems arise in distinguishing between direct investment and portfolio investment (OECD, 1993).

In principle, an FDI database should include:

- new equity investments as well as long-term credits;
- reinvested earnings, respectively consolidated losses;
- changes in the net value of assets.

It should involve only investments stemming from establishing, acquiring or expanding an affiliated subsidiary corporation or branch but not portfolio investments (Brewer, 1991). In reality, though, available data related to net flows are based on the capital account of the balance of payments statistics. By definition, these data exclude invested profits and consolidated losses as well as revaluation of the capital stock.

For the most part, the figures reported in this chapter are based on data related to cumulated flows (in value terms) which are collected and published by OECD, IMF, UNIDO and UN–ECE, supplemented by data from national statistics. Despite all the shortcomings explained above, these data allow us to identify the basic trends and patterns both for the group of CEE–FSU countries as a whole as well as for single countries.

ASSESSMENT OF THE CURRENT SITUATION

Conditions of FDI

The key to FDI is a legal and institutional framework setting the scene for productive investment in general. After the collapse of the old system, the CEE–FSU countries suffered from such problems as oversized and overstaffed companies, unclear property rights, seriously distorted prices, irrational tax and tariff systems, weak financial institutions and exaggerated bureaucratic regulations. Meanwhile, the CEE–FSU countries have taken significant steps towards a market-oriented system – though some have moved more quickly and some more slowly. Legal provisions regulating FDI have already been installed in all CEE–FSU countries, although the level of elaboration of the legal framework differs substantially from country to country (for more details see Chapter 13).

All countries have started comprehensive privatization programmes. Concepts and legislation, however, vary widely and so does public and political support. The same is true with respect to the current state of the privatization process. It is therefore not easy to examine its impact on FDI. According to the OECD (1993) report, there are again three main groups of countries:

1. Hungary is considered as the leader, although the game is still running. Its privatization policy is more 'open' to foreigners than those of other countries. This may explain why Hungary has been very successful in attracting foreign capital.
2. The Czech Republic, Poland, Russia and the Ukraine are placed in the middle. They put more emphasis on distributing the property to their population and less on pulling in investors from abroad.
3. Albania, Bulgaria and Belarus are at the bottom of the scoreboard. Their road to privatization is cobbled with uncertainties which may discourage foreigners.

This ranking may be different in some cases. It can be argued that with respect to privatization there is no point in placing Russia and the Ukraine in the middle – together with the Czech Republic and Poland. However each ranking is more or less arbitrary. In this case, the criterion is the technique of privatization: there is no doubt that mass privatization poses some impediments to FDI. It should be noted that, although to varying degrees, most CEE–FSU countries restrict FDI to some 'strategic' sectors such as defence, aviation, shipping, energy or banking.

Despite the manifold legal and institutional obstacles, all CEE–FSU countries use a wide variety of instruments in setting incentives to influence an investment decision by increasing the profit accruing to the potential investment or by reducing the risks attached to it. The most important are fiscal instruments (such as preferential tax rates, tax exemption and tax credits) but also non-financial instruments (such as import protection or the establishment of free-trade enterprise zones).

In the literature, there is controversy about how the pattern of international direct investment will be affected by government actions. An OECD (1991) report on 'investment incentives and disincentives' came to ambiguous conclusions. However an unfavourable economic and political climate cannot easily be surmounted by special incentive government actions.

Apart from enhancing the attractiveness of CEE–FSU countries to foreign investors by implementing a sound legal and institutional framework, there is much more to do to improve the knowledge of foreigners about which opportunities CEE–FSU countries may offer them. An inquiry among a sample of 163 entrepreneurs, business consultants and bankers of Western countries who were regarded as potential investors in CEE–FSU countries indicates that their reluctance is mainly caused by the lack of transparency within the

Table 12.1 Obstacles to FDI in CEE–FSU (a sample of 163 respondents from developed market economies)

Factor	Frequency of quotation, %
Lack of information about potential partners	97
Difficulties in assessing the potential of enterprises	89
Complicated legal structure	71
Lack of transparency of the economy	67
Insufficient stability of the political and/or economic situation	44
Lack of transparency of the decision-making process	36
Language barriers	21

Source: Sereghyová (1993).

local economy rather than by bureaucratic administrative procedures (Table 12.1).

The Flows of FDI into CEE

Overall trends

Although some FDI trickled into the CMEA countries in the 1970s and 1980s, a dynamic development only started after 1989 when the new democratic governments committed themselves to economic transformation. From

Table 12.2 FDI flows into CEE–FSU countries by recipient countries, 1989–92

	Number of projects[a]				Net flows (US$ m)			
	1989	1990	1991	1992	1989	1990	1991	1992
Bulgaria	30	140	900	1200	–	4	56	42
Czechoslovakia	60	1600	4000	6000	257	188	592	1054
Czech Republic	–	–	–	3120	–	–	–	983
Slovak Republic	–	–	–	2875	–	–		71
Hungary	1000	5700	9100	13000	–	311	1459	1471
Poland	90	2800	4800	10100	–7	88	117	185[b]
Romania	5	1500	8000	20700	–	–18	37	73[c]
Total above	1185	11740	26800	51000	–	573	2261	2825
Former Yugoslavia	–	3900	–	–	–	189[d]	137[d]	–
Slovenia	–	–	1000	1650	–	–2	41	113
Former Soviet Union	1300	2900	3900	15300	–	–	–	–
Belarus	–	40	280	710	–	–	–	–
Estonia	–	100	1100	2662	–	–	–	–
Latvia	–	50	295	1300	–	–	–	–
Lithuania	–	20	220	2300	–	–	–	–
Russia	–	1500	2022	3500	–	–	–	100
Ukraine	–	70	400	900	–	–	–	–
Grand total	–	–	–	–	–	–	2502	3855

Notes:
– Data not available.
[a] Registered at the end of the year.
[b] January–September.
[c] January–November.
[d] January–October.

Source: UN–ECE (1993, 1994).

the end of 1989 to the end of 1992, the number of foreign projects skyrocketed – according to the database of the UN–ECE (1993) – from about 2500 to about 70,000 (Table 12.2). Thus it is fairly reasonable to assume that at present more than 100,000 foreign investment projects are registered in CEE–FSU countries.

The large number of registered projects overstates the level of FDI into CEE. Only an estimated average of 50 per cent of all projects are virtually in operation (OECD, 1993). A large proportion of companies are just an accommodation address. Besides, only very few companies have made substantial investments. The average size of foreign equity involvement is minimal and the typical FDI in CEE–FSU countries is rather small.

Table 12.3 Stocks[a] of FDI in CEE–FSU countries by recipient countries, 1989–92 (US$ m)

	1989	1990	1991	1992
Bulgaria	–	–	300	320
Czechoslovakia	256	436	1100	1900
Czech Republic	–	–	–	1669
Slovak Republic	–	–	–	231
Hungary	550	1450	3300	4300
Poland	100	352	680	1400
Romania	–	113	269	538
				8458
Total above	–	–	5649	
Former Soviet Union	837	1328	5500[b]	–
Belarus	53	101	–	–
Estonia	45	48	180[b]	–
Latvia	9	27	121[b]	–
Lithuania	14	15	120[b]	–
Russia	617	959	800[b]	–
Ukraine	24	52	670[b]	–

Notes:
– Data not available.
[a] Cumulative flows at the end of the year.
[b] October.

Source: OECD (1993).

The mushrooming of projects formally registered must be attributed to foreign activities in trade and other services. In these sectors, foreigners mostly invested just the minimum deposit demanded by law. Large-scale investments (in the mining and in the manufacturing branches) are small in number.

Consequently flows of capital have increased at a much slower pace than the number of projects registered. In 1992, flows to CEE–FSU countries amounted to just US$3.8 bn or a little more (Table 12.2).[3] For comparison, at the same time global FDI financed by OECD countries reached about US$175 bn; flows to CEE–FSU countries amounted to less than 2 per cent of the total.

Stock figures (derived from cumulative flows) indicate that at the end of 1992 not more than US$15 bn were invested in CEE–FSU countries (Table 12.3). With respect to total worldwide FDI stocks – approximately US$1.5 trillion – this is a *quantité négligeable* (Jungnickel, 1993). On the other hand, this indicates that there still exists an enormous potential for FDI in CEE–FSU countries.

Geographical distribution

With respect to recipient country preferences, there is a clearcut ranking: foreign investors favour Hungary, Poland and the Czech Republic. Hungary has been able to attract the lion's share (30 per cent) of foreign capital but Poland and the Czech Republic are catching up strongly. According to recent national statistics, the amount of FDI stocks in Poland jumped from US$1.4 bn at the end of 1992 to US$3 bn at the end of 1993, and in the Czech Republic from US$1.7 bn to US$2.2 bn. In these three countries alone, the accumulated FDI flows accounted for about half of the FDI attracted by all CEE–FSU countries.

It is remarkable enough that the successor states of the Soviet Union are more and more becoming an attractive place for Western FDI, too. Especially the Ukraine and the Baltic states could raise their share in total FDI projects significantly. At the end of 1992 nearly 6000 joint ventures were registered in Estonia, Latvia and Lithuania, many more than existed at the same time in Russia (3500).

Flows of FDI to CEE–FSU countries stem mainly from Western developed market economies. The geographical pattern differs widely, but on average Germany dominates clearly: in 1991 and 1992, more than two-fifths of reported FDI came from this country (Table 12.4). The other most important donor countries were Austria, the USA and the Netherlands.

Germany ranks among the top five donor countries in all CEE–FSU countries, but it is not the first everywhere (Table 12.5). That means that the fears about 'German domination' in CEE–FSU countries are basically exaggerated. Recent statistics indicate that even in the Czech and in the Slovak Republics,

Table 12.4 FDI flows into CEE–FSU countries from OECD donor countries, 1991 and 1992

	1991		1992	
Donor countries	(US$ m)	(%)	(US$ m)	(%)
Total OECD countries	1654	100.0	2366	100.0
of which:				
Austria	361	21.8	397	16.8
France	210	12.7	167	7.0
Germany	725	43.8	988	41.6
Japan	185	11.1	–	–
The Netherlands	145	8.7	364	15.5
USA	–	–	397	16.8

Note: – Data not available.

Source: Love (1993).

the predominance of its two western neighbouring nations – Germany and Austria – is apparently becoming a matter of the past (Sereghyová, 1994).

There is no simple explanation for the different clusters: geographic proximity as well as traditional economic and cultural links are perhaps the main cause. The high share of French investment in Romania or of Finland in Estonia, for instance, may be explained by language ties. Sometimes, though, the ranking is strongly influenced by incidents such as large-scale engagements of single investors.[4]

The bulk of FDI into CEE–FSU countries has come from West European countries. The only important overseas investors are those from the USA which hold not only the top place in Russia and Hungary but are among the leaders in all other CEE–FSU countries, too. Japan, one of the leading investing countries in the world, has been conspicuously reluctant to enter the CEE–FSU countries. This is in line with the typical wait-and-see attitude of Japanese investors observed in other parts of the world.

The high regional concentration of investments within the individual countries is quite notable. Most of the foreign investors go either to the capital city or to regions of industrial agglomeration. In Russia, for example, the bulk of FDI is concentrated in Moscow City and the Central Region, and in Hungary in Budapest City and the western parts of the country. This does not come as a surprise: it is the best way to take advantage of externalities which are strategically important for foreign investors.

Table 12.5 Top five FDI donor countries in selected CEE–FSU recipient countries, 1992/93 (ranking by stocks; percentage shares in brackets)

	Donor countries ranking				
Recipient countries	1st	2nd	3rd	4th	5th
Bulgaria[a]	Greece (–)	Germany (–)	Austria (–)	Italy (–)	Russia (–)
Czech Republic[b]	Germany (31)	USA (28)	France (13)	Belgium (7)	Austria (–)
Slovak Republic[c]	Austria (–)	Germany (–)	USA (–)	Netherl. (–)	France (–)
Hungary[d]	USA (–)	Germany (–)	Austria (–)	UK (–)	France (–)
Poland[e]	Germany (37)	Sweden (8)	USA (8)	Austria (7)	France (5)
Romania[f]	France (–)	USA (–)	Germany (–)	Italy (–)	UK (–)
Estonia[g]	Finland (51)	Russia[i] (22)	Sweden (11)	USA (3)	Germany (3)
Russia	USA (61)	Italy (6)	–	–	Germany (4)
Ukraine[h]	Italy (–)	USA (–)	Germany (–)	Sweden (–)	Spain (–)

Notes:
[a] 31 March 1993.
[b] 31 December 1993.
[c] 31 December 1992.
[d] 1 August 1993.
[e] 1 July 1992.
[f] 1 January 1992.
[g] 1 January 1993.
[h] 31 March 1993.
[i] CIS.

Source: OECD (1993).

Sectoral concentration

A general trend in worldwide FDI is that 'it started everywhere in services' (Inotai, 1992). The CEE–FSU countries are no exception to this. The bulk of projects are in commerce, transportation, banking, insurance and other consumer and business services. However in this respect one has to make a distinction between the number of the projects and the amount of investment made within and outside the service sector. In value terms, the sectors of energy, mining and manufacturing attract most of the capital. This is because these sectors are much more capital-intensive than the service branches.

Due to the insufficient database, it is difficult to draw general conclusions about the industrial composition of FDI in CEE–FSU countries. From German FDI statistics (which appear to be fairly reliable) one can conclude that on average manufacturing is the major recipient of foreign capital: at the end of 1992 about 60 per cent of stocks of German FDI in CEE–FSU countries were allocated in this sector (Table 12.6).

Although it could be expected that labour- and capital-intensive industries such as production of consumer goods and food processing offer the best opportunities, these industries generally seem to provide only limited scope

Table 12.6 Structure of German FDI in CEE–FSU countries by selected branches, 1989 and 1992, %[a,b]

			Memo items:	
Sectors	1989	1992	Spain 1992	Portugal 1992
Manufacturing	89.7	58.2	66.0	66.0
of which:				
Chemical industry	3.8	3.3	17.3	11.6
Engineering	13.8	9.2	6.4	4.2
Motor vehicles	–	26.7	22.9	5.7
Electrical equipment	2.9	5.2	7.3	28.3
Trade	3.6	10.2	2.9	3.0
Banking, insurance, investment funds[c]	6.7	32.6	31.1	31.0

Notes:
– Data not available.
[a] Stocks at end of year.
[b] Including China.
[c] Including other activities.

Source: Deutsche Bundesbank (1994).

for FDI: 45 per cent of total investment in manufacturing was concentrated in just four branches, namely chemical industry, engineering, vehicle building and electrical equipment (Table 12.6). There are at least two explanations for this (Schmidt, 1993).

First, in labour- and capital-intensive industries, technologies in most cases are relatively simple, hence the possibilities that foreign firms may gain firm-specific advantages are quite limited. In those industries, subcontracting is the dominant form of foreign investment.

Second, the main interest of foreign investors is not to take advantage of sweatshop labour. Most of them look for a long-term engagement. This may explain why the structure of German FDI in CEE–FSU countries differs significantly from the structure which is typical for German FDI in developing countries. It is rather similar to that in Spain and Portugal, two of the preferred West European target countries for German FDI.

Presently, the main strategy of German companies is to build up 'prolonged workbenches' in labour-intensive industries. They hire firms (for example, firms producing industrial switches, computer keyboards or headlights and brakes for cars) which can be employed as suppliers for their home production base. The relatively short distance between domestic plants and foreign subsidiaries makes it easy to meet even tight delivery schedules. This gives producers in most CEE–FSU countries an edge on their Asian rivals.

Commodity specialization and trade orientation

Initially, the structural pattern of FDI was more or less accidental. Recently, a relatively big share of fresh investment has been channelled into the manufacturing sector (and into manufacturing subdelivery bases). This indicates that a reorientation of foreign investors is under way: the structure of FDI comes closer to the comparative advantages of the countries than it was in the past. Consequently one can expect different patterns in different countries according to their respective comparative advantages and levels of development (Dunning, 1991; Sereghyová, 1994).

Much research has been devoted to analysing the contribution of FDI to industrial restructuring and especially to establishing an export base. By and large, FDI seems to be more export-oriented than oriented towards local markets, but due to lack of data this point remains controversial in the literature. Presumably it is correct to say that multinationals generally start FDI as export bridgeheads for securing their own domestic markets or for serving international markets; later they turn to supplying the recipient countries' markets when local demand has increased as a result of industrialization and growing income and the recipient countries' markets offer new sales opportunities.

In this respect, foreign investors have often been criticized that their exports of resource-based and labour-intensive products have a much larger share in total trade than their exports of 'sophisticated goods'. However the obvious importance of inter-industry exports at the early stage of industrialization does not come as a surprise: the pattern is fully in line with the theory of economic development. This can be expected to change when the recipient countries have approached the state of intra-industry production.

Intra-firm trade plays an increasingly important role in the foreign trade orientation of FDI. This also has a strong impact on the imports of recipient countries. Intra-firm imports consist mainly of capital goods to establish foreign affiliates and of 'sophisticated' intermediate products used for local processing which is often considered as a factor weakening the progress of industrialization in the recipient country. However this pattern of intra-firm imports rather reflects the local availability of inputs at the respective stage of industrialization. It will change quickly in the ongoing process of reindustrialization.

The Effects of FDI

It is often claimed by the CEE–FSU countries that the contribution of FDI to building up the recipient country's new capital stock is relatively small. Indeed, at first sight, the impact of FDI remains disappointing if measured

Table 12.7 Stocks of FDI (end of year) relative to GDP in selected CEE–FSU countries, %

	1991	1992
Bulgaria	–	0.3
Czechoslovakia	3.4	5.8
Czech Republic	–	7.0
Slovak Republic	–	2.6
Hungary	10.0	11.4
Poland	0.6	1.3
Romania	0.6	1.3
Former Soviet Union	–	–
Estonia	–	1.8[a]
Russia	–	0.3[a]
Ukraine	–	0.9[a]

Notes:
– Data not available.
[a] October.

Source: OECD.

against the expectations and needs of the CEE–FSU countries. The amount of invested capital at the end of 1992 on average amounted to about 1.5 per cent of GDP (Table 12.7). Only in two countries, Hungary and – by a wide margin – the Czech Republic, did the accumulated stocks of FDI reach a significantly higher relative level.

Whatever the reason for the modest capital inflows, magnitudes that would close the 'capital gap' should not be expected (see Chapter 13). Historical experience of LDCs in the 1970s and 1980s shows that the net annual flows of FDI averaged only 0.4 per cent of total investment over a twenty-year period. In addition, only a few countries' inflows were persistently clearly above the average (for example, Malaysia); most of the others were clearly below the average (for instance, India); some countries' shares exhibited stability while others experienced significant changes from one year to another (Brewer, 1991).

Even if there are large increases in FDI flows in the next two or three years – which is unlikely – it would take several years before the cumulative effect could be substantial. So far, the CEE–FSU countries cannot rely on growing FDI flows alone; the bulk of capital must be mobilized at home.

CONCLUSIONS

Economists and policy makers in CEE–FSU countries often complain that foreign companies are reluctant with respect to large-scale investments. They are right. The number of projects started is actually impressive but the amount of invested capital is still relatively low. However even a brief analysis of FDI into CEE–FSU countries appears to confirm that these flows have been consistent with what follows from economic theory and conventional wisdom.

FDI is only one out of the several possible forms of a company's international involvement. A company in search of such an involvement faces a trade-off in the method of entering a foreign market: it will opt for an equity arrangement only under certain conditions – if it can identify significant ownership, locational and internalization advantages. Otherwise it will choose a strategy like exporting or subcontracting. Apparently the conditions for Western investments in CEE–FSU countries still leave much to be desired (Donges and Wieners, 1993; Welfens, 1993):

1. The legislation should guarantee private property (or a prompt and full compensation at market values in the event of expropriation) and the repatriation of capital up to Western standards. In this respect further improvements need to be made.

2. The acquisition of real estate and land is handled in a different way in different countries, but everywhere it is still more or less restricted. FDI would be encouraged by allowing foreigners to acquire the real estate necessary to the business.
3. The registration and licensing procedures are often fathomless and the activities submitted to authorization or barred to foreigners are frequently vaguely formulated. Formulas such as 'prejudicial to the country's economic interest' should be stated more precisely.
4. The legislation on taxes and duties often lacks transparency. Sometimes foreign investors are preferred to local investors; sometimes they are discriminated against. Rules, procedures and preferences need to be clarified.
5. Privatization is still a sensitive issue in most countries. In principle, foreign investors are welcome to participate in the privatization process but, in fact, they may often be discouraged by opaque and complicated procedures. Governments in CEE–FSU countries should recognize that the market for the run-down and overstaffed state-owned enterprises is far from a seller's market. More efforts need to be made to privatize these enterprises directly to foreigners.

The policy framework of the CEE–FSU countries in search of FDI appears to be ambivalent. It consists of various forms of concessions and subsidies, on the one hand, and a complex system of controls and regulations, on the other. This reflects the governments' desire to obtain the highest possible benefit from FDI in terms of technology, capital and managerial know-how but at the same time to restrict foreign ownership and control of the economy. The concern of recipient countries to preserve economic sovereignty may be understandable.

However, the economic effect of most regulations and controls imposed on multinationals is detrimental, reducing rather than increasing the benefits from FDI. There is some evidence in the literature that many governments are obliged to offer concessions and subsidies only to compensate for the controls and regulations they impose on foreigners. A considerable number of studies dealing with incentives to FDI have concluded that they are more harmful than useful (Brewer, 1991).

First, incentives may be inappropriate with respect to the recipient country's factor endowment. A common contention in the literature is the high capital intensity of multinationals in recipient countries (especially in LDCs) relative to that of locally owned firms. It is argued that such capital-intensive technologies are disregarding relative scarcities which are not 'appropriate' to the (mostly) labour-rich and capital-scarce countries, and may adversely affect employment opportunities.

Second, incentives may affect the recipient country's trade performance. A crucial point is the demand of multinationals for protected markets. Granting protection, recipient countries may be pushed towards a strategy of import substitution instead of export promotion. Many LDCs which were successful in attracting FDI followed import substitution. In this case, however, multinationals will consider the incentives provided by tariffs and quotas as 'artificial' and only limited in time. Indeed, these incentives may not be a strong inducement for foreign investors to go abroad.

Finally, incentives may also have an impact on the forms of inflow of foreign capital – whether multinationals choose greenfield investments, joint ventures or mergers. In many CEE–FSU countries, governments have a preference for joint ventures – although the welfare effects of this strategy are uncertain.

Several studies based on interviews with managers of multinationals report that they regard factors such as resource endowments, level of economic development, future growth performance, market size, infrastructure facilities and political stability to be much more important in their investment decision than concessions and subsidies. Studies based on regression analysis of empirical data on FDI flows come to the same result. Obviously most multinationals regard such incentives as too volatile, transitory or even illusory. Tax holidays, for example, are usually given to firms only during the early days of their operations when they are least likely to show profits. Therefore governments in CEE–FSU countries should primarily pay attention to creating a general and consistent framework for foreign investors – only then can they hope to participate adequately in international capital flows. FDI cannot be switched on like an electric light; to get the reputation of an attractive harbour for FDI needs some time – and some effort, too.

NOTES

1. The author would like to thank Birgit Sander and the participants of the conference on 'Transforming Economies and European Integration' for valuable comments on an earlier draft of the text of this chapter.
2. For useful reviews see Agarwal, Gubitz and Nunnenkamp (1991) and Stehn (1992).
3. The preliminary figure for 1993 recently published by the ECE is US$3.9 bn.
4. Flows can be especially 'biased' by such transactions. For instance, in the Czech Republic, the share of US capital in total FDI in 1993 jumped to 45 per cent while the share of German capital dropped to 14 per cent. This was due to a large-scale investment of Philip Morris (about US$190 m) into a joint venture with the Czech company Tabák Kutná Hora (Sereghyová, 1994).

REFERENCES

Agarwal, J.P. (1989), 'Determinants and structural development of FDI in Pacific-Rim developing countries', Kiel Working Paper 382, Kiel Institute of World Economics.

Agarwal, J.P., Gubitz, A. and Nunnenkamp, P. (1991), 'Foreign direct investment in developing countries. The case of Germany', Kieler Studien 238, Tübingen.

Alter, R. and Wehrlé, F. (1993), 'Foreign direct investment in Central and Eastern Europe. An assessment of the current situation', *Intereconomics*, **28**(3), 126–31.

Brewer, T.L. (1991), 'Foreign direct investment in developing countries. Patterns, policies and prospects', The World Bank Working Papers, New York.

Caves, R.E. (1993), 'Japanese investment in the United States: lessons for the economics of foreign investment', *The World Economy*, **16**(3), 279–300.

Deutsche Bundesbank (1994), 'Kapitalverflechtungen mit dem Ausland', Beilage zur Zahlungsbilanzstatistik, Frankfurt a. M.

Donges, J.B. and Wieners, J. (1993), 'Foreign investment in Eastern Europe's transformation process', mimeo.

Dunning, J.H. (1980), 'Towards an eclectic theory of international production: some empirical tests', *Journal of International Business Studies*, **11**(1), 9–31.

Dunning, J.H. (1991), 'The prospects for foreign direct investment in Eastern Europe', University of Reading Discussion Papers in International Investment and Business Studies, No. 155.

Hill, B. (1985), 'The role of direct foreign investment in developing Asian countries', *Weltwirtschaftliches Archiv*, **121**, 355–82.

Inotai, A. (1992), 'Foreign direct investment in reforming CMEA countries: facts, lessons and perspectives', in Klein, M.W. and Welfens, J.J. (eds), *Multinationals in the New Europe and Global Trade*, Berlin, Heidelberg, New York: Springer Verlag, 129–48.

Jungnickel, R. (1993), 'Recent trends in foreign direct investment', *Intereconomics*, **28**(3), 118–25.

Love, A.R. (1993), 'Aid in transition', Report of the Development Assistance Committee 1993, Paris.

OECD (1991), *Investment Incentives and Disincentives: Effects on International Direct Investment*, Paris: OECD.

OECD (1993), 'Foreign direct investment in Central and Eastern Europe. Policies and trends in fourteen economies in transition', OECD, Paris, July.

Parry, T.G. (1985), 'Internalization as a general theory of foreign direct investment: a critique', *Weltwirtschaftliches Archiv*, **121**(3), 564–9.

Rugman, A.M. (1985), 'Internalization is still a general theory of foreign direct investment', *Weltwirtschaftliches Archiv*, **121**(3), 570–75.

Sander, B. and Schmidt, K.-D. (1993), 'Explaining foreign direct investment (FDI) in Central East European reform countries – what should we know?', in *Entrepreneurship in East European Countries in the Framework of Increasing East–West Economic Compatibility*, Universitat de Barcelona, 1–18.

Schmidt, K.-D. (1993), 'Foreign direct investment of German companies in Central and East European countries', in *Entrepreneurship in East European Countries in the Framework of Increasing East-West Economic Compatibility*, Universitat de Barcelona.

Schmidt, K.-D. and Naujoks, P. (1993), 'Western enterprises on eastern markets', Kiel Working Paper No. 607, Kiel Institute of World Economics.

Sereghyová, J. et al. (1993), 'Entrepreneurship in Central East Europe. Conditions, opportunities, strategies', Heidelberg.
Sereghyová, J. (1994), 'Recent development of foreign investment in the former CSFR and the Czech Republic', Prague, mimeo.
Stehn, J. (1992), 'Ausländische Direktinvestitionen in Industrieländern – Theoretische Erklärungsansätze und empirische Evidenz', Kieler Studien 245, Tübingen.
UN–ECE (1993), *Economic Survey of Europe in 1992–1993*, New York: United Nations Economic Commission for Europe.
UN–ECE (1994), *Economic Survey of Europe in 1993–1994*, New York: United Nations Economic Commission for Europe.
Welfens, P.J.J. (1993), 'The growth of the private sector: privatization and foreign direct investment in Eastern Europe', in Siebert, H. (ed.), *Overcoming the Transformation Crisis. Lessons for the Successor State of the Soviet Union*, Tübingen: J.C.B. Mohr (Paul Siebeck) Publishing, 119–66.

Discussion of Chapter 12

Rumen Gechev

THE ROLE OF FOREIGN INVESTMENT DURING THE BULGARIAN TRANSITION TO A MARKET ECONOMY

It is well known, as pointed out by Klaus-Dieter Schmidt in Chapter 12, that both the direction of movement and the amount of foreign investments depend mainly on the parameters of the business environment and the political stability in a long-term perspective. Political will and intentions can influence investment decisions but they cannot determine them. In this respect, decisions to invest in the Bulgarian economy depend on the opportunities it offers for a sufficiently high expected rate of return, the associated risk of the investment and the access to reliable markets.

For the period 1990–93, the total sum of FDI in Bulgaria is US$200–220 m or as little as 1 per cent of the total amount of these investments in Eastern Europe, amounting, according to UN–ECE, to about US$20 bn. Hungary ranks first with nearly US$7 bn, followed by Russia (more than US$3 bn), the Czech Republic (US$2 bn, Romania US$755 m and Slovakia US$380 m). The fact that Bulgaria lags behind Hungary (a country comparable both in the size of its population and in the market potential) by the order of 30 times speaks for itself. What are the reasons for such a disturbing tendency?

The continuing economic recession proved the inadequacy of the 'shock therapy' approach which Bulgaria chose to follow. Many aspects of the country's economic life have registered a positive change during the last four years. One could mention, for instance, the privatization of more than 50 per cent of the trade and services sectors, the elimination of the consumer goods deficit on the domestic market, the positive results from the restructuring of the banking system, a certain degree of trade reorientation in the direction of Western Europe and so on. The majority of macroeconomic indicators, however, continue to go from bad to worse.

Thus the total GDP decline for the 1990–93 period exceeds 40 per cent. After plunging by over 50 per cent, the industrial sector shows certain signs of increased activity, mainly in the petrochemical industry. But in a number of key industries such as electronics, machine-tool engineering, the chemical industry and instrument engineering the picture is getting bleaker. The decline in agricultural production is substantial as well. From this point of view, what is dangerous is not only the shrinking GDP itself, but the undesirable trends in its structure, manifested in the drop of potential interest for direct investment.

The collapse in the real sector of the economy has undermined the base of the financial and budgetary stabilization of the country. The total debt of the government and of the SOEs to the banks at the end of April 1994 amounts to as much as 590 bn lev. For the sake of comparison, the 1993 GDP was 290 bn lev. The budget deficit can hardly be expected to fall below the range of 6–7 per cent of the GDP, and the balance of payments is being managed mainly through the assistance of the IMF and the World Bank. At the beginning of 1994, the country went through a severe foreign exchange crisis, when in the course of several days only, the exchange rate of the lev to the US dollar depreciated from 46–47 lev to a high of 65 lev per dollar. This embarrassed and gravely disturbed not only the foreign exchange market; it also made questionable the fulfilment of the government's budget plan, and undermined the implementation of the business plans of both the private and state-owned companies.

Following the 1994 debt reduction and rescheduling deal with the London Club commercial banks, Bulgaria has resumed servicing its foreign debt. Should the government fail to negotiate and secure the influx of new sources of foreign finance, the foreign exchange reserve of the central bank will be incapable of coping with a new depreciation of the currency. Given the brittle financial equilibrium and the unsettled problems in the real sector of the economy, the attraction of FDI could play a significant role in curbing the recessionary tendencies and creating conditions for gradual economic upturn and revival.

In the opinion of foreign and mainly Western experts, the Bulgarian legislative regime for foreign investments is one of the most liberal in Eastern Europe. The law of 1992 regulating foreign investment in Bulgaria settles the conditions and rules for carrying out economic activity in the country by foreign persons. Under 'foreign person' the act means: a legal person registered abroad; a partnership which is not a legal person and has been registered abroad; a physical person – a foreign national with permanent residence abroad.

According to the law, foreign persons enjoy equal opportunities for economic activities with local entities with the exception of several special cases. Special permissions or licences are required for certain activities such as manufacturing of arms and military equipment and the trade therein, banking and insurance, prospecting and extraction of natural resources from the territorial sea zone, the continental shelf or the exclusive economic zone.

Foreign persons can acquire property rights over buildings and limited property rights over real estate or land. So far this has not proved to be a considerable barrier to foreign investment since the Bulgarian legislation makes it possible for leasehold of the land to continue as long as the respective economic activity is carried out on it (production of goods or services).

The banking activity of foreign banks and banking institutions is regulated and licensed by the Board of Directors of the Bulgarian National Bank. Since the share of capital in the newly established private banks, compared to the capital of the state-owned commercial banks, is still rather low, the entry of foreign bank capital would assist the formation of genuine bank competition. However, with a view to protecting the national interests and the need to give the banking sphere time to adapt to the new conditions, the process of permitting foreign bank capital to penetrate the country initially is subject to the licensing regime.

Foreign physical and legal persons can open accounts with Bulgarian banks both in local and foreign currency without any quantitative restrictions, and they can manage these accounts practically under a completely liberalized regime. The only requirement they must comply with, when transferring foreign exchange abroad, is to prove they have paid all taxes due. Given the internal convertibility of the lev, profits made in this currency can be converted into foreign currencies and expatriated under these conditions.

In 1990 some 140 joint ventures were registered in the country; in 1991 their number grew to 900, and in 1992 their number increased by another 300. At the beginning of 1994 the number of registered joint ventures exceeded 3500. Despite this high dynamism, however, Bulgaria lags many-fold by this indicator behind Hungary (13,000 joint ventures in 1992), Romania and the Czech Republic.

However, the unit size, the origin and the sectoral breakdown of the foreign capital are not particularly favourable. The average size of a foreign interest in an individual company is in the range of US$85–100,000, that is, these are mainly small investments, almost entirely in the sectors of trade and services. The total amount of FDI in industry is estimated at slightly above US$10 m. The geographical concentration of FDI in the country is rather uneven – it is predominantly focused round Sofia and Plovdiv (the second biggest city) mainly because of the sizeable local markets and the availability of suitable infrastructure.

Concerning origin, the greatest activity is manifested on the part of Turkish capital (279 joint ventures), Greek capital (202 joint ventures) and Russian capital (151 joint ventures), closely followed by companies from Middle Eastern countries. West European and US companies are insignificantly represented: their presence is merely symbolic. Such a structure of the origin of

FDI is not very favourable for the country. Foreign investment is important not only as an additional capital resource but also as a possibility for transfer of technologies, as a source of managerial experience and potential for opening up new markets. The economic and technological involvement with insufficiently well-developed countries will not foster the successful integration of the Bulgarian economy in the European structures and in the world economy at large.

The agreements with the EU and EFTA mark a definite step forward, but they are far below the existing potential. The share of Western Europe in Bulgarian exports has grown from 10–12 per cent at the end of the 1980s to about 35 per cent at the beginning of 1994. This growth, however, can hardly compensate for the huge losses of markets to the East.

The EU and EFTA agreements envisage a certain asymmetry in the foreign trade regulations in favour of Bulgarian exports. Thus, on the one hand, the market preferences granted by the EU and EFTA could attract Western capital, and on the other, these investments would allow for the manufacturing of goods meeting world standards. Unfortunately in actual trade, this asymmetry at present is in inverse proportion. The West increased its exports to Bulgaria to a larger extent than Bulgaria did in the direction of the West. The Bulgarian trade deficit with the EU alone exceeds US$300 m. Given these circumstances, Western companies simply lack stimuli to invest in Bulgaria, as the internal market is limited, while the Western markets are difficult to access. The trade balance figures are positive only in respect to the Balkan region countries (US$550 m in 1993).

What can be done in the short and in the medium run for a tangible stimulation of the foreign investors' interest? First of all, several important legislative acts, such as the stock exchange law, could be invoked. Stock exchanges in Bulgaria are still in their infancy, and without the regulation and expansion of their activity one can hardly expect them to act as a key intermediary in the process of privatization, including the participation of foreign capital. Two other bills regulating bankruptcy are also directly linked with the possibility of making the SOEs, earmarked for privatization, more attractive for potential investors. Bulgaria has a number of potentially good manufacturing enterprises in electronics, certain engineering industries, pharmaceutical industry, electric- and motor-truck engineering, textiles and the food-processing industry.

In order to attract foreign capital in the manufacturing branches, it is imperative that the economic policy of the government be directed to the real sector of the economy. Alongside the decisive curbing of inflation (still ranging around 60 per cent annually) and foreign exchange rate stabilization, the government should direct its efforts to pursuing preferential policy towards manufacturing. Tax breaks, credit preferences, and a system of export stimuli are necessary for the companies from the manufacturing sector. This means a new investment and industrial policy.

What Bulgaria needs is the adoption of a system of national priorities in the economy, which should also include measures facilitating the access of foreign capital and the optimization of its sectoral structure. The long-term objective of turning Bulgaria into a developed market economy is inconceivable without the preservation and development of those of the existing manufacturing industries and enterprises which have good future prospects. To meet this objective, Bulgaria urgently needs the application of a measured, well-selected and only temporary targeted protection policy.

This task presupposes a reassessment of the foreign trade policy of the country. The economic losses incurred as a result of the unnecessary politicization of trade relations with the East European countries are far too heavy. It is necessary to restore the Bulgarian presence in its traditional markets as the national market is quite limited. Besides, Bulgaria could be used by Western investors as a springboard for production, export, and re-export to the CIS zone countries. In a number of cases this is a possible and favourable move for them in order to minimize the business risk involved in direct investment in regions of high political risk and a more unstable economic environment. Moreover, the expected joining of GATT will diminish the tariff and non-tariff barriers for Bulgarian exports. It is in the common interest to make use of these opportunities.

István Ábel

The chapter written by K.-D. Schmidt addresses one of the most crucial issues of the transition. Foreign investment itself, with its contribution to major factors determining the outcome of the transition, is one of the 'engines of transition', as the author states. His approach is based on the large literature on FDI and surveys most of the theories explaining the functions of FDI, the propagation mechanism of its effects and the factors determining it. As there is no generally accepted theory, this survey is very helpful and inspiring indeed. In my comments I shall not concentrate on the theories mentioned and presented in the chapter. Instead, I shall continue on the path K.-D. Schmidt laid down in his chapter and I shall try to touch other potentially important aspects of the current developments in the CEECs with respect to FDI.

Why is FDI an especially important factor determining the success of transition? First of all, because the recovery from the slump which occurred in all transforming economies has numerous prerequisites, like change in management approaches, introduction of new technologies, changes in micro-behavioural responses, access to foreign markets and, among other things, fresh capital. Under the current circumstances, nothing can bring all of these necessities to the CEECs so effectively as FDI.

What is the reason, then, that FDI is not widely encouraged in all these economies? There are basically two main factors influencing the flow of FDI into CEE. One is evidently the process of privatization as this creates space and incentives for foreign investors to enter the market. The other factor is the state of the financial services industry as, without a well-functioning banking system, doing business is extremely difficult both for foreigners and locals.

Taking the first factor, namely privatization, one can observe that there is a certain resistance, particularly to those forms of privatization which would involve more intensive participation of foreigners. The reason for this is mainly political. There is a certain ideological opposition to foreigners taking over the crown jewels of the country currently struggling with an economic collapse.

To identify this barrier to economic recovery it must be pointed out that conservative parties as well as liberals or even socialists are equally committed to privatization and are equally aware that this cannot be successful without foreign participation. There is only one political force, namely nationalists, who adamantly oppose privatization by FDI. The real danger to economic recovery and eventual cooperation with the modern world economy currently is not represented by the socialist revival but rather by the threat of nationalism as a base for official policies. Although this statement might sound surprising and apologetic for the current shifts in the political focus, voters of most countries in the region seem to share this view when voting nationalists out of the parliaments in the last elections in Hungary and Poland.

The importance of the financial sector and privatization in promoting FDI points to an emphasis on the importance of bank privatization in CEE. A certain type of bank privatization, of that with a strategic Western partner, is particularly instructive in this respect. A strategic partner would bring not only capital, improved management, modern information technology and new products, but cheaper funding as well. And this is probably even more important than any other factor for paving the way to economic recovery. Without improving the supply of funds, there is no hope for major improvements in the conditions for restructuring enterprises and creating the basis for economic recovery.

The chapter also addresses the issue of the sectoral structure of FDI in different countries and different years. The sectoral concentration alone is important and well presented in the chapter; however, the shifts in the focus of FDI during the stages of capital inflow have not been analysed. The targeted sectors change over time, starting with trade and approaching financial sectors only at a later stage of development. This issue could be the topic of further research based on the important results presented in this chapter.

13. Putting foreign direct investment in Eastern Europe into perspective: turning a macroeconomic failure into a microeconomic success story

Richard Stern

INTRODUCTION[1]

When the former Eastern bloc embarked on economic transformation, a potentially vast new market with over 300 million consumers opened between the Elbe River and the Pacific Ocean. Each country inherited an obsolete capital stock which was incapable of generating the growth necessary to revive these economies in a market setting. Though well educated (relative to countries with similar levels of per capita GDP outside the region) and perhaps highly skilled, the productivity per worker was assumed to be low relative to Western countries whose workforces enjoy similar levels of education. Low productivity per worker is attributed to the lack of proper incentives generated by the centrally planned system and to the dearth of modern equipment. Available domestic capital for investment has been in short supply due to the small pool of funds and to the inefficient allocation system. Policy makers hoped that the allure of a vast market combined with the prospects for economic transformation to a market-based system would attract large amounts of foreign direct investment (FDI).

FDI has traditionally been viewed as an external source of capital which can be used to augment domestic savings. Particularly in less developed economies where savings rates do not meet the capital requirements for investment leading to sustained growth, FDI offers a potential remedy for domestic capital shortages. In practice FDI is unlikely to completely solve the problem of insufficient capital, though it can at least 'prime the pump' for economic growth. In addition to filling the savings–investment gap, FDI could also serve as a conduit for the transfer of technology, technical expertise and new production methods.

The purpose of this chapter is to assess the progress and analyse some problems related to FDI into Central and Eastern Europe and the former Soviet Union (CEE–FSU). It is suggested that the traditional goals of FDI, namely complementing shortfalls in national savings to fill the investment gap, will not happen in Eastern Europe, at least in the short run. At the macro-level, the combination of the recession in Western Europe, the USA and Japan and the high levels of political and economic risk faced by all CEE–FSU countries make the original aims of FDI, the catalyst for economic recovery, untenable. At the micro-level, economic, legal, and in some cases, political reform have not progressed quickly enough to convince many potential investors about the security of their investment.

The theoretical literature on FDI covers a wide range of issues. As it is analysed in more detail in Chapter 12, here I shall focus my attention only on some specific issues relevant to the further discussion in this chapter.

The macroeconomic justification for FDI is that it augments savings and total investment, which should eventually result in economic growth, and hence more demand for all goods produced in the economy. In the development strand of the literature, FDI was seen as one solution to the savings–investment gap.

At the microeconomic level, the literature turns to the impact of FDI on firm productivity. The relevant conclusions of this 'industrial organization' approach to FDI (see Helpman, 1984; Krugman, 1983; Rugman, 1986 as well as Chapter 12 of this volume) suggest that the main advantage to hosting foreign-owned firms is that, in addition to different or newer technology, foreign firms possess intangible productive assets, such as technological know-how, marketing skills and export contacts.[2] In the industrial organization approach, a firm's primary motivation to invest in a foreign country is to increase its market size and hence take advantage of scale effects. In addition, the placement of the firm's foreign operations might be a strategic location for both domestic and international trade.

Perhaps the most relevant theoretical application of the industrial organization approach to FDI is the concept of spillover effects. That is, the transfer of technology and human capital that comes from FDI should increase the productivity per worker within the firm. As experienced workers leave firms, they carry new knowledge to other firms either within the industry or not and this transfer of knowledge will increase the productivity of the new firm. The spillover effect is characterized by many domestic firms reaping the productivity benefits of the initial injection of foreign physical and human capital. We argue below that it is the spillover effects which substantially contribute to economic growth and thus a prudent policy would be to try to attract FDI into those industries which are likely to generate the largest spillover effects.

IS FOREIGN DIRECT INVESTMENT COMING INTO CEE–FSU?

At the beginning of 1990, business people and analysts believed that the level of FDI flows into CEE–FSU would bridge the gap between domestic savings and investment capital needs (Stern, Bunt and Thomas, 1993). *Ex-ante*, for FDI to fulfil this function there must be sufficient domestic capital (as well as financial and non-financial infrastructure) already in place so that the foreign capital is used productively. The second necessary condition is that there is a sufficient market structure to move capital to its most productive use and that capital is actually deployed into those sectors.

Arguably CEE–FSU countries do not satisfy these necessary conditions (Welfens, 1992) and thus even if they were able to attract the level of capital required, there was no guarantee that it would be used to its fullest extent, given the state of economic reform in most of the countries of the region even in 1994. Table 13.1 gives some estimates of the total level of capital required (foreign plus domestic) to generate substantial economic growth.

Though the figures in Table 13.1 are unrealistically high,[3] they give a rough idea of the level of foreign capital that would be needed to sustain strong economic growth. Borensztein and Montiel (1991) argue that even small investment rates may achieve satisfactory rates of growth in CEE–FSU, primarily due to the existing endowment of a well-educated labour force. Given the characteristics of the labour force, the marginal product of capital is extremely high, so high that foreign capital generates increasing returns to scale.[4] Thus a little foreign capital goes a longer way in CEE–FSU countries than in other parts of the world and thus the capital requirements listed might be cut substantially.

However, even if the figures were cut by two-thirds, it is clear that CEE–FSU countries would not receive this level of FDI. As of October 1993, total cumulative committed (not necessarily disbursed) FDI into the region has reached US$14.6 bn, which falls far short of any figure listed (UN–ECE, 1993, p. 2).[5] It is important to note that the UN–ECE figures are cumulative commitments, not disbursements, and that the capital requirements listed in Table 13.1 are in-place capital requirements. In order to understand how much FDI has flowed into the region and into which sectors, it is necessary to look at the distribution and structure of FDI into CEE–FSU.

Macro- and Micro-Level Distribution of FDI[6]

Not surprisingly, the countries with the highest growth rate of FDI and cumulative level of FDI are the Visegrad-4. Hungary leads the group with US$3.9 bn as of October 1993 (with US$1 bn in new projects during the

Table 13.1 Estimates of annual investment needs in CEE–FSU

Estimate, year	Regional coverage	Policy target	Period (years)	Average annual investment requirement (US$ bn)
Begg et al., 1991	CEE-6	Doubling GDP per capita (7% p.a.)	10	103–226
Fitoussi and Phelps, 1991	CEE-6	Aver. labour prod. as France in 1990	10	110 (net) 180 (gross)
Rodrik and Collins, 1991	CEE-6 and FSU	1. Aver. labour prod. as developed West in 1991	10	CEE-6: 421 (net) FSU: 1164 (net)
	CEE-6 and FSU	2. 7% p.a. average GDP growth	10	CEE-6: 344 (net) FSU: 571 (net)
Gross and Steinherr, 1991	Visegrad-4 and FSU	Average GDP/capita as EU in 1990	10–15	V-4: 126 (net) FSU: 687 (net)
Ochel, 1991	CEE-6	4–5% p.a. average GDP growth	from 1996	75–98 (gross)
	FSU	3–4% p.a. average GDP growth	from 1996	106–116 (gross)
Boote, 1992	CEE-6	EU productivity level (implicit 12.5% p.a. GDP growth)	10	260 (gross)
Korolev and Lushchin, 1992	FSU	Maintain 1992 output level	1991–95	299–321 (gross)

Source: Lankes (1993), p. 27.

first quarter of 1993 alone), the Czech Republic with US$1.4 bn, 1993, and Poland with US$1.8 bn. Despite the staggering growth rates of FDI, the calculated ratio of FDI/GDP is small in all countries (see Chapter 12). FDI in the southern tier of East European countries, Bulgaria, Romania and Albania, is almost negligible; finally, FDI in the FSU has just begun to flow despite political and economic instability, with the highest levels of FDI flowing into Russia (US$2.9 bn). Total FDI into the Visegrad-4 almost doubles the level of FDI into the CIS countries in 1993.

From the UN–ECE (1993) database, it is clear that roughly 60 per cent of all FDI is flowing into the manufacturing sector. In all the countries surveyed, the engineering industry has received the largest inflow of foreign capital within the manufacturing sector. This subsector includes non-electrical engineering, office equipment and computers (not surprisingly), electrical equipment, communications equipment and transport equipment. These items are heavily demanded goods, and all are actually produced in the donor country (or at least outside the recipient country) and thus constitute a transfer of hardware but neither the knowledge to build it nor the substantial investment to set up production – obviously this is less productive in the long run for the recipient country, but less of a financial commitment for the donor country.

The next highest concentration of FDI is in services, which requires less capital per venture and constitutes a smaller overall transfer of technology. In sheer number terms, this sector constitutes the number of projects committed. Telecommunications, transport and construction constitute less than 7 per cent of total FDI in all the countries surveyed. This result seems surprising, given that at least with respect to telecommunications, most CEE–FSU countries are engaging either a West European or American telecommunications company to replace the existing archaic 'phone system.

Not surprisingly, foreign trade (included in total trade operations) accounts for roughly only 22 per cent of all FDI ventures. The main reason is that, at present, Western markets are fairly closed to goods from CEE–FSU – especially those which might compete with similar goods produced in the EU. From an investor's standpoint, it does not make sense to base expected future income streams on the ability to export to the West. FDI into CEE–FSU is only rational in the short and medium terms if it is profitable in domestic and perhaps other CEE–FSU markets.

Finally, as in the West, FDI is restricted by the host countries in critical areas such as defence and strong restrictions are in place for FDI into the financial – especially banking – sector. In most cases special permission is required by the government and limitations on the extent of FDI are in force in all countries.[7]

The size of capital investment from foreign sources has been falling steadily since 1990. Most countries have abolished minimum capital requirements as well as maximal ceilings for some sectors. In Hungary, the average initial foreign investment in 1990 was about US$360,000 and by 1994, the average in the Visegrad-4 countries dropped to US$250,000 and to a low of less than US$20,000 in Romania. At the same time, the share of foreign ownership in joint ventures has dropped below 50 per cent, despite the governmental guarantees and legal protections to repatriate initial investments and profits offered by most countries (OECD, 1993, pp. 81–2).

The drop in average capitalization and thus the scope and investment in CEE–FSU is not too surprising, given the level of uncertainty and risk currently facing these countries. One plausible explanation can be found in the literature on irreversible investment. Briefly, many investments, particularly in physical plants and equipment, once undertaken are likely to have little value in alternative uses, or at least a low resale value. This means that such irreversible investments can be considered, from the standpoint of the investor, to be sunk costs – not recoverable if the investor chooses to withdraw from the activity. Thus when an investor evaluates a particular project, he/she considers not only its current expected return but also the expected return to waiting and undertaking the project only if more favourable conditions prevail in the future. When uncertainty about the future is high, waiting and investing only under favourable conditions may have higher value. Furthermore, if uncertainty is expected to be resolved to some extent in the future, it is even more likely that waiting is the more profitable strategy.[8]

Thus individual countries need to allay investor fears through appropriate governmental/legal guarantees (to be discussed later), transparent policies and a stable enough economic environment (with manageable inflation and a relatively stable exchange rate). These requirements are extremely difficult to achieve – especially during the process of transition – and thus potential investors are following the most prudent course and waiting.

Systemic Problems Facing Host Countries' Ability to Attract FDI

Why has FDI fallen far short of the enormous capital requirements? The potential explanations can be divided up into host and donor country categories. From the host (CEE–FSU) country side, the most obvious disincentive is the lack of stability (political and economic) during the period of transition. In particular, CEE–FSU economies are still mixed, partially privatized and partially still state owned;[9] there are still many domestic distortions – especially in capital markets – which prevent both financial deepening and efficient transfers of capital.[10] The existence of severe capital market distortions adds to the difficulty of calculating a rational rate of return, which is a strong deterrent to FDI.

Second, problems with the legal framework will prevent FDI from flowing. Unless the legal framework and the tax systems are clearly defined, FDI will not flow into the host country because investors feel that their investments are not secure. A study of the OECD (1993) divides the CEE–FSU into three groups with respect to the development of the legal framework surrounding FDI:

1. The Visegrad-4 have developed corporate and commercial law structures which incorporate FDI into the general legal framework.
2. The second group of countries, Bulgaria, Romania, the Baltics and Russia have a patchwork of laws which govern FDI – some inherited from the communist days, some new. These countries have pieced together a series of laws that are barely adequate to cover the main issues but add uncertainty because of the possibility of changes.
3. The third group consists of countries such as Albania, Belarus, Ukraine and Kazakhstan which have only the basic legal essentials for any type of business including FDI.

Not surprisingly, foreign investors tend to concentrate capital in the first group of countries.

Third, even if financially wide markets do exist, financially deep markets do not yet exist. Thus domestic financing is realistically limited to bank lending rather than securities-based raising of capital. Debt leverage is extremely risky in CEE–FSU due to the fact that the old bad debt problem has yet to be solved. Finally, perhaps the most unstudied problem facing FDI into CEE–FSU lies in the issue of contracting. The question is, given the uncertainty and incomplete markets (as above), can foreign investors write contracts that would be mutually beneficial to both sides in order to forge an effective deal? That is, foreign investors need a contracting structure that would grant them enough security of investment (both in the form of repatriation of profits and investment and in the form of access to markets to sell output) while at the same time providing net positive benefit to the host country. In reality for the foreign investor, this translates into either a guaranteed market for the output of the investment (either access to domestic markets, preferential access to domestic markets, or guaranteed access to foreign markets), some form of buyback agreement, or counter trade. For the host country, this translates into a technology transfer and/or human capital transfer (with the hope of positive spillovers into other industries) plus guaranteed employment and labour retraining.

The most common contractual arrangements between foreign investors and host enterprises are either counter trade or buyback arrangements because the foreign investor is guaranteed a market for output and limits risk as no money changes hands *per se*. In addition, with these types of agreement, the incentive to maximize the firm's objective function is high on both the owner's and manager's side. With a buyback agreement, the manager is producing for a specific market and thus must gear output toward satisfying demand. Thus the principal-agent problem is minimized.

Other sorts of agreements, such as joint ventures (without specific output agreements) with majority holding by the foreign partner, could be subject to principal-agent problems because the manager is less likely to care about a firm in which he/she has little or no stake or decision-making authority.

The contractual arrangement problem has been borne out by the statistical data collected by the OECD. Enterprises with foreign capital are characterized by low start-up costs and are concentrated in relatively low-risk industries where workers do not need much retraining, such as manufacturing (where markets for output domestically and internationally are assured) and engineering (where workers are traditionally well trained and where there is high and sustainable domestic demand in each country).

Problems Inhibiting Donor Country FDI

For the donor companies, the main motivations for investment into CEE–FSU are to penetrate and capture domestic markets, to establish a production base for intra-regional sales, and to set up low-cost production bases (especially due to the combination of low cost – relative to Western Europe, Japan, and the USA – and reputedly highly skilled labour) for exporting to Western markets. Part of the reason why Western firms have not invested as heavily into CEE–FSU as expected is due to the worldwide recession which strongly affected the USA in 1991 and then spread to Europe and Japan. In addition, despite the fact that Germany is Europe's largest FDI donor country, it has had to divert much of its available resources to integrating the eastern sector with the rest of the economy and to resettlement of ex-Soviet troops as a part of the unification terms. Thus Germany's level of FDI has not lived up to the *ex-ante* predictions.

Second, CEE exports have limited access to Western markets, despite the positive step toward EU market liberalization by the 1992 Europe Agreements (EAs). However, these agreements, as discussed in Part One, have specifically excluded CEE exports (such as agriculture and steel) which pose a threat to EU domestic markets. This phenomenon is one factor limiting the flow of FDI into CEE.

In addition, informal restrictions, such as lack of marketing expertise and contacts, pose an even stronger barrier than formal trade restrictions, due to the fact that the problem is harder to pinpoint. These 'intangibles' might well be solved over time, as CEE–FSU firms learn new Western-style techniques, but this will not help in the short run. Thus without direct access to export markets, foreign investors are less likely to commit funds to invest mainly in the domestic markets unless they expect that the foreign market will eventually open up. Profit margins in Western countries for goods produced with low-cost labour and other inputs are much higher than in CEE–FSU, because firms tend to price to the market.

Other reasons for the low level of investment into CEE–FSU include the lack of political and economic stability (as discussed above) and the exchange rate risk. Because none of the CEE–FSU currencies are fully convertible,[11] there is always a risk that investment in hard currency will not be recoverable if the domestic currency cannot be converted back to hard currency. In addition, until the transition process is over, all economies are subject to persistent inflationary pressure.[12] Inflationary pressure will force devaluations or depreciations of the currency depending upon the regime. Thus, unless FDI is grounded in a hard currency with guarantees of full repatriation of the investment in hard currency, investors are wary of sinking large amounts of money into CEE–FSU.

HOW LITTLE PIECES OF FDI CAN GO A LONG WAY

Though the level of FDI into CEE–FSU is not going to be sufficiently high to fill the savings–investment gap, even in small quantities it can have a strong impact on revitalizing certain sectors. Eventually these sectors could lead the economy into a pattern of economic growth.

The literature on endogenous economic growth (Helpman and Krugman, 1985; Grossman and Helpman, 1989a, 1989b, 1989c; Romer, 1990) provides a relevant application to FDI. The literature concludes that endogenous, sustained economic growth is based on three premises. First, technological change lies at the heart of economic growth because it provides the incentive for continuous capital accumulation which in turn produces greater output and productivity per worker. Second, technological change arises from a competitive market situation where there is commitment to maintaining an environment which facilitates further advances (that is, educational infrastructure and R&D funds). Third, in order for technological change to occur, there has to be an existing technology base on which to build. Romer (1990) argues that once the instructions for working with raw materials have been made, they can be reproduced, modified and adapted costlessly; thus the real cost of technological change is 'sunk' with the primary idea and the future use of the technology is a positive spillover effect.

The literature also concludes that the larger the economy's stock of human capital and the larger its capacity to trade, the greater the speed of economic growth. The idea is that the more integrated economies are, the larger the effective stock of human capital (or access to that stock), and thus the easier it is to learn new production techniques.

Applied to FDI, the argument is as follows. If we accept the premise that the labour force is both well educated and well trained in CEE–FSU countries, then what is needed to revitalize industries is the application of new technology, new production and management techniques, and perhaps some start-up capital. These necessary conditions can only be met if the economy generates the requirements itself, or if the economy 'imports' them from abroad. To import human and physical capital through conventional trade is not yet feasible.[13] Thus the main avenue through which technology can be transferred is FDI. That is, FDI flows into critical sectors[14] (for example, computer development) can not only generate strong industry-specific growth, but it can also spill over into other sectors. If strategic investment were to occur in a few of these critical areas, in the medium term economic growth could be led by these sectors.

In addition, if FDI facilitates technology, managerial technique, or production technique transfer, then the marginal productivity of one unit of foreign capital is higher than that of one unit of domestic capital (embedded in which, presumably, is a relatively lower level of technology and old managerial techniques). And if spillover effects are generated from the foreign capital, the marginal productivity of FDI becomes even higher.

Thus, if FDI is targeted to building up critical sectors (that is, if FDI is considered as part of any industrial policy or programme) and if markets continue to develop (as distortions are removed), the necessary conditions for economic growth will be in place in the medium and in the long term.[15] Host country policy makers should choose sectors based on current and projected future contributions to domestic production first, keeping the idea of exportability in mind but putting a smaller weight on the product's potential tradeability in an *ex-ante* cost–benefit analysis.

APPROPRIATE POLICIES TO STIMULATE FDI INTO CRITICAL SECTORS

The main way to overcome the problem of attracting FDI is to present an economy which is growing, in which markets work efficiently (especially financial markets) and access to foreign markets is liberalized. Short of that, countries will have to rely on legal and industrial policies to help attract foreign capital. Current policy tools available to host countries to attract FDI into CEE–FSU include the legal framework governing FDI, the tax system, and market-based incentives either existing or evolving. The legal and tax systems are codified by laws that are relatively easy to access, but to assess how conducive the market environment is to FDI is a difficult task.[16] Thus the purpose of this section is to highlight the ways in which FDI can be targeted to certain sectors and the associated costs to the host country.

The legal system, including the commercial code, provides the foundation for FDI. Without a solid legal framework guaranteeing the rights and responsibilities of the host and donor countries, codifying rules of conduct, formalizing rights of transfer, competition and distribution of profits and investments, no potential investor will invest. Thus a fully articulated and transparent legal system is a necessary condition for FDI. As mentioned above, only the Visegrad-4 countries fully meet this necessary condition.

Tax incentives are a common way of offsetting the excessive risk of investing in CEE–FSU. At the same time, the more stable countries (the Visegrad-4) have reduced the tax incentives and are moving toward neutral treatment of foreign and domestic firms. The main tax incentives are on the disposition and repatriation of profits. Corporate income tax breaks vary from country to country but, as a general rule, the more unstable the country, the more widespread the tax relief.

In general, tax incentives are the simplest and most common means of attracting FDI. But tax incentives are neither sufficient for the donor country nor necessarily beneficial for the host country on net. For the donor country, political and economic instability (especially macroeconomic) can easily outweigh the positive benefits of a tax break. For the host country, the loss of tax receipts – especially if tax exemptions are widespread – translates into the loss of a revenue source for the government budget. These revenue shortfalls may not be worth the benefit of FDI. At the same time, extending tax incentives to a few sectors *ad hoc* raises the question of transparency. Without a transparent system, investors will be less likely to commit funds to the recipient country. Thus a system of tax incentives needs to be worked out carefully.

Finally, the extension of market incentives to a potential foreign investor is an especially controversial topic for the countries in transition. More specifically incentives could include government-granted monopoly power or guarantees of limited domestic market entry, preferential trade arrangements for the importation of inputs or export of outputs, the guarantee of a specific exchange rate for repatriation of profits, or special tariffs protecting the investor from other foreign competition. All these special arrangements might make FDI more attractive to the investor but, at the same time, might be economically dangerous for the host country.

In particular, these treatments effectively inhibit the development of open and contestable markets, one of the goals of economic reform and one of the most difficult aspects of reform for the government to put in place. Effectively these policies inhibit competition and might be detrimental to economic growth especially if all the profits are repatriated and none of the technology or skills can spill over. Second, once applied, these special arrangements are difficult to remove.[17] A firm that receives protection for five years is likely to be able to extend it to ten years. Such protection might lead to inefficient production and lack of competition.

CONCLUSIONS AND EXTENSIONS

The purpose of this chapter was to analyse and assess FDI into CEE–FSU from two different perspectives. At the macroeconomic level, FDI has obviously failed to reach the proportions needed to generate economic growth in CEE–FSU in the short run. However at the microeconomic level, it might facilitate the transfer of technology and technical know-how that in themselves might ultimately generate economic growth if applied to the 'right' sectors.

Given the pattern of FDI into CEE–FSU since 1990, it is clear that the utility of FDI lies not in its ability to fill the savings–investment gap within a short period; rather the goals of FDI should be scaled down to a more 'realistic' level. In particular, we argue that FDI should be viewed as a means for technology transfer (both in terms of human capital and physical capital) into specific sectors which can contribute to economic growth in the medium and long terms. In addition to machinery and investment capital, the use of foreign management styles and techniques is an integral part of the diffusion of foreign investment.

Appropriate government policy to target and stimulate FDI into certain industries might facilitate its more successful deployment. At the same time government policy can help, with the existence of the market, to guide FDI into the 'critical' sectors of the economy, where its overall positive impact will be the highest.

Because only aggregated FDI data were used in the discussion, it was only possible to paint a broad-brush sketch of the situation. The next logical empirical step should be a systematic analysis of firm-level data by comparing the productivity levels of enterprises receiving FDI and those receiving only domestic capital. On the theoretical front, it is important to see whether FDI is indeed a better substitute for trade in generating economic growth.

NOTES

1. The author wishes to thank Dr Hans Peter Lankes for providing the forum to study foreign direct investment.
2. For a good description of the industrial organization approach see Aitken and Harrison (1993) and Graham and Krugman (1991), appendix B.
3. In the sense that with the possible exception of the Visegrad-4, striving toward European Union levels of development in the next ten years is unlikely to happen.
4. The source of the increasing returns is the spillover effects that can be generated by new technologies. Specifically, foreign capital is more productive than domestic capital because high technology, advanced training, and years of experience are embedded in it.
5. This figure is hard to pinpoint since it is calculated using national sources with various exchange rate schemes applied to local currencies.
6. The data used in this subsection are taken from OECD (1993), UN–ECE (1993) and UNIDO (1992).
7. For example, foreign banks need special permission to invest more than 10 per cent of the founding capital in a Hungarian bank.
8. An excellent discussion of the irreversible investment argument can be found in Borensztein and Montiel (1991).
9. It should be noted, however, that there is a high level of variation between countries from the Visegrad-4 economies posting the highest levels of economic activity generated by the private sector to some of the non-Russian republics of the CIS in which the private sector contributes little to GDP. The point here is that no country in the region has privatized all the sectors it intends to and thus some sectors are still subject to protection (including subsidies) and other distortions.
10. The most advanced capital market in the region is arguably in the Czech Republic, where most of the banking sector has been privatized and a security market has been set up. At the same time, as discussed in Chapter 10, the Czech Republic has not fully dealt with the bad debt problem, and many banks would be technically insolvent if the bad loans were called in. In addition, the securities market is barely functional due to the dearth of viable securities.
11. Arguably, some CEE currencies such as the Czech koruna, the Hungarian forint, and the Polish zloty are all convertible for current account transactions; however none have capital account convertibility.
12. The inflationary bias is partially due to the fact that until privatization programmes are complete, the social safety net is in place, and the tax system operates smoothly, government expenditures and revenues are hard to predict. Besides, in some countries, such as Russia, there is a tendency to print money to cover government shortfalls.
13. The constraints on hard currency trade are binding because the demand for CEE–FSU goods in the West is low due to poor product quality and low technological content.
14. 'Critical' sector is defined as here as either an industry whose products are used widely in the production process or one in which the skills learned and technology used can be applied to other sectors.
15. The point at which economic growth takes place occurs when enough firms applying the new technology (increasing returns) are in the market to generate industry-and economy-wide increasing returns. For more in-depth detail about the mechanism which translates firm-specific growth into economy-wide growth, see Stern (1992) and Murphy, Schleifer and Vishny (1989).
16. The factual information in this section comes from OECD (1993).
17. This is the argument made against 'infant industry' protection in the trade literature.

REFERENCES

Aitken, B. and Harrison, A. (1993), 'Do domestic firms benefit from foreign direct investment?', mimeo.

Borensztein, E. and Montiel, P.J. (1991) 'Savings, investment, and growth in Eastern Europe', International Monetary Fund, Washington, DC, June.

Graham, E.M. and Krugman P.R. (1991), 'Foreign direct investment in the United States', Institute for International Economics, Washington, DC.

Grossman, G.M. and Helpman, E. (1989a), 'Comparative advantage and long run growth', NBER Working Paper No.2809, Cambridge: National Bureau for Economic Research.

Grossman, G.M. and Helpman, E. (1989b), 'Growth and economic welfare in a small open economy', NBER Working Paper No. 2970, Cambridge: National Bureau for Economic Research.

Grossman, G.M. and Helpman, E. (1989c), 'Product development and international trade', *Journal of Political Economy*, **97**(6), December, 1261–83.

Helpman, E. (1984), 'A simple theory of international trade with multinational corporations', *Journal of Political Economy*, **92**(3), June, 451–71.

Helpman, E. and Krugman, P.R. (1985), *Market Structure and Foreign Trade: Increasing Returns, Imperfect Competition and the International Economy*, Cambridge, Mass.: MIT Press.

Krugman, P.R. (1983), 'The new theories of international trade and the multinational enterprise', in Kindleberger, C.P. and Audretsch, D.B. (eds), *The Multinational Corporation in the 1980s*, Cambridge, Mass.: MIT Press.

Lankes, H.P. (1993), 'Foreign direct investment', European Bank For Reconstruction and Development, London, mimeo.

Murphy, K., Schleifer, A. and Vishny, R. (1989), 'Industrialization and the Big Push', *Journal of Political Economy*, **97**(5), October, 1003–26.

OECD (1993), 'Foreign direct investment in Central and Eastern Europe: policies and trends in fourteen economies in transition', OECD, Paris, July.

Romer, P.M. (1990), 'Endogenous technological change', *Journal of Political Economy*, **98**(5), p. 2, October, S71–S102.

Rugman, A. (1986), 'New theories of the multinational enterprise: an assessment of internalization theory', *Bulletin of Economic Research*, **398**(2), 101–18.

Stern, J., Bunt, K. and Thomas, N. (1993), 'Foreign direct investment to the countries of Central and Eastern Europe', Working Paper No. 2, National Economic Research Associates, London.

Stern, R.E. (1992), 'Financial market efficiency, increasing returns, and economic growth in post-socialist economies', Ph.D. dissertation, University of California, Berkeley, September.

UN–ECE (1993), 'Statistical survey of recent trends in foreign investment in East European Countries', Note to the Secretariat, United Nations Economic Commission for Europe, November.

UNIDO (1992), 'Foreign direct investment in Central and Eastern European countries: recent developments and determinants', United Nations Industrial Development Organization, June.

Welfens, P. (1992), 'Privatization and foreign direct investment in East-European transformation: theory, options and strategies', Volkswirtschaftsliche Diskussionsbeitrage no. 167, Westfalische Wilhelms-Universität, Münster.

Discussion of Chapter 13

Gancho Ganchev

The chapter by Richard Stern deals with the problem of FDI to Eastern Europe from an interesting point of view. The author argues that the macroeconomic approach is not sufficient to explain the dynamics of Western direct investment into the reforming CEECs and has to be complemented with a microeconomic one, emphasizing the spillover effect of technology transfer.

According to the author, the main reason for the gap between the high investment requirements and the modest capital inflow to the reforming countries is, on the one hand, the incomplete market infrastructure and the economic uncertainty in the recipient countries and, on the other, the limited market access of the Eastern imports in the donor countries. The latter aspect has especially negative effects, given one of the main entry arguments of foreign investors – to establish a low-cost productive base and meet some demand in the West.

The first question to be asked about the confrontation between macro- and micro-levels is that, taking into account the high uncertainty in the reforming countries, it becomes evident that there is no contradiction between high potential profits (high marginal productivity) of foreign investment (and, respectively, high investment demand) in Eastern Europe, and low foreign capital inflow. The explanation is that the expected rate of return on foreign investment is low, primarily due to the inherent high risks in these countries. Put differently, the economic policy task comes back to the necessary efforts to reduce the uncertainty in the reforming countries. It follows also that we return to the traditional problems of the post-communist countries – poor legal infrastructure, lack of deep financial markets, banking system burdened by bad loans and so on.

In this respect, however, the author follows the traditional Western point of view, separating the CEECs into the 'Visegrad-4' and 'the rest'. For example, Bulgaria is cited as having a 'patchwork' of laws which govern FDI in contrast with the Visegrad-4 which supposedly possess commercial and company law structure, incorporating FDI. In fact, Bulgaria is the only post-communist country whose legal system has nothing to do with a 'patchwork' model. Bulgaria was the first reforming country to adopt a new constitution in order to subordinate the whole legal system to the principles of the civil society and market economy, in contrast to all the other former socialist countries still living under reformed communist constitutions and restructuring their legal system on a 'patchwork' basis. Of course, this alone does not imply that Bulgaria is more advanced on the path of transformation but, from the point of view of consistency and stability of the legal environment, the Bulgarian way has its merits.

Concerning the spillover effect, it can be argued that the same obstacles impeding FDI from the macroeconomic point of view are hampering the process of technology transfer. For example, the market infrastructure is just emerging and most markets are in their embryonic form. Other factors such as educational infrastructure, available research funds, high initial technological level, large effective human capital stock (or access to that stock), are severely affected by the transformational recession (in Kornai terms) and have negative impact on the spillover capacities of the economies in transition.

On the other hand, the spillover effect is not necessarily connected with FDI. There are other channels and forms of technology transfer – licensing, OPT and the like. Finally, it is not quite clear in principle whether a macroeconomic failure can be transformed into a microeconomic success story. The main difference between macro and micro is the level at which information is aggregated. Consequently, the macroeconomic failure is also a microeconomic one, but expressed in different terms.

To conclude, the spillover effect of FDI should be expected to be negatively influenced by the same factors which affect adversely the inflow of foreign capital from a macroeconomic point of view. One of the main reasons why the Western companies are not investing in the East – the limited access of Eastern exports to developed countries – will have a negative impact both on the volume of FDI and on the diffusion of the new technologies. The transition uncertainty in general is the main common cause for the modest expected spillover effect and for the low expected returns on investment. The two problems have to be resolved simultaneously.

Annex NACE classification of economic activities

NACE no.	Description
11	**Extraction and briquetting of solid fuels**
12	**Coke ovens**
13	**Extraction of petroleum and natural gas**
14	**Mineral oil refining**
15	**Nuclear fuels industry**
16	**Production and distribution of electricity, gas, steam and hot water**
161	Generation and distribution of electric power
162	Gasworks: gas distribution
163	Production and distribution of steam, hot water, compressed air; district heating plants
17	**Water supply; collection, purification and distribution of water**
21	**Extraction and preparation of metalliferous ores**
211	Extraction and preparation of iron ore
212	Extraction and preparation of non-ferrous metal ores
22	**Production and preliminary processing of metals**
221	Iron and steel industry (as defined in the ECSC Treaty), excluding integrated coke ovens
222	Manufacture of steel tubes
223	Drawing, cold rolling and cold folding of steel
224	Production and preliminary processing of non-ferrous metals
23	**Extraction of minerals other than metalliferous and energy-producing minerals; peat extraction**
231	Extraction of building materials and refractory clays
232	Mining of potassium salt and natural phosphates
24	**Manufacture of non-metallic mineral products**
241	Manufacture of clay products for constructional purposes
242	Manufacture of cement, lime and plaster
243	Manufacture of concrete, cement or plaster products for constructional purposes
243.1	Manufacture of asbestos-cement products
243.6	Manufacture of ready-mixed concrete
244	Manufacture of articles of asbestos (except articles of asbestos-cement)
245	Working of stone and of non-metallic mineral products

NACE no.	Description
246	Production of grindstones and other abrasive products
247	Manufacture of glass and glassware
248	Manufacture of ceramic goods
25	**Chemical industry**
251	Manufacture of basic industrial chemicals and manufacture followed by further processing of such products
255	Manufacture of paint, painter's fillings, varnish and printing ink
256	Manufacture of other chemical products, mainly for industrial and agricultural purposes
257	Manufacture of pharmaceutical products
258	Manufacture of soap, synthetic detergents, perfume and toilet preparations
259	Manufacture of other chemical products, chiefly for household and office use
259.1	Manufacture of photographic chemical material (sensitized photographic film, plate, paper, etc., and auxiliary products)
259.2	Manufacture of polishes and the like for household use (shoe, furniture and floor care products, metal polishes, car polishes, etc.)
26	**Man-made fibres industry**
31	**Manufacture of metal articles (except for mechanical, electrical and instrument engineering and vehicles)**
311	Foundries
312	Forging; drop forging, closed dieforging, pressing and stamping
313	Secondary transformation, treatment and coating of metals
314	Manufacture of structural metal products (incl. integrated assembly and installation)
315	Boilermaking, manufacture of reservoirs, tanks and other sheet-metal containers
316	Manufacture of tools and finished metal goods except electrical equipment
316.5	Manufacture of domestic heating appliances and kitchen heating appliances of all kinds
316.6	Manufacture of metal furniture (including safes)
319	Other metal workshops not elsewhere specified
32	**Mechanical engineering**
321	Manufacture of agricultural machinery and tractors
322	Manufacture of machine-tools for working metal, and of other tools and equipment for use with machines
323	Manufacture of textile machinery and accessories; manufacture of sewing machines
324	Manufacture of machinery for the food, chemical and related industries
325	Manufacture of plant for mines, the iron and steel industry and foundries, civil engineering and the building trade; manufacture of mechanical handling equipment
326	Manufacture of transmission equipment for motive power
327	Manufacture of other machinery and equipment for use in specific branches of industry
328	Manufacture of other machinery and equipment

NACE no.	Description
33	**Manufacture of office machinery and data-processing machinery**
34	**Electrical engineering**
341	Manufacture of insulated wires and cables
342	Manufacture of electrical machinery (comprising electric motors, electricity generators, transformers, switches, switchgear and other basic electrical plant)
343	Manufacture of electrical apparatus and appliances for industrial use; manufacture of batteries and accumulators
344	Manufacture of telecommunications equipment, electrical and electronic measuring and recording equipment, and electro-medical equipment
345	Manufacture of radio and television receiving sets, sound reproducing and recording equipment and of electronic equipment and apparatus (except electronic computers); manufacture of gramophone records and prerecorded magnetic tapes
346	Manufacture of domestic type electric appliances
347	Manufacture of electric lamps and other electric lighting equipment
348	Assembly and installation of electrical equipment and apparatus (except for work relating to the wiring of buildings)
35	**Manufacture of motor vehicles and of motor vehicle parts and accessories**
351	Manufacture and assembly of motor vehicles (including road tractors) and manufacture of motor vehicle engines
352	Manufacture of bodies for motor vehicles and of motor-drawn trailers and caravans
353	Manufacture of parts and accessories for motor vehicles
36	**Manufacture of other means of transport**
361	Shipbuilding
362	Manufacture of standard and narrow-gauge railway and tramway rolling-stock
363	Manufacture of cycles, motor-cycles and parts and accessories thereof
364	Aerospace equipment manufacturing and repairing
37	**Instrument engineering**
371	Manufacture of measuring, checking and precision instruments and apparatus
372	Manufacture of medical and surgical equipment and orthopaedic appliances (except orthopaedic footwear)
373	Manufacture of optical instruments and photographic equipment
374	Manufacture of clocks and watches and parts thereof
41/42	**Food, drink, and tobacco industry**
411	Manufacture of vegetable and animal oils and fats
412	Slaughtering, preparing and preserving of meat (except the butchers' trade)
413	Manufacture of dairy products
414	Processing and preserving of fruit and vegetables

NACE no.	Description
415	Processing and preserving of fish and other sea foods fit for human consumption
416	Grain milling
417	Manufacture of spaghetti, macaroni, etc.
418	Manufacture of starch and starch products
419	Bread and flour confectionery
420	Sugar manufacturing and refining
421	Manufacture of cocoa, chocolate and sugar confectionery
422	Manufacture of animal and poultry foods (including fish meal and flour)
423	Manufacture of other food products
424	Distilling of ethyl alcohol from fermented materials; spirit distilling and compounding
425	Manufacture of wine of fresh grapes and of beverages based thereon
427	Brewing and malting
428	Manufacture of soft drinks, including the bottling of natural spa waters
429	Manufacture of tobacco products
43	**Textile industry**
431	Wool industry
432	Cotton industry
433	Silk industry
434	Preparation, spinning and weaving of flax, hemp and ramie
435	Jute industry
436	Knitting industry
437	Textile finishing
438	Manufacture of carpets, linoleum and other floor coverings, including leathercloth and similar supported synthetic sheeting
438.1	Manufacture of carpets, carpeting, rugs, etc. from all types of fibres
438.2	Manufacture of linoleum and similar floor coverings (on paper, board or textile base)
439	Miscellaneous textile industries
44	**Leather and leather goods industry (except footwear and clothing)**
441	Tanning and dressing of leather
442	Manufacture of products from leather and leather substitutes
45	**Footwear and clothing industry**
451	Manufacture of mass-produced footwear (excluding footwear made completely of wood or of rubber)
453	Manufacture of ready-made clothing and accessories
455	Manufacture of household textiles and other made-up textile goods (outside weaving-mills)
456	Manufacture of furs and of fur goods
46	**Timber and wooden furniture industries**
461	Sawing and processing of wood
462	Manufacture of semi-finished wood products
463	Manufacture of carpentry and joinery components and of parquet flooring
464	Manufacture of wooden containers
465	Other wood manufactures (except furniture)

NACE no.	Description
466	Manufacture of articles of cork and articles of straw and other plaiting materials (including basketware and wickerwork); manufacture of brushes and brooms
467	Manufacture of wooden furniture
47	**Manufacture of paper and paper products; printing and publishing**
471	Manufacture of pulp, paper and board
472	Processing of paper and board
473	Printing and allied industries
474	Publishing
48	**Processing of rubber and plastics**
481	Manufacture of rubber products
482	Retreading and repairing of rubber tyres
483	Processing of plastics
49	**Other manufacturing industries**
491	Manufacture of articles of jewellery and goldsmiths' and silversmiths' wares; cutting or otherwise working of precious and semi-precious stones
492	Manufacture of musical instruments
493	Photographic and cinemato-graphic laboratories
494	Manufacture of toys and sports goods
495	Miscellaneous manufacturing industries
50	**Building and civil engineer-ing**
500	General building and civil engineering work (without any particular specialization) and demolition work
501	Construction of flats, office blocks, hospitals and other buildings, both residential and non-residential
502	Civil engineering; construction of roads, bridges, railways, etc.
503	Installation (fittings and fixtures)
504	Building completion work
	Manufacturing industry
1/4	**Industry**
5	**Building and civil engineering**

Index